# Beginning Smartpl Web Development

Building JavaScript, CSS, HTML and Ajax-based Applications for iPhone, Android, Palm Pre, BlackBerry, Windows Mobile, and Nokia S60

## Gail Rahn Frederick
### with Rajesh Lal

Apress®

President and Publisher: Paul Manning
Lead Editor: Tom Welsh
Technical Reviewer: James Pearce
Editorial Board: Clay Andres, Steve Anglin, Mark Beckner, Ewan Buckingham, Gary Cornell, Jonathan Gennick, Jonathan Hassell, Michelle Lowman, Matthew Moodie, Duncan Parkes, Jeffrey Pepper, Frank Pohlmann, Douglas Pundick, Ben Renow-Clarke, Dominic Shakeshaft, Matt Wade, Tom Welsh
Coordinating Editor: Debra Kelly
Copy Editors: Patrick Meader, Katie Stence, and Sharon Terdeman
Compositor: MacPS, LLC
Indexer: BIM Indexing & Proofreading Services
Artist: April Milne
Cover Designer: Anna Ishchenko

Distributed to the book trade worldwide by Springer-Verlag New York, Inc., 233 Spring Street, 6th Floor, New York, NY 10013. Phone 1-800-SPRINGER, fax 201-348-4505, e-mail orders-ny@springer-sbm.com, or visit http://www.springeronline.com.

For information on translations, please e-mail info@apress.com, or visit http://www.apress.com.

Apress and friends of ED books may be purchased in bulk for academic, corporate, or promotional use. eBook versions and licenses are also available for most titles. For more information, reference our Special Bulk Sales–eBook Licensing web page at http://www.apress.com/info/bulksales.

The source code for this book is available to readers at http://www.apress.com. A "live" version of the source code is maintained by the author at http://learntheweb.com/books.

# Contents at a Glance

# Contents

# About the Authors

**Gail Rahn Frederick** is a mobile software architect, Mobile Web enthusiast, and instructor of standards-based Mobile Web development. Her mobile applications and Mobile Web sites have been deployed to 10+ mobile operators in 6+ countries in North America and Europe. Gail teaches Mobile Web development for smartphones and other devices, including defensive programming and other survival tips for the mobile ecosystem, at Learn the Mobile Web (http://learnthemobileweb.com) and Portland Community College (http://www.computers.pcc.edu). At Medio Systems (http://medio.com), she leads a mobile software team developing personalized search and discovery products with a focus on mobile analytics. Gail lives at the base of an extinct volcano in Portland, Oregon.

**Rajesh Lal** is an author, designer, developer, and technology evangelist working at Nokia in Mountain View. Rajesh has been involved in Mobile UI/UX design for the past five years and has hands-on experience with a variety of mobile devices, including Sony Mylo, Windows Mobile, Apple iPhone, Nokia S60, and Maemo devices. He has authored multiple books on gadgets and widgets and enjoys taking an objective and pragmatic approach to design. His blog on design and user experience can be found at http://abcofdesign.com.

# About the Technical Reviewers

**James Pearce** has the Mobile Web in his veins, having worked at Argogroup, AnywhereYouGo, and, a decade ago, as founder of mobile blog WAPtastic. He was most recently CTO at dotMobi. James develops and runs a range of contemporary mobile web sites and services, and writes and speaks extensively on the topic. He can be found online at `http://tripleodeon.com`.

**Rocco Georgi** is co-founder and CTO of London-based PavingWays Ltd., a consulting company that helps customers expand their business to the Mobile Web and mobile devices. He has been working as a web developer since 1999. At PavingWays Ltd., he specializes in bringing web-based applications to mobile devices of any kind. As an active writer and conference speaker on topics such as mobile web development and mobile widgets, Rocco shares his experiences with the community.

**A. Todd Emerson** has held leadership positions at mobile data solutions companies since 2000. Todd has launched white-label mobile data solutions at US and European mobile operators, and his solution designs include a wide array of mobile-centric technologies including Mobile Web, rich client, data synchronization, messaging, and voice recognition. Tens of millions of mobile subscribers actively use Todd's solutions. In addition to his work with mobile operators, Todd is the founder of Kikata, a business solutions company that focuses on delivering emerging technology solutions (RFID, mobility, VoIP, and cloud-based infrastructure) to small and mid-sized businesses.

# Acknowledgments

To my partner Kim, thank you for your love and patience while I spent days, nights, and weekends writing this book. Your support is everything to me. I'm back now.

To Fish and Chips, we can't wait to meet you.

To Debra Kelly, Tom Welsh, Steve Anglin, and everyone at Apress, thank you for guiding me through the publishing labyrinth and for providing candid feedback to improve my book. Your good humor through the ups and downs of my pregnancy is deeply appreciated.

To Rajesh Lal, thank you for contributing your mobile design and usability expertise in Chapters 6 and 7. Nokia is lucky to have you.

To my technical reviewers James Pearce, Rocco Georgi, and Todd Emerson, thank you for your detailed analysis of every chapter of this book. Your efforts immeasurably improved its quality and timeliness.

To Andrea Trassati of dotMobi, Francois Daost of W3C, Bennett Marks of Nokia and formerly OMA, and Luca Passani of WURFL, the mobile industry veterans who contributed interviews and reviewed selected portions of the text, your assistance was invaluable. Thank you.

To John T. Keith at Cloud Four, thank you for allowing me to use your innovative mobile browser research.

To Rob, Brian, and everyone at Medio, thank you for graciously encouraging me to follow this dream.

To Luni, without your mentorship, I would still be writing C++ for Windows desktops.

To the memory of Dr. Karl Stockhausen, whom we lost to melanoma during the writing of this book, I am blessed to have known such a brilliant, caring, upstanding, outspoken, hilarious, and occasionally ornery young man. You inspire me to live bravely.

And, of course, to Nixon, our trusty black Labrador, who curled up nearby for most of the writing of this book, thank you for never complaining, not even once. Yes, I am finally ready to throw the ball for you at Mt. Tabor Park.

Gail Rahn Frederick

I want to extend my thanks to Steve Anglin and Gail Frederick for giving me this great opportunity, and to Debra Kelly for all her support. I also want to thank Samir, my mentor, who makes me feel excited about everything I do and points me in the right direction.

Rajesh Lal

# Introduction

I believe in the W3C's principle of One Web—that services and information on the web should be thematically consistent and accessible to all kinds of devices, without regard to differences in presentation capabilities. Informally, the One Web principle means that if I write my grocery list online at home in Firefox, I should be able to view the list and check off my purchases at the grocery store using my mobile phone. That said, the Mobile Web and its ecosystem are unique in many ways—in access patterns, user behaviors, browser technologies, and client capabilities.

A recent mobiThinking report coined the maxim "utility is the engine of the Mobile Web". This phrase has become my mantra for Mobile Web development and I encourage you to adopt it as well. Mobile Web content succeeds when it solves a real problem for a user on the move. Driving directions, public transportation, business listings, news headlines, social networking, and banking are all examples of content that succeeds on the Mobile Web because real people using mobile phones in their daily lives find this information to be relevant, local, and immediately available.

The Mobile Web is experiencing exponential growth. It's the Desktop Web circa 1994. Everyone knows it is time to jump on board, but few understand how to get started. This book argues that a standards-based approach to Mobile Web development, with a deep knowledge of web and mobile standards and a healthy skepticism for rushed standardization efforts, provides the best methodology for building web content for mobile devices.

This book is written for web developers and designers who are beginning to explore the Mobile Web. No prior experience with mobile devices is assumed. The first two parts of the book introduce you to the basic concepts, standards, and conventions of Mobile Web development. The third part teaches you mobile design and usability principles and specialized enhancements for powerful web browsers on smartphones. The final part of the book shows you how to optimize, validate, test, and deploy a Mobile Web site on the public Internet and into the mobile ecosystem.

I hope you find the book to be an enlightening guide and accurate reference for mobilizing Web content and maximizing its reach on the Mobile Web. Best wishes in your mobile adventures.

Gail Rahn Frederick

# Getting Started with Mobile Web Development

Part 1 introduces the mobile industry, mobile users, and the Mobile Web. You'll meet web policymakers, authors of mobile best practices, and drafters of Mobile Web standards. You'll learn to evaluate a standard or best practice and judge its appropriateness for your mobile web project.

With this knowledge of the ecosystem, you'll prepare for a mobile web development project by setting up a development environment, selecting an IDE, and configuring a web server with common mobile MIME types. Then you'll extend Firefox with add-ons for viewing mobile web pages on the desktop, using mobile emulators and actual mobile devices for more accurate views of the Mobile Web.

Once the development environment is ready, you'll examine the markup and scripting languages that drive rich, lightweight web experiences on all kinds of mobile devices, especially smartphones. You'll study HTML, XHTML-MP, and WML, then style mobile markup using CSS. Finally, you'll review best practices for coding web pages for mobile devices.

# Chapter 1

# Introduction to Mobile Web Development

Mobile is a totally new medium. Best practices from the desktop world simply do not apply. The unique attributes of the mobile device, ecosystem and user require new best practices for Mobile Web development.

This book teaches you the syntax, semantics, and ecosystem of the Mobile Web. You will learn to build adaptive, responsive, and standards-compliant Mobile Web sites guaranteed to work on any mobile browser. Simple development tips and techniques will improve web usability on small screens. You will enrich your Mobile Web site for advanced smartphone browsers (browsers in high-end mobile phone with integrated Internet features such as email and desktop-capable Web browsing) capable of rendering full HTML and proprietary extensions. After development, you learn to test thoroughly on actual mobile devices, optimize Mobile Web pages for network transport, and maximize survival in the mobile ecosystem by avoiding transcoding.

The Mobile Web is the Wild West. The big guns control the ecosystem, and shootouts are commonplace. A determined individual can stake a claim, build a homestead, and establish a community, and independent outposts flourish in remote locations. But the best way to survive is to show up armed. The most effective weapons for a mobile developer in the Wild West include:

- deep technical understanding of mobile standards and best practices
- critical thinking skills and a healthy sense of skepticism
- fanatical devotion to syntactic correctness
- an appreciation of the needs of mobile users

A standards-based approach to Mobile Web development ensures compliance and usability across mobile browsers and platforms. Knowing all the rules—and knowing when to ignore the rules—is necessary for success on the Mobile Web.

# Mobile Web vs. Desktop Web

Fundamentally, there is one Web. Its content is standardized markup, styles, scripts, and multimedia viewable using web browsers. In this book, by convention, we call this the Web the Desktop Web. It is what we surf in Firefox or Opera or Internet Explorer on our desktops, laptops, and netbooks.

The Web is a vast collection of servers linked by TCP/IP computer networks. Many of these servers, known as web servers, implement the Hypertext Transfer Protocol (HTTP) to share documents and files. Web servers provide access by Uniform Resource Identifiers (URIs) to text files, markup documents, and binary resources.

In an HTTP request, the client sends a web server the URI of the desired resource and a collection of request headers, one of which contains a list of MIME types that advertise the content types supported on the client.

In an HTTP response, the web server sends the client the document itself (markup, text, or binary) and another set of headers, one of which contains the MIME type describing the file type of the document transmitted to the client.

The Mobile Web uses the plumbing of the Desktop Web and adds new MIME types, markup languages, document formats, and best practices to provide web content optimized for the small screens, resource constraints, and usability challenges of web browsers on mobile devices.

The Mobile Web introduces new components into the web ecosystem, including:

- Markup languages and styles optimized for mobile devices
- MIME types that differentiate mobile markup from desktop HTML
- Browser clients with a wide variety of capabilities
- Network proxies that further adapt your content to cater for those clients

If the Mobile Web is the Wild West, then the Desktop Web is an island paradise. The Desktop Web is a safe and well-understood development environment driven by client technologies steeped in established standards. At the time of this writing, the Desktop Web is nearly 20 years old. Desktop browser clients are public, free, freely available, and frequently updated. Only a handful of software vendors and open-source projects produce the dominant web browsers in use today, reducing the testing burden for cross-platform web development. In the desktop ecosystem, if a web page reaches the destination browser, its markup is almost always left unaltered en route by intermediary servers on the Internet. Network owners and Internet Service Providers (ISPs) are not interested in optimizing and improving the web experience through automated markup adaptation and content repackaging (see Table 1-1 for a list of the characteristics that define the Mobile Web and the Desktop Web).

Desktop Web filtering software can prevent viewing of objectionable web pages, but web filters work by blocking page *access* rather than adapting page *syntax*.

Mobile Web development is a new discipline for these reasons:

- *The Mobile Web ecosystem is totally new.* The Mobile Web uses the plumbing of the Desktop Web, but it has new best practices and new gotchas derived from the unique attributes of mobile devices. Desktop metaphors do not apply. Bandwidth consumption is a concern, even for smartphones. Rich Web 2.0 features such as JavaScript frameworks and Asynchronous JavaScript and XML (AJAX) must be used judiciously, or you risk draining battery power. Operators frequently control and block traffic to Mobile Web sites. Transcoding proxies often attempt to reformat mobile markup en route to a mobile browser. Finally, defensive programming is essential to reduce exposure to transcoders and mobile network problems.

- *The Mobile Web user is totally new.* Mobile Web users have unique usage patterns and navigation methods. Mobile users are keenly goal-directed and location-aware. Roaming in and out of coverage areas, mobile users count network access problems among the top factors affecting the Mobile Web browsing experience. In fact, cost-sensitive mobile users prefer to cancel the network transaction rather than risk a chargeable mistake.

- *The Mobile Web browser is totally new.* The mobile browser has unique benefits, quirks, and workarounds. Partial and flawed implementations of web standards are commonplace. Improperly formatted web pages can have drastic effects on mobile devices, including crashing the browser or resetting the device. Advanced web features such as JavaScript and AJAX are highly desirable but drain battery life. With more than a dozen mobile browser vendors in the marketplace, the burden of ensuring compliance with web standards falls to OEMs and operators.

**Table 1-1.** *Characteristics of the Mobile Web and Desktop Web*

|  | Mobile Web | Desktop Web |
| --- | --- | --- |
| **Average Session Length** | 2 – 3 minutes | 10 – 15 minutes |
| **Minimum Screen Size** | 90 × 60 | 800 × 600 |
| **Maximum Screen Size** | 240 × 400 for popular devices | Unlimited |
| **Browser Vendors** | 12+ and growing | Two with market share over 5% |
| **Browser Bugs** | Frequent. Permanent, except for smartphones with updatable OSes. | Rare and patchable |
| **W3C[1] Standards** | Spotty. Sometimes ignored or challenged by mobile industry. | Mature and accepted |
| **Markup Languages** | WML<br>CHTML<br>XHTML Basic<br>XHTML-MP<br>XHTML<br>HTML | XHTML, HTML |
| **JavaScript and AJAX** | Not on 90% of mobile devices. Available as ECMAScript-MP and JavaScript. Document Object Model (DOM) and supported events vary. Proprietary APIs are common. | Usually available |
| **Addressable Clients** | 3 billion mobile subscribers worldwide | 1 billion total notebooks, desktops and servers |

# Mobile Markup Languages

Today's mobile devices include standards-based, but not necessarily standards-compliant, mobile browsers that allow users to view web content in several mobile markup languages, including:

- XHTML and HTML
- XHTML Mobile Profile (XHTML-MP)
- CHTML (iMode)
- Wireless Markup Language (WML)

---

[1] World Wide Web Consortium, http://w3.org

# HTML and XHTML

HTML is the luxury automobile of mobile markup languages. As the standard markup language of the web, HTML is well-known among web developers and designers. Many mobile browsers support the full tag set of HTML, but, those browsers might not enable a satisfactory user experience for direct viewing of desktop HTML websites. The screen resolution, storage, and bandwidth limits of a mobile device necessitate optimized markup and styles—and of course, mobile users expect dedicated services appropriate to their mobility.

XHTML combines the tag set of HTML with the strict syntax compliance of XML. Mobile browsers process and render XML-formatted markup more easily than the loose syntax rules of HTML. XHTML is the best markup choice for HTML-capable mobile browsers.

Smart mobile browsers in Android, iPhone, Nokia Series 60, Windows Mobile, and BlackBerry devices all support XHTML, HTML, JavaScript, and AJAX. This feature set and the optional additions of adequate client-side caching and CSS extensions form a foundation for interactive Mobile Web applications. This book describes how to build advanced web applications for smartphone browsers.

**NOTE:** Mobile Web sites targeting only smartphones can use the full feature set of HTML 4 and, in the near future, HTML 5. However, HTML and XHTML use on a Mobile Web site comes at a price. Using HTML and XHTML sacrifices compatibility with high-volume featurephones (low-cost, mass-market mobile phones with fewer features) that use older browsers. (Featurephone users surf the Mobile Web in strikingly high numbers—despite the smartphone hype.) Using desktop markup also invites transcoders—network appliances designed to optimize the Desktop Web for mobile devices by reformatting markup—to misinterpret the markup as intended for desktop browsers and machine readapt it for mobile browsers. This book teaches you strategies for both situations: how to maximize HTML compatibility for mobile browsers and how to avoid double-transcoding of mobile-optimized HTML.

# XHTML Mobile Profile

Specified and maintained by the Open Mobile Alliance (http://openmobilealliance.org), XHTML Mobile Profile (XHTML-MP) is the de facto standard markup for the Mobile Web. As its Mobile Profile suffix indicates, this markup language is a subset of XHTML deemed useful for mobile computing devices, including phones:

- XHTML-MP 1.0 sets the base tags for mobile markup.
- XHTML-MP 1.1 adds the <script> tag and support for mobile JavaScript.

- XHTML-MP 1.2 adds more form tags and text input modes. At the time of writing, many mobile browsers do not support XHTML-MP 1.2.

Virtually all new Mobile Web sites use XHTML-MP to reach mobile users.

This markup language introduces to the Mobile Web the familiar concept of separating markup structure and presentation. XML-formatted markup defines the document structure and Cascading Style Sheets (CSS) control the presentation. Most XHTML-MP mobile browsers support Wireless CSS, CSS Mobile Profile, and/or CSS 2. Yes, *most* means that not all mobile browsers that support XHTML-MP also support CSS. Welcome to the wild world of Mobile Web development! This book teaches you how to use a device database to identify mobile browser quirks such as shoddy CSS support, so you can adapt your markup accordingly. Fortunately, mobile browsers are rapidly improving in their adherence to web standards and general quality levels.

XHTML-MP is the markup language specified by the second version of the Wireless Application Protocol (WAP). A technically inaccurate but popular industry synonym for XHTML-MP is WAP2.

## WML

Wireless Markup Language (WML) is an older, simpler markup language for low-power mobile devices. It was standardized at the Wireless Application Protocol Forum (now the Open Mobile Alliance) in 1998. WML is a dialect of Extensible Markup Language (XML) that uses a deck and card metaphor. A single markup document can contain multiple user interface (UI) screens, or *cards*. WML was designed to display text on monochrome mobile devices with extremely limited memory and processing power. A mobile developer writes WML in plaintext using an integrated development environment (IDE) or text editor or generates the code using a server-side web scripting language. In some mobile networks, WML gateway servers compile the markup into binary format for compact (and hence faster) transmission to the device. A WML-capable mobile browser decompiles and renders the binary WML or renders textual WML directly.

WML has two major versions: WML 1.1and WML 1.3. Among other advances, WML 1.3 introduced support for color images. Today, virtually all mobile browsers support WML 1.3 and other markup languages. About 5% of mobile devices in use today in the USA support *only* WML in the browser; the other 95% support and prefer XHTML-MP, XHTML, and/or HTML.

WML is the markup language specified by the first version of the WAP specification. For this reason, the mobile industry also refers to WML as WAP1. This is technically incorrect as the WAP specifications cover the entire the protocol stack (including the markup itself), but the synonym endures nonetheless.

WML is considered the legacy language of the Mobile Web. It's old-fashioned enough that the Apple iPhone stands alone in its modernity by specifically dropping support for WML in its Web-capable mobile browser. Despite its age, the simple structure and compact binary format of WML make it an attractive markup language to use with simple Mobile Web applications or to provide a textual Mobile Web experience for older mobile phones.

For example, the Trimet public transit system in Portland, OR, offers a simple WML site for looking up schedules for buses and light rail. Every stop on every transit route is identified by a unique numeric ID posted prominently at the stop. Trimet site users enter the stop ID into a WML form to find the next expected arrival times of buses and trains at the stop. The site also allows transit schedules to be browsed by route number or location. The Trimet transit site has a constrained but important feature set for mobile users. Its small document sizes make for fast performance on even 2G mobile networks. Because the site uses WML, virtually every mobile phone in use today can view transit schedules. WML is a great choice to maximize a municipal Mobile Web site's availability to a diverse population of transit riders. You can find the Trimet WML site for transit schedules at `http://wap.trimet.org`. (Many other Mobile Web sites and apps are available for Trimet riders, including many that target the iPhone and other smartphones. See `http://trimet.org/apps/` for more information.)

## Other Mobile Markup Languages

This book focuses on the widely used markup languages on the Mobile Web: XHTML, HTML, XHTML-MP, and WML. There are other standardized mobile markup languages that were not widely adopted. Some of these markups predate reliable Internet access on mobile devices or were subsumed by later, more popular standards. These markup languages merit brief mention but no further discussion.

### HDML

WML might be the legacy language of the Mobile Web, but it is not the first markup language viewable on a mobile phone. That honor belongs to HDML (Handheld Device Markup Language), a WML precursor designed by Openwave (formerly Unwired Planet), a mobile infrastructure provider and browser vendor. HDML was submitted to the W3C in 1997, but never standardized nor widely adopted. However, HDML was influential in shaping the syntax and usability of WML.

Mobile phones in the mid 1990s were monochrome, and most were limited to three-line displays. Some of these primitive devices included support for rendering HDML documents. HDML browsers were notoriously stringent about syntax correctness.

As a tinkerer, I once prototyped a forms-based web site in HDML for my analog mobile phone. The web site worked, but I gave up because the browser enforced tiny maximum file sizes for HDML documents. It didn't help that the browser was also utterly undiscoverable to the average user. I frequently crashed the browser with invalid HDML syntax during development, and at each crash, my HDML phone would print the file name and line number of the C source code that I offended. Fun times!

## CHTML

I-mode mobile devices on the Japanese DoCoMo mobile network use an HTML subset called Compact HTML (CHTML) for rendering web content. The Japanese mobile browser company Access created CHTML and submitted it to the W3C for standardization in 1998. CHTML uses the structure of HTML with a severely constrained tag set to deliver web content to very small information appliances like low-end mobile phones. CHTML excludes support for these HTML features:

- Images in JPEG format (GIF format is supported)
- Tables
- Image maps
- Multiple fonts and styles (only one font is supported on I-mode devices)
- Background colors and images
- Frames
- Style sheets

CHTML is found only on mobile devices in the Japanese market, while I-mode services in CHTML are being rapidly reimplemented in XHTML.

### XHTML Basic

XTML Basic is a recommended mobile markup language that was a transitional step in the downgrade from HTML to XHTML-MP for limited mobile devices. Recommended in 2000 by the W3C, its tag support was expanded by the Open Mobile Alliance to create XHTML-MP.

Many mobile browsers support the XHTML Basic DTD, but Mobile Web developers prefer to work in the more widely supported XHTML-MP.

## Mobile Scripting Languages

Client-side scripting in mobile browsers used to be the exclusive domain of smartphones, but this is rapidly changing. By 2010, many mass-market mobile devices will support ECMAScript-MP, or *mobile JavaScript*. Mobile JavaScript is a fantastic tool for creating interactive Mobile Web experiences. As with any client-side mobile technology, testing JavaScript on actual mobile devices is critical for effective development because testing on emulators and in Firefox might not uncover syntax problems and performance issues that can occur on the target mobile device.

Mobile and desktop JavaScript have virtually identical syntax. The mobile version is stringent about ending lines with semicolons. Mobile JavaScript reduces the supported character sets and excludes computationally intensive language elements. It differs from its desktop counterpart in the extent of its DOM and event support in the mobile browser. DOM and event support can vary from one browser vendor and version to another. On-device testing is critical for success with mobile JavaScript.

Client-side scripting can also reduce Mobile Web browsing performance. Mobile users can disable JavaScript execution. Because of this, even markup designed for mobile devices that support JavaScript must gracefully adapt to a non-scripted environment. Flexible Mobile Web design implements markup first and iteratively enhances it with client-side scripting. This book teaches device awareness and content adaptation techniques that enable conditional inclusion of scripting to target only mobile browsers with support for JavaScript.

> **NOTE:** WML provided its own scripting language, WMLScript. WMLScript is linked from WML documents and supports form validation, dialog boxes, card navigation, and URI navigation. WMLScript is not discussed in this book; instead, we focus on JavaScript and ECMAScript-MP, forward-looking scripting languages for client-side scripting in mobile browsers.

# Mobile Style Sheets

Style sheets for mobile markup documents conform to one of three CSS dialects. The best mobile browsers support CSS2, the style standard used with XHTML and HTML on the Desktop Web. Mobile browsers that support XHTML-MP use Wireless CSS and/or CSS Mobile Profile, independent but related subsets of CSS2 that enable limited browsers to support common style properties. Mobile CSS subsets remove computationally intensive CSS features such as property inheritance and 3D element alignment.

# Mobile Industry Groups and Standards Bodies

Adherence to Mobile Web industry standards and best practices is important for flexible and cross-platform development. Several Internet and mobile industry bodies govern Mobile Web standards and recommended best practices, including:

- *W3C*: This body standardizes mobile markup languages and publishes best practices documents for Mobile Web development and testing.

- *Open Mobile Alliance* (formerly WAP Forum): This body standardizes mobile markup and style languages and other mobile technologies designed to be interoperable across devices, geographies, and mobile networks.

- *dotMobi* (http://mtld.mobi): This body controls the .mobi top-level domain, the content of which must be device-adaptive and compatible with mobile devices. This body also publishes best practices for Mobile Web development and nurtures mobile developers, marketers, and operators with online communities.

- *Mobile Marketing Association*: This body centralizes technology recommendations and best practices for marketing and advertising on mobile devices.

- *Open Mobile Terminal Platform (OMTP)* (www.omtp.org/): This operator-sponsored mobile industry group standardizing mobile-device access from Web applications.

Mobile Web development is a young discipline and is experiencing an explosion of standards and best practices activity. A wise Mobile Web developer is well-versed in these industry documents and uses critical thinking to decide which best practices apply when developing Mobile Web content targeting geographies and mobile device models.

# The Mobile Ecosystem

The mobile ecosystem is a rich, chaotic, and thrilling world. As a Mobile Web developer, you can expect to come into contact with several parts of the ecosystem. OEMs and mobile software vendors control the mobile-browser software that ships on mobile devices. The mobile operator sells mobile phones and network service. The operator controls mobile device access to the Web. Independent mobile developer communities are often organized around a mobile platform or service component. Developer communities provide camaraderie and technical interactions with peers working in the industry on Mobile Web and application projects.

## EXERCISE 1. BROWSE THE MOBILE WEB

Familiarize yourself with the Mobile Web by browsing the Web on different kinds of mobile phones. Find or borrow a few devices from different manufacturers with different screen sizes and modalities (especially touchscreens). At a minimum, use at least one featurephone and one smartphone. Next, use the mobile devices to do the following:

1. Navigate to and launch the web browser.

2. Browse mobile-optimized web pages. If you have trouble finding mobile-optimized sites, use a mobile search engine such as Google (http://google.com), Yahoo! (http://yahoo.com), or Bing (http://bing.com). Next, look in the *Mobile Web* search results category for links to Mobile Web pages.

3. Browse desktop web pages.

4. Use a mobile search engine to search for a nearby restaurant, find its phone number, and then find driving directions from your current location to the restaurant.

Record your experiences as you browse the Web on mobile devices with varying capabilities, then answer these questions:

- How easy or hard was it to find the web browser on the mobile phone? How many keypresses did it take to launch the browser?

- Were Mobile Web pages viewable on the phone? Were they usable? Why or why not?

- Were desktop web pages viewable on the phone? Were they usable? Why or why not?

- Were desktop web pages presented in an adapted or transcoded view? How did this view of the web affect your browsing experience?

- Which mobile search engine did you select? Why? Could you easily distinguish between web- and mobile-optimized web search results?

- How easy did you find it to search for a nearby restaurant on the phone? Could you click the phone number to start a call to the restaurant? Were the driving directions available and accurate?

Finally, make sure that each mobile device used in this exercise has a data plan that allows browsing the public Internet.

# Code Samples

Code and markup in this book was written in Eclipse PDT using PHP 5 on a Windows-desktop computer. The code is hosted in a Linux, Apache, MySQL, and PHP (LAMP) environment. The theme for the sample code in this book is a fictional fresh produce market called Sunset Farmers' Market.

You can find code samples, errata, and other information from this book at `http://learnthemobileweb.com/books/`. Also, you can browse to `http://learnto.mobi/books/` on a mobile device to view code samples in a mobile browser.

# Summary

In the introduction, I evaluated the foundational differences between the Desktop Web and the Mobile Web. I introduced the uniqueness in mobility that necessitates mobile-markup languages targeting the small form-factors of mobile devices and goal-directed mobile users. I also introduced you to the markup and scripting languages of the Mobile Web, and I casually mentioned a few outlier languages of historical significance only. I surveyed the mobile ecosystem and introduced you to mobile-industry groups and standards bodies.

In the next chapter, I'll show you how to set up a Mobile Web-development environment and take advantage of several methods for browsing the Mobile Web from a desktop computer.

# Chapter 2

# Set Up Your Mobile Web Development Environment

In this chapter, you'll learn how to set up your Mobile Web development environment.

Mobile Web development requires many of the traditional tools for web development: a server-side scripting language, a robust integrated development environment (IDE) with support for scripting and markup languages, a configurable web server, and a browser for viewing and testing web pages. File comparison and source code control tools are strongly recommended to track and manage changes to your project.

As a Mobile Web developer, you require new tools, web server configuration, and web-browser configuration to complete your development environment. The IDE provides you with syntax coloring and autocomplete for mobile markup languages. However, you must also extend your web server configuration to support mobile MIME types. You can configure Firefox, a flexible and open web browser, to mimic a mobile device and enable desktop browsing of the Mobile Web. You can also use mobile phone emulators for a more accurate view of the Mobile Web on a specific mobile browser or device, but you should use mobile-specific test tools to test your content and its interoperability with real handsets.

You can view Web pages in a mobile context using one of three tools, listed here in order of increasing authenticity:

1. *Firefox with mobile add-ons* allows the browser to impersonate mobile devices, so you can view of Mobile Web documents. Firefox is a convenient developer tool for testing mobile markup, but it is a poor visual imitation of an actual mobile device. It is suitable only for developer testing.

2. *Mobile browser emulators* execute the actual mobile browser code (or close to it) to simulate all browser features, including document rendering. This is a closer approximation of the actual behavior of mobile browsers; however, you should be aware that emulators are not available for many types of handset.

3. *Mobile browsers on actual mobile devices* are the best tools for examining the behavior of a web page on a mobile device. Testing on an actual mobile device most accurately represents how mobile users interact with web pages see Chapter 11 for more information about testing Mobile Web pages).

# Recommended IDEs

An IDE is a set of developer tools that facilitate designing, programming, executing, and debugging a web application (or any other type of software).

Mobile Web development does not require a specific IDE. The choice is yours, provided that the IDE supports web development in any markup language. Web development employs a markup language and a server-side runtime language (PHP, Java, .NET, and so on) to build web documents, as well as CSS and JavaScript files for styling and client-side interactivity, respectively.

An IDE should provide syntax coloring and autocomplete, and surface syntax errors for the markup, scripting languages, and ideally, the CSS. Some IDEs can import web development project settings from other IDEs. Pick the IDE that makes you most productive and do not hesitate to switch if you are unsatisfied with its usability. You will spend a lot of time building your Mobile Web development project in the IDE, so it is important to choose one that supports efficient web development.

Web developers usually choose an IDE based on its support for a server-side runtime language. Markup language support is built into every mature IDE. Table 2-1 lists popular web development IDEs by development platform and their runtime language support. All of these IDEs support HTML, XHTML, and provide at least modest support for mobile markup languages.

Adobe Dreamweaver and other dedicated web design environments are suitable for producing Mobile Web page layouts, but lack the runtime language support to convert a layout into a Mobile Web application.

Figure 2-1 shows a screenshot of a simple PHP template for an XHTML-MP webpage, as viewed in Eclipse PHP Development Tools. Figure 2-2 shows the same PHP template in NetBeans.

**Table 2–1.** *Popular Web Development IDEs by Platform and Runtime Language*

| IDE | Development Platform | Web Runtime Language(s) | License | URL |
|-----|---------------------|------------------------|---------|-----|
| Eclipse | Windows<br>Linux<br>Mac OS | C/C++<br>Java<br>PHP<br>Python | Free and open source | http://eclipse.org |
| Microsoft Visual Studio | Windows | .NET<br>C#<br>C/C++<br>Python (requires add-on)<br>Ruby (requires add-on) | Proprietary | http://www.microsoft.com/visualstudio/ |
| Komodo | Windows<br>Linux<br>Mac OS | Perl<br>PHP<br>Python<br>Ruby | Proprietary | http://www.activestate.com/komodo/ |
| NetBeans | Windows<br>Linux<br>Mac OS<br>Solaris | C/C++<br>Groovy<br>Java<br>PHP<br>Python<br>Ruby | Free and open-source | http://netbeans.org |
| NuSphere PhpED | Windows | PHP | Proprietary | http://www.nusphere.com/products/phped.htm |
| Aptana Studio | Windows<br>Linux<br>Mac | PHP<br>Python<br>Ruby on Rails | Dual-licensed. Free and open-source. Proprietary for Pro version. | http://aptana.com/studio |
| Zend Studio | Windows<br>Linux<br>Mac | PHP | Proprietary | http://www.zend.com/en/products/studio |

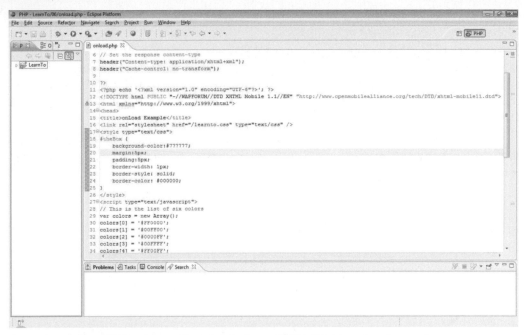

**Figure 2–1.** *Eclipse PHP Development Tools 3.3 viewing an XHTML-MP 1.1 markup document*

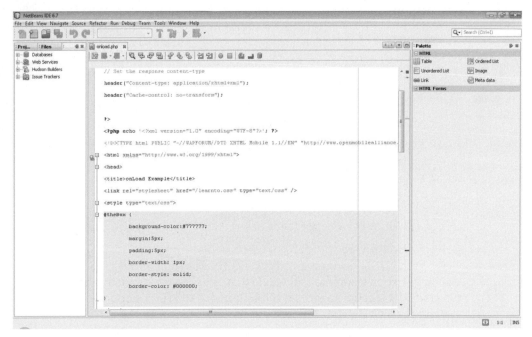

**Figure 2–2.** *NetBeans PHP 6.7 viewing an XHTML-MP 1.1 markup document*

# Mobile MIME Types

Mobile MIME types (or content types) identify the format of Mobile Web content. Text documents containing mobile markup, binary files containing viewable or playable content like ringtones, wallpaper and videos, and binary executable mobile applications are differentiated by web servers and browser clients in an HTTP transaction using MIME types.

MIME types are used in several ways during an HTTP transaction between a Mobile Web browser and web server—and by the transcoders or proxies that lie between them:

- *Mobile Browser*: The mobile browser sends a list of supported MIME types as the value of the Accept HTTP request header. The Accept request header advertises the content types supported on the mobile device. Unfortunately, some mobile devices are known to report content support inaccurately in this request header. Web servers consider the values in this header and consult a database of mobile device characteristics to determine the best content to send in the HTTP response.

- *Web Server*: The web server is configured to associate file extensions of mobile content with mobile MIME types. (Web servers generally come preconfigured to support mobile MIME types. However, the webmaster must manually add the additional mobile MIME types.) The MIME type associated with a web document is used as the value of the Content-Type header in the HTTP response. When the web server returns a file to a mobile browser and uses the correct mobile MIME type, the mobile browser knows how to interpret the file: as a web page, mobile application, wallpaper, ringtone, video, and so on. (In some cases, the browser itself might not render the file, but it will prompt the user to save or install it.)

- **Transcoders and gateways**: You will often encounter transforming HTTP proxy servers between the device and your web server. These proxy servers can inspect the Accept and Content-Type headers when deciding how to manipulate the original content on behalf of the device. For example, a PNG image might be transformed into a GIF image, or an HTML document might be converted to XHTML.

- **Server-Side Runtime Languages**: You can override the MIME type associated with a document using a server-side runtime language. Listing 2-1 shows sample PHP code that uses a built-in function at the start of the script to set the MIME type for an HTTP response that contains an XHTML-MP document.

**Listing 2-1.** *Set the MIME Type for a HTTP Response with PHP*

```
<?php
header('Content-Type: application/vnd.wap.xhtml+xml');
?>
```

Mobile MIME type configuration on a web server is critical to the mobile accessibility of web content. The mobile browser uses the MIME type in the HTTP response to determine whether the web document should be viewed in the browser, viewed by launching a mobile OS component (such as setting an image as wallpaper), or viewed by launching a native mobile application (such as playing a video in the video player).

Table 2-2 lists MIME types for some of the Mobile Web's common file types.

**Table 2-2.** *MIME Types for Common Mobile File Types*

| MIME Type(s) | File Extension(s) | Contents | Common Uses |
|---|---|---|---|
| `application/vnd.wap.xhtml+xml`<br>`application/xhtml+xml` | xhtml | XHTML-MP markup | Mobile Web pages |
| `text/html` | html (or htm on Windows servers) | HTML markup | Mobile Web pages for HTML-capable smartphones and mobile devices |
| `text/css` | css | CSS1, CSS2, and Wireless CSS | Cascading style sheets for Mobile Web documents |
| `application/javascript`<br>`text/javascript` | js | JavaScript | Scripting language used with HTML and XHTML-MP 1.1 and 1.2 |
| `multipart/mixed` | - | MIME multipart-encoded document | Allows markup and related web resources (images, CSS, scripts, and so on) to be downloaded in a single HTTP response envelope |
| `text/vnd.wap.wml` | wml | WML markup | Lightweight Mobile Web pages for older or low-end mobile devices |
| `text/vnd.wap.wmlscript` | wmls | WML Script | Scripting language used with WML |
| `audio/mp3`<br>`audio/mpeg` | mp3 | MP3 audio | Ringtones and full track music |
| `audio/x-midi` | midi | MIDI audio | Ringtones |
| `image/gif` | gif | GIF image | Wallpapers |
| `image/jpg`<br>`image/jpeg` | jpg<br>jpeg | JPG image | Wallpapers |
| `image/png` | png | PNG image | Wallpapers |
| `video/3gpp` | 3gp | 3GP video | Mobile video |
| `video/mp4` | mp4 | MPEG4 video | Mobile video |

# Web Server Configuration

File extensions for mobile markup and related mobile documents are associated with MIME types. Web servers hosting Mobile Web content must be configured to associate mobile file extensions with the correct MIME type. The process of adding new MIME types into web server configuration is different for each model of web server.

## Apache

The Apache web server uses the AddType directive in *mod_mime* configuration to add new MIME types into mime.types, httpd.conf, or .htaccess configuration files.

Apache's mime.types and http.conf files are global web server configuration files. These files control the overall behavior of the Apache web server.

Apache uses .htaccess files for local or directory-specific Apache configuration. The contents of an .htaccess file affect the directory (and all subdirectories) in which it is placed. The Apache Project (http://httpd.apache.org) recommends that you use .htaccess files only when access to the main Apache configuration file is restricted. (For example, it recommends you use .htaccess use in a shared web-hosting environment where users have nonadministrative access to control their own web documents, but not to the overall Apache server.) Excessive use of .htaccess files impacts server performance.

The AddType configuration directive specifies a MIME type and a list of file extensions to be served with the MIME type using this format:

```
AddType <MIME type> <file extension> [<file extension>] ...
```

Listing 2-2 shows an.htaccess configuration file that adds support for mobile MIME types. This file associates both .xhtml and .xhtm file extensions with the MIME type for XHTML-MP markup. Similarly, the .wml file extension is associated with the MIME type for WML markup, while the .wmls file extension is mapped to the MIME type for WML Script.

**Listing 2-2.** *Apache .htaccess Configuration for Mobile MIME Types*

```
# Add Mobile MIME types for XHTML-MP, WML, and WML Script file extensions
AddType application/vnd.wap.xhtml+xml .xhtml .xhtm
AddType text/vnd.wap.wml .wml
AddType text/vnd.wap.wmlscript .wmls
```

## Microsoft IIS

The Microsoft Internet Information Services (IIS) web server provides user interface, command-line, and programmatic methods for managing MIME type associations with file extensions.

In addition to using the IIS management applications for MIME type configuration, IIS 7 introduces command-line syntax for managing MIME types. Listing 2–3 shows a command that associates .xhtml files containing XHTML-MP markup with the application/vnd.wap.xhtml+xml MIME type.

**Listing 2-3.** *Adding a MIME Type into Microsoft IIS 7 at the Command Line*

```
appcmd set config /section:staticContent ^
 /+"[fileExtension='.xhtml',mimeType='application/vnd.wap.xhtml+xml']"
```

These Microsoft TechNet articles provide more information about managing MIME types through the IIS management applications or scripting:

- *IIS 4 and 5*: http://technet.microsoft.com/en-us/library/bb742440.aspx

- *IIS 6*: www.microsoft.com/technet/prodtechnol/WindowsServer2003/Library/IIS/cd72c0dc-c5b8-42e4-96c2-b3c656f99ead.mspx?mfr=true

- *IIS 7*: http://technet.microsoft.com/en-us/library/cc725608(WS.10).aspx

## Nginx

Nginx (http://nginx.net/) is a lightweight Web server that is well suited to serving static files. On busy sites, a common configuration is to have a server such as Apache or IIS providing the dynamic page generation proxied behind an nginx instance that takes care of images, style sheets, and other static files without the accompanying resource requirements.

You can use the *types* directive to make configuring MIME types in nginx.conf straightforward. Listing 2-4 shows an example command that associates the .xhtml file extension with the MIME type for XHTML-MP markup and the .wml file extension with the MIME type for WML markup.

**Listing 2-4.** *Adding MIME Types into Nginx*

```
types {
  application/vnd.wap.xhtml+xml    xhtml;
  text/vnd.wap.wml    wml;
}
```

## Mobile Web Browsers on the Desktop

Your Mobile Web development environment is not complete without tools for viewing web pages in a mobile context. The most convenient developer tool for viewing Mobile Web pages is Firefox. Firefox can be configured to impersonate a mobile device and provide a rough approximation of how web content might render on mobile devices. Mobile browser emulators, desktop software that simulates a mobile device or a mobile browser, bring you a step closer to actual mobile device behavior. An emulator uses the same browser engine that you find on a mobile device; however, because it doesn't run in the same execution environment, you cannot always use this approach to detect client-side performance problems. The most accurate way to view web pages in a mobile context is to use an actual mobile device because this will likely let you see the effects of network latency and any proxies present.

> **NOTE:** If you develop Mobile Web content primarily for iPhone, Android, or Nokia Series 60 3<sup>rd</sup> Edition or later, you should also use a WebKit browser such as Apple Safari (`http://apple.com/safari/`) or Google Chrome (`http://google.com/chrome`). Browsers in these mobile devices use WebKit. Safari and Chrome are WebKit-based desktop browsers that allow user-agent modification and provide code inspectors.

## Firefox and Mobile Add-Ons

Firefox is an open-source, standards-compliant, and extensible web browser from the Mozilla Foundation that you can customize easily using add-ons. Add-ons are extensions and themes developed in the XUL (XML User Interface Language, `https://developer.mozilla.org/en/XUL`) programming language. Mozilla hosts a directory of add-ons at `https://addons.mozilla.org/`.

> **NOTE:** In case you were wondering, the acronym XUL, pronounced as *zool*, is indeed a play on the god Zuul from the classic geek movie, *Ghostbusters*. In that movie, Sigourney Weaver's character is possessed by Zuul and famously declares: "There is no Dana. There is only Zuul."

XUL the programming language uses XML to define the user interface and JavaScript for application logic. The XUL slogan reads: "There is no data. There is only XUL."

In case you were *really* wondering, the XML namespace used in XUL documents is shown in Listing 2-5. Who says that developers don't have a sense of humor?

**Listing 2-5.** *Namespace URI for XML-Based XUL Programming Language Used in Firefox Extensions*

```
http://www.mozilla.org/keymaster/gatekeeper/there.is.only.xul
```

The next step is to download and install several add-ons that work together to allow Firefox to mimic a mobile device and render web documents written in mobile markup languages. Start by downloading the latest version of Firefox at `http://www.mozilla.com/en-US/products/firefox/`. The following sections will explain how to install and use the add-ons. After you install all the add-ons, restart Firefox to enable them in the browser.

After installing the extensions in this section and restarting Firefox, view the Tools ➤ Add-ons dialog box in Firefox. Figure 2-3 shows the Add-ons dialog box with several extensions installed.

**Figure 2-3.** *Add-ons dialog box in Firefox 3.0.11 after installing mobile add-ons*

## XHTML Mobile Profile

The XHTML Mobile Profile add-on provides support for the
`application/vnd.wap.xhtml+xml` MIME type. This add-on allows Firefox to view XHTML-MP Mobile Web documents in the browser window. Without this extension, Firefox prompts the user to save an XHTML-MP document as a file.

Version 0.5.3 of the XHTML Mobile Profile add-on also adds support for the
`multipart/mixed` MIME type. Multipart encoding is a mobile-markup optimization that bundles a markup document and its dependent resources (images, CSS, scripts, and so on) into an envelope for transmission in a single HTTP response. Many mobile browsers and operators support multipart encoding for Mobile Web content. This add-on displays the HTML component of a multipart-encoded document in the browser window. For more information about multipart encoding, see Chapter 9.

Install XHTML Mobile Profile by browsing in Firefox to `https://addons.mozilla.org/en-US/firefox/addon/1345` and clicking the Add to Firefox button.

This add-on has no options and needs no configuration. When enabled, it allows XHTML-MP and multipart-encoded mobile markup to be viewed in a browser window.

## wmlbrowser

The wmlbrowser add-on allows Firefox to render WML documents in the browser window. Its WML rendering is suitable for developing and debugging WML code, and its layout of WML documents weakly resembles the actual display on mobile devices. Regardless, I still strongly recommend testing on emulators and actual mobile devices. You will learn more about WML in Chapter 3.

Without this extension, Firefox prompts the user to save a WML document as a file.

Install wmlbrowser by browsing in Firefox to `https://addons.mozilla.org/en-US/firefox/addon/62` and clicking the Add to Firefox button.

This add-on likewise has no options and needs no configuration. When enabled, it allows WML mobile markup to be viewed in the browser window.

You can see a screenshot of wmlbrowser rendering the sample WML document at `http://learnto.mobi/02/wml-var.wml` (see Figure 2-4).

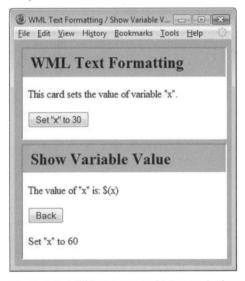

**Figure 2-4.** *A WML document with two cards viewed in Firefox 3.0.11 with wmlbrowser add-on*

## User Agent Switcher

The User Agent Switcher add-on enables Firefox to change the user-agent value that identifies the browser to web servers in HTTP transactions. This add-on sets the value of the `User-Agent` HTTP request header to one of many user-agents configured by the user. Mobile Web developers use User Agent Switcher to mimic the user-agents of mobile devices. Web sites detect mobile devices using the `User-Agent` request header and use it as the basis for content adaptation. Step one to impersonate a mobile device in Firefox is to send the phone's user-agent in web requests.

Without this extension, Firefox always sends its default user-agent in HTTP requests.

Install User Agent Switcher by browsing in Firefox to `https://addons.mozilla.org/en-US/firefox/addon/526` and clicking the *Add to Firefox* button.

This add-on allows the user to save user-agents from many sources. When enabled, the Tools ➤ Default User-Agent menu allows the user to easily change the value of the `User-Agent` HTTP request header.

Figure 2-5 is a screenshot of the Options dialog box for User Agent Switcher.

**Figure 2-5.** *The Options dialog box for the User Agent Switcher Add-On*

The Options dialog box is found by selecting the Tools ➤ Default User-Agent ➤ Edit User-Agents menu item. This dialog allows you to view and modify the list of installed user-agents. See Appendix A for sample user-agents from mobile devices. The mobile developer community mobiForge (`http://mobiforge.com`) also provides a pre-packaged set of mobile user-agents for User Agent Switcher. See `http://mobiforge.com/developing/blog/user-agent-switcher-config-file` and look for the attachment to the blog post.

Figure 2-6 selects a value from the list of installed user-agents in User Agent Switcher.

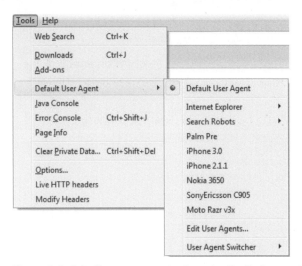

**Figure 2-6.** *Selecting a user-agent value using the Tools menu in Firefox 3.0.11*

Use the *Tools* menu to change the value of the `User-Agent` request header to a value previously added in the Options dialog box.

## Modify Headers

The Modify Headers add-on allows rule-based modification of HTTP request headers sent by Firefox. Mobile Web developers use this extension to modify Firefox request headers to exactly match those sent by a mobile device. Step two to impersonate a mobile device in Firefox is to send the exact set of HTTP request headers sent by the phone in web requests.

It is possible to modify the `User-Agent` request header using Modify Headers but recommended to use instead the more robust support in the User Agent Switcher add-on.

Without this extension, Firefox sends its default set of HTTP request headers when making requests to web servers.

Install Modify Headers by browsing in Firefox to `https://addons.mozilla.org/en-US/firefox/addon/967`and clicking the *Add to Firefox* button.

Figure 2-7 shows the Modify Headers menu item in the Tools Menu of Firefox.

**Figure 2-7.** *Modify Headers dialog box is available in the Tools menu of Firefox 3.0.11*

The Modify Headers add-on uses a dialog box to configure simple rules for changing the HTTP request headers sent in Firefox. Each rule adds, modifies or filters (suppresses) a single request header. Rules are executed sequentially and may be individually enabled and disabled.

The example rules in Figure 2-8 change several request headers in Firefox:

- They add `MSISDN: 5035551212`.

- They update the `Via` header to `Via: 127.0.0.1`.

- They update the `Connection` header to `Connection: close`.

- They remove the `Keep-Alive` header.

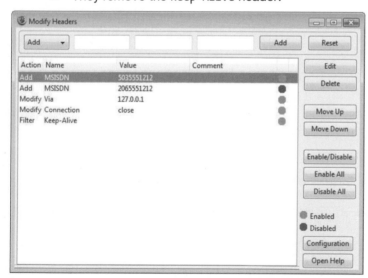

**Figure 2-8.** *The Modify Headers configuration dialog box with sample rules*

The second MSISDN rule is not executed because it is disabled.

By default, Modify Headers modifies Firefox request headers only when the Modify Headers dialog box is open, but that setting may be changed by clicking the *Configuration* button on the dialog.

It can be helpful to view Firefox request headers while you are writing rules to modify them to mimic a mobile device. The Live HTTP Headers add-on displays HTTP request and response headers in a Firefox window. Or, browse to http://learnto.mobi/view.php from Firefox to view request headers.

See Appendix B for samples of HTTP request headers from mobile devices.

## Live HTTP Headers

The Live HTTP Headers add-on allows users to view request and response headers from HTTP transactions in Firefox. Mobile Web developers review HTTP headers to check that Firefox is accurately impersonating a mobile device and to gain a deeper understanding of the HTTP transaction.

Without this extension, Firefox surfaces only a summary of header information in the Tools ➤ Page Info dialog.

Install Live HTTP Headers by browsing in Firefox to https://addons.mozilla.org/en-US/firefox/addon/3829 and clicking the Add to Firefox button.

Figure 2-9 shows the Live HTTP Headers menu item in the Tools menu of Firefox.

**Figure 2-9.** *The Live HTTP Headers dialog box available in the Tools menu of Firefox*

Next, select the Tools ➤ Live HTTP Headers menu item to open its dialog box (see Figure 2-10).

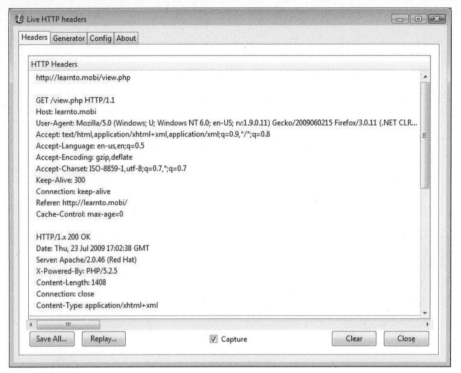

*Figure 2-10.* The Live HTTP Headers dialog box displaying Headers  and add-on configuration

The Live HTTP Headers dialog box displays a real-time stream of HTTP request and response headers. Clear the *Capture* checkbox to pause header collection. Use the Config tab to change add-on configuration. Its configuration settings allow developers to filter the web content for which headers are viewed and saved.

This add-on adds a pane to Firefox's *Page Info* dialog that displays the request and response headers for the web document, as shown in Figure 2-11.

*Figure 2-11. Live HTTP Headers adding Headers to Firefox's Page Info dialog box*

## Small Screen Renderer

The Small Screen Renderer add-on creates a view in Firefox that displays web pages on a very small screen, similar to that of a mobile device. This add-on is designed to provide an approximation of how a web page might be displayed on the small screen of a mobile device. Mobile Web developers use the add-on as a sanity check, so they can have a reasonable degree of confidence that their page layouts are adequate for small screens. However, testing Mobile Web pages in emulators and actual mobile devices provides a much more accurate view of mobile browser page rendering.

Without this extension, Firefox renders web pages in the entirety of the browser window. Install Small Screen Renderer by browsing in Firefox to `https://addons.mozilla.org/en-US/firefox/addon/526` and clicking the Add to Firefox button.

This add-on has no options and no configuration. When enabled, small-screen view can be toggled in Firefox's View menu.

Select View ➤ Small Screen Rendering to enable and disable small-screen viewing of web pages in Firefox, as shown in Figure 2-12.

**Figure 2-12.** *Toggling Small Screen Rendering in the View menu of Firefox*

The Small Screen Rendering add-on simulates how a web page might be viewed on a mobile device. For example, Figure 2-13 shows a small screen view of CNN's desktop web site in Firefox.

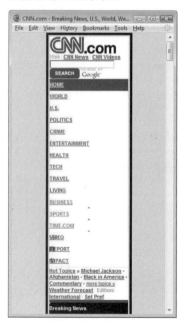

**Figure 2-13.** *Small Screen Rendering of* www.cnn.com *in Firefox*

# Firebug

The Firebug add-on allows live editing and debugging of HTML, CSS, and JavaScript in any web page. Firebug provides DOM inspection and assessments of web site performance. Mobile web developers use Firebug to review markup and style syntax, find errors, debug client-side scripts, and improve performance.

Without this extension, Firefox does not allow editing of web content viewed in a browser window. Other extensions provide JavaScript debugging, DOM inspection, and performance indicators. Firebug aggregates these important features of web-development tools into a single extension and provides clean integration into the Firefox browser.

Install Firebug by browsing in Firefox to `https://addons.mozilla.org/en-US/firefox/addon/1843` and clicking the Add to Firefox button. Or, visit the Firebug website at `http://getfirebug.com/`.

This add-on has options that control the web pages that Firebug can inspect and the types of web content to be inspected. Figure 2-14 shows the Tools ➤ Firebug menu in Firefox.

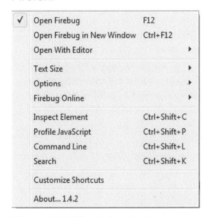

**Figure 2-14.** *The Tools ➤ Firebug menu in Firefox*

When the extension is enabled, press F12 or use the Tools ➤ Firebug ➤ Open Firebug menu item to open Firebug. Figure 2-15 shows Firebug displaying the HTML and CSS for a desktop web page. This screen is also used to edit the page markup.

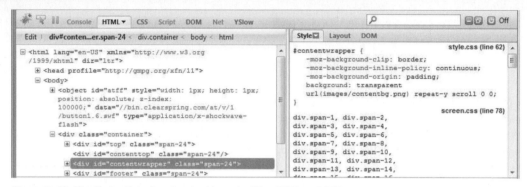

**Figure 2-15.** *The Firebug interface for viewing and editing HTML and CSS*

# Mobile Browser Emulators

Mobile device OEMs and software vendors provide products that emulate mobile devices and browsers, allowing a developer to simulate using a handset, running mobile applications, and browsing the Mobile Web. Emulators are important debugging tools for Mobile Web developers. A mobile emulator provides a general sense of how a web page renders on the mobile device. However, *the best debugging method is to test your Mobile Web application on an actual mobile device*.

There are three types of mobile emulators relevant for Mobile Web development:

- Mobile **device** *emulators* simulate the mobile phone OS and mobile applications. The emulator simulates a running mobile device. Users can access the native features of the device, use the mobile browser, and run and debug third-party applications. Mobile device OEMs make device emulators available for free to the mobile developer community.

- Mobile **browser** *emulators* simulate only the mobile-browser application. These emulators allow users to view web pages using the same application that runs on mobile devices. Browser vendors make browser emulators available for free to the mobile developer community.

- Mobile **infrastructure** *emulators* simulate the mobile device and its dependent services in the mobile ecosystem. Blackberry smartphones from RIM (Research in Motion) communicate with enterprise servers to manage email and Internet access. RIM provides emulators that simulate Blackberry devices and enterprise services, allowing mobile developers to test in an end-to-end simulation of the Blackberry environment.

Mobile Web developers can run multiple mobile emulators to analyze how their Mobile Web pages display in a wide variety of mobile devices and mobile browsers. Figures 2-

16 through 2-22 show CNN's Mobile Web site (http://m.cnn.com) as it displays in a sampling of mobile emulators.

**Figure 2-16.** *CNN Mobile viewed in iPhone Emulator*

**Figure 2-17.** *CNN Mobile viewed in Android 1.5 Emulator*

**Figure 2-18.** *CNN Mobile viewed in Palm Pre Emulator*

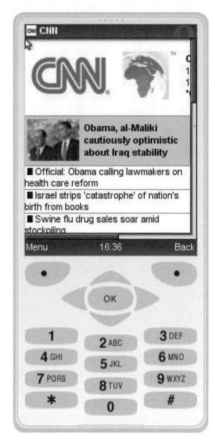

**Figure 2-19.** *CNN Mobile viewed in Opera Mini Emulator*

**Figure 2-20.** *CNN Mobile viewed in Openwave v7 Emulator*

Select Skin: Nokia N70 ▾  [ Update ]

**Figure 2-21.** *CNN Mobile viewed in dotMobi Emulator using Nokia N70 skin*

**Figure 2-22.** *CNN Mobile viewed in WinWAP Emulator*

Table 2-3 lists mobile emulators useful in Mobile Web development. You can visit
`http://learnthemobileweb.com/mobile-web-emulators/` for the latest list of mobile
emulators.

**Table 2-3.** *Mobile Device, Browser and Infrastructure Emulators*

| Emulator Name | Emulator Type | URL | Description |
| --- | --- | --- | --- |
| 3 | 3 | `http://developer.palm.com/` | SDK contains Palm Pre emulator. |
| iPhone SDK | Device | `http://developer.apple.com /iPhone/program/` | Contains an iPhone Simulator. Runs only on Mac OS X. |
| Android SDK | Device | `http://developer.android.com /sdk/` | SDK contains Android emulator. |
| Windows Mobile 6 SDK | Device | `http://msdn.microsoft.com/en- us/windowsmobile/bb264327.aspx` | SDK contains emulators and skins for Windows Mobile devices. |
| Nokia Mobile Browser Simulator 4.0 | Browser | `www.forum.nokia.com/info /sw.nokia.com/id/db2c69a2-4066- 46ff-81c4-caac8872a7c5 /NMB40_install.zip.html` | Emulates XHTML, XHTML-MP and WML as rendered on Nokia devices. |
| RIM Blackberry Simulators | Device Infrastruct-ure | `www.blackberry.com/developers /downloads/simulators/index.shtml` | Simulators for Blackberry devices and Blackberry Enterprise Server |
| Opera Mini Simulator | Browser | `www.opera.com/mini/demo/` | Simulates Opera Mini, a proxy solution for delivering advanced mobile browsing to featurephones supporting the J2ME or BREW runtime environments. |
| YoSpace SmartPhone Emulator | Device | `www.yospace.com/index.php /spedemo.html` | Demo of commercial device emulator. |
| Openwave Phone Simulator V7 | Browser | `http://developer.openwave.com /dvl/tools_and_sdk/phone_ simulator/` | Emulator for popular mobile browser installed on featurephones. Renders XHTML-MP and WML. |
| WinWAP Simulator | Browser | `www.winwap.com/desktop_ applications/browser_emulator` | Simulates a WML mobile browser found on Windows Mobile devices. Free 30-day trial. |

## Actual Mobile Devices

The best and most accurate method for viewing and testing Mobile Web pages is to use an actual mobile device. Mobile Web developers keep many phones in close reach for on-device testing during development. Because the actual battery-powered mobile device is involved instead of desktop software, on-device testing surfaces rendering and performance problems in mobile browsers that are missed in Firefox and emulator testing.

If investing in mobile phone service and devices is not an option, commercial alternatives such as DeviceAnywhere (http://deviceanywhere.com/) provide access to mobile devices in-network in many geographical areas. Mobile device manufacturers and network operators frequently offer loaned and leased devices to members of their developer and partner programs. You can learn more about testing Mobile Web content on mobile devices in Chapter 11.

# Other Development Tools

File-comparison and source code control utilities are also useful for Mobile Web development. These tools can be integrated into IDEs and are also available as standalone software products.

## File Comparison

File comparison utilities provide line-by-line visual inspection and merging of the differences in text files. File comparison is handy for tracking changes between iterations of a source code file. Used in conjunction with an IDE and source code control, a file-comparison tool allows you to track and manage changes to source code files in a web development project.

You can find several open source and/or free file-comparison utilities available for Windows, including WinMerge (http://winmerge.org/), ExamDiff (http://www.prestosoft.com/edp_examdiff.asp), and WinDiff from Microsoft (http://support.microsoft.com/kb/159214).

Linux and UNIX operating systems include the built-in `diff` command. For Mac OS X, Apple also provides a free FileMerge utility as part of Apple Developer Tools.

In addition to standalone tools, CVS and SVN version control clients (see Figure 2-23) come bundled with file comparison and merge utilities. It is a software development best practice to use a file-comparison tool to review modifications to each file, or *diff the changes*, before committing updated code to a source-control repository.

> **NOTE:** Geek slang for the act of comparing text files is *doffing*. The term *diff* is the name of an early UNIX file-comparison program.

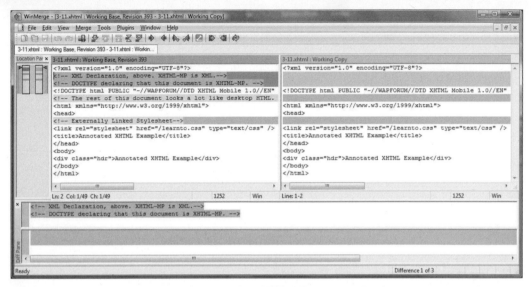

*Figure 2-23. Comparison (in Tortoise SVN client) of an XHTML-MP document showing comment removals*

## Source Code Control

Source code control (or source control or version control) is the practice of storing and managing revisions to text (and binary) files used in a software project. Source code control allows software teams to work on the same files simultaneously and manage merging changes into a single authoritative copy. Each file revision is owned by a user and commited to a central or distributed source code repository. When multiple users make conflicting changes to a file, the source-control system might attempt to automatically merge the revisions into a single updated file. If an automatic merge cannot be performed, the system uses file-comparison features to guide the user through a manual merge of code changes.

Source code management brings sanity and control to a software project, especially when the development team is distributed. Its client/server architecture allows clients in any geography and operating system to interact with a source code repository. A centralized source-control server stores source code files and their annotated-revision histories and manages user permissions. Developers use GUI or command-line client applications to update local source files to the latest repository versions, reserve files to edit exclusively, and upload (or commit) modified files back to the repository. Developers should include clear and human-readable comments describing changes to source code when committing them to the repository.

Two popular and reliable open source version control systems are CVS and SVN. Systems such as *git* and *mercurial* have also emerged as contemporary alternatives in recent years.

Concurrent Version System (CVS, http://www.nongnu.org/cvs/) is the older of the two systems. It is easy to install and widely deployed, but it shows its age and increasing obsolescence with expensive branching and tagging, server support restricted to UNIX, and some well-documented issues in handling advanced file-management scenarios.

Subversion (SVN, http://subversion.tigris.org/) promotes itself as the successor to CVS and fixes many of CVS's biggest flaws. SVN is truly cross-platform with servers and clients available on Windows, Linux, and OS X. It provides command-line clients and Tortoise SVN (http://tortoisesvn.tigris.org/), a powerful and truly excellent Windows GUI client with shell integration for managing source code transactions (see Figure 2-24).

Both CVS and SVN require a system administrator or OS expert with administrative privileges to install the server and create the repository. Source code clients are available from the open source projects, as well as numerous third-party developers. You can install CVS and SVN clients easily on any operating system. CVS and SVN are cross-platform tools, which means that client applications on any OS can access a server installed on a supported OS.

**NOTE:** Inconsistency in line break characters used across OSes is an annoyance in cross-platform software development. For example, when a Windows developer saves and commits changes to a source code file with UNIX-style line breaks, the file can also be updated to include Windows-style line breaks. The source-control system will recognize the updated code and line breaks as source code changes, causing unnecessary complexity when reviewing differences between file revisions. If your project includes developers using multiple OSes, set a convention for line-break format in source code files. IDEs and text editors include options to choose the default line-break format.

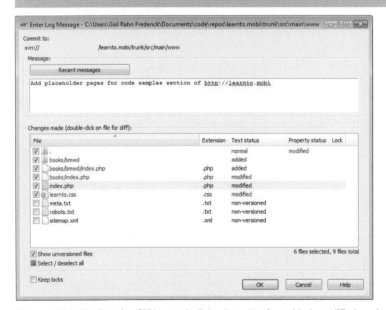

*Figure 2-24. The Tortoise SVN commit dialog box showing added, modified, and uncontrolled files*

## EXERCISE 2. IMPERSONATE A MOBILE DEVICE IN FIREFOX

In this exercise, you will impersonate a mobile device in Firefox and browse the Mobile Web using the extensions introduced in this chapter. Firefox impersonates a mobile device by:

- Supporting mobile MIME types

- Rendering mobile markup formats

- Sending the same HTTP request headers as a mobile device

Firefox mimics the HTTP request characteristics of a mobile browser or mobile device, but it makes no attempt to replicate its browsing behavior.

Use the user-agents from Appendix A and the HTTP request headers from Appendix B to modify Firefox to impersonate a mobile device:

- Use the User-Agent Switcher add-on to set the user-agent to a mobile device.

- Use the Modify Headers add-on to update Firefox request headers to match those from a mobile device.

- Use the Live HTTP Headers add-on to view request headers and confirm that they match the samples from actual mobile devices in Appendix B.

Next, browse XHTML-MP and WML documents on the Mobile Web. Impersonate mobile devices with varying capabilities, and browse the Mobile Web as the iPhone, Palm Pre, SonyEricsson C905, and LG VX9100 devices.

After you accomplish the preceding steps, answer these questions:

1. Can you coerce multiple Mobile Web experiences from the same domain? For example, http://cnn.com has both XHTML-MP and WebKit-optimized XHTML Mobile Web sites.

2. How does the content on the mobile version relate to the desktop web site? Are site themes consistent between Desktop Web and Mobile Web?

3. Mobile users are goal-oriented and remain on a Mobile Web site for three minutes or less. Are you able to complete common tasks on the Mobile Web site in this timeframe? (For example, on a weather web site, how easy is it to find the weather forecast for your city? On a travel web site, how quickly can you find arrival information for a flight?)

4. For which user-agents did the web site redirect to mobile-optimized markup? Which user-agents received desktop markup? Why?

Now repeat this exercise using mobile emulators. How does the presentation of Mobile Web pages change between Firefox and the emulators?

The presentation of Mobile Web pages can also change from device to device. Observe these variations and formulate hypotheses about why mobile browsers vary in displaying the same web page and why Mobile Web sites modify presentation and behavior for mobile user-agents. See Chapter 4 for more information about content adaptation.

# Summary

In this chapter, you learned how to install and configure the tools used in Mobile Web development. You selected an IDE based on its support for markup authoring and your choice of server-side scripting language, and you learned the most common MIME types used on the Mobile Web and how to configure your web server to support them. You also learned discussed three methods to view and debug Mobile Web pages: Firefox with add-ons, mobile browser emulators, and actual mobile devices. You selected file comparison and source-control utilities to manage Mobile Web source code. In the exercise, you used Firefox and mobile emulators to impersonate mobile devices and browse the Mobile Web.

In the next chapter, you'll examine the syntax of mobile markup languages and style sheets. You will also study relevant best practices from industry organizations and standards bodies.

# Part II

# The Syntax of the Mobile Web

Part 2 explores the markup, scripting languages, and device databases that enable device-aware mobile web development. You'll learn about the markup languages that drive rich, lightweight web experiences on all kinds of mobile devices, especially smartphones. You'll study HTML, XHTML-MP, and WML, style mobile markup using CSS, and get to know the best practices for coding web pages for mobile devices.

You'll learn to use databases of mobile device characteristics to identify web traffic from mobile phones, and adapt markup to target mobile devices and mobile browser versions.

For capable mobile devices, you'll iteratively enrich a mobile web site with client-side interactivity powered by ECMAScript-MP, JavaScript, and AJAX. You'll also examine the differences in DOM structure between mobile browsers, and delve into strategies for cross-platform scripting in a mobile environment.

# Chapter 3

# Mobile Markup Languages

Now that your development environment is set up, you will explore markup and styling languages that comprise Mobile Web pages. Web browsers on mobile devices are capable of rendering multiple markup languages. This chapter details the most widely adopted mobile markups: HTML, XHTML, XHTML-MP, and WML. I will also cover the mobile-appropriate CSS variants that style the presentation of XHTML-MP, XHTML and HTML documents.

This chapter is a thorough introduction to the syntax and semantics of *mobile* markup language. It is not intended to teach the desktop HTML and XHTML tag sets or detail all tags and attributes in each language. Many syntax references are available online or in other publications. See `http://learnthemobileweb.com/books/` for links to markup guides on the web.

## Selecting a Mobile Markup Language

Unfortunately, no single mobile markup language is universally appropriate for mobile devices. Mobile phone and mobile browser capabilities vary dramatically. Your Mobile Web site should select the best markup known to be supported by the mobile device, modifying its syntax and presentation to provide the best possible Mobile Web experience while avoiding known incompatibilities. This powerful mobile development technique is called *content adaptation* and is explained in detail in Chapter 4.

Markup languages may also be selected to target only browser support. This strategy makes no attempt to detect and avoid browser or device quirks, but simply redirects mobile devices to versions of a Mobile Web site based on support for the markup language.

Here are some general guidelines for choosing a mobile markup language:

- *XHTML*: Targeted to advanced mobile devices and smartphones. Increasingly, mobile browsers support XHTML in addition to XHTML-MP and WML. Mobile Web development in XHTML looks to the future, focusing on creating usable experiences on small screens with the rich tag set of XHTML. XHTML may not be supported on mainstream featurephone devices. It is critical to ensure browser support for web standards using a device database. Device awareness and content adaptation are detailed in Chapter 4.

- *XHTML-MP*: Targeted to mainstream featurephone mobile devices. Also suitable for most advanced mobile devices and smartphones, except the iPhone. XHTML-MP is the standard language for Mobile Web development.

- *WML*: Targets older mobile devices and browsers that do not support XHTML-MP or are known to have severe XHTML-MP implementation bugs. Not suggested for, but supported by all mobile devices and smartphones except for the iPhone and iPod Touch. Mobile Web development in WML looks to the past, ensuring support with legacy mobile devices. WML is suitable for textual Mobile Web content with minimal graphics where small document size is a priority.

To maximize compatibility with mobile devices, it is strongly recommended to first implement a Mobile Web site in XHTML-MP to support mainstream mobile devices and smartphones. If your Mobile Web site targets only a small number of smartphone models whose users are known to heavily browse the Web, consider creating smartphone-optimized Mobile Web sites using the full tag set of XHTML and including JavaScript and AJAX for a richer user experience. Read more about mobile JavaScript and AJAX in Chapter 5 and enhancing mobile markup for smartphones in Chapter 7.

New Mobile Web sites should almost never be coded in WML. Convince yourself that XHTML-MP is not an option before creating new WML markup.

# XHTML

XHTML is XML-formatted HTML. It uses the full tag set of HTML and conforms to the rigorous syntax requirements of XML. XHTML is widely used on the desktop web. As a rule, all smartphone browsers support XHTML, and increasingly, mobile browsers on new Internet-savvy featurephones also support XHTML.

This book assumes familiarity with the full tag set of XHTML as used in desktop web development. See `http://learnthemobileweb.com/books/` for links to XHTML language references.

XHTML is recommended for smartphone-optimized Mobile Web sites that provide a rich user experience to advanced mobile devices. An iPhone-optimized or WebKit-optimized Mobile Web site might use XHTML and WebKit CSS extensions to generate a compelling user experience for touchscreen smartphones. A Mobile Web site targeting

BlackBerry devices might combine XHTML with proprietary BlackBerry JavaScript APIs to provide location-aware web content in smart BlackBerry browsers.

However, there are many, many technical and ecosystem considerations when developing Mobile Web pages in XHTML rather than XHTML-MP. Using desktop markup in a Mobile Web site reduces device compatibility, impacts browser performance and tempts transcoders to incorrectly re-format the markup to provide an "optimized view" for mobile devices. Many concerns can be mitigated with markup optimization and defensive programming techniques. All of these considerations are addressed in subsequent chapters of this book.

> **NOTE:** Mobile browsers supporting XHTML, CSS, JavaScript, and AJAX are called "full Web" browsers.

## Why Not HTML?

HTML is widely supported in mobile browsers. But, the user pays a performance penalty for poorly formatted HTML markup, so XHTML is strongly preferred for Mobile Web development.

HTML is notoriously relaxed about its syntax. Desktop web browsers do an adequate job of inferring corrections to invalid HTML markup. Indeed, a 2008 study by Opera showed that only 4.13% of web pages comply with web markup and scripting standards. *More than 95% of web pages use invalid markup and scripting.* Clearly, the desktop web browser must identify markup errors and render a web page that matches the *intent* of the markup.

XHTML uses the tag set of HTML and enforces the rigorous syntax requirements of XML. Mobile Web developers use the rigorous XHTML dialect of HTML to generate syntactically valid markup for mobile browsers. Valid markup simplifies the browser's job and keeps it focused on rendering rather than detecting code errors and determining developer intent. The limited processing power and memory of mobile devices make valid markup syntax a priority.

## HTML 5

HTML 5 is the next major release of the foundational language of the Web. It is currently a draft recommendation undergoing active revision at the W3C (http://www.w3.org/TR/html5/) with joint participation by the Web Hypertext Application Technology Working Group (WHATWG, http://whatwg.org/). HTML 5 will be the next standard for markup and APIs supported in Web browsers. For developer convenience, the W3C maintains a document describing the differences between HTML 4 and HTML 5 at http://dev.w3.org/html5/html4-differences/.

If XHTML has been bidding to supersede HTML, then the relevance of HTML 5 is that it folds the two syntaxes together as equally valid ways to express the abstract DOM representation of HTML. The HTML 5 specification updates and combines HTML 4, XHTML 1, and DOM Level 2 HTML. HTML5 replaces XHTML 1 as the normative XML serialization format for HTML. Developers can use either the forgiving HTML syntax or rigorous XML syntax to format an HTML 5 document.

HTML 5 includes the following new and updated features:

- A new HTML doctype: `<!DOCTYPE html>`.

- New structural markup elements (i.e., `<header>`, `<nav>`, `<footer>`, `<section>`, etc.)

- Backwards-compatible parsing rules for HTML and XHTML.

- New `<audio>` and `<video>` markup elements for multimedia content.

- More `type` values for the `input` element, allowing native selection of dates, times, colors, and numbers.

- Frames are removed from HTML (with the exception of `<iframe>`, which is newly sandboxed).

- APIs for 2D drawing, media playback, media type registration, drag and drop, and cross-document messaging.

- Web application caches for offline browsing.

WHATWG and the W3C estimate that HTML 5 will reach Candidate Recommendation phase in 2012, at which point the entire specification will be mature enough for implementation in desktop and mobile browsers. That said, some components of HTML 5 are already implemented in the latest releases of desktop Web browsers and, at this writing, mobile browsers for Android and iPhone mobile devices.

One area of HTML 5 that draws intense browser vendor interest, especially for mobile browsers, is its Web application cache functionality. Also called "offline browsing," this feature of HTML 5 allows users to interact with Web applications even when a network connection is unavailable. HTML 5 is poised to dramatically increase Mobile Web usability for the common mobile use case of users moving in and out of network coverage. Offline caching allows a Web application to declare which markup, scripting, style, and data files are required for the application to run without accessing the network, enabling the browser to cache these files, and provide application access to the cached versions until network coverage is restored.

Smartphone browser vendors are racing to adopt features of HTML 5 as they gain industry consensus during the standardization process. Especially advanced mobile browsers do already, or soon will, support offline caching, new multimedia elements, and native controls for advanced input formats. Given that HTML 5 is a major revision to markup and API standards, and that it introduces significant new processing burdens for mobile devices, we can expect delays in HTML 5 adoption on lower-end mobile devices and fragmented standards support as HTML 5 is introduced across the mobile browser landscape.

# XHTML-MP

XHTML Mobile Profile (XHTML-MP) is a subset of XHTML targeting the limited capabilities of mobile devices. It is currently considered the de facto standard language for Mobile Web development. XHTML-MP is suitable markup for browsers in all kinds of mobile devices from resource-limited featurephones to smartphones and advanced mobile devices. This section explains the syntax of XHTML-MP 1.0.

XHTML-MP is XML. It conforms to the strict syntax requirements of XML.

> **NOTE:** XHTML-MP is a subset of XHTML and a superset of XHTML Basic (an early mobile markup language not discussed in this book). A notable difference between XHTML Basic and XHTML-MP is that the former does not support CSS.

Because XHTML and XHTML-MP are related, we learn XHTML-MP by subtraction. Starting with XHTML for the desktop web, we change the DTD, remove unsupported tags and attributes, and add mobile-specific language features to arrive at the features set of XHTML-MP.

## Example XHTML-MP Document

Listing 3-1 is an example of a very simple XHTML-MP document. This listing can be viewed in a browser at `http://learnto.mobi/books/bmwd/03/3-1.xhml`. View the example in a mobile browser or emulator to observe how document content is displayed in the browser.

**Listing 3–1.** *Example Annotated XHTML-MP Document*

```
<?xml version="1.0" encoding="UTF-8"?>
<!-- XML Declaration, above. XHTML-MP is XML.-->
<!-- DOCTYPE declaring that this document is XHTML-MP. -->
<!DOCTYPE html PUBLIC "-//WAPFORUM//DTD XHTML Mobile 1.0//EN"
"http://www.wapforum.org/DTD/xhtml-mobile10.dtd">
<!-- The rest of this document looks a lot like desktop HTML. -->
<html xmlns="http://www.w3.org/1999/xhtml">
<head>
<!-- Externally Linked Stylesheet-->
<link rel="stylesheet" href="/learnto.css" type="text/css" />
<title>Annotated XHTML Example</title>
</head>
<body>
<div class="hdr">Annotated XHTML Example</div>
</body>
</html>
```

# DTDs for XHTML-MP

As with any markup language, XHTML-MP identifies itself in a markup document with a unique DTD. Here are DTDs for XHTML-MP 1.0 and 1.1, the two revisions used widely on the Mobile Web. Only one DTD is allowed at the top of each XHTML-MP document.

```
<!DOCTYPE html PUBLIC "-//WAPFORUM//DTD XHTML Mobile 1.0//EN"
"http://www.wapforum.org/DTD/xhtml-mobile10.dtd">
```

```
<!DOCTYPE html PUBLIC "-//WAPFORUM//DTD XHTML Mobile 1.1//EN"
"http://www.openmobilealliance.org/tech/DTD/xhtml-mobile11.dtd">
```

Functional differences between XHTML-MP 1.0 and XHTML-MP 1.1 are described later in this section.

# XHTML Elements Not Supported in XHTML-MP

XHTML-MP is a strict subset of XHTML. Some XHTML tags are not appropriate for use in the resource-constrained rendering environment of a mobile browser. To preserve performance and portability, XHTML Mobile Profile excludes several tags and attributes from the XHTML standard.

Table 3-1 lists XHTML tags that are unsupported in XHTML-MP.

**Table 3-1.** *XHTML Elements Unsupported in XHTML-MP*

| XHTML Element | Reason for Exclusion |
|---|---|
| frame, frameset, iframe, noframes | Frames have significant browser memory requirements, including new DOM instances. Frames are not usable on small screens. |
| applet | Java applets are not supported in mobile browsers or natively on mobile devices. Java SE is not supported on mobile devices.(Outside of the browser, many mobile phones can run applications written in Java ME. Sidekick devices from Danger, a Microsoft subsidiary, uses a proprietary Java SDK based on Java SE and Java ME.) |
| area, map | Image maps are not supported nor easy to use on mobile devices. |
| basefont | Specify default font styles using CSS. |
| bdo | Bidirectional text is not supported. |
| button | Use <input type="submit"> for push buttons. |
| center | Use CSS to align page elements. |
| col, colgroup | Only basic tables are supported. See the next section for details. |
| del, ins, s, strike | Use CSS to style text to appear as deleted from, inserted into, or struck from the document. |
| dir, menu | Use CSS to style text to appear as directory or menu lists. |
| font | Use CSS to specify font styles. |
| legend | Basic forms are supported. Legends are not supported in fieldsets. |

| XHTML Element | Reason for Exclusion |
|---|---|
| noscript, script | Supported only in XHTML-MP 1.1 and later. |
| sub, sup | Mobile devices provide limited fonts. Subscripts and superscripts are supported. |
| tbody, tfoot, thead | Basic tables are supported. Grouping table header, body and footer elements is not supported. |
| tt | Use CSS to style text to appear as teletype text. |
| u | Underlining is a universal indicator of link labels. Underlined text that is not a link is not usable on small screens and strongly discouraged. However, if underlining is absolutely required, it may be accomplished using the text-decoration: underline; CSS directive. |
| xmp | Use CSS or the pre element to style text to appear preformatted. |

In addition, links in XHTML-MP using the <a> tag do *not* support the target attribute that traditionally opens link targets as popups or in new browser tabs or windows. Only a select few smartphone browsers support tabbed browsing and/or opening multiple browser windows. See Chapter 7 for more information about optimizing mobile markup for advanced mobile browsers.

The XHTML elements supported in the Mobile Profile standard allow rich web interfaces to be developed that are usable on small mobile phone screens. XHTML-MP's removal of legacy tags used for fancy text layouts (font, basefont, dir, menu, del, ins, s, strike, tt, etc.) supports a cleaner separation of content and presentation in Mobile Web documents. (This separation is imperfect. For example, the body tag still supports a bgcolor attribute.) XHTML-MP markup tags are used to specify Mobile Web content and CSS is used to style its presentation.

# Updated and Mobile-Specific Features in XHTML-MP

XHTML Mobile Profile simplifies some XHTML elements. However, it also introduces new syntax for mobile-specific language features. This section describes syntax differences between XHTML-MP and XHTML and new additions to the markup language targeting mobile browsers and mobile use cases.

## URI Schemes

Mobile browsers that support XHTML-MP also allow mobile-specific URI schemes as link targets in the href attribute of the <a> tag. These schemes enable common mobile use cases in Mobile Web content.

The tel: URI schemes allow mobile users to click a link to initiate a phone call. The format of a tel: URI is tel:<phone number>. The phone number to dial on the mobile device is embedded directly into the URI. The markup example below illustrates the use of the `tel:` scheme. (Hyphens are provided for human readability and are ignored by the dialer on the mobile device.)

```
Call <a href="tel:+1-503-555-1212">+1-503-555-1212</a> for Information
```

The `wtai:` scheme is used to initiate phone calls and add contact phone numbers to the mobile device's address book. This scheme uses a different URI format for each task. The format for initiating a phone call from the mobile device is `wtai://wp/mc;<phone number>`. To add a contact into the mobile address book, use the `wtai://wp/ap;<phone number>;<name>` scheme. The markup examples below illustrate both uses of the `wtai:` scheme:

```
Call <a href="wtai://wp/mc;+15035551212">+1-503-555-1212</a> for Information
```

```
<a href="wtai://wp/ap;+15035551212;Information">Add to Address Book</a>
```

Unfortunately, the `tel:` and `wtai:` URI schemes are not universally supported in mobile browsers. In general, older mobile browsers prefer `wtai:` while newer browsers support `tel:`. Some browsers do allow use of both schemes. Use a device database to determine which of the two protocols are supported by a specific model of mobile device. See Chapter 4 for more information about device databases and content adaptation.

The `sms:` URI scheme initiates a SMS message. The format of this scheme is `sms:<phone numbers>?<action>`, where `<phone numbers>` is a comma-separated list of phone numbers and `<action>` is an optional token to specify more information about the text message, such as the message body. The markup examples below show uses of this scheme:

```
<a href="sms:+15035551212,+15035551234">Text us with a Question</a>
<a href="sms:+15035551212?body=Ask+a+Question">Text me with a Question</a>
```

The `mmsto:` URI scheme initiates an MMS message. The format of this scheme is `sms:<phone numbers>;<action>`, where `<phone numbers>` is a comma-separated list of phone numbers and `<action>` is an optional token to specify more information about the text message.

```
<a href="mmsto:+15035551212">Send us a Photo</a>
<a href="mmsto:+15035551212?subject=Photo">Send us a Photo</a>
```

The `sms:` and `mmsto:` URI schemes are not universally supported in mobile browsers. Consult a device database and perform on-device testing to determine their actual support levels in mobile browsers.

## Forms

XHTML-MP provides basic support for forms. The `<form>` element supports `action`, `enctype`, and `method` attributes to specify, respectively, the URL to submit form data, the MIME encoding to use for form contents and the HTTP request method used to submit the form. The `<form>` attributes `name` and `target` from XHTML are not supported.

Valid child elements of `<form>` include `<fieldset>`, `<p>`, and `<table>`. The `<input>` elements of a form must be contained inside one of these child tags. In the `<input>` element, the new `title` attribute specifies a softkey label to display when the input element is focused. As in XHTML, CSS may be used to customize the visual style of the form and its input fields.

The code sample in Listing 3-2 illustrates the use of `<form>` and `<input>` elements in XHTML-MP. This listing can be viewed in a browser at `http://learnto.mobi/books/bmwd/03/3-2.xhml`. View the example in a mobile browser or emulator to observe the form behavior. Figure 3-1 displays Listing 3-2 in the Android emulator.

**Figure 3-1.** *XHTML-MP Forms in Android Emulator*

**Listing 3-2.** *XHTML-MP Forms*

```
<?xml version="1.0" encoding="UTF-8"?>
<!DOCTYPE html PUBLIC "-//WAPFORUM//DTD XHTML Mobile 1.0//EN"
"http://www.wapforum.org/DTD/xhtml-mobile10.dtd">
<html xmlns="http://www.w3.org/1999/xhtml">
<head>
<link rel="stylesheet" href="/learnto.css" type="text/css" />
<title>XHTML-MP Form</title>
</head>
<body>

<form action="/signup.php" method="post">
<p>Join the Sunset Farmers&apos; Market email list:</p>
<fieldset>
<label>First Name: <input type="text" name="firstname" size="7" title="First"/></label>
<label>Email: <input type="text" name="email" size="10" title="Email"/></label>
</fieldset>
<p>
```

```
<input type="submit" src="send.jpg" value="Join List" title="Join List"/>
</p>
</form>

</body>
</html>
```

## Tables

Tables are greatly simplified in XHTML-MP but still retain some useful features. The `<table>` element can contain only `<caption>` and `<tr>` child elements, (which in turn can contain `<td>` and `<th>` child elements to represent the table cells). The `cellpadding` and `cellspacing` attributes are not supported. Instead, use CSS to style tables, rows, columns, and individual cells. Table rows and cells can be aligned using CSS or the `align` and `valign` attributes. Both header and data cells (`<th>` and `<td>` tags) can span blocks in the table's grid using `colspan` and `rowspan` attributes. All other visual components of tables, including background colors, fonts, and visual differentiation of header and footer rows, are controlled using CSS.

The code sample in Listing 3-3 displays a basic `<table>` element in XHTML-MP. This listing can be viewed in a browser at `http://learnto.mobi/books/bmwd/03/3-3.xhml`. View the example on an emulator or mobile device to observe how a table displays in a mobile browser. Figure 3-2 displays Listing 3-3 in an Android emulator.

**Figure 3-2.** *XHTML-MP Table in Android Emulator*

**Listing 3-3.** *XHTML-MP Table*

```
<?xml version="1.0" encoding="UTF-8"?>
<!DOCTYPE html PUBLIC "-//WAPFORUM//DTD XHTML Mobile 1.0//EN"
"http://www.wapforum.org/DTD/xhtml-mobile10.dtd">
<html xmlns="http://www.w3.org/1999/xhtml">
<head>
<link rel="stylesheet" href="/learnto.css" type="text/css" />
<title>XHTML-MP Table</title>
</head>
<body>

<table class="borderOne">
<caption>Today&apos;s Freshest Produce</caption>

<tr align="center" valign="top">
<th>Vegetable</th>
<th>Price</th>
<th>Vendor</th>
</tr>

<tr align="left" valign="top">
<td class="vegName">Broccoli</td>
<td class="vegPrice">$1.50/lb</td>
<td class="vegVendor">Mt. Tabor Farms</td>
</tr>

<tr>
<td align="center" valign="middle" class="special" colspan="3">Special! <a
href="/specials.php">$3 for 3 heirloom tomatoes at Booth 201.</a></td>
</tr>

<tr align="left" valign="top">
<td class="vegName">Goat Cheese</td>
<td class="vegPrice">$4.00 / wedge</td>
<td class="vegVendor">Portland Organic Dairy</td>
</tr>

</table>

</body>
</html>
```

# Links and Access Keys

Navigating between links and scrolling the browser window are difficult tasks on mobile devices. Recognizing this limitation, XHTML-MP provides a method to accelerate link activation in the <a> tag using the mobile phone keypad. Access keys are numeric shortcuts associated with a link. Pressing the shortcut key activates the link.

Use the accesskey attribute of the <a> tag to create numeric shortcuts. Valid accesskey values are the numbers 0–9. Using the accesskey attribute usually does *not* display the shortcut key on the screen. The developer must generally provide a visual cue for users to know which number key activates the link. (Here, a device database can identify browsers that do display access keys.)

This code sample activates the link when the user presses the 1 key:

```
<div>1. <a href="/" accesskey="1">Home</a></div>
```

Access keys are commonly combined with ordered lists (<ol> and <li> tags) to create navigation menus in XHTML-MP. By definition, ordered lists display item numbers, so there is no need to also add a visual cue for the user.

The code sample in Listing 3-4 displays a menu of links with access keys using ordered lists in XHTML-MP. This listing can be viewed in a browser at http://learnto.mobi/books/bmwd/03/3-4.xhtml. View the example in a mobile browser or emulator to observe the behavior of access keys. Figure 3-3 displays Listing 3-4 in the Android emulator.

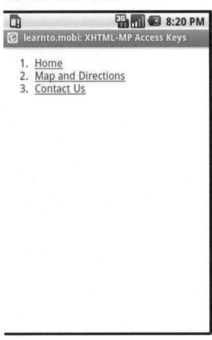

**Figure 3-3.** *XHTML-MP Access Keys in Android Emulator*

**Listing 3-4.** *XHTML-MP Access Keys*

```
<?xml version="1.0" encoding="UTF-8"?>
<!DOCTYPE html PUBLIC "-//WAPFORUM//DTD XHTML Mobile 1.0//EN"
"http://www.wapforum.org/DTD/xhtml-mobile10.dtd">
<html xmlns="http://www.w3.org/1999/xhtml">
<head>
<link rel="stylesheet" href="/learnto.css" type="text/css" />
<title>XHTML-MP Access Keys</title>
</head>
<body>

<ol>
<li><a href="/" accesskey="1">Home</a></li>
<li><a href="/map.php" accesskey="2">Map and Directions</a></li>
<li><a href="/contact.php" accesskey="3">Contact Us</a></li>
```

```
</ol>

</body>
</html>
```

An alternate way to access keys in a Mobile Web document is to note the access key in plaintext brackets after the link target. This pattern is useful when embedding access keys into horizontal menus and inline in text paragraphs. The example XHTML-MP below displays the access key value in this manner:

```
Browse to <a href="/article.php?id=123" accesskey="8">the next article</a> [8] for …
```

## Embedded Objects

The `<object>` and `<param>` tags are supported in XHTML-MP, but caveats apply. These tags are used to embed multimedia files into web documents. However, many media types, especially Flash and video formats, are not commonly supported in mobile browsers. Use a device database to ensure that the media format is supported before embedding media into a document.

# Common Implementation Bugs

The XHTML-MP language is standardized and widely accepted in the mobile industry. Unfortunately, the same cannot be said for its rendering engines in mobile browsers. Mobile browsers have flaws and may also suffer deliberate lack of support for markup languages and features. An XHTML-MP document may render with slight or obvious differences across browser versions and models.

The most common XHTML-MP implementation differences in mobile browsers are the following:

- The browser may have a small number of installed fonts. Heading elements (`<h1>` … `<h6>`) may span only two or three font sizes. In general, developers have very little control over font selection in XHTML-MP. See the CSS for Mobile Devices section of this chapter for details.

- Tables may render poorly enough to avoid altogether.

- The user interface for single and multiple select lists vary in display.

- Document titles may be displayed inline in the browser window, in the window chrome, or not displayed at all.

- Image alignment and cropping may not be supported using CSS. Incorrect or incomplete support for CSS style directives.

- Default padding and margin properties in the CSS box model may vary.

The devil is in the details with XHTML-MP implementation bugs. The burden is on the Mobile Web developer to create well-formed and valid markup syntax and test using actual mobile devices and browsers to ensure that markup renders as expected on supported devices. Many developers find the W3C Mobile Web Best Practices (http://www.w3.org/TR/mobile-bp/) to be a helpful guide for producing standards-compliant and usable Mobile Web content. For more about effective mobile browser and web site validation and testing strategies, see Chapters 9 and 10.

Some implementation flaws are egregious enough to be tracked by device databases, allowing Mobile Web developers to programmatically avoid problematic syntax. This technique is described in Chapter 4.

## XHTML-MP 1.1

XHTML-MP 1.1 adds support for the <script> and <noscript> tags, DOM events and a dialect of the ECMAScript scripting language, i.e., JavaScript or its mobile-optimized cousin ECMAScript MP. AJAX is possible in XHTML-MP 1.1 for mobile browsers known to support an XmlHttpRequest variant and sufficient DOM properties and methods. See Chapter 5 for information about JavaScript and AJAX on mobile devices.

Similarly to XHTML, scripts can be referenced externally or written inline in an XHTML-MP document. The markup snippet below imports an external JavaScript file into an XHTML-MP document:

```
<script type="text/javascript" src="http://learnto.mobi/lib.js" />
```

Here is an example of a JavaScript function declared inline in a XHTML-MP 1.1 document:

```
<script type="text/javascript">
function handleOnClick() {
        // Get the new image URL
        var newSrc = "http://learnto.mobi/img/screamer_icon.png";

        // Update the image URL
        document.getElementById("theImg").src = newSrc;
}
</script>
```

Below, an XHTML-MP image tag associates the inline JavaScript function above with its onclick event:

```
<img id="theImg" src="/logo.png"width="140" height="50" alt="Logo"
onclick="handleOnClick();"/>
```

This syntax is identical to that used in XHTML desktop web development. Browser event models may be restricted in mobile browser. See Chapter 5 for more about JavaScript for mobile browsers.

> **NOTE:** The MIME type text/javascript must be used to identify JavaScript and ECMAScript MP in XHTML-MP 1.1 markup documents.

## XHTML-MP 1.2

XHTML-MP 1.2 is the latest revision to the markup standard. It adds support for text input modes, objects and events. XHTML-MP 1.2 is a new standard, adopted in March 2008, and is not yet widely adopted in mobile browsers. It is not discussed further in this book.

### Best Practices for XHTML-MP Web Development

Mobile Web development in XHTML-MP has many uniquenesses and quirks. These beginning best practices will help you produce usable Mobile Web pages in XHTML-MP.

- *Simple, fast-loading page designs win*. Mobile users browse across often-congested mobile networks. Simple Mobile Web pages with compact byte sizes produce a responsive user experience.

- *Mobile users pay per KB.* Some mobile subscribers pay per kilobyte of downloaded data, and reward mobile users by providing a streamlined Mobile Web browsing experience. Strip unnecessary whitespace and comments from your markup. Consider the total kilobyte size of your mobile markup and linked external resources. (See Chapter 8 for more Mobile Web optimization tips.)

- *Pages must be readable without Images or CSS*. Some cost- and bandwidth-conscious mobile users browse without downloading images. Your Mobile Web pages must be readable and usable without images. Specify `alt` text and image sizes in the markup to make page layouts without images resembling the intended design. Some mobile browsers have faulty support for CSS, so at a minimum your Mobile Web page must be readable without CSS.

- *Scrolling sucks*. This scientific principle summarizes the difficulty that many mobile users (especially on featurephones) experience trying to scroll up and down to view the entirety of a Mobile Web page. Mobile browsers scroll as few as three lines of text per user click. That equates to one frustrated user pressing the Down key ten times to view a thirty-line article snippet. Balance the amount of content on a single page with the network delay incurred to fetch the next Mobile Web document.

# CSS for Mobile Devices

Most mobile browsers support one or more of three Cascading Style Sheet (CSS) standards: CSS2, Wireless CSS, and CSS Mobile Profile. Additionally, some smartphones with WebKit browsers support parts of the CSS3 standard. Some older mobile devices support no CSS at all (but these devices are not browsing the Internet in significant numbers and would be good candidates for Mobile Web content in WML).

# CSS2

CSS2 is markup styling for the desktop web, standardized by the W3C (http://www.w3.org/TR/CSS2/) and well understood by web developers. Full web mobile browsers support the entire CSS2 specification, and even parts of CSS3 in some cases.

# Wireless CSS and CSS Mobile Profile

Wireless CSS and CSS Mobile Profile are tightly related, but independent mobile subsets of CSS2 used to style XHTML-MP documents.

Wireless CSS is a CSS2 subset standardized by the Open Mobile Alliance. Its most recent version, 1.2, was released in September 2007. This CSS variant adds three mobile-specific CSS extensions to support scrolling marquee text, text input formats, and access keys mappings. All of these mobile extensions are now obsolete and should not be used in new Mobile Web projects. The marquee style properties in Wireless CSS were retired in favor of the marquee features in CSS3.

> **NOTE:** Wireless CSS specifies style exceptions for documents presented in the Chinese, Japanese, and Korean character sets. Refer to the Wireless CSS specification for more information.

CSS Mobile Profile is a CSS2 subset—with some features borrowed from CSS3—that is standardized by the W3C. It is intended to provide a common subset of styles for resource-constrained mobile devices where implementation of the full CSS standard is not possible. The W3C's goal is to align CSS Mobile Profile with Wireless CSS as much as possible.

Despite the independence of the two mobile CSS standards, there is a measure of compatibility and interoperability between them. The Wireless CSS 1.2 standard (authored by the Open Mobile Alliance) attests to their compatibility:

> *Since both CSS2 variants follow CSS user agent semantics, conforming Wireless CSS user agents will accept valid W3C CSS Mobile Profile style sheets.*

Both mobile CSS subsets support core CSS syntax and properties including selectors, inheritance, the box model, shorthand properties, generic font families, and absolute and relative font sizes. Both mobile dialects comply with existing CSS syntax standards and can be validated with a CSS validator. However, because the two dialects are subsets of desktop CSS, there are notable absences in the mobile specifications. Optional features in the mobile specifications may be freely omitted by browser vendors while still claiming compliance to the standard. This is a source of significant frustration for new Mobile Web developers. Table 3-2 provides developers with a list of the exact differences between CSS2 and its mobile subsets.

Here are a few notable oddities or omissions in Wireless CSS and CSS Mobile Profile. Wireless CSS leaves the `inherit` property value as optional for many properties and, therefore, often unimplemented in mobile browsers. Also in Wireless CSS, the `display` property requires only the `none` value. Values commonly used in desktop styling, like `block`, `table`, `inline`, and `inherit` are optional and often left unimplemented in browsers. The absence of display property values complicates the construction of complex page layouts. In CSS Mobile Profile, box positioning using the `position`, `bottom`, `top`, `left`, `right`, and `z-index` properties is left as entirely optional in the standard.

Overall, Wireless CSS is a more restricted subset and an older standard targeted at Web browsers on resource-limited mobile devices. CSS Mobile Profile adds in much more of the CSS2 standard to enable richer web documents but risks full support on mass-market mobile browsers.

Table 3-2 describes the key differences between CSS2, Wireless CSS, and CSS Mobile Profile.

**Table 3-2.** *CSS2 Properties with Optional, Limited, or No Support in Mobile CSS Dialects*

| CSS2 Property | Description | Wireless CSS | CSS Mobile Profile |
|---|---|---|---|
| `background-color` | Background color for a block element. | The inherit value is optional in the standard. | Full support |
| `background-attachment` | Specifies how background attaches to browser window. | The inherit value is optional in the standard. | Full support |
| `background-image` | Specifies a background Image. | The inherit value is optional in the standard. | Full support |
| `background-position` | Position of background image. | Supported values are top, center, bottom, left, and right. The inherit value is optional in the standard, as are length and percentage values. | Supported values are top, center, bottom, left, right, and inherit. |
| `border-color,` `border-top-color,` `border-right-color,` `border-bottom-color,` `border-top-color,` | Sets color of box border for document element. | The inherit value is optional in the standard. | Full support |

| CSS2 Property | Description | Wireless CSS | CSS Mobile Profile |
|---|---|---|---|
| border-style, border-top-style, border-right-style, border-bottom-style, border-top-style | Sets style of box border for document element. | Supported values are none, solid, dashed, and dotted.<br><br>Optional values are hidden, double, groove, ridge, inset, outset, and inherit. | Supported values are none, solid, dashed, dotted, and inherit. |
| border-width, border-top-width border-right-width, border-bottom-width, border-top-width | Sets width of box border for document element. | The inherit value is optional. | Full support |
| display | Display model or instructions for a document element. | Supported value is none. If an element is visible, it should not declare a display property in CSS.<br><br>All other values are optional. | Supported values are inline, block, list-item, none, and inherit. |
| float, clear | Float control for the document element. | The inherit value is optional. | Full support |
| font-family | Font family used for text in the document element. | Supported values are generic font names and inherit. Optional to allow specific font names.<br>Only a very small number of fonts are preinstalled on most mobile devices. Specifying a font by name is not recommended. | Full support<br><br>Only a very small number of fonts are preinstalled on most mobile devices. Specifying a font by name is not recommended. |

| CSS2 Property | Description | Wireless CSS | CSS Mobile Profile |
|---|---|---|---|
| font-size | Font size used for text in the document element. | Supported values are absolute sizes, relative sizes, and inherit.<br><br>Absolute sizes are xx-small, x-small, small, medium, large, x-large, and xx-large.<br><br>Relative sizes are smaller and larger.<br><br>Numeric and percentage values are optional in the standard. | Supported values are absolute sizes, relative sizes, and inherit. |
| font-style | Visual styling used for text in the document element. | Supported values are normal, italic, oblique, and inherit. | Full support |
| font-variant | Font variations used for text in the document element. | Supported values are normal, small-caps, and inherit. | Full support |
| font-weight | Type weight used for text in the document element. | Supported values are normal, bold, and inherit.<br><br>Numeric or bolder and lighter values must be supported but may map to normal and bold values. | Full support |
| height, width | Width and height of the document element. | Supported values are numeric length, percentage, and auto.<br><br>The inherit value is optional. | Full support |

| CSS2 Property | Description | Wireless CSS | CSS Mobile Profile |
|---|---|---|---|
| list-style-image | Image used to delimit list items. | Supported values are URL, none, and inherit. | Full support |
| list-style-position | Position of icon or character used to delimit list items. | Optional | Not supported |
| list-style-type | Icon or character used to delimit list items. | Supported values are disc, circle, square, decimal, lower-roman, upper-roman, lower-alpha, upper-alpha, none, and inherit. | Same |
| margin, margin-bottom, margin-left, margin-right, margin-top | Sets width of box margin for document element. | The inherit value is optional. | Full support |
| outline, outline-color, outline-style, outline-width | Outline styles in box model. | Not supported | Optional |
| overflow, overflow-style | Overflow styles used to specify marqueed text. Borrowed from CSS3 specification. | Not supported. Instead, use deprecated value -wap-marquee for the display property. | Supported overflow value is auto. Supported overflow-style value is marquee. |
| padding, padding-bottom, padding-left, padding-right, padding-top | Sets width/height of box padding for document element. | The inherit value is optional. | Full support. |
| position, bottom, left, right, Top | Positioning a block element by specifying its fixed, absolute, or relative coordinates. | Not supported | Optional |

| CSS2 Property | Description | Wireless CSS | CSS Mobile Profile |
|---|---|---|---|
| text-align | Specifies alignment of text in a document element. | Supported values are left, right, center, and inherit.<br><br>The justify value is optional. | Full support |
| text-decoration | Specifies adornment styles for text elements. | Supported values are blink, underline, and none.<br><br>Optional values are inherit, overline, and line-through. | Supported values are blink, underline, inherit, and none. |
| text-transform | Transforms the case of text in a document element. | Supported values are capitalize, uppercase, lowercase, none, and inherit. | Full support |
| vertical-align | Specifies vertical alignment for the content of a document element. | Supported values are top, middle, bottom, and baseline.<br><br>All other values are optional. | Supported values are top, middle, bottom, baseline, and inherit. |
| visibility | Specifies whether the document element is visible. | Supported values are visible and hidden.<br><br>Optional values are collapse and inherit. | Full support |
| white-space | Specifies how to format whitespace in the document element. | Supported values are normal, pre, nowrap, and inherit. | Full support |
| z-index | Specifies the 3D (front and back) alignment for overlapping elements. | Not supported | Optional |

## Determining CSS Support on a Mobile Device

It can be difficult to determine actual CSS support levels in mobile browsers. Few browser manufacturers provide public documentation about their supported standards. The best ways to diagnose CSS support in a mobile browser are to:

- *Consult browser manufacturer documentation, if available.* See `http://learnthemobileweb/books/` for links to browser documentation.)

- *Consult a device database.* See Chapter 4 for details.

- Use *public mobile browser test pages to troubleshoot CSS support.* See Chapter 10 for details.

- *Create your own CSS test pages that demonstrate CSS property support.* Test widely on mobile browsers. Contribute this information to the Mobile Web developer community. See Chapter 12 for details.

## Best Practices for Mobile CSS

Effective CSS for mobile browsers combines common sense, on-device testing, and strict syntax adherence. These beginning best practices and the W3C Mobile Web Best Practices can help you get started:

- *All numeric property values must include units.* Label all numeric property values with units. Technically, CSS with unlabelled numeric values is invalid, but desktop browsers are notoriously lenient in this regard. Don't make the mobile browser do the work to guess your units. Declare them in the CSS. For example, this `margin` property is invalid CSS because the margin widths and heights are unlabelled with units:

  ```
  margin: 4 0 2 0;
  ```

  This CSS statement is corrected to specify pixels as the unit of measure:

  ```
  margin: 4px 0px 2px 0px;
  ```

- *Use generic values for* `font-family` *and relative values for* `font-size`. The developer has virtually no control over the fonts installed on mobile devices. Use the simpler of the generic `font-family` values (`serif`, `sans-serif`, and `monospace`) and absolute or relative `font-size` values for flexible page styles that render as consistently as possible across mobile browser and devices.

- *The only reliable `border-style` is `solid`.* Advanced browsers may support additional border styles, such as `dashed`, `dotted`, `grooved`, or `ridged`, but only solid border lines render well on small screens.

- *Test for URL delimiter compatibility.* Mobile browsers have CSS implementation quirks.

# External, Internal, and Inline Stylesheets

XHTML-MP, XHTML, and HTML all support styles and style sheets included in a markup document in three ways: externally, internally, and inline.

External stylesheets are linked from the document header (i.e., inside the `<head>` tag) using a link reference with a `stylesheet` relationship and `text/css` MIME type. This syntax makes all styles in the .css file available for use in the document body. Here is an example of an externally-linked stylesheet:

```
<link href="http://learnto.mobi/mobile.css" type="text/css" rel="stylesheet"/>
```

A less common method for embedding external stylesheets is specified in the WAP CSS standard. Style sheets can be externally references into a markup document using an XML processing instruction:

```
<?xml-stylesheet href="http://learnto.mobi/mobile.css" media="handheld" type="text/css" ?>
```

Internal style sheets are included in the document header (again, inside the `<head>` tag) using the `<style>` tag. Here, the CSS content is written into the document rather than stored in an external .css file. The example below illustrates the syntax of an internal style sheet:

```
<style type="text/css">
#theBox {
        background-color:#777777;
        margin:5px;
        padding:5px;
        border-width: 1px;
        border-style: solid;
        border-color: #000000;
}

.nav {
        margin: 3px;
}
</style>
```

When external or internal style sheets are used, styles are associated with XHTML-MP elements using `class` or `id` attributes, or by using selectors in the CSS document itself. See the code sample below for example uses of `class` and `id` attributes in mobile markup.

```
<div id="theBox"> </div>

<div class="nav"><a href="/">home</a></div>
```

An inline style uses the `style` attribute on any markup element (or tag) to specify its style. Inline styles are not named and not reusable across markup elements. An inline style overrides a style defined externally or internally for a document element. The code sample below uses an inline style to apply a background color to a single table cell:

```
<td style="background-color: #FAFAD2;">Yellow</td>
```

There are performance and caching implications of the choice of method to embed styles in a markup document. External style sheets are reusable across Mobile Web documents, but they increase the total download time for the first document that references the style sheet, because a round-trip to the web server is required to retrieve the CSS file. External CSS files may or not be cached by the mobile browser, potentially increasing the number of server requests to load a Mobile Web page. However, compact CSS file sizes and HTTP caching directives can increase the likelihood that the style sheet will be cached in the browser. As a result, cached, external style sheet provides an overall performance gain as the user browses subsequent Mobile Web pages. See Chapter 8 for more information about caching directives in HTTP response headers.

Internal style sheets provide no reuse advantage and have the overhead of copying styles into each Mobile Web document. But, internal style sheets render quickly in the browser because the styles are delivered in the same server response as the markup. Also, many Web server frameworks provide tools to minimize an internal style sheet by writing out only the styles actually referenced by the markup elements, minimizing the impact of internal styles on the final document size.

Inline styles are not reusable, provide no client-side performance or caching gains, inflate the markup document's file size, and violate the separation of content and presentation. Think carefully when using inline styles in a Mobile Web document. External or internal style sheets are almost always a better choice.

## Media Selectors and Media-Dependent Style Sheets

The CSS2 standard uses media selectors for conditional inclusion of style sheets in a Mobile Web document, as in the following XHTML markup:

```
<link rel="stylesheet" type="text/css" media="handheld" href="foo.css" />
```

Here, the `media` attribute and `handheld` value tells a web browser that the declared style sheet is appropriate only for mobile devices. Media selectors are also used on the desktop web to activate a new style sheet when printing web content.

Unfortunately, media-dependent style sheets are supported only in smartphone browsers. Mass-market mobile browsers do not support media dependencies in style sheet declarations. Therefore, the use of media selectors in practice is restricted to a limited selection of powerful mobile devices.

Further, the underlying premise of media dependencies is arguably invalid for the Mobile Web. Media dependencies assume that desktop markup is appropriate for mobile devices so long as the style sheet is optimized. Regardless of the breadth of media selector support in mobile browsers, this premise makes little sense for the Mobile Web. Desktop markup is heavyweight and optimized for huge screen sizes. A superior approach provides a Mobile Web site whose design, markup, and styles are optimized for mobile devices. Simplifying the style sheet and crossing your fingers about markup compatibility is not adequate. Your mobile users will thank you for considering them.

Make it easy for a mobile browser to render your Mobile Web page. *Avoid media selectors.* Instead, provide device-adaptive mobile markup and include only the styles and style sheets that are appropriate for the mobile device.

# WML

WML is an XML-based markup language for mobile devices. Predating XHTML-MP and not supporting style sheets, WML is considered the legacy language of the Mobile Web. It is in use on the Mobile Web, but its prevalence is declining rapidly in favor of newer and more powerful markups. This discussion of WML syntax is included for completeness only.

WML is *not* a good choice for new Mobile Web projects (unless there is a compelling geographic or demographic reason to target users with older mobile devices). Mainstream Mobile Web development is done using newer markup languages, like XHTML-MP and HTML. However, mobile developers are often asked to maintain and upgrade existing services, so familiarity with WML is still important.

> **NOTE**:  There are three versions of the WML standard: 1.1, 1.2,and 1.3. WML 1.1 and 1.3 were widely adopted in mobile browsers. This book discusses only WML 1.3, which was standardized in 2000. (There is a WML 2.0 standard but it can be ignored as it was never adopted by browsers.)

WML inherits the strict syntactic rules of XML. Strict syntax compliance is essential when developing WML pages because WAP gateways and browsers are both inflexible in processing invalid markup. WAP gateways tend not to be able to convert invalid WML into the WMLC bytecode required to send to the handset. In contrast with HTML rendering, WAP gateways often try *not* to fix syntax errors to recover a partially-compliant WML document, preferring instead to render nothing or an error message. Older mobile browsers, some still in use today, may crash the application or even reset the phone when encountering invalid WML or WMLC bytecode. Regardless of the gateway and browser tolerance threshold for invalid markup, the burden is always on the developer to produce valid WML web content.

## SYNTAX RULES FOR XML-BASED MARKUP LANGUAGES

XML-based markup languages must conform to strict syntax rules. These markup languages must be both well-formed and valid. A well-formed XML document obeys XML syntax rules. A valid XML document adheres to the DTD of the XML dialect in use. The XML 1.0 standard enforces the following rules, for example:

- XML declaration is recommended (suggested, but not required).

- DOCTYPE declaration is required in the document prolog.

- Tags must be properly nested and closed, or self-closed singletons.

- Tags and attributes must be lowercased.

- Attribute values must be surrounded by quotation marks. (Not single quotes. Not assumed quotes.)

WML, XHTML-MP, and XHTML are XML-based markup languages.

Here is an example WML document that breaks all the XML syntax rules. Can you spot the errors?

```
<wml>
<card ID=start title='Example of Invalid WML'>
<P>This markup is invalid.
</card>
</wml>
```

The WML code sample above has the following syntax errors:

- XML declaration is missing.

- DOCTYPE declaration is missing.

- ID attribute of <card> tag is uppercase. (Well-formed WML requires lowercase tags.)

- Value of the id attribute of the <card> is not delimited.

- Value of the title attribute of the <card> tag is delimited with single quotes.

- <p> tag is uppercase. (Well-formed WML requires lowercase tags.)

- <p> tag has an open tag but not matching close tag.

Syntax correctness is a virtue. Especially in WML browsers, rendering poorly-formed or invalid markup can have drastic negative effects, including crashing the browser application and powering off the mobile device.

Here, the invalid WML document is revised to be well-formed and valid XML. The corrections are bolded.

```
<?xml version="1.0" encoding="utf-8"?>
<!DOCTYPE wml PUBLIC "-//WAPFORUM//DTD WML 1.3//EN"
"http://www.wapforum.org/DTD/wml13.dtd">
<wml>
<card id="start" title="Example of Valid WML">
<p>This markup is valid.</p>
</card>
</wml>
```

The W3C Markup Validator (http://validator.w3.org/) is an online tool to help you find and resolve syntax problems in XML-based mobile markup. Additionally, source code is available for download and local installation. Markup validation is discussed further in Chapter 10.

For more information about the XML 1.0 standard, see the W3C recommendation for the latest edition at http://www.w3.org/TR/xml/.

WML uses a card metaphor to structure information. One WML document is called a *deck*. A WML *deck* contains one or more *cards*. One *card* is displayed at a time in the mobile browser. Internal links allows the user to browse cards in a deck without the device having to make further requests over the network.

Listing 3-5 is an annotated example of a WML document with multiple cards. Bolded sections show the tag hierarchy for documents and cards and two link formats for navigating between cards in a deck. Other features in the sample document include bolded text and a link that initiates a phone call when clicked.

Listing 3-5 can be viewed in a browser at http://learnto.mobi/books/bmwd/03/3-5.wml.

**Listing 3-5.** *Annotated Sample WML Document*

```
<?xml version="1.0" encoding="utf-8"?>
<!-- XML Declaration, above. WML is XML.-->
<!-- This construct is an XML comment. -->
<!-- DOCTYPE declaring that this document is WML 1.3. There are also declarations for
WML 1.1 and 1.2. Developer should only use WML 1.3.-->
<!DOCTYPE wml PUBLIC "-//WAPFORUM//DTD WML 1.3//EN"
"http://www.wapforum.org/DTD/wml13.dtd">
<!-- The root tag in a WML document is <wml>. -->
<wml>
<!-- WML uses a card metaphor. A WML document (or deck) may contain several cards. Each
card needs a unique ID and name. -->
<!-- The "&apos;" token below is an XML entity. XML entities are used to encode
characters that may impede document processing if left in their original form. -->
<card id="start" title="Sunset Farmers&apos; Market">
<!-- All textual content in a card must be contained in a <p> tag. -->
<p>Welcome to the <b>Sunset Farmers&apos; Market</b>!</p>
<p>Visit us every Wednesday afternoon in the city center for farm-fresh fruit,
vegetables and plants.</p>
<!-- Anchor is one of the linking techniques in WML. -->
<p><anchor>Contact Us
<go href="#contact"/>
</anchor>
</p>
</card>

<!-- Subsequent cards in the deck are not displayed unless user navigates there by
clicking links.-->
<card id="contact" title="Contact Us">
<p>Contact the Sunset Farmers&apos; Market at <a href="wtai://wp/mc;5035551234">503-555-
1234</a>.</p>
<p><a href="#start">Home</a></p>
</card>

<!-- WML is XML. Make sure that every open tag has a matching close tag.-->
</wml>
```

# Tag Hierarchy

WML documents and cards adhere to a strict tag hierarchy. The root tag of a WML document is <wml>.

Valid child tags of <wml> are:

- <head>: Defines document metadata and access control using the <meta> and <access> tags. Zero or one <head> tags are allowed in a document.

- <card>: Defines a card to display in the browser. One or more <head> tags are allowed in a document.

- <template>: Defines global event handlers and commands for the deck. Zero or one <template> tags are allowed in a document.

- 

Valid child tags of <card> are:

- <p>: Contains text, images, and links. Most user-accessible and visible content in a WML card is child content of this tag. Zero or more <p> tags are allowed in a card.

- <pre>: Contains preformatted text. Zero or more <pre> tags are allowed in a card.

- <do>: Contains commands and actions. Zero or more <do> tags are allowed in a card.

- <timer>: Activates time-based events. Zero or one <timer> tags are allowed in a card.

- <onevent>: Specifies tasks based on different card-level events. Zero or more <onevent> tags are allowed in a card.

# Special Characters

WML is XML. Any character that is escaped in XML using an entity must also be escaped in WML. These characters are used as XML syntax delimiters. When they are intended as plaintext data in the document, they must be escaped from their literal form.

Table 3-3 lists predefined entity names in the XML and WML 1.3 standards.

**Table 3-3.** *PreDefined XML and WML Entities*

| Character Name | Character | Entity | Related Standard |
|---|---|---|---|
| Ampersand | & | &amp; | XML |
| Apostrophe | ' | &apos; | XML |
| Quotation Marks | " | &quot; | XML |
| Right Angle Bracket | > | &gt; | XML |
| Left Angle Bracket | < | &lt; | XML |
| Non-Breaking Space | ' ' (whitespace) |   | WML |
| Soft Hyphen | | &shy; | WML |

Of course, because WML is XML, it is perfectly valid to reference characters numerically using the &#x<hexadecimal>; or &#<decimal>; character reference formats. However, beware of limited characters sets, language settings regional firmware variations on mobile devices. Make sure to test any use of extended or unusual characters on actual mobile devices.

In addition, the dollar-sign character (i.e. $) is reserved in WML to reference variables that are substituted with values derived from state stored in the browser. A WML variable is delimited with the dollar sign and parentheses, i.e. $(variableName). Here is an example that displays the value of a WML variable inline in a paragraph:

```
<p>The value of <b>x</b> is: $(x)</p>
```

To display a single dollar sign inline as a currency notation, duplicate the character, as shown in the following code:

```
<p>The value of <b>x</b> is: $$100.</p>
```

See the **User Input and Variables** section below for more about WML variables.

# Header and Metadata

A WML document contains a single (but optional) header section (in the <head> tag) that stores document metadata and access controls.

Document metadata is defined using the <meta> tag. It has the same syntax as its HTML counterpart. Many <meta> tags are allowed in a WML header. HTTP response headers can be embedded into the document using the http-equiv and content attributes:

```
<meta http-equiv="Cache-Control" content="no-cache" />
```

The <meta> tag expresses any metadata formatted as name-value pairs using the name and content attributes:

```
<meta name="Author" content="Gail Rahn Frederick" />
```

By default, cards in a WML deck are public and can be linked to from any other deck at any URL. Using an `<access>` tag in the document header, deck access can be restricted by domain and path URL components. The `domain` attribute specifies the URL domain of other WML decks that can link to this document. Its default value is the current domain. The `path` attribute specifies the root URL path of other WML decks that can link to this document. Its default value is the root path ("/"), making all documents on the current domain able to link to this deck.

Note that this access control is implemented in the browser, and does not replace a server-side security policy for page access.

The following examples illustrate uses of the `<access>` tag.

All documents on the `learnto.mobi` domain can access this WML deck:

```
<access domain="learnto.mobi" />
```

All documents on the current domain can access this WML deck:

```
<access path="/" />
```

All documents on the `learnto.mobi` domain whose paths start with `/02/` can access this WML deck:

```
<access domain="learnto.mobi" path="/02/" />
```

Listing 3-6 is an example WML document that uses <meta> and <access> tags in the document header. This listing can be viewed in a browser at `http://learnto.mobi/books/bmwd/03/3-6.wml`.

**Listing 3-6.** *WML Document Header*

```
<?xml version="1.0" encoding="utf-8"?>
<!DOCTYPE wml PUBLIC "-//WAPFORUM//DTD WML 1.3//EN"
"http://www.wapforum.org/DTD/wml13.dtd">
<wml>
<head>
<meta http-equiv="Cache-Control" content="no-cache" />
<meta name="Author" content="Gail Rahn Frederick" />
<access domain="learnto.mobi" />
</head>
<card id="start" title="Sunset Farmers&apos; Market">
<p>Welcome to the <b>Sunset Farmers&apos; Market</b>!</p>
<p>Visit us every Wednesday afternoon in the city center for farm-fresh fruit,
vegetables and plants.</p>
</card>

</wml>
```

# Text Formatting

WML allows only basic control over text formatting. Font selection, font sizes, line colors, background colors, and other fine-grained text formatting is not available in WML because the language specification predates powerful mobile devices, and CSS-like styling is also not available in the specification.

In a card, text is displayed inside either the <p> or <pre> tags. The <p> tag delimits paragraphs. It has two attributes that control paragraph display. The align attribute specifies the paragraph's horizontal alignment. The default value is left, but right and center may also be used for alternate display. The mode attribute specifies whether to wrap paragraph text across multiple lines. The default value is wrap, causing paragraphs to wrap across lines. The nowrap attribute value forces the paragraph to render on a single line. The paragraph may be displayed as marqueed text. Or, horizontal scrolling must be used to view the paragraph.

Table 3-4 lists all the WML text formatting tags.

**NOTE:** Use the mode attribute with care. Its value is sticky across paragraphs. Indicating a mode attribute on a <p> tag sets that wrapping mode for all subsequent paragraphs until the attribute is next declared.

**Table 3-4.** *WML Text Formatting Tags*

| WML Tag | Description | Example |
|---------|-------------|---------|
| <b> | Bold text. | Bring your <b>reusable</b> shopping bags. |
| <i>> | Italicized text. | Welcoming <i>all</i> farmers. |
| <u>> | Underlined text. | Accept <u>no</u> substitute. |
| <big>> | Text in bigger font. | <big>Open 24 Hours</big> |
| <small>> | Text in smaller font. | I like <small>turnips</small>. |
| <em>> | Emphasized text. Text is usually formatted as italic. | I <em>really</em> like fruit. |
| <strong>> | Strong text. Text is usually formatted as bold. | <strong>I mean it!</strong> |
| <pre>> | Pre-formatted text. Text and whitespace is rendered exactly as entered in markup. | <pre>H  E  L  L  O</pre> |
| <br/>> | Line break. | <br/> |

Basic text formatting tags are allowed only inside a WML paragraph (`<p>` tag), with the exception of `<pre>`. The `<pre>` tag is peer with `<p>` and is a direct child tag of `<card>`. Text formatting tags can be mutually nested, and multiple styling is valid, as long as the resulting markup remains well-formed and valid. For example, in the WML paragraph markup below, the word "brown" displays as bolded and italicized in a mobile browser:

```
<p>The <i>quick <b>brown</b> fox</i> jumps over the lazy dog.</p>
```

Mobile browsers take liberties with rendering text formatting tags in WML. Test WML documents in actual mobile browsers to confirm that text formatting tags produce the desired visual effect.

Listing 3-7 is an example WML document that uses all the text formatting tags. This listing can be viewed in a browser at `http://learnto.mobi/books/bmwd/03/3-7.wml`. Figure 3-4 displays Listing 3-7 in Opera Mini, WinWAP, and Openwave V7 emulators.

**Listing 3-7.** *WML Text Formatting*

```
<?xml version="1.0" encoding="utf-8"?>
<!DOCTYPE wml PUBLIC "-//WAPFORUM//DTD WML 1.3//EN"
"http://www.wapforum.org/DTD/wml13.dtd">
<wml>
<!-- NOTE: WML browsers take liberties with implementing text formatting!-->
<card id="text" title="WML Text Formatting">
<p>Welcome to the <b>Sunset Farmers&apos; Market</b>!</p>
<p>Visit us <em>every Wednesday afternoon</em> in the city center for farm-fresh fruit,
vegetables and plants.</p>
<p>Our vendors are <strong>sustainable family farms</strong> whose harvest was picked
the <big>very same day</big>.</p>
<p>We accept <i>credit cards</i>, <u>cash</u> and <small>checks</small>.</p>
<pre>Hope     to     see     you     s o o n!</pre>
</card>
</wml>
```

**Figure 3-4.** *WML Text Formatting in Opera Mini, WinWAP, and Openwave V7 Emulators*

# Links

WML uses three tag formats for creating hyperlinks. The `<a>` tag navigates to a URL. The `<anchor>` and `<do>` tags navigate to URLs and can also execute tasks that include WML variables. See the "Variables and User Input" section for other examples of using WML variables in tasks.

## <a> Tag

The first format is the familiar `<a>` tag that specifies the link location in the `href` attribute. Use the # anchor token to link to a card in a document using the card's ID. These examples show common uses of the `<a>` tag to create hyperlinks.

Here is an external link to the first card in a WML document:

```
<a href="http://learnto.mobi/books/bmwd/03/3-5.wml">Listing 3-5</a>
```

Here is an external link to a specific card in a WML document, identifying the card by its id (`contact`):

```
<a href="http://learnto.mobi/books/bmwd/03/3-5.wml#contact">Contact us</a>
```

Here is an internal link to a card in the current WML document:

```
<a href="#contact">Contact us</a>
```

## <anchor> Tag

The second format for creating hyperlinks in WML documents is the `<anchor>` tag. It is used when the link target may be internal navigation, a URL or a state change for a browser variable. (Browser variables are discussed in the "Variables" section later in this chapter.) The `<anchor>` tag has this format:

```
<anchor title="txt">label task</anchor>
```

The italicized anchor tag components are:

- *txt* is an optional short textual link title with a maximum of five characters. This value is often displayed as a tooltip. WML browsers are free to display or ignore the title.

- *label* is a text link label displayed in the WML document.

- *task* is a WML tag indicating the action to take when the link is activated.

> **NOTE:** The actions specified in `<anchor>` and `<do>` tags are WML tasks. WML tasks allow navigation changes and manipulate values of WML variables. To learn about WML variables, see the "Variables" section later in this chapter.

Four possible tags may be used in the *task* component of the `<anchor>` tag: `<go>`, `<prev>`, `<refresh>`, and `<noop>`. Table 3-5 lists the tags, descriptions, and syntax examples.

**Table 3–5.** *Task Elements of WML Anchor Tag*

| WML Tag | Description | Examples |
|---|---|---|
| `<go>` | Navigates to a URL. Uses attributes and subtags to specify HTTP method, send query variables, and set browser variable state.<br><br>See the "User Input and Variables" section for more examples of using this WML variables and sending their values in HTTP GET and POST requests. | `<go href="http://learnto.mobi/" />`<br><br>`<go href="http://learnto.mobi/" method="get">`<br>`  <setvar name="x" value="123"/>`<br>`</go>`<br><br>`<go href="http://learnto.mobi/" method="post">`<br>`  <postfield name="x" value="123"/>`<br>`</go>` |
| `<prev>` | Navigates to the previous card in the browser history. Optionally, updates values of WML browser variables. | `<prev/>`<br><br>`<prev>`<br>`  <setvar name="x" value="123"/>`<br>`</prev>` |
| `<refresh>` | Refreshes the current card in the deck, updating values for one or more WML variables. | `<refresh>`<br>`  <setvar name="x" value="123"/>`<br>`</refresh>` |
| `<noop>` | Performs no action. | `<noop/>` |

The following examples illustrate the use of each action.

Here is an external link to a WML document:

```
<anchor>Listing 3-5 <go href="http://learnto.mobi/books/bmwd/03/3-5.wml"/></anchor>
```

The above example is equivalent to constructing a link using the `<a>` tag:

```
<a href="http://learnto.mobi/books/bmwd/03/3-5.wml">Listing 3-5</a>
```

Here is an `<anchor>` link that sends a POST request with two variables:

```
<anchor>Send Info <go href="http://learnto.mobi/submit" method="post">
  <postfield name="x" value="123"/>
  <postfield name="y" value="456"/>
</go>
</anchor>
```

This <anchor> task navigates to the previous card in the browser history:

```
<anchor>Go Back <prev/></anchor>
```

The <anchor> example below refreshes the current page and changes the value of a WML variable:

```
<anchor>Update <refresh>
  <setvar name="x" value="789"/>
</refresh>
</anchor>
```

## <do> Tag

The third format for creating links in WML is the <do> tag. The <do> tag is similar to the <anchor> tag in that both navigate to cards, URLs, or execute tasks when activated by the user. The <anchor> tag is activated when the user clicks a textual link label. In contrast, the <do> tag is activated by selecting a browser user interface component, usually a function key, soft key, or menu item. This tag is used to extend the general browser interface with deck-specific commands, rather than necessarily placing the action in the body of the page.

The <do> tag has this format:

```
<do type="type" label="label" name="name" optional="optional"> task img</do>
```

The italicized tag components are:

- *type* is the browser command to associate with this task. See Table 3-6 for values of this attribute.

- *label* is a text label to display in the browser and associate with this command. If not provided, the browser uses general labels based on the tag's *type* value.

- *name* is an optional internal text name for the element. Naming a <do> tag is used to identify a general command at the deck level and override it using a <do> tag with an identical name in a card.

- *optional* is a Boolean value (true or false) indicating whether the browser may ignore this tag. The default value for this attribute is false.

- *task* is a WML tag indicating the action to take when the link is activated. See Table 3-5 for a list of valid task tags in WML.

- *img* is an optional WML <img> tag of a selectable image that activates the link.

The *type* attribute specifies the general browser command that is associated with the task in the <do> tag. The presentation of general browser commands is decided by the browser. Developers cannot control the presentation. The browser is free to implement <do> tags using system menus, function keys, labeled soft keys, software buttons, hard keys, or any other methods that makes sense on the mobile device.

**Table 3-6.** *Type Attribute Values of WML Do Tag*

| Type Value | Description |
| --- | --- |
| accept | The accept or OK function of the WML browser. |
| delete | The delete function of the WML browser. |
| help | The help function of the WML browser. |
| options | The options function of the WML browser. |
| button | Creates a button to be rendered on the browser screen. |
| prev | The previous navigation function of the WML browser. |

This example <do> tag navigates to a new WML document when the user activates the browser help function:

```
<do type="help" name="helpdoc" optional="false">
  <go href=""http://learnto.mobi/help.wml" />
</do>
```

The <do> tag can also associate a browser command with an image displayed on the screen. The example below associates the delete function with a GIF image:

```
<do type="delete">
  <go href="http://learnto.mobi/delete">
    <setvar name="x" value="123"/>
  </go>
  <img src="/delete-icon.gif" alt="Delete"/>
</do>
```

Listing 3-8 is an example of a WML document that uses all the link tags. This listing can be viewed in a browser at http://learnto.mobi/books/bmwd/03/3–8.wml. Figure 3-5 displays Listing 3-8 in the OpenWave v7 Emulator.

**Listing 3-8.** *WML Links*

```
<?xml version="1.0" encoding="utf-8"?>
<!DOCTYPE wml PUBLIC "-//WAPFORUM//DTD WML 1.3//EN"
"http://www.wapforum.org/DTD/wml13.dtd">
<wml>
<card id="text" title="WML Links">
<do type="help" label="Info" name="helpdoc" optional="false">
  <go href="#market" />
</do>
<p>Welcome to the <a href="#market">Sunset Farmers&apos; Market</a>!</p>
</card>

<card id="market" title="Market Info">
<p>Visit us <em>every Wednesday afternoon</em> in the city center for farm-fresh fruit,
vegetables and plants.</p>
<p>Contact us at <a href="wtai://wp/mc;5035551234">503-555-1234</a>.</p>
<p><anchor>Go Back<prev/></anchor></p>
```

```
</card>

</wml>
```

**Figure 3-4.** *WML Browser Menu with Info Menu Item Generated from WML Do Tag in Listing 3-8*

# Images

WML handles images in a similar manner to HTML and XHTML-MP. The `<img>` tag embeds an image into a document. Its `src` attribute specifies the image URL. Its `alt` attribute contains a textual description of the image. Its `width` and `height` attributes set the image dimensions. Vertical image alignment relative to the current text line is possible using the `align` attribute, whose value can be `top`, `middle`, or `bottom`. Table 3-7 describes the possible values of the `align` attribute.

**Table 3-7.** *Values of the `align` Attribute of the WML `<img>` Tag*

| Attribute Value | Description |
| --- | --- |
| top | Aligns the top of the image with the top of the line. |
| Middle | Aligns the middle of the image with the middle of the line. |
| Bottom | Aligns the bottom of the image with the bottom of the line. |

Here is an example `<img>` tag in WML that is aligned with the bottom of the current line:

```
<img src="http://learnto.mobi/img/screamer_icon.png" alt="Learn the Mobile Web"
width="96" height="88" align="bottom" />
```

> **TIP:** Always provide width, height, and alt attributes for images. Specifying these attributes allows the mobile browser to layout the markup document and display meaningful information to the user while the image file is still downloading.

It is important to remember that not all mobile devices support all image formats. GIF, JPG, and PNG image formats may or may not be renderable in a mobile browser. In addition, an older, black-and-white image format called Wiress Bitmap (WBMP) is supported in all WML browsers. Consult a device database to find the image formats supported on a mobile device. See Chapter 4 for more about device awareness and content adaptation. Some mobile browsers allow the user to disable viewing and downloading images. Make sure your page design degrades gracefully in the absence of images. For example, some WML browsers automatically add a line break after each image.

Listing 3-9 contains an image embedded in a WML document. This listing can be viewed in a browser at `http://learnto.mobi/books/bmwd/03/3-9.wml`. Figure 3-6 displays Listing 3-9 in the OpenWave V7 Emulator.

**Listing 3-9.** *WML Images*

```
<?xml version="1.0" encoding="utf-8"?>
<!DOCTYPE wml PUBLIC "-//WAPFORUM//DTD WML 1.3//EN"
"http://www.wapforum.org/DTD/wml13.dtd">
<wml>
<card id="image" title="WML Images">
<p><img src="http://learnto.mobi/img/screamer_icon.png" width="96" height="88"
alt="Screaming Geek" align="bottom"/> Visit <a href="http://learnto.mobi">Learn the
Mobile Web</a> to learn about mobile web development.</p>
</card>
</wml>
```

*Figure 3-6. Image rendering in WML in Openwave V7 Emulator*

## Tables

WML supports primitive tables to display data in a grid format. WML tables do not allow cell styles, alignment, or cells spanning multiple rows or columns. The `<table>` tag in WML supports only a single attribute, `columns,` whose value is an integer number of columns to expect in the table. The `columns` value is a clue to the browser to optimize document rendering.

Table row and data cell tags, `<tr>` and `<td>` respectively, are the only valid child and grandchild tags of the `<table>` tag. Text formatting, images, and links are allowed inside the `<td>` tag of a table cell. WML tables must be embedded inside a paragraph.

Here is a WML table with three columns:

```
<table title="Produce" columns="3">
<tr>
<td><b>Vendor</b></td>
<td><b>Booth</b></td>
<td><b>Products</b></td>
</tr>
<tr>
<td>Rising Moon Farms</td>
<td>105B</td>
<td>Eggplant, Peppers</td>
</tr>
<tr>
<td>Summerfield Fungi</td>
<td>803</td>
<td>Mushrooms</td>
</tr>
</table>
```

Table-based page layout in WML is *strongly discouraged* because of unexpected problems with rendering across mobile browsers and platforms. See Figure 3-7 for an example of odd cell alignments when rendering a table whose content is wider than the screen width.

The best use of WML tables that I have encountered is viewing image thumbnails in a grid. When image thumbnails are sized to respect the width of the browser window, grid-based image viewing and selection is very effective in WML.

Listing 3-10 displays a WML table. This listing can be viewed in a browser at `http://learnto.mobi/books/bmwd/03/3-10.wml`. Figure 3-7 displays Listing 3-10 in the Openwave V7 Emulator.

**Listing 3-10.** *WML Tables*

```
<?xml version="1.0" encoding="utf-8"?>
<!DOCTYPE wml PUBLIC "-//WAPFORUM//DTD WML 1.3//EN"
"http://www.wapforum.org/DTD/wml13.dtd">
<wml>
<!-- NOTE: WML browsers take liberties with cell alignment in table rendering!-->
<card id="text" title="WML Tables">
<p>Today&apos;s Fresh Vegetables</p>
<p><table title="Title" columns="2">
<tr>
<td><b>Produce</b></td>
<td><b>Price</b></td>
</tr>
<tr>
<td>Broccoli</td>
<td>$$0.99/lb</td>
</tr>
<tr>
<td>Red Peppers</td>
<td>$$1.25 each</td>
</tr>
<tr>
<td>Jerusalem Artichokes</td>
```

```
<td>$$1.00 each</td>
</tr>
</table></p>
</card>
</wml>
```

```
Today's Fresh
Vegetables
Produce    Price
           $0.99/
Broccoli
           lb
Red        $1.25
Peppers    each
        ⬍ Options
```

**Figure 3-7.** *WML tables in Openwave V7 Emulator*

## Timers

Timers in WML allow card navigation using timeouts. Using its `value` attribute, the `<timer>` tag in WML specifies a duration *in tenths of seconds* to wait before timing out.

Here is an example `<timer>` tag that waits 5 seconds before expiring:

```
<timer value="50"/>
```

When the timer expires, the `ontimer` event in the parent `<card>` tag fires. The ontimer event specifies a URL to load in the WML browser. The example below navigates the browser to a card in the current WML deck:

```
<card id="timer" title="Welcome" ontimer="#next">
```

The `ontimer` event navigates to any URL, including external cards and documents, as in this example:

```
<card id="timer" title="Welcome" ontimer="http://learnto.mobi/books/bmwd/03/3-
7.wml#expired">
```

Timers are part of the WML event model, a rich model for handling navigation and user events in cards and across WML documents. The event model is not studied further in this book. See `http://learnthemobileweb.com/books/` for web resources to learn more about WML events and event handlers.

Listing 3-11 specifies a WML timer and its timeout behavior. This listing can be viewed in a browser at `http://learnto.mobi/books/bmwd/03/3-11.wml`. View the example in a mobile browser or emulator to observe the timeout navigation behavior. Figure 3-8 displays Listing 3-11 in the Openwave V7 Emulator.

**Figure 3-8.** *WML Timers before and after expiration in Openwave V7 Emulator*

**Listing 3-11.** *WML Timers*

```
<?xml version="1.0" encoding="utf-8"?>
<!DOCTYPE wml PUBLIC "-//WAPFORUM//DTD WML 1.3//EN"
"http://www.wapforum.org/DTD/wml13.dtd">
<wml>
<card id="timer" title="Welcome" ontimer="#next">
<timer value="50"/>
<p>Sunset Farmers&apos; Market...</p>
</card>
<card id="next" title="Sunset Market">
<p>Welcome to the Sunset Farmers&apos; Market! Every Wednesday afternoon in the city
center.</p>
</card>
</wml>
```

# Variables

WML documents can define and manage untyped variables. Unlike a desktop web browser, these are stored in the browser's state and persist between pages. Variables in WML have deck scope. Their values are set through user input or static declarations. Variable values can be updated as the user navigates between cards.

Here is a simple WML tag that sets the value of the variable x to the untyped value `blueberries`:

```
<setvar name="x" value="blueberries"/>
```

The `<setvar>` tag sets the `name` and `value` of a WML variable using its attributes. The `<setvar>` tag is valid inside a WML *task*, a WML tag that performs a navigation, refresh, or URL action.

**NOTE:** The <anchor> and <do> tags execute WML tasks. A WML task is a navigation action that can include setting values or WML variables. Valid WML actions include navigating to a URL, displaying the previous card in the history, refreshing the current card and taking no navigation action. See Table 3-5 for a list of WML tasks.

HTML and XHTML-MP both use a <form> tag to surround user input fields and manage form submission. WML does not use forms. Instead, WML uses tasks to upload variable values to a server. Values of WML variables can be sent to a web server as HTTP GET query parameters or HTTP POST postdata.

Here is an example of setting a variable value in a WML task. When the user selects the Next Page link in the <anchor>, the <go> tag and <setvar> subtag cause the browser to set the value of the variable x to 123 and navigate to the card with ID card2.

```
<anchor>Next Page<go href="#card2">
   <setvar name="x" value="123"/>
   </go>
</anchor>
```

The example below refreshes the current card and changes the value of the variable x to 456. The variable value is displayed in the paragraph and may change when the card is refreshed.

```
<p> The value of X is $(x).<br/>
<anchor>Update X<refresh>
   <setvar name="x" value="456"/>
   </refresh>
 </anchor>
</p>
```

Remember, WML variables are scoped to the deck. Variable values can be established and change as the user navigates between the cards of a deck and the decks of a site.

WML tasks can similarly be used to upload variable values to a server. Assuming that the WML variable x was initialized previously in the deck to the value 123, this code sends a HTTP GET request to a web server and submits the value of x as the value of the query parameter fruit.

```
<anchor>Send Fruit to Server
   <go href="http://learnto.mobi/?fruit=$(x)" method="get" />
:escape</anchor>
```

When the anchor link is activated, the mobile browser will navigate to http://learnto.mobi/?fruit=123. Notice that the variable is formatted as $(x:escape), not $(x). Using the :escape suffix forces the WML browser to escape the value of the variable. Variables may also be declared with two other suffixes, :noescape and :unescape, to force no variable escaping and remove variable escaping, respectively.

If a HTTP POST transaction is desired, then the <postfield> tag is used instead of <setvar>, as in this example. When the anchor link is activated, the browser will navigate to http://learnto.mobi/ and send fruit=123 in the request's postdata.

```
<anchor>Send Fruit to Server
  <go method="post" href="http://learnto.mobi/">
  <postfield name="fruit" value="$(x)"/>
  </go>
</anchor>
```

An example WML document that shows how to manipulate WML variable values and submit them to a web server is shown in Listing 3-12. In the first card, the user sets the value of the variable x to blueberries when navigating to the next card. In the second card, the value of x is displayed on the screen. The user can navigate back, update x to peaches or bananas, or submit the value of x to the web server by activating <anchor> links. This listing can be viewed in a browser at http://learnto.mobi/books/bmwd/03/3–12.wml. View the example in a mobile browser or emulator to observe the variable behavior. Figure 3-9 displays Listing 3-12 in the Openwave V7 Emulator.

**Figure 3-9.** *WML Variables in Openwave V7 Emulator*

**Listing 3-12.** *WML Variables*

```
<?xml version="1.0" encoding="utf-8"?>
<!DOCTYPE wml PUBLIC "-//WAPFORUM//DTD WML 1.3//EN"
"http://www.wapforum.org/DTD/wml13.dtd">
<wml>
<card id="setx" title="WML Variables">
<p>What is your favorite fruit?</p>
<p>
  <!-- This task sets the value of x. -->
  <anchor>Set to Blueberries <go href="#showx">
  <setvar name="x" value="blueberries"/>
  </go>
  </anchor>
</p>
</card>

<card id="showx" title="Show Variable Value">
<p>Your favorite fruit is $(x).</p>
<p>
  <anchor>Back <go href="#setx"/></anchor>
</p>

<!-- These two task updates the value of x. -->
```

```
<p>
<anchor>Set to Peaches<refresh>
<setvar name="x" value="peaches"/>
</refresh>
</anchor>
<br/>
<anchor>Set to Bananas<refresh>
<setvar name="x" value="bananas"/>
</refresh>
</anchor>
</p>

<!-- This task sends the value of x to the server as the variable fruit. -->
<p>
<anchor>Send Fruit to Server
   <go href="http://learnto.mobi/?fruit=$(x:escape)" method="get" />
</anchor>
</p>
</card>
</wml>
```

# User Input

So far, we have set static values for WML variables using the `<setvar>` tag. Values for WML variables can also be set with user input. WML supports list selection and text user input modes.

This WML `<input>` tag controls textual user input. Its `name` attribute sets the variable name. Its `size` attribute specifies the width in characters of the input field. Its `maxlength` attribute sets the maximum character length of the user input.

```
<input name="name" size="5" maxlength="10"/>
```

To shield user-entered characters from display, set the input `type` attribute to `password`:

```
<input type="password" name="pwd" size="5" maxlength="5"/>
```

To enforce formats at user text entry, which is helpful for keypad text entry, use the optional `format` and `emptyok` attributes, as in the example below.

```
<input name="age" size="5" format="*N" emptyok="true"/>
```

The `emptyok` attribute is Boolean and indicates that the user is allowed to leave the text input blank.

The `format` attribute specifies a text format that user input must match. The `*N` attribute value indicates that an unlimited number of numeric characters may be entered. Text formats follow the syntax of an one-character optional modifier and an one-character descriptor , where valid descriptors are specified using the notation described in Table 3-8.

**Table 3-8.** *Text Format Descriptors for the WML* `<input>` *Tag*

| Token | Description |
| --- | --- |
| A | A symbol or uppercase alphabetic character. |
| a | A symbol or lowercase alphabetic character. |
| N | A numeric character. |
| X | A symbol, uppercase alphabetic or numeric character. |
| x | A symbol, lowercase alphabetic or numeric character. |
| M | A symbol, uppercase alphabetic or numeric character. When multiple characters are entered, the browser keeps the first character as uppercase and changes the rest to lowercase. |
| m | A symbol, lowercase alphabetic or numeric character. When multiple characters are entered, the browser keeps the first character as lowercase and changes the rest to uppercase. |

Table 3-9 lists the two valid text format modifiers. The modifier is entered before the descriptor in the `format` attribute value.

**Table 3-9.** *Text Format Modifiers for the WML* `<input>` *Tag*

| Token | Description |
| --- | --- |
| 1...9 | A single-digit number specifies the maximum characters to be entered. |
| * | The asterisk modifier indicates that an unlimited number of characters may be entered. |

Here are some examples of common text formats used in WML text input:

- *\*N*: Unlimited number of numeric characters.
- *10N*: Up to ten numeric characters, used to enter a U.S. telephone number.
- *\*A*: Unlimited uppercase alphabetic characters.
- *\*M*: Unlimited mixed case characters. The first character is uppercase and all subsequent characters are lowercase.

An example WML document that captures user text entry, displays it in a card, and submits the values to a web server is shown in Listing 3-13. In the first card, the user inputs text into three fields. In the second card, the user-entered text is displayed on the screen. The user sends the values to the web server by activating the `<anchor>` link. This listing can be viewed in a browser at `http://learnto.mobi/books/bmwd/03/3-13.wml`.

View the example in a mobile browser or emulator to observe the user input behavior. Figure 3-10 displays Listing 3-13 in the Openwave V7 Emulator.

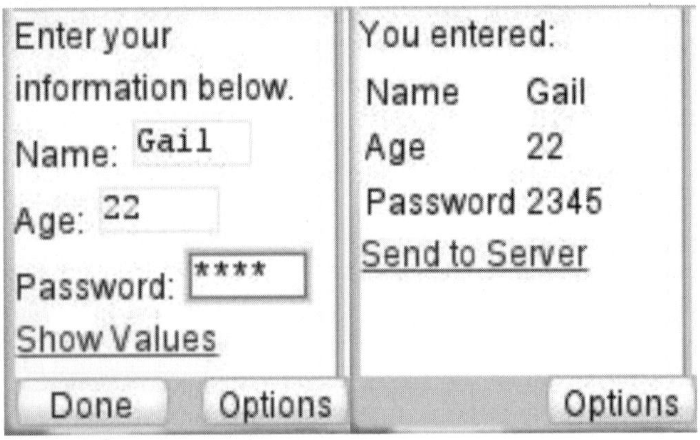

**Figure 3-10.** *WML Text Entry in Openwave V7 Emulator*

**Listing 3-13.** *WML Text Entry*

```
<?xml version="1.0" encoding="utf-8"?>
<!DOCTYPE wml PUBLIC "-//WAPFORUM//DTD WML 1.3//EN"
"http://www.wapforum.org/DTD/wml13.dtd">
<wml>
<card id="input" title="WML Text Input">
<p>
Enter your information below.<br/>
Name: <input name="name" size="5"/><br/>
Age:  <input name="age" size="5" format="*N"/><br/>
Password:  <input type="password" name="pwd" size="5" format="*N"/><br/>
</p>
<p>
<anchor>Show Values<go href="#card2"/></anchor>
</p>
</card>

<card id="card2" title="Show Values">
<p>
You entered:<br/>
<table columns="2">
<tr><td>Name</td><td>$(name)</td></tr>
<tr><td>Age</td><td>$(age)</td></tr>
<tr><td>Password</td><td>$(pwd)</td></tr>
</table>
</p>
<p>
<anchor>Send to Server
  <go href="http://learnto.mobi/" method="get">
  <setvar name="name" value="$(name)"/>
  <setvar name="age" value="$(age)"/>
  <setvar name="pwd" value="$(pwd)"/>
  </go>
</anchor>
</p>
```

```
</card>
</wml>
```

User input for list selection in WML is accomplished using the `<select>` and `<option>` tags in a manner similar to HTML and XHTML-MP. The `<select>` tag identifies the list. Its `name` attribute sets the variable name. Its `multiple` attribute uses a Boolean value to indicate that the list allows multiple items to be selected.

This WML sample code allows the user to select a single favorite fruit option from a list:

```
<select name="fruit">
<option value="blueberry">Blueberries</option>
<option value="apple">Apples</option>
<option value="peach">Peaches</option>
</select>
```

The similar WML code below allows the user to select many favorite fruits from the list. Note the use of the `multiple` attribute to mark the list as accepting multiple selected items. The value of a multiple selection list is a semi-colon delimited list of all selected values.

```
<select name="fruit" multiple="true">
<option value="blueberry">Blueberries</option>
<option value="apple">Apples</option>
<option value="peach">Peaches</option>
</select>
```

WML browsers take liberties with rendering select lists. Single-select lists may be drawn as drop-down lists or displaying multiple items and allowing only one to be selected. Multiple-select lists are usually drawn displaying multiple items.

Figures 3-11 and 3-12 display single-select and multiple-select lists, respectively, in the Openwave V7 Emulator.

**Figure 3-11.** *Single-Select List in Openwave V7 Emulator*

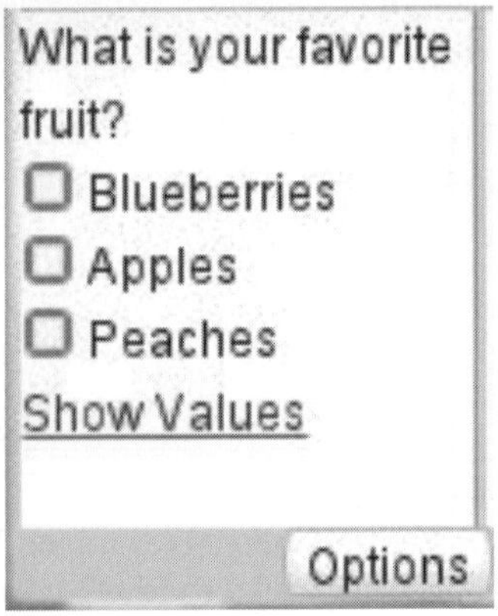

**Figure 3-12.** *Multiple-Select List in Openwave V7 Emulator*

Listing 3-14 is a WML document that lets the user select an item from a list and displays the selected value to the user. In the first card, the user selects their favorite fruit from a list. In the second card, the user-selected fruit is displayed on the screen. This listing can be viewed in a browser at `http://learnto.mobi/books/bmwd/03/3-14.wml`. View the example in a mobile browser or emulator to observe the user input behavior.

**Listing 3-14.** *WML List Input*

```
<?xml version="1.0" encoding="utf-8"?>
<!DOCTYPE wml PUBLIC "-//WAPFORUM//DTD WML 1.3//EN"
"http://www.wapforum.org/DTD/wml13.dtd">
<wml>
<card id="input" title="WML List Input">
<p>
What is your favorite fruit?
<select name="fruit">
<option value="blueberry">Blueberries</option>
<option value="apple">Apples</option>
<option value="peach">Peaches</option>
</select>
</p>
<p>
<anchor>Show Values<go href="#card2"/></anchor>
</p>
</card>

<card id="card2" title="Show Values">
<p>
Favorite Fruit: $(fruit)<br/>
</p>
</card>
</wml>
```

# Other WML Language Features

WML has surprisingly comprehensive features considering its age and target devices. This chapter does not discuss all features of the markup language. These WML language features are left as reader research exercises:

- A rich event model.

- Deck-level templates for card menus and behavior using the ‹do› tag.

- WMLScript, a companion scripting language for client-side form validation, mathematical computations, showing dialog boxes, and console debugging.

- Openwave language extension to enable try/catch exception handling.

- Openwave language extension to allow browsers to spawn child WML display contexts and pass variables from child context to parent at exit.

Browse to http://learnthemobileweb.com/books/ for links to WML references and helpful documentation.

> **TIP:** The best way to test mobile markup is on actual mobile devices. This is especially true for WML browsers that are known to take liberties with markup rendering.

## EXERCISE 1: EXPERIMENT WITH MOBILE MARKUP

Experiment with the mobile markup languages in this chapter. Create WML, XHTML-MP, and XHTML markup documents. Validate markup syntax using the W3C Validator or ready.mobi. View the markup in Firefox, mobile emulators and on actual mobile devices.

Use these page suggestions or create your own:

- Excerpt your favorite book or magazine in a Mobile Web page. Format and style the text using features from the markup language.

- Find scores for your favorite sports team online or in a newspaper. Create a sports page including a game summary and the score.

- Create a login page that accepts a username and password and displays it on the screen. Is this possible in all markup languages without scripting?

- Create tables of text and images.

- Create a mobile version of a popular desktop web page.

Answer these questions:

1. How does the authoring experience change between the mobile markup languages?

2. Are certain markup languages better suited to certain page designs? Why?

3.  What is the total byte size for each markup document? How could this size be reduced?

4.  Which markup languages produce the best user experience? Answer this question by testing on mobile devices of varying capabilities.

Challenge yourself to implement the same pages in WML, XHTML-MP, and HTML. How do the features of the markup language hinder or facilitate the user experience? How would your markup change for smaller and larger screen sizes?

# Summary

In this chapter, you learned three mobile markup languages and methods for styling XHTML-MP and HTML markup using mobile CSS. We reviewed strategies for selecting a markup language for Mobile Web development. We introduced best practices for syntax and styling of Mobile Web documents.

In the next chapter, we explore device awareness and content adaptation, powerful techniques for tailoring mobile markup to the mobile browser and mobile device. We use a device database to identify web requests from different types of mobile phones and adapt mobile markup to target mobile device and browser capabilities.

# Chapter 4

# Device Awareness and Content Adaptation

Your new knowledge of mobile markup syntax and best practices makes you ready to adapt Mobile Web content to increase compatibility and usability across mobile devices and browsers. Adapting a Mobile Web site to target mobile browser and device capabilities is achieved by applying two core principles of Mobile Web development: device recognition and content adaptation.

Device awareness is attained by inspecting the User-Agent and other HTTP request headers to identify Web traffic from mobile devices and provide information about device characteristics. Developers use a device database and accompanying API to identify the device that originates the Web request. Once the device is identified, the device database provides detailed properties about the mobile device and its browser.

For example, a Mobile Web developer might pass the User-Agent request header value that follows to a device database API:

```
Mozilla/5.0 (iPhone; U; CPU iPhone OS 2_2_1 like Mac OS X; en-us)
AppleWebKit/525.18.1 (KHTML, like Gecko) Version/3.1.1 Mobile/5H11
Safari/525.20
```

The device database identifies this Web client as an Apple iPhone running version 3.1.1 of its operating system and using a Safari Web browser. With an identified device, the Mobile Web developer can use the API to learn more about the iPhone model. The device database reports that its screen size is 320 x 480 pixels, the screen can rotate between landscape and portrait orientations, its browser supports JavaScript and AJAX, and the tel: protocol is preferred for embedding phone numbers as links in Web pages, among other characteristics.

Several open-data, open-source and proprietary mobile device databases provide mobile browser and device characteristics to developers. This chapter examines two popular device databases: WURFL and DeviceAtlas.

Content adaptation is the process of optimizing mobile markup to target the capabilities and avoid the flaws of the mobile device and its browser. Basic content adaptation identifies Web requests from mobile devices and desktop browsers, sending the former to a Mobile Web site and the latter to a desktop-optimized Web site. More advanced content adaptation uses device characteristics (obtained through device awareness) as criteria for changing the functionality or design of the Mobile Web site. Content adaptation groups mobile devices and browsers according to shared capabilities, identifies the ways in which a Mobile Web site might adapt, and implements rules for adapting the site to each device group.

This chapter describes how to use device awareness to identify mobile devices and implement content adaptation in a Mobile Web site.

# Device Awareness

Device awareness is the process of using information in a Web request to identify a mobile browser or device and determine its capabilities. Learning the mobile device characteristics allows a Mobile Web site to make choices about adapting mobile markup, styles, scripting, and page layout to provide the best possible mobile user experience. This section describes the mechanics of device awareness and example implementations using two popular device database technologies.

## Using HTTP Request Headers to Identify Mobile Devices

Device awareness identifies mobile devices and browsers by inspecting the metadata in the HTTP headers of a Web request. Three request headers are especially important in identifying a device:

The `User-Agent` header identifies the mobile browser and almost always also identifies the mobile device manufacturer and model.

The `X-Wap-Profile` header provides a URL to a User Agent Profile in Resource Description Framework (RDF) file format (an XML dialect used for W3C specifications). The User Agent Profile is a document that describes the capabilities of the mobile device and browser. Some mobile devices provide the User Agent Profile URL in the `Wap-Profile` or `profile` headers.

The `Accept` header provides a list of MIME types for content supported in the browser or device.

Listing 4-1 shows HTTP request headers for the Blackberry Curve 8310, a smartphone made by Research in Motion. The `User-Agent`, `X-Wap-Profile`, and `Accept` headers are in bold type for readability.

**Listing 4-1.** *HTTP Request Headers for Blackberry Curve 8310*

```
Accept-Language: en-US,en;q=0.5
x-wap-profile: "http://www.blackberry.net/go/mobile/profiles/uaprof/8310/4.2.2.rdf"
Host: learnto.mobi
Accept-Charset: ISO-8859-1,UTF-8,US-ASCII,UTF-16BE,windows-1252,UTF-16LE,windows-1250
User-Agent: BlackBerry8310/4.2.2 Profile/MIDP-2.0 Configuration/CLDC-1.1 VendorID/102
```

```
Accept:
application/vnd.rim.html,text/html,application/xhtml+xml,application/vnd.wap.xhtml+xml,t
ext/vnd.sun.j2me.app-descriptor,image/vnd.rim.png,image/jpeg,application/x-
vnd.rim.pme.b,application/vnd.rim.ucs,image/gif;anim=1,application/vnd.wap.wmlc;q=0.9,ap
plication/vnd.wap.wmlscriptc;q=0.7,text/vnd.wap.wml;q=0.7,*/*;q=0.5
profile: http://www.blackberry.net/go/mobile/profiles/uaprof/8310/4.2.2.rdf
Via: BISB_3.4.0.56, 1.1 pmds166.bisb1.blackberry:3128 (squid/2.7.STABLE6)
Cache-Control: max-age=259200
Connection: keep-alive
```

You might be wondering why you don't have enough information to implement device awareness without using a device database API if a mobile device provides request headers identifying itself and its capabilities. Unfortunately, request headers alone are insufficient for device awareness. Headers can be missing from HTTP requests from mobile devices or, if present, can contain inaccurate values. For example, the X-Wap-Profile header is notorious in the mobile industry for containing an invalid URL or, if valid, a URL that points to an inaccurate User Agent Profile description. The Accept header value can omit supported MIME types, and it provides an incomplete assessment of content support on the device. For example, a mobile browser displays GIF images when the image/gif MIME type is part of the header value, but the header does not convey that GIF images over 100K fail to display due to exhausted browser memory. A device database is designed to convey exactly this kind of capability to Mobile Web developers. The User-Agent is provided on every Web request, contains accurate information, and is generally sufficient to identify the mobile device and browser models, but not their capabilities.

See Appendix B for more examples of HTTP request headers from mobile devices, as well as to learn how to capture and view these headers using a mobile browser.

> **NOTE:** In an attempt to protect Mobile Web developers from device limitations, a transcoder deployed in the mobile network might change the values of HTTP request headers and might mask the identity of mobile devices. See Chapter 12 for more information about determining when a Web request is proxied through a transcoder and how to use the modified headers to discover the mobile device originating the request. Some device database APIs automatically determine the originating device for transcoded Web requests. With other device databases, the burden is on the caller to check alternate request headers and provide this information to the API.

## Using a Device Database to Obtain Device Capabilities

A device database is the most accurate method for identifying mobile devices and determining their characteristics. The developer tools used in device awareness are a device database and its accompanying API. The device database might be a physical file in XML, JSON, or other format, or it might be a set of database tables intended for import into an existing relational database management system (DBMS). Device database vendors provide APIs for many popular web runtime frameworks.

The HTTP headers sent by a device in a Web request are the primary inputs that a device database API uses to identify the mobile device and browser. Some APIs use only the User-Agent header value for device identification, while other APIs prefer the entire set of request headers. Once the device is recognized, the API provides the developer with a unique device identifier that is used as a key to look up device and browser characteristics. Some device database APIs combine device identification and characteristic retrieval into a single, optimized API call.

## WURFL Device Database

The Wireless Universal Resource File (WURFL, http://wurfl.sourceforge.net) is an open-data mobile device database and open-source API that provides access to a community-driven database of mobile device and browser characteristics. The WURFL project is about ten years old. You can learn more about WURFL from the interview with its co-creator, Luca Passani, which you will find in a sidebar later in this section.

WURFL recognizes almost all known mobile devices and tracks many device characteristics. WURFL rarely misidentifies a mobile device, but when that happens, it is easy to communicate with the database maintainers and contribute device information that corrects the problem.

WURFL stores device data in an XML format. The device database is one large XML file, wurfl.xml, which at the time of writing contains about 13MB of device information. Device characteristics are textual and categorized into groups. (The WURFL API allows lookup by characteristic and group names.) The WURFL database is hierarchical, which means that mobile device models in the database inherit capabilities from ancestor devices. An ancestor device can be an earlier device model or a virtual device that represents a version of a mobile OS or browser. At every step in the hierarchy, device capabilities can be updated to match the actual functionality of mobile device families or an individual device.

### INTERVIEW WITH LUCA PASSANI, CO-CREATOR OF WURFL

Luca Passani is the co-creator of the WURFL device database and API. Formerly of Openwave and AdMob, Passani now leads WURFL development and advocates for the rights of content owners and developers on the Mobile Web.

FREDERICK: Describe your motivation for creating WURFL?

PASSANI: While working for developer marketing within Openwave since 2001, the rest of the good Developer Marketing team and I were doing a great job at evangelizing about WAP and the Openwave WAP SDK. Developers liked the tool, but one point that was reiterated was, "Guys, it's not an Openwave world alone. You have Nokia, you have Ericsson, you have PDAs, and we would like to support them all." For this reason, I was asking Openwave if they would sponsor a free tool for developers. In the middle of the .com bubble burst, money was tight, so the answer was no. But the company was OK with me leveraging the open source model and the community on WMLProgramming to create an open-source developer tool.

After all, they were also asking me to help developers migrate from WML to XHTML-MP, so timing was great. That was how WURFL was born in January 2002.

After that, the only way was up. WURFL was free, open, and it worked. In 2007, I left Openwave and, after a [period] with AdMob, I created my own company around the idea of providing professional support around WURFL.

FREDERICK: How does WURFL differentiate itself from [other device database products] in the marketplace?

PASSANI: At the cost of sounding arrogant, I think the question should be phrased more fairly, "How do others differentiate from WURFL?" There is really no open-source competition to WURFL, but there are multiple commercial initiatives. Their story is typically about "better data, better documentation, better tools, and/or better support than WURFL."

Honestly, I have seen first-hand that the "better data" part only refers to a subset of devices; for the rest, even commercial solutions copy from WURFL. As far as the API goes, I honestly believe the latest releases of Java and PHP API are better than commercial solutions in terms of speed, openness, and flexibility.

As far as tools and support are concerned, now that I have a company, [you can] expect improvement in that area, too.

FREDERICK: How is device data sourced and verified? What is the role of the community here?

PASSANI: The community is everything. Not only is the community adding the data, but [it is] also placing existing data under scrutiny. There is a process in place. In order to become a contributor, you need to be approved. After you are approved, your submissions are monitored, and, if you don't abide by the WURFL conventions, your contributor credentials will be revoked. I have a small staff of people doing the check on submissions and also adding device information.

As far as data quality is concerned, it varies. Popular devices will typically get a lot of attention, so information is most probably correct. On the other hand, a weird Motorola [mobile device] from Kazakhstan spotted in the logs will find its way into WURFL, some basic info will be set through UAProf, but thorough validation of the device is more unlikely to take place.

One important aspect to mention, though, is that, because of its openness, a lot of companies will adopt WURFL and set up their own business intelligence to correct information that does not work for them. A lot of times this information is fed back into WURFL. Other times it is not, which is a shame [because] sharing device information is key to fixing the problem for everyone and being able to use our time on our business model. In my opinion, using time on rediscovering the wheel is not a wise use of resources.

---

The WURFL database can be customized and extended using patch files, XML files in the same format as the main database that are applied sequentially to add new devices and override device capabilities. For example, the WURFL maintainers provide a patch file that identifies desktop Web browsers.

You can browse and search the master WURFL device data repository at http://wurflpro.com/. Browsing the repository is a human-readable way to discover the capabilities for a mobile device. Figures 4-1 and 4-2 display screenshots of wurflpro.com taken while searching for the Palm Pre device. Figure 4-1 shows all search results for the *Pre* model name. Figure 4-2 shows the WURFL database entry for the Palm Pre with webOS version 1.2.

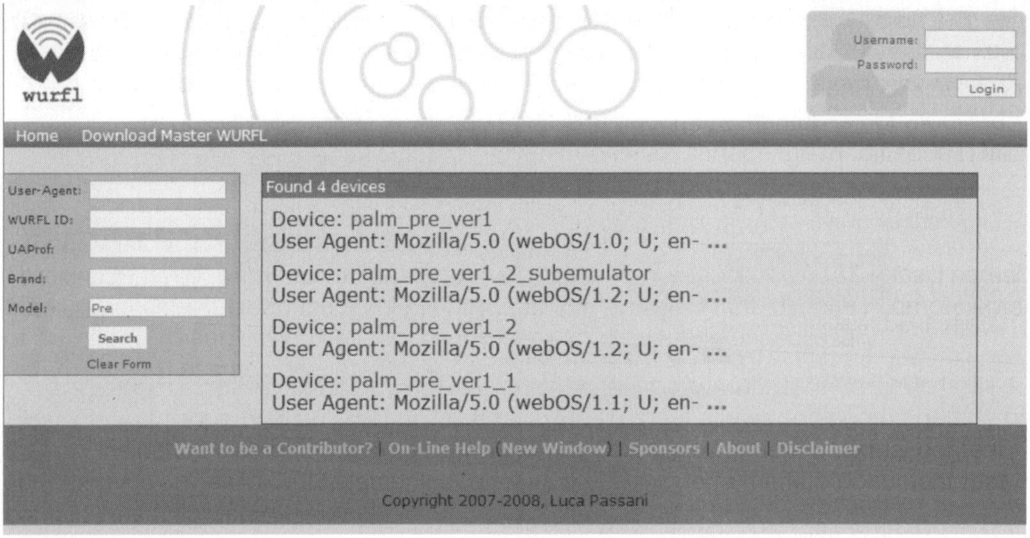

**Figure 4-1.** *Search results for* Pre *showing Palm Pre Device versions in the WURFL public repository at wurflpro.com*

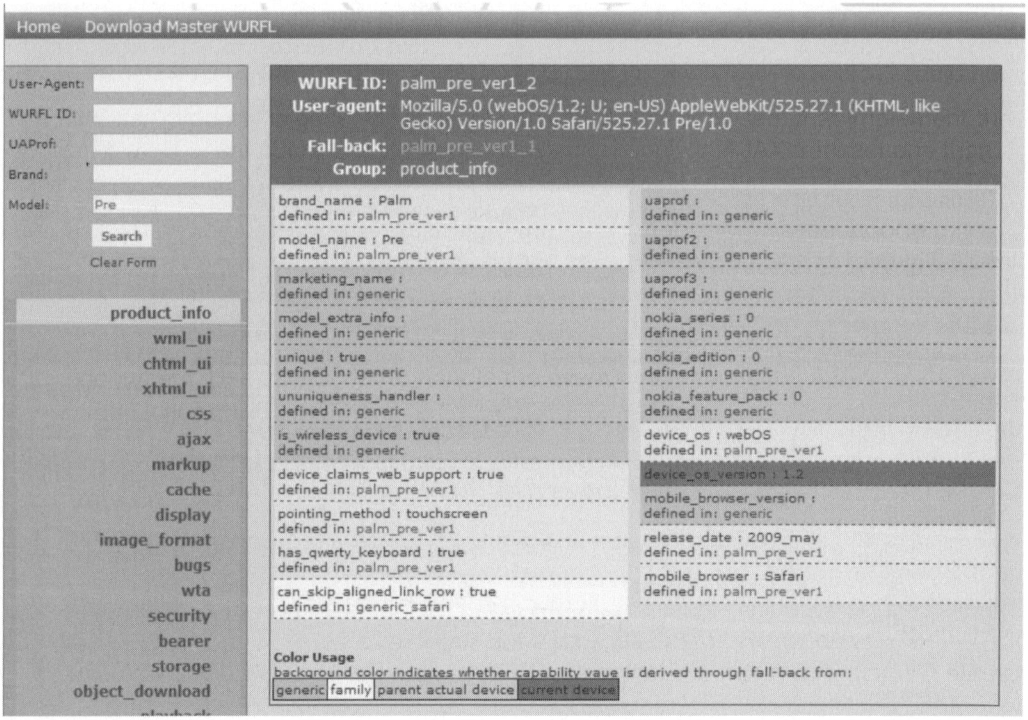

**Figure 4-2.** *Device entry for Palm Pre with webOS version 1.2 in the WURFL public repository at wurflpro.com*

Figure 4-2 shows off several features of the WURFL device database. The WURFL device ID of the Palm Pre with webOS version 1.2 is palm_pre_ver_1_2. Its ancestor entry in the device hierarchy is the "fall-back" device, palm_pre_ver_1_1. The screenshot shows all the device characteristics in the product_info group. This group provides basic mobile device product information. Each characteristic in the group is shaded with a background color that indicates where in the device hierarchy the value is defined. Dark and light green characteristics are defined in the current device or its immediate parent. These values are considered the most reliable because they are defined close in the hierarchy to the actual device. Characteristic values defined more distantly up the device hierarchy, at the level of a virtual device family or OS version or browser version, are shaded yellow. Capabilities defined at the root of the device database hierarchy are shaded red to indicate that they are most distantly defined and often, the least reliable.

The WURFL project provides object-oriented device database APIs for Java, PHP, and .NET Web runtime frameworks licensed under the GPL. The API provides methods for recognizing a mobile device from the HTTP request or User-Agent header value, as well as for obtaining device characteristics by group or characteristic name.

You can download the WURFL database, patch files, and API implementations from the WURFL SourceForge site at http://wurfl.sourceforge.net/.

Follow these steps to install and use the WURFL database and PHP API:

1. Download the WURFL PHP API into an accessible location on your Web server.

2. Download the main WURFL database and patch file(s) into an accessible location on your Web server.

3. Configure the PHP API by customizing a wurfl-config.xml file.

4. Write PHP code that initializes the WURFL API using wurfl-config.xml.

5. Write PHP code that recognizes a mobile device using the HTTP request headers or User-Agent.

6. Write PHP code that uses the API to obtain device characteristics.

The first step required to use the WURFL API is that you download the latest version of the PHP API from the WURFL SourceForge software download site at http://sourceforge.net/projects/wurfl/files/. This section describes installation for version 1.1 of the PHP API. Next, you install the software distribution into an accessible location on your Web server. This section assumes that the PHP API is installed into a directory named wurfl-php-1.r1.

The second step required to use the WURFL API in PHP is that you download and install the WURFL database and patch file(s) to an accessible location on your Web server. Create a writable directory for caching WURFL device data to disk for fast lookups.

The third step required to use the WURFL API in PHP is that you configure the API installation. In PHP, you initialize the WURFL API by customizing a wurfl-config.xml file that provides the file locations of the main WURFL database, patch files. Listing 4-2 is an example wurfl-config.xml file that indicates that the main WURFL database, patch files, and disk cache directory are all located in the same directory as the configuration file. For your reference, an annotated version of `wurfl-config.xml` is available at http://wurfl.sourceforge.net/nphp/wurfl-config.xml.

**Listing 4-2.** *Example wurfl-config.xml Configuration File for WURFL PHP API*

```xml
<?xml version="1.0" encoding="UTF-8"?>
<wurfl-config>
    <wurfl>
        <main-file>wurfl.xml</main-file>
        <patches>
            <patch>web_browsers_patch.xml</patch>
            <patch>bots_and_spider.xml</patch>
        </patches>
    </wurfl>
    <persistence>
        <provider>file</provider>
        <params>dir=cache</params>
    </persistence>
    <cache>
        <provider>null</provider>
    </cache>
</wurfl-config>
```

In Listing 4-2, the `<main-file>` element specifies the location of the main WURFL device database. The `<patch>` elements specify the location of any WURFL patch files used to modify the database contents. All file locations are absolute paths or relative paths from the `wurfl-config.xml` file location. The `<persistence>` element can specify one of several caching mechanisms for WURFL device data. The listing opts for a simple, file-based cache provider, and the `<params>` element specifies the cache directory (again, relative to the location of the configuration file itself) that should contain the cache files.

The fourth step required to use the WURFL API in PHP is that you write PHP code that initializes the WURFL API using `wurfl-config.xml`. Begin by finding the path to the PHP installation directory from the first step. After creating the configuration file in the third step, find its absolute path. This line shows an example absolute path to a configuration file:

```
/home/webuser/learnto.mobi/html/books/bmwd/04/wurfl/wurfl-config.xml
```

Listing 4-3 uses the WURFL API installation directory and configuration file path in a PHP code snippet that initializes the API. Note that the WURFL API installation directory in the `require_once` statement above is *relative* to the location of the file containing the PHP code (although you could also provide an absolute path; they are equally valid in PHP). The configuration file location is an absolute path.

**Listing 4-3.** *Example WURFL API Initialization in PHP*

```php
require_once('wurfl-php-1.r1/WURFL/WURFLManagerProvider.php');
$wurflConfigFile =
"/home/webuser/learnto.mobi/html/books/bmwd/04/wurfl/wurfl-config.xml";
$wurflManager =
WURFL_WURFLManagerProvider::getWURFLManager($wurflConfigFile);
```

The fifth step required to use the WURFL API in PHP is that you write PHP code that recognizes a mobile device using Web request headers. Here, the WURFL API provides three options for device recognition. The first (and preferred) API variant uses the entire set of HTTP request headers to identify the device, as in the following PHP code:

```
$device = $wurflManager->getDeviceForHttpRequest($_SERVER);
```

The variable `$device` is a `WURFL_Device` object that you can use in the sixth step to obtain device characteristics. The second API variant for device recognition uses only a User-Agent string (or value of the `User-Agent` HTTP request header) to identify the device, as in this PHP example:

```
$device = $wurflManager->getDeviceForUserAgent($_SERVER['HTTP_USER_AGENT']);
```

You use the third API variant for device recognition only when the WURFL ID for a device is already known. Here, you use the ID as the identifying parameter for the device in the database. In the code sample that follows, the Palm Pre device ID is used from Figure 4-2.

```
$device = $wurflManager->getDevice("palm_pre_ver_1_2");
```

The sixth and final step required to use the WURFL API in PHP is that you write PHP code that uses the API to obtain characteristics for the newly identified device. You can use the methods and properties of the `$device` instance of the `WURFL_Device` class (obtained in the fifth step) to obtain characteristic values.

The `WURFL_Device` object provides `id` and `fallback` properties that identify the current device ID and the ID of the immediate ancestor in the device hierarchy, respectively. Its `getCapability` and `getAllCapabilities` methods find device capability values.

The `getCapability` method returns the value of one device characteristic:

```
$bestMarkup = $device->getCapability('preferred_markup');
```

The `getAllCapabilities` method returns an Array of all device capabilities and values. The array can then be dereferenced to find individual capability values, as in the following code sample:

```
$props = $device->getAllCapabilities();
$bestMarkup = $props['preferred_markup'];
$modelName = $props['model_name'];
$isMobileDevice = $props['is_wireless_device'];
```

All characteristic values are PHP strings (even Boolean values).

## Common WURFL Device Characteristics

Table 4-1 lists several commonly used device characteristics from the WURFL device database. You obtain the values of these characteristics for a device using the `getCapability` or `getAllCapabilities` methods of the `WURFL_Device` object, as demonstrated in the preceding section.

You can find the complete set of WURFL device characteristics documented at http://wurfl.sourceforge.net/help_doc.php.

**Table 4-1.** *Commonly Used Device Characteristics in WURFL Device Database*

| Characteristic Name | Characteristic Group | Type | Description |
|---|---|---|---|
| brand_name | product_info | string | Indicates the brand name of the mobile device (such as LG, Apple, and Nokia). |
| model_name | product_info | string | Indicates the model name of the mobile device (such as VX9100, iPhone, and N96). |
| is_wireless_device | product_info | string <br><br> Valid values are *true* or *false*. | Indicates whether the device is a recognized mobile device or browser. This value is *false* for desktop browsers, robots, and spiders. |
| device_claims_web_support | product_info | string <br><br> Valid values are *true* or *false*. | Indicates whether the mobile browser claims to support Web standards (such as HTML, JavaScript, and AJAX). |
| ajax_support_javascript | Ajax | string <br><br> Valid values are *true* or *false*. | Indicates whether the mobile browser reliably supports JavaScript functionality. |
| preferred_markup | Markup | string | Indicates the markup language best supported by the browser on the mobile device. |
| resolution_width | Display | string Valid values are numeric. | Indicates the screen width. |
| resolution_height | display | string Valid values are numeric. | Indicates the screen height. |

## Code Samples Using the WURFL API

The code samples in Listing 4-4 and 4-5 illustrate how to use the WURFL PHP API and device database to view and use device property values in Mobile Web pages.

Listing 4-4 is a Mobile Web page in XHTML-MP that uses the WURFL PHP API to view mobile device characteristics from the WURFL device database. It contains the `formatBoolean`, `formatArray`, and `writeCapability` utility functions to format device characteristics for display in the Web page. These functions are not related to the WURFL API. After the function declarations, a standard page header is included (which is also unrelated to the WURFL API). The next two sections of code initialize the WURFL API and obtain a `WURFL_Device` instance that identifies the mobile device or desktop Web browser making the Web request. Finally, you call the `getCapability` method of `WURFL_Device` is called repeatedly to obtain several device characteristics.

You can view the result of Listing 4-4 by browsing to http://learnto.mobi/books/bmwd/04/4-4.php in a desktop or mobile browser.

**Listing 4-4.** *Sample Code for WURFL Property Viewer*

```php
<?php
// Format a boolean capability value
function formatBoolean($value) {
    return $value ? ("Yes") : ("No");
}

// Format an array capability value
function formatArray($value) {
    $output = "[";
    join(',', $value);
    $output .= "]";
    return $output;
}

// Output a capability list item
function writeCapability($name, $value) {
    $output = '<li><span class="capaName">' . $name . '</span>? <span
class="capaValue">';
    if (is_bool($value)) {
        $output .= formatBoolean($value);
    } else if (is_array($value)) {
        $output .= formatArray($value);
    } else {
        $output .= $value;
    }
    $output .= '</span></li>';
    return  $output;
}

// Define constants used in the page header and footer
define("TITLE", "WURFL Device Info");
// Include header markup
require ("../../../includes/header.php");

// Initialize WURFL
require_once('./wurfl-php-1.r1/WURFL/WURFLManagerProvider.php');
```

```
$wurflConfigFile = "/home/webadmin/learnto.mobi/html/books/bmwd/04/wurfl/wurfl-
config.xml";
$wurflManager = WURFL_WURFLManagerProvider::getWURFLManager($wurflConfigFile);

// Get the device making the HTTP request
$device = $wurflManager->getDeviceForHttpRequest($_SERVER);

// Use the WURFL API to display mobile device characteristics
?>
<p>WURFL Device Characteristics</p>
<ul>
<?= writeCapability("User-Agent", $_SERVER['HTTP_USER_AGENT']) ?>
<?= writeCapability("Brand Name", $device->getCapability('brand_name')) ?>
<?= writeCapability("Model Name", $device->getCapability('model_name')) ?>
<?= writeCapability("Pointing Method", $device->getCapability('pointing_method')) ?>
<?= writeCapability("Screen Width", $device->getCapability('resolution_width')) ?>
<?= writeCapability("Screen Height", $device->getCapability('resolution_height')) ?>
<?= writeCapability("Mobile Device", $device->getCapability('is_wireless_device')) ?>
<?= writeCapability("Supports Web Standards", $device-
>getCapability('device_claims_web_support')) ?>
<?= writeCapability("Preferred Markup", $device->getCapability('preferred_markup')) ?>
<?= writeCapability("Supports Access Keys", $device-
>getCapability('access_key_support')) ?>
</ul>

<p>Click here to try <a href="4-5.php">the WURFL switcher</a>.</p>

<?
// Include footer markup
require ("../../../includes/footer.php");
?>
```

Figure 4-3 shows screenshots of Listing 4-4 when impersonating the Nokia N96 and Samsung T919 devices in Firefox. Notice how the device information changes in each screenshot.

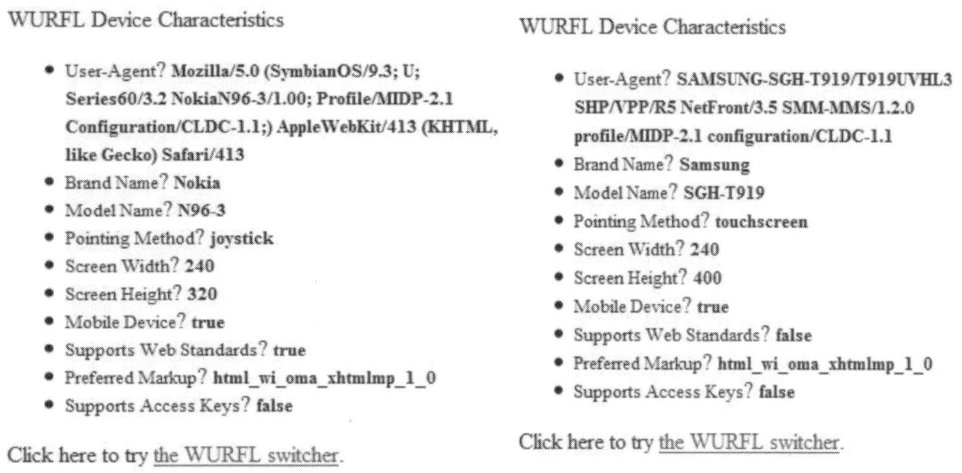

**WURFL Device Characteristics**

- User-Agent? **Mozilla/5.0 (SymbianOS/9.3; U; Series60/3.2 NokiaN96-3/1.00; Profile/MIDP-2.1 Configuration/CLDC-1.1;) AppleWebKit/413 (KHTML, like Gecko) Safari/413**
- Brand Name? **Nokia**
- Model Name? **N96-3**
- Pointing Method? **joystick**
- Screen Width? **240**
- Screen Height? **320**
- Mobile Device? **true**
- Supports Web Standards? **true**
- Preferred Markup? **html_wi_oma_xhtmlmp_1_0**
- Supports Access Keys? **false**

Click here to try the WURFL switcher.

**WURFL Device Characteristics**

- User-Agent? **SAMSUNG-SGH-T919/T919UVHL3 SHP/VPP/R5 NetFront/3.5 SMM-MMS/1.2.0 profile/MIDP-2.1 configuration/CLDC-1.1**
- Brand Name? **Samsung**
- Model Name? **SGH-T919**
- Pointing Method? **touchscreen**
- Screen Width? **240**
- Screen Height? **400**
- Mobile Device? **true**
- Supports Web Standards? **false**
- Preferred Markup? **html_wi_oma_xhtmlmp_1_0**
- Supports Access Keys? **false**

Click here to try the WURFL switcher.

**Figure 4-3.** *Screenshots of the Mobile Web Page in Listing 4-4 for the Nokia N96 and Samsung T919*

Listing 4-5 is a PHP script that uses a HTTP 302 redirect to send desktop and mobile browsers to different destination URLs. The mobile industry refers to this type of script, one that conditionally redirects browsers to different destinations based on device characteristics, user choice, or the entered domain name, as a *switcher* or *mobile switcher*. (You can learn more about this subject in Chapter 10, which discusses how to deploy your scripts.)

The sample switcher code in Listing 4-5 begins by identifying the redirect targets for desktop and mobile browsers as absolute URLs on the current domain. Next the code initializes the WURFL PHP API, then uses the WURFL API to populate the $device variable with a WURFL_Device instance that identifies the mobile device or desktop browser originating the Web request. Next, the script checks the value of the WURFL characteristic, is_wireless_device, to determine whether the client is a desktop or mobile device, applying a known bug fix for the unusual situation where the WURFL API unexpectedly provides an Array as the return value from the getCapability method for devices identified as desktop browsers. The HTTP 302 redirect is implemented by checking the value of the is_wireless_device property and redirecting mobile and desktop browsers to the appropriate location using the Location HTTP response header.

You can view Listing 4-5 by browsing to http://learnto.mobi/books/bmwd/04/4-5.php in a desktop or mobile browser. Notice that the following redirect rules are implemented:

- Desktop browsers are redirected to http://learnto.mobi/books/bmwd/04/desktop.php.

- Mobile browsers are redirected to http://learnto.mobi/books/bmwd/04/mobile.php.

- When a Location response header is used, the body of the HTTP response is blank.

**Listing 4-5.** *Sample Code for WURFL Switcher*

```php
<?php
// This script decides whether the client is a mobile device and redirects to Desktop or
Mobile Web content as appropriate.

// The URI redirect location for desktop browsers
$desktopRedirect = "/books/bmwd/04/desktop.php";

// The URI redirect location for wireless browsers
$mobileRedirect = "/books/bmwd/04/mobile.php";

// Initialize WURFL
require_once('./wurfl-php-1.r1/WURFL/WURFLManagerProvider.php');
$wurflConfigFile = "/home/webadmin/learnto.mobi/html/books/bmwd/04/wurfl/wurfl-
config.xml";
$wurflManager = WURFL_WURFLManagerProvider::getWURFLManager($wurflConfigFile);

// Get the device making the HTTP request
$device = $wurflManager->getDeviceForHttpRequest($_SERVER);
// Is this device a mobile device?
$isMobileDevice = $device->getCapability('is_wireless_device');
```

```
// When WURFL identifies some desktop web browsers, an array for this capability. Choose
the first value of such an array.
if (is_array($isMobileDevice)) {
        $isMobileDevice = $isMobileDevice[0];
}

// Implement the HTTP 302 redirect by adding a response header, routing to the mobile
user experience for mobile devices.
// Confusing comparison - $isMobileDevice is a string, not a boolean
if ($isMobileDevice == "true") {
    header("Location: " . $mobileRedirect);
}
else {
    header("Location: " . $desktopRedirect);
}

exit;

?>
```

Figure 4-4 contains screenshots of Listing 4-5 when browsed using Firefox in two scenarios: the first scenarios relies on the default desktop user-agent, and second scenario has Firefox impersonate the Samsung T919. Notice that the desktop and mobile browsers are identified properly and redirected to the appropriate locations.

## Device is Desktop Web Browser!

- Back to Chapter 04

home

## Device is Mobile Browser!

- Back to Chapter 04

home

*Figure 4-4. Screenshots of the Mobile Web Page in Listing 4–5 executed in Firefox and Samsung T919*

### Contributing Device Data to WURFL

WURFL is a community-driven device database with active third-party developers and contributors of device information. The WURFL developer community is centralized on the WMLProgramming Yahoo Group at http://tech.groups.yahoo.com/group/wmlprogramming/. You can join this active group to ask and answer questions about the device database, the API, device recognition, and Mobile Web programming in general.

All Mobile Web developers are welcome and encouraged to contribute to the WURFL community, especially by providing device characteristic information and HTTP request headers. To learn how to become a WURFL contributor, follow the instructions on the WURFL SourceForge web site at http://wurfl.sourceforge.net/contribute.php and the WURFL Public Repository at www.wurflpro.com/static/become_a_contributor.htm.

## DeviceAtlas Device Database

DeviceAtlas is a commercial device database and API provided by dotMobi, which claims that it is the fastest and most accurate tool for recognizing mobile devices. The DeviceAtlas database is an aggregation of device information from operators, manufacturers, WURFL, and other sources. It is available with commercial licensing terms that range from a free, single-server developer license to affordable annual fees for two server licenses and negotiable enterprise license terms. See http://deviceatlas.com/licences for more information about DeviceAtlas licensing.

DeviceAtlas stores device data in JSON format. The device database is one JSON file. Device characteristics are stored hierarchically, similarly to WURFL, to ensure a compact JSON data file, but the device hierarchy is hidden from API users. Desktop browsers, robots, spiders, proxy servers, and transcoders are all recognized in the DeviceAtlas database.

With a commercial license, the DeviceAtlas database can be customized and extended privately or publicly by contributing device information through a Mobile Web test suite or using the DeviceAtlas web site (http://deviceatlas.com).

The DeviceAtlas web site contains a wealth of device information and reports available to registered users. Site registration is free. The device database is browsable and searchable in the Devices section of the site (http://deviceatlas.com/devices). Figures 4-5, 4-6, 4-7, and 4-8 show what you might see when browsing the DeviceAtlas site.

Figure 4-5 shows what you see when browsing the list of Alcatel mobile devices known to DeviceAtlas.

**Figure 4-5.** *DeviceAtlas browsing of Alcatel mobile device models*

Figure 4-6 show what you see when using DeviceAtlas to search results for *Pre*. This search query finds the device database entry for the Palm Pre mobile device.

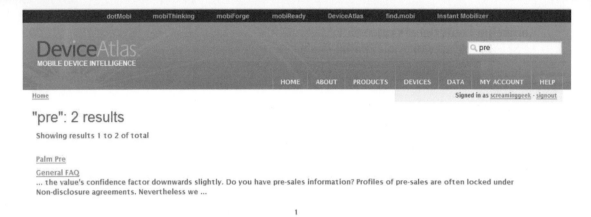

**Figure 4-6.** *DeviceAtlas search results for Pre*

Figure 4-7 show what you see when using DeviceAtlas to view the device database entry for the Palm Pre. It displays an image of the mobile device and its characteristics. The web site optionally displays your contributions to the characteristics of this device, as well as characteristics with conflicting values from the original data sources.

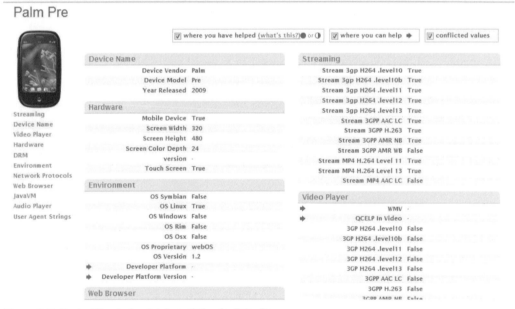

**Figure 4-7.** *DeviceAtlas device database listing for Palm Pre*

Clicking a characteristic in Figure 4-7 allows registered site users to edit device information. Figure 4-8 shows the DeviceAtlas user interface for editing the screen-height characteristic for the Palm Pre. User-edited device information is moderated before it is included in the public DeviceAtlas database.

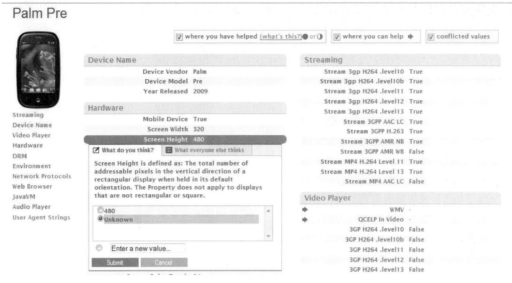

**Figure 4-8.** *Editing a device characteristic in DeviceAtlas*

The DeviceAtlas device database API is available for Java, .NET, PHP, Python, and Ruby Web runtimes. The object-oriented API provides methods for recognizing a mobile device from the `User-Agent` header value and obtaining device characteristics individually or as an array. This section describes the installation and use of the DeviceAtlas PHP API.

You can visit `http://deviceatlas.com/downloads` to download the DeviceAtlas API and documentation; download instructions for the DeviceAtlas device database are provided once a commercial license is obtained from dotMobi.

Follow these steps to install and use the DeviceAtlas database and PHP API:

1.  Download the DeviceAtlas API into an accessible location on your Web server.

2.  Download the DeviceAtlas JSON database into an accessible location on your Web server.

3.  Write PHP code that initializes the DeviceAtlas API.

4.  Write PHP code that recognizes a mobile device by User-Agent and obtains characteristic values for the mobile device.

First, you use the DeviceAtlas API to download the latest version of the PHP API from the DeviceAtlas download site. This section describes how to install version 1.3.1 of the PHP API. You install the software distribution into an accessible location on your Web server; this section assumes that you install the PHP API into a directory named `deviceatlas`. The software distribution contains the PHP API, a sample JSON file, and the API documentation.

Second, you use the DeviceAtlas API in PHP to download and install the DeviceAtlas JSON database file to an accessible location on your Web server. DeviceAtlas is a commercial database, and you download the JSON database file using instructions provided by dotMobi with the commercial license. (A free, single-server developer license is available for DeviceAtlas.)

Third, you use the DeviceAtlas API in PHP to write PHP code that initializes the API. You initialize the API by including the API class file and providing a relative or absolute path to the JSON device database. Listing 4-6 shows an example of PHP initialization code for DeviceAtlas; it uses the deviceatlas API installation directory (from the first step) and a relative path to the JSON device database file (from the second step) to initialize the API. The $tree variable is an internal tree representation of the device database that is passed as a parameter when using the API to identify mobile devices and obtain device characteristics.

**Listing 4-6.** *Code Sample for DeviceAtlas API Initialization*

```
// Initialize DeviceAtlas
include 'deviceatlas/Mobi/Mtld/DA/Api.php';
$tree = Mobi_Mtld_DA_Api::getTreeFromFile("deviceatlas/20091028.json");
```

Fourth, you use the DeviceAtlas API in PHP is to write PHP code that recognizes a mobile device by User-Agent and obtains characteristic values for the mobile device. In the DeviceAtlas API, device recognition and property retrieval are combined into a single method call. DeviceAtlas provides two API methods to obtain all characteristics for a device in a PHP array: Mobi_Mtld_DA_Api::getProperties and Mobi_Mtld_DA_Api::getPropertiesAsTyped. The code sample that follows illustrates how to use these methods:

```
$props = Mobi_Mtld_DA_Api::getProperties($tree, $_SERVER['HTTP_USER_AGENT']);
$propsTyped = Mobi_Mtld_DA_Api::getPropertiesAsTyped($tree,
$_SERVER['HTTP_USER_AGENT']);
```

The $props variable is an array of device characteristic names and string values. The $propsTyped variable is an array of characteristic names with values typed as string, integer, or boolean, according to the DeviceAtlas device characteristics documentation specified in the next section.

The API also provides methods to retrieve individual property values as untyped strings or values typed as string, integer, or boolean, according to the DeviceAtlas device characteristics documentation. The code sample that follows illustrates how to use these different API calls:

```
$prop = Mobi_Mtld_DA_Api::getProperty($tree, $_SERVER['HTTP_USER_AGENT'], 'model');
$propBool = Mobi_Mtld_DA_Api::getPropertyAsBoolean($tree, $_SERVER['HTTP_USER_AGENT'],
'mobileDevice');
$propInt= Mobi_Mtld_DA_Api::getPropertyAsInteger($tree, $_SERVER['HTTP_USER_AGENT'],
'displayWidth');
$propString = Mobi_Mtld_DA_Api::getPropertyAsString($tree, $_SERVER['HTTP_USER_AGENT'],
'vendor');
```

After executing this code sample, $prop and $propString are strings, $propBool is a Boolean value, and $propInt is an integer. In the DeviceAtlas API, untyped characteristic values are always PHP strings.

## Common DeviceAtlas Device Characteristics

Table 4-2 lists several commonly used device characteristics from the DeviceAtlas device database. You obtain the values of these characteristics for a device using the getProperty, getAllProperties, and getPropertyAs… methods of the Mobi_Mtld_DA_Api object, as demonstrated in the preceding section.

You can find the complete set of DeviceAtlas device characteristics documented at http://deviceatlas.com/properties.

**Table 4-2.** *Common Device Characteristics in DeviceAtlas Device Database*

| Characteristic Name | Type | Description |
| --- | --- | --- |
| isBrowser | boolean | Indicates whether the device is a desktop browser. |
| vendor | string | Indicates the brand name of the mobile device (such as LG, Apple, and Nokia). |
| model | string | Indicates the model name of the mobile device (such as VX9100, iPhone, and N96). |
| mobileDevice | boolean | Indicates whether the device is a recognized mobile device or mobile browser. |
| markupSupport | string | Lists the enumerated set of markup languages supported on the device. |
| displayWidth | integer | Gets the screen width. The related usableDisplayWidth property gets the addressable horizontal pixels in the browser, taking into account padding and scrollbars. |
| displayHeight | integer | Gets the screen height. The related usableDisplayHeight property gets the addressable vertical pixels in the browser, taking into account padding and scrollbars. |

## Code Samples Using the DeviceAtlas API

The code samples in Listing 4-7 and 4-8 illustrate how you can use the DeviceAtlas PHP API and device database to view and manipulate device property values in Mobile Web pages.

Listing 4-7 is a Mobile Web page in XHTML-MP that uses the DeviceAtlas PHP API to view mobile device characteristics from the DeviceAtlas device database. This listing is similar to Listing 4-4, the WURFL Property Viewer, except that it uses a different device database API.

**Listing 4-7.** *Sample Code for DeviceAtlas Property Viewer*

```php
<?php

// Define any constants
define("TITLE", "DeviceAtlas Device Info");

// Include our header
require ("../../../includes/header.php");

// Format a boolean capability value
function formatBoolean($value) {
        return $value ? ("Yes") : ("No");
}

// Format an array capability value
function formatArray($value) {
        $output = "[";
        join(',', $value);       $output .= "]";
        return $output;
}

// Output a capability list item
function writeCapability($name, $value) {
        $output = '<li>' . '<span class="capaName">' . $name . '</span>? <span
class="capaValue">';
        if (is_array($value)) {
                formatArray($value);
        } else if (is_bool($value)) {
                formatBoolean($value);
        } else {
                $output .= $value;
        }
        $output .= '</span></li>';
        return  $output;
}

// Initialize DeviceAtlas
include 'deviceatlas/Mobi/Mtld/DA/Api.php';
$tree = Mobi_Mtld_DA_Api::getTreeFromFile("deviceatlas/20091028.json");

// Get the user-agent making the HTTP request. This value is used in property lookups
$userAgent = $_SERVER['HTTP_USER_AGENT'];

// Get all DeviceAtlas properties for the device.
$props = Mobi_Mtld_DA_Api::getProperties($tree, $userAgent);
```

```
// Show the UA, whether the request originates from a mobile device, and a few browser
characteristics
?>

<p>DeviceAtlas Device Characteristics</p>
<ul>
<?= writeCapability("User-Agent", $userAgent) ?>
<?= writeCapability("Vendor Name", $props['vendor']) ?>
<?= writeCapability("Model Name", $props['model']) ?>
<?= writeCapability("Desktop Browser", $props['isBrowser']) ?>
<?= writeCapability("Mobile Device", $props['mobileDevice']) ?>
<?= writeCapability("Screen Dimensions", $props['displayWidth'] . ' x ' .
$props['displayHeight']) ?>
<?= writeCapability("Touchscreen", $props['touchScreen']) ?>
<?= writeCapability("Supported Markups", $props['markupSupport']) ?>
<?= writeCapability("Supports HTTPS", $props['https']) ?>
</ul>

<p>Click here to try <a href="4-8.php">the DeviceAtlas switcher</a>.</p>

<?
// Include our footer
require ("../../../includes/footer.php");
?>
```

Like Listing 4-4, Listing 4-7 contains the formatBoolean, formatArray, and
writeCapability utility functions to format device characteristics for display on the Web
page. These functions are not related to the DeviceAtlas API. After the function
declarations, a standard page header is included (which is also unrelated to the
DeviceAtlas API). The next two sections of code initialize the DeviceAtlas API and use
the Mobi_Mtld_DA_Api::getProperties method to obtain an untyped array of all device
characteristic values for the mobile device or desktop Web browser making the Web
request. Finally, the $props array of string values is dereferenced repeatedly to obtain
the device characteristics.

You can view the results of Listing 4-7 by browsing to
http://learnto.mobi/books/bmwd/04/4–7.php in a desktop or mobile browser.

Figure 4-9 shows the results of Listing 4-7 when impersonating the Nokia N96 and
Samsung T919 devices in Firefox. Notice how the device information changes in each
screenshot.

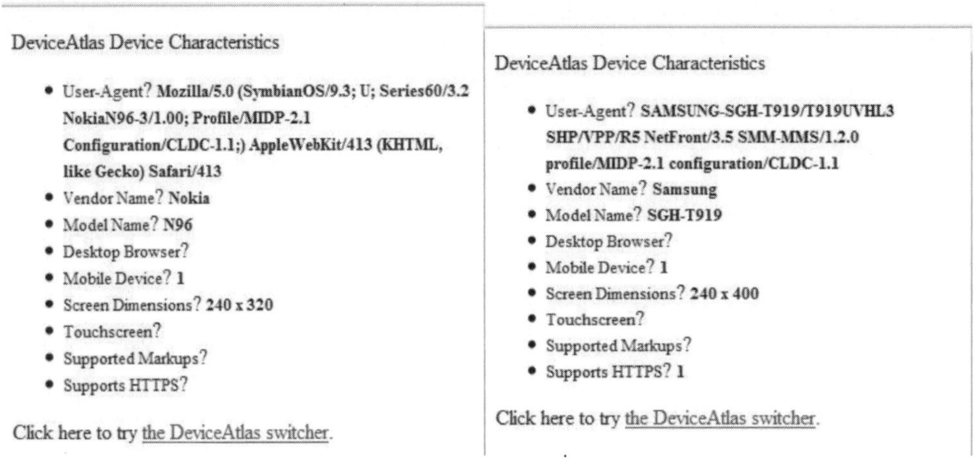

DeviceAtlas Device Characteristics

- User-Agent? **Mozilla/5.0 (SymbianOS/9.3; U; Series60/3.2 NokiaN96-3/1.00; Profile/MIDP-2.1 Configuration/CLDC-1.1;) AppleWebKit/413 (KHTML, like Gecko) Safari/413**
- Vendor Name? **Nokia**
- Model Name? **N96**
- Desktop Browser?
- Mobile Device? **1**
- Screen Dimensions? **240 x 320**
- Touchscreen?
- Supported Markups?
- Supports HTTPS?

Click here to try the DeviceAtlas switcher.

DeviceAtlas Device Characteristics

- User-Agent? **SAMSUNG-SGH-T919/T919UVHL3 SHP/VPP/R5 NetFront/3.5 SMM-MMS/1.2.0 profile/MIDP-2.1 configuration/CLDC-1.1**
- Vendor Name? **Samsung**
- Model Name? **SGH-T919**
- Desktop Browser?
- Mobile Device? **1**
- Screen Dimensions? **240 x 400**
- Touchscreen?
- Supported Markups?
- Supports HTTPS? **1**

Click here to try the DeviceAtlas switcher.

**Figure 4-9.** *Screenshots of the Mobile Web Page in Listing 4–7 for the Nokia N96 and Samsung T919*

Listing 4-8 is a *switcher*, a PHP script that uses a HTTP 302 redirect to send desktop and mobile browsers to different destination URLs. Listing 4-8 is similar to Listing 4-5, except that it relies on the DeviceAtlas device database API.

The sample switcher code in Listing 4-8 begins by identifying the redirect targets for desktop and mobile browsers as absolute URLs on the current hostname. Next, the listing initializes the DeviceAtlas PHP API, then uses the DeviceAtlas API to obtain the value of the $isMobileDevice variable, a typed Boolean value for the database characteristic mobileDevice that indicates whether the value of the User-Agent request header is a mobile device. The HTTP 302 redirect is implemented by checking the value of the $isMobileDevice variable. Finally, Listing 4-8 redirects mobile and desktop browsers to the appropriate location using the Location HTTP response header.

You can see Listing 4-8 in action by browsing to http://learnto.mobi/books/bmwd/04/4-8.php in a desktop or mobile browser. Notice that the listing implements the following redirect rules:

- Desktop browsers are redirected to http://learnto.mobi/books/bmwd/04/desktop.php.

- Mobile browsers are redirected to http://learnto.mobi/books/bmwd/04/mobile.php.

- When a Location response header is used, the body of the HTTP response is blank.

**Listing 4-8.** *Sample Code for DeviceAtlas Switcher*

```php
<?php
// This script decides whether the client is a mobile device and redirects to Desktop or
Mobile Web content as appropriate.

// The absolute URI redirect location for desktop browsers
$desktopRedirect = "/books/bmwd/04/desktop.php";
```

```
// The absolute URI redirect location for wireless browsers
$mobileRedirect = "/books/bmwd/04/mobile.php";

// Initialize DeviceAtlas
include 'deviceatlas/Mobi/Mtld/DA/Api.php';
$tree = Mobi_Mtld_DA_Api::getTreeFromFile("deviceatlas/20091028.json");

// Get the user-agent making the HTTP request. This value is used in property lookups
$userAgent = $_SERVER['HTTP_USER_AGENT'];

// Get all DeviceAtlas properties for the device.
$isMobileDevice = Mobi_Mtld_DA_Api::getPropertyAsBoolean($tree, $userAgent,
'mobileDevice');

// Do the HTTP 302 redirect by adding a response header.
if ($isMobileDevice) {
    header("Location: " . $mobileRedirect);
}
else {
    header("Location: " . $desktopRedirect);
}

exit;

?>
```

Figure 4-10 contains screenshots of Listing 4–8 as seen from Firefox when using the default desktop user-agent and when impersonating the Samsung T919. Notice that the desktop and mobile browsers are identified properly and redirected to the appropriate locations.

## Device is Desktop Web Browser!

- Back to Chapter 04

home

## Device is Mobile Browser!

- Back to Chapter 04

home

**Figure 4-10.** *Screenshots of the Mobile Web Page in Listing 4-8 executed in Firefox and Samsung T919*

### Contributing Device Data to DeviceAtlas

Representatives from dotMobi, the creators of DeviceAtlas, were invited to contribute an interview for this book; see Chapter 12 for an interview with Andrea Trassati, co-creator of DeviceAtlas and WURFL device databases, about the future of the Mobile Web.

DeviceAtlas provides Test Application for DeviceAtlas (TA-DA), a Mobile Web application that profiles devices and incorporates their characteristics into the public database. A developer browses to TA-DA (http://ta-da.mobi) on the mobile device and executes tests that determine hardware, software, and web browser characteristic values (see http://deviceatlas.com/ta-da-documentation for detailed TA-DA documentation).

As a registerd DeviceAtlas user, you can view and edit device characteristics on the DeviceAtlas web site (http://deviceatlas.com). Edited device data is merged into your private JSON file, and after dotMobi review, might be incorporated into the public database.

dotMobi also owns the mobiForge mobile developer community (http://mobiforge.com), where device information and Mobile Web development techniques are discussed in blogs and forums.

> **NOTE:** The W3C term for device database is *device description repository*. The standards organization recommends its DDR-Simple API (www.w3.org/TR/DDR-Simple-API/) as a standard API for accessing device repositories and retrieving device characteristics. At the time of this writing, DeviceAtlas implements the W3C DDR-Simple API, but WURFL does not yet provide an implementation of this standard.

# Content Adaptation

Content adaptation is the strategy of customizing mobile markup, styles, and scripts for groups of mobile devices with common capabilities. Content adaptation uses the principles of device awareness to identify devices and browsers and group them according to shared properties. Device group membership becomes the criteria for customizing Web content according to your adaptation rules.

The DeviceAtlas Data Explorer is a helpful tool for displaying device data visually and uncovering candidate groups. Using Data Explorer, you select a device property and view the distribution of property values across mobile devices. You can also compare the values of pairs of device properties.

Figure 4-11 illustrates how you can use Data Explorer to view support for XHTML-MP 1.1 (the prerequisite markup language for mobile JavaScript and AJAX) across mobile devices. Figure 4-12 shows a comparison of mobile browser support for XHTML-MP 1.1 and 1.2 using Data Explorer. You can browse to http://deviceatlas.com/explorer to use Data Explorer as a registered DeviceAtlas user.

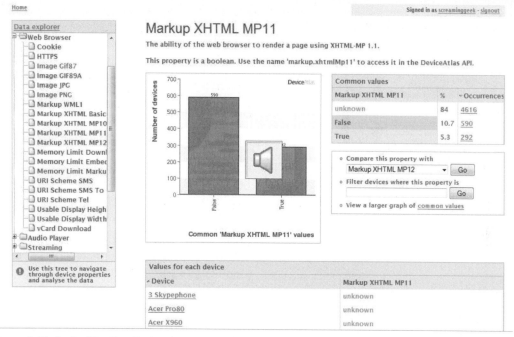

**Figure 4-11.** *DeviceAtlas Data Explorer showing support for XHTML-MP 1.1 on mobile devices*

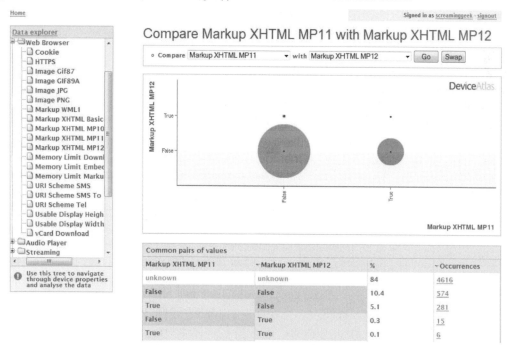

**Figure 4-12.** *DeviceAtlas Data Explorer comparing support for XHTML-MP 1.1 and XHTML-MP 1.2 on mobile devices*

Content adaptation rules are created by the Mobile Web developer or designer. Content adaptation can change the syntax, design, and functionality of a Mobile Web site. It is important to remember that content adaptation consists of more than creating conditional execution in Web runtime templates. Effective content adaptation adapts the Mobile Web user experience to the capabilities and limitations of the mobile device. It improves the user experience on smartphones and streamlines the user experience on featurephones. It surfaces only mobile content known to be compatible on the device. For example, consider mobile markup for a navigational menu. On the iPhone, the menu might be styled to appear like a native OS menu. On JavaScript-capable mobile devices, the menu might pop up when an image is clicked. On phones not supporting scripting, the menu might always be present in the page footer. Content adaptation principles provide a developer framework to implement each menu and use that menu only for the appropriate groups of devices.

The first principle of content adaptation is to embrace, expect, and manage diversity. Mobile devices come in a multitude of operating systems, browser versions, screen sizes, input modes, modalities, and navigation methods. Content adaptation is a strategy that allows a single Mobile Web application to adapt and present the markup, styles, and scripting that provide the best user experience for each mobile device, browser, and user. The best Mobile Web applications exploit the strengths of each mobile platform.

Once you design your Mobile Web site and decide which mobile devices to target with it, you can implement content adaptation in three steps. First, divide the target mobile devices into groups based on shared capabilities, guided by the available characteristics in your device database. Second, decide the ways in which the Mobile Web site can adapt its design and functionality. Third, use the device groups and identified site adaptations to write rules for exactly how the site changes for each group. After you establish your rules, implement the device groups and conditional adaptations in the Web runtime language. You might find it useful to iterate these steps to home in on an achievable content adaptation strategy for your Mobile Web site.

## Creating Device Groups

Device groups are created by sorting the universe of supported mobile devices into classes based on shared capabilities, ensuring that all supported devices belong to at least one group. Device groups become the atomic unit of customization when implementing content adaptation in the Web runtime framework.

The number of groups and choice of classification criteria are arbitrary and tightly related to the Mobile Web project requirements. For simple Mobile Web sites, grouping devices based on screen size might be sufficient for customizing the user experience. More complex Mobile Web projects might require additional device groups based on browser capabilities, such as support for CSS2, XHTML, JavaScript, and AJAX. Mobile Web sites targeting a single phone model, such as iPhone-specific Web sites, might not need to group devices or implement content adaptation.

Remember the breadth of the mobile device landscape when considering your device classification. At the time of writing, the screen sizes (in pixels) of devices browsing the Mobile Web range between 128 x 128 and 800 x 480. Mobile devices feature widely variable navigation methods, including keypads, joysticks, styli, and finger gestures on a touchscreen. Older mobile devices support only WAP markup standards but newer smartphones adhere to the latest Web standards. Device groups do not need to be mutually exclusive and might also consider browser or device limitations. For example, creating a group for all mobile devices known to render XHTML tables poorly can be useful for developers in adapting an interface to avoid table use.

Browsing the device database and viewing mobile devices and device characteristics can help you choose the best criteria for classifying the supported devices into groups.

For example, a Mobile Web site targeting all mobile devices might use these device groups for content adaptation; note that a device can belong to more than one group:

- *Group 1*: Browsers supporting JavaScript and AJAX

- *Group 2*: Devices with a screen width of 320 pixels or greater

- *Group 3*: Devices with a screen width between 240 and 319 pixels

- *Group 4*: Devices with a screen of less than 240

- *Group 5*: Browsers supporting only WML

Group 5 was created to identify older mobile devices and direct them to a low-fi experience. Groups 2, 3, and 4 were created to segment all device screen sizes into three classes. These groups are scaling targets for dynamic images. Group 1 was created to enable a dynamic, scriptable mobile user experience for smartphones.

A Mobile Web site targeting only smartphones browsers that adhere to Web standards might use more specific device groups for content adaptation. The device groups that follow segment devices into useful classes when devices are already known to support XHTML, CSS2, and JavaScript:

- *Group 6*: Browsers supporting AJAX

- *Group 7*: Browsers using the WebKit rendering engine

- *Group 8*: Devices with touchscreens activated using a finger

- *Group 9*: Devices with touchscreens activated using a stylus

- *Group 10*: Browsers where orientation changes are detected using the JavaScript `onresize` event

- *Group 11*: Browsers where orientation changes are detected using the JavaScript `onorientationchange` event

- *Group 12*: Devices with portrait screen sizes (screen height is greater than width)

- *Group 13*: Devices with landscape screen sizes (screen width is greater than height)

Group 6 identifies mobile browsers with sufficient AJAX support to provide a dynamic, scriptable, mobile user experience. Note that not all smartphones have browsers that support AJAX, and some AJAX implementations have performance limitations, so not all smartphones are considered to support AJAX (see Chapter 5 for more information about mobile AJAX). Group 7 identifies mobile browsers that are built from the open-source WebKit rendering engine. WebKit support provides proprietary CSS extensions that many Mobile Web designers find useful. Groups 8 and 9 identify touchscreen mobile devices; these devices require clickable regions of a Mobile Web page to be enlarged to make it easier for a stylus or finger to activate the link.

Notice that the smartphone device classification does *not* consider screen width. Many smartphones support easy switching between portrait and landscape modes, so adapting content to a fixed screen width is problematic. Instead, a Mobile Web developer can use the `onresize` or `onorientationchange` JavaScript events to update the user interface when the device orientation changes (see Chapter 5 for more about mobile JavaScript). Groups 10 and 11 identify mobile devices that enable you to detect orientation changes using JavaScript. Groups 12 and 13 identify devices where the screen orientations do not change or cannot be detected in JavaScript.

## Choosing Adaptation Points

Once device groups are established, review the design and functionality of the Mobile Web site to find components that can be adapted to exploit the capabilities of browsers and devices in each group. Here, an expert Mobile Web designer can be extremely helpful by creating a reference design (a site layout targeted at a single mobile device or screen size) and envisioning how it might change across device groups (see Chapter 6 for details about Mobile Web design and usability on smartphones).

The goal of this step is to identify simple, achievable adaptations that improve the user experience for capable mobile devices and streamline the user experience for limited mobile devices. Adaptations might include changing or removing design components, scaling and transcoding graphics, modifying CSS, or updating dynamic page components using AJAX.

For example, a Mobile Web site targeting all mobile devices might adapt in the following ways:

- Dynamically update some page content using AJAX
- Scale images to accommodate different screen sizes
- Vary the length of text passages
- Provide a one-page WML site for compatibility with older browsers

A Mobile Web site targeting only smartphones might adapt in these ways:

- Dynamically update all page content using AJAX
- Style components using WebKit CSS extensions

- Increase the font or block size of links

- Provide an alternate style sheet optimized for landscape screen orientations

# Writing Content Adaptation Rules for Device Groups

The third step in content adaptation requires that you create rules for implementing content adaptations across the device groups. This step specifies exactly how the Mobile Web site design or functionality changes to fulfill the spirit of the adaptation.

For a Mobile Web site targeting all mobile devices, the following rules might define how you implement adaptations for each device group:

- *Adaptation*: Dynamically update its content using AJAX.

    a. *Group 1*: Update markup to XHTML-MP 1.1 and include AJAX functionality.

    b. *Not in Group 1*: Use XHTML-MP 1.0 and exclude AJAX functionality

- *Adaptation*: Scale images to accommodate different screen sizes.

    a. *Group 2*: Scale images to a maximum width of 300 pixels.

    b. *Group 3*: Scale images to a maximum width of 220 pixels.

    c. *Group 4*: Scale images to a maximum width of 150 pixels.

- *Adaptation*: Vary the length of text passages.

    a. *Group 2*: Each text passage has a maximum length of 750 characters.

    b. *Group 3*: Each text passage has a maximum length of 500 characters

    c. *Group 4*: Each text passage has a maximum length of 250 characters.

- *Adaptation*: Provide a one-page WML site for compatibility with older browsers.

    a. *Group 5*: Redirect to the one-page WML site.

    b. *Not in Group 5*: Do not redirect to the one-page WML site.

For a Mobile Web site targeting only smartphones, these rules might define how you implement adaptations:

- Adaptation: Dynamically update all page content using AJAX.

    a. *Group 6*: Include AJAX functionality.

    b. *Not in Group 6*: Exclude AJAX functionality.

- Adaptation: Style components using WebKit CSS extensions.

  a. *Group 7*: Include WebKit extensions in the CSS.

  b. *Not in Group 7*: Exclude WebKit extensions from the CSS.

- Adaptation: Increase the size of links.

  a. *Group 8*: Add 20px of padding to all clickable text and image links. Use CSS to increase font sizes for text links.

  b. *Group 9*: Add 10 pixels of padding to all clickable text and image links and use CSS to increase font sizes for text links.

  c. *Not in Group 8 or 9*: Don't include any CSS or padding changes for clickable text and image links.

- Adaptation: Provide an alternate style sheet optimized for landscape screen orientations.

  a. *Group 10*: Use the JavaScript `onresize` event to switch between portrait and landscape style sheets.

  b. *Group 11*: Use the JavaScript `onorientation` event to switch between portrait and landscape style sheets.

  c. *Group 12*: Disregard the alternate style sheet.

  d. *Group 13*: Use only the alternate style sheet.

## Implementing Content Adaptation

After you decide your device groups, adaptation points, and content adaptation rules are decided, your final step is to use your chosen Web runtime framework to implement content adaptation in the Mobile Web application. This section contains PHP code samples using the WURFL device database and PHP API to classify mobile devices into groups and implement a single point of content adaptation.

Listing 4-9 shows how to create a Mobile Web page that adapts its style sheet to provide an improved user experience for touchscreen mobile devices. For touchscreen devices, the font sizes and selectable areas for the menu and footer links are enlarged to accommodate touch gestures from human fingers better.

**Listing 4-9.** *Content Adaptation for Touchscreen Devices Using WURFL Device Database and API*

```
<?
// Initialize WURFL
require_once('./wurfl-php-1.r1/WURFL/WURFLManagerProvider.php');
$wurflConfigFile = "/home/webadmin/learnto.mobi/html/books/bmwd/04/wurfl/wurfl-
config.xml";
$wurflManager = WURFL_WURFLManagerProvider::getWURFLManager($wurflConfigFile);

// Get the device making the HTTP request
$device = $wurflManager->getDeviceForHttpRequest($_SERVER);
```

```php
// Does the device have a touchscreen?
$pointingMethod = $device->getCapability('pointing_method');
$isTouchscreen = ($pointingMethod != null) && (stripos($pointingMethod, "touchscreen")
!== FALSE);
?>
<?php echo '<?xml version="1.0" encoding="UTF-8"?>'; ?>
<!DOCTYPE html PUBLIC "-//WAPFORUM//DTD XHTML Mobile 1.0//EN"
"http://www.wapforum.org/DTD/xhtml-mobile10.dtd">
<html xmlns="http://www.w3.org/1999/xhtml">
<head>
<meta name="HandHeldFriendly" content="true" />
<meta name="viewport" content="width=320,initial-scale=1.0, user-scalable=no" />
<title>Content Adaptation with WURFL</title>
<style type="text/css">
.hdr {
  text-align: center;
  font-variant: small-caps;
  font-size: large;
  margin: 2px 0px 4px 0px;
}
.ad {
  margin: 8px;
  text-align: center;
}
.adImg {
  border: 0px solid;
  margin-bottom: 2px;
}
.adtext {
  margin: 0px;
}
.intro {
  font-size: small;
  margin: 4px 2px;
}
ol.menu {
  list-style-type: none;
  margin: 0px;
  padding: 0px;
  text-align: left;
}
ol.menu li {
  color: #000000;
  background-color: #aaffaa;
<? // Enlarge menu list items for touchscreen devices
if ($isTouchscreen) { ?>
  margin: 0px;
  padding: 0px;
  width: 100%;
<? } else { ?>
  margin: 2px;
  padding: 2px 6px;
<? } ?>
}
<? // Enlarge the menu links for touchscreen devices.
if ($isTouchscreen) { ?>
ol.menu a {
```

```
      margin: 5px;
      padding: 10px;
      color: #000000;
      text-align: left;
      font-size: large;
      display: block;
}
<? } ?>
.ftr {
      text-align: center;
<? // Enlarge the footer content for touchscreens.
if ($isTouchscreen) { ?>
      font-size: large;
      margin: 4px;
      width: 100%;
<? } else { ?>
      font-size: small;
      margin: 4px 0px 2px 0px;
<? } ?>
}
</style>
</head>
<body>
<h1 class="hdr">Sunset Farmers&apos; Market</h1>
<div class="ad">
<a href="#"><img class="adImg" src="berry_ad.jpg" width="200" height="40" alt="Fresh
Raspberries This Week" /></a><br/>
<a class="adtext" href="#">fresh raspberries this week</a>
</div>
<div class="intro">Visit us every Wednesday afternoon in the city center for farm-fresh
fruit, vegetables and plants.</div>
<ol class="menu">
<li><a href="#">About the Market</a></li>
<li><a href="#">Seasonal Favorites</a></li>
<li><a href="#">Hours &amp; Directions</a></li>
<li><a href="#">Our Local Farmers</a></li>
<li><a href="#">Stall Map</a></li>
</ol>
<div class="ftr">Call <a href="tel:+15035551234" class="ctc">503-555-1234</a> for market
info</div>
</body>
</html>
```

The PHP script in Listing 4-9 starts by initializing the WURFL PHP API and identifying the device originating the Web request. It checks the value of the pointing_method device database characteristic to determine whether the mobile device includes a touchscreen. The variable $isTouchscreen is a Boolean flag indicating that the device has a touchscreen. Listing 4-9 implements an adaptive style sheet where CSS declarations and properties change for touchscreen devices. For touchscreens, the code removes all padding and margins from list items with the ol.menu li style. The ol.menu a style is used only for touchscreens to increase the font size and selectable regions for menu links. The code also modifies .ftr style to enlarge the font size and margins for footer content. Modifying the style sheet is sufficient to implement content adaptation for touchscreen mobile devices; the XHTML-MP markup need not change.

Instead of implementing an adaptive style sheet, Listing 4-9 could have chosen to import one of two external, static and cacheable style sheets that are optimized for either touchscreen or non-touch devices. This approach requires an additional network transaction to complete the page display, but could reduce bandwidth requirements for subsequent page views if you cache the style sheet in the browser.

You can see Listing 4-9 in action by browsing to http://learnto.mobi/books/bmwd/04/4–9.php in a mobile browser for touchscreen or non-touch mobile devices.

Figure 4-13 displays the XHTML-MP Mobile Web page from Listing 4-9 in two forms: first, it shows the emulated mobile browser for the touchscreen Android G1 device; second, it shows Firefox impersonating the non-touchscreen Nokia 5310. Notice how the menu links and footer content adapt to accommodate both screen modes.

**Figure 4-13.** *Listing 4-9 in the touchscreen Android G1 emulator and non-touchscreen Nokia 5310*

# Content Adaptation on the Mobile Web

Let's review an example of content adaptation on the public Mobile Web. Amazon.com is a worldwide Internet-retailing powerhouse. Its content-adaptive Mobile Web presence targets three groups of mobile devices: touchscreen smartphones, smartphones without touchscreens, and featurephones.

For all device groups, Amazon.com makes its Mobile Web site available at the same URL as the Desktop Web site (http://amazon.com), implementing user-agent switching to route mobile browsers to one of the three mobile user experiences. Mobile Web pages are lightweight desktop HTML and served with the text/html MIME type. Amazon.com enables mobile commerce using cookies and HTTPS. The site assumes that all mobile browsers support HTTPS and cookies, even when user-agents are provided that are known not to implement these Web technologies properly. (In addition, HTTPS transactions and cookies could be transformed or blocked by mobile operator gateways and transcode—see Chapter 12 for a discussion of gateways, transcoders, and the mobile ecosystem.)

For touchscreen smartphones like the iPhone, Palm Pre, Android, and similar mobile devices, Amazon.com provides an image-rich Mobile Web experience using less than 10k of mobile markup per page and linking to external product, navigation, and rating images. The home page contains featured products and a prominent link to route users to the Desktop Web site. Search result pages display product details and use JavaScript to show an expanded view that includes buttons to add the item directly to your shopping cart. Product pages include a larger picture, more product information, and similar JavaScript interactivity to show customer and editorial reviews.

Figure 4-14 captures the Amazon.com touchscreen-user experience for the home page, search results for *teddy bear*, and a teddy bear product page, respectively. You can view the Amazon.com touchscreen-user experience by browsing to `http://amazon.com` using a touchscreen smartphone. Impersonate the Apple iPhone, Palm Pre, or Android G1 to observe the Amazon.com touchscreen experience.

**Figure 4-14.** *Amazon.com user experience for touchscreen smartphones*

You can see content adaptation occurring within the touchscreen-optimized Amazon.com site. Figure 4-15 shows subtle icon variations on the Amazon home page between the Android G1 and Palm Pre touchscreen smartphone models.

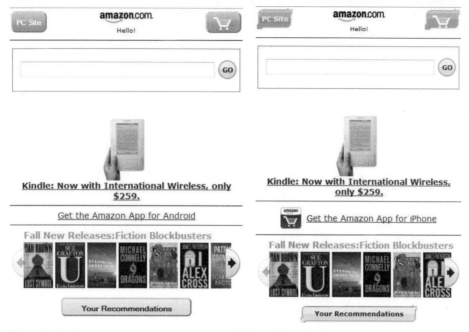

**Figure 4-15.** *Amazon.com home pages for an droid G1 and Palm Pre touchscreen smartphones*

Amazon.com provides a similar user experience for smartphones without touchscreens. Mobile Web pages are image-rich and provide product details, but provide fewer instances of JavaScript interactivity. Page design is optimized for non-touch devices, and it features smaller fonts, smaller clickable images, and the increased use of background colors to distinguish page sections.

Figure 4-16 captures the Amazon.com touchscreen user experience for the home page, search results for *teddy bear*, and a teddy bear product page, respectively. You can view the Amazon.com smartphone user experience by browsing to http://amazon.com using a touchscreen smartphone; you can impersonate the BlackBerry Curve 9800 or Nokia N96 to observe the Amazon.com smartphone experience.

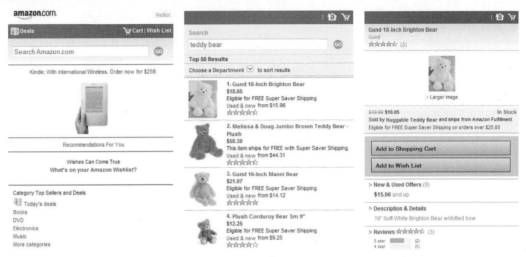

**Figure 4-16.** *Amazon.com user experience for smartphones without touchscreens*

For featurephones, Amazon provides a lean Mobile Web experience with minimal images and external resources. Amazon.com's featurephone Mobile Web pages average about 2K of markup, reference only one external style sheet, and link to two or fewer images. Product pages show only product information summaries and require the user to click links to view reviews and product details. Amazon.com targets casual browsers in its featurephone user experience. Its content adaptation choices create a streamlined user experience that loads quickly on mobile devices and minimizes vertical scrolling, but requires multiple Web transactions to view the complete product information.

Figure 4-17 captures the Amazon.com featurephone user experience for the home page, search results for *teddy bear*, and a teddy bear product page, respectively. You can view the Amazon.com featurephone-user experience by browsing to http://amazon.com using a mobile device. In this case, you impersonate the Nokia 5310 to observe the Amazon.com featurephone experience.

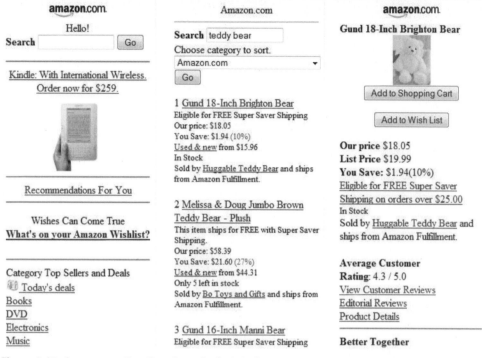

**Figure 4-17.** *Amazon.com User Experience for Featurephones*

Two facets of the Amazon.com content adaptation strategy stand out. First, some touchscreen mobile devices with Web-capable browsers are miscategorized as featurephones at the time of this writing. The Samsung T919 (marketed as the Behold) is one example of a popular touchscreen mobile phone that would be better served with the touchscreen smartphone version of Amazon.com. Second, outside of its compact size, nothing in the featurephone Amazon.com site indicates that its HTML markup is already optimized for mobile devices. This might make the Mobile Web site a target for transcoding. In contrast, the Amazon.com sites for smartphones and touchscreens contains `<meta>` tags indicating that the markup is already mobile-optimized. Chapter 12 discusses transcoding and defensive programming techniques.

### EXERCISE 4: ANALYZE CONTENT ADAPTATION ON THE MOBILE WEB

This exercise challenges you to find and analyze an example of content adaptation on the Mobile Web. Can you find an adaptive Mobile Web site? When you are browsing an adaptive site, can you deduce its content adaptation rules by browsing the site as you impersonate various mobile devices?

- Impersonate mobile devices in Firefox as you browse the Mobile Web, using the user-agents from Appendix A and the request headers from Appendix B, as necessary.

- Browse Mobile Web sites until you find a content-adaptive site.

- View the adaptive Mobile Web site impersonating a wide variety of smartphones and featurephones. At a minimum, view the site as an iPhone, Blackberry, or other smartphone, and LG VX9100.

Note how the Mobile Web site design and functionality changes with the impersonated mobile device.

Next, answer these questions:

1. In what ways does the site design adapt to mobile devices? Look for changes in image dimensions, formats, amounts of text on the page, and layout changes.

2. How does the site design adapt to touchscreen devices?

3. Does the Mobile Web site provide a richer experience for smartphone browsers? Does the site provide optimized versions for specific smartphone models such as Android G1, iPhone, or Palm Pre?

4. Does the Mobile Web site conditionally include advanced features such as JavaScript or AJAX for supported mobile browsers?

For extra credit, deduce a Mobile Web site's device groups and content adaptation rules by impersonating mobile devices with different screen sizes, markup-language support, and input methods.

# Summary

This chapter introduces device awareness, a method to identify mobile devices and query device and browser capabilities. You learned how to implement device awareness in PHP using two industry-leading device databases: WURFL and DeviceAtlas. Mobile Web sites use device awareness to implement content adaptation.

Content adaptation groups mobile devices by shared capabilities and adapts Web content to provide the best possible user experience for each supported mobile device. You learned how to create a content adaptation strategy using a three-step process: classifying mobile devices into groups, identifying site adaptation points, and writing rules to customize the design and functionality of the adaptation points for each device group. Finally, you reviewed a real-world example of content adaptation on the Mobile Web by browsing Amazon.com's touchscreen, smartphone, and featurephone Mobile Web sites.

The next chapter examines JavaScript and AJAX support in Web browsers on mobile devices.

# Chapter 5

# Adding Interactivity with JavaScript and AJAX

Using mobile JavaScript and Asynchronous JavaScript and XML (AJAX) can increase the interactivity of a dynamic Mobile Web site, mitigate its impact on a mobile network, and improve usability on smartphones and other devices with advanced mobile browsers.  This chapter introduces client-side scripting using JavaScript and AJAX on supported mobile devices, providing development tips, code samples, and suggestions for avoiding common pitfalls. Of course, scripting functionality should be conditionally included in a Mobile Web page, allowing the page to maintain compatibility with older mobile browsers that do not support these advanced features.

With mobile JavaScript, the devil is truly in the details. The mobile JavaScript standard, EcmaScript Mobile Profile, allows proprietary API extensions, so expect to encounter fragmentation and inconsistent event models in mobile browser implementations. Many mobile browsers support the desktop JavaScript standard, EcmaScript, but even these advanced browsers provide inconsistent event models. For this reason, testing any mobile JavaScript features on actual mobile devices (not emulators) is strongly recommended.

AJAX is a method for building dynamic web applications that uses JavaScript to asynchronously update the information displayed on a web page through background requests to a web server. The good news about mobile AJAX is that there really is no special technology known as "mobile AJAX". AJAX is AJAX, in a desktop or mobile context. Any AJAX differences between mobile browsers are due to fragmentation in the underlying JavaScript implementation. As you will see in this chapter, creating AJAX features for mobile browsers is possible with only a small amount of client-side scripting. Mobile AJAX is generally implemented in practice with dynamic response documents requested from the web server that are not XML but rather XHTML fragments or JavaScript Object Notation (JSON, http://json.org). The name AJAX is often "adjusted" accordingly to AJAH HTML ( or AJAJJSON (. These two formats (HTML and JSON, respectively) are more easily interpreted by mobile browsers than XML.

# Iterative Development Approach

Mobile JavaScript is a powerful but fragmented technology. When adding JavaScript and AJAX features to a Mobile Web site, I strongly advise you to adopt an iterative development approach. Build and test your Mobile Web site in its entirety before introducing any client-side scripting. Provide a usable Mobile Web experience even when scripting is unsupported or disabled in the browser. As with desktop browsers, mobile users can—and do—disable JavaScript execution to increase browsing performance and security.

Use content adaptation techniques to conditionally add one JavaScript or AJAX feature for supported mobile browsers. After adding the feature, observe the functional and performance changes on a few supported browsers. Broadly test and debug the feature on all targeted mobile browsers, making sure your Mobile Web content adapts gracefully when scripting is not supported on the device.

Iterate the process of adding a client-side scripting feature, observing its performance ramifications and broadly testing the feature. In this way, your library of mobile JavaScript and AJAX functionality is verified as it grows. It also saves you the hassle of debugging a problematic JavaScript library in its entirety. This approach is very similar to progressive enhancement, a web development strategy that focuses first on developing content (in markup), then enhances the content with presentation (in CSS), and finally adds client-side scripting (in JavaScript).

# JavaScript in Mobile Browsers

JavaScript is used for client-side scripting in web pages. It is a superset of the standardized ECMAScript, a common scripting reference model adopted by desktop and most mobile browsers. JavaScript can be used to respond to events that occur as a user interacts with a web page. For example, JavaScript form validation occurs as users move focus between form elements or submit a completed form. JavaScript is also useful for constructing dynamic user interface elements in HTML, such as menus. JavaScript includes a Document Object Model (DOM) for manipulating markup and document functionality. DOM manipulation is the foundation of AJAX technology, which is discussed in the section "AJAX in Mobile Browsers" later in this chapter.

Mobile and desktop JavaScript share some of the same pitfalls. API fragmentation requires browser detection and conditional code to include only the JavaScript supported on the mobile device. Debugging JavaScript can be tedious and browser-dependent. It is difficult to implement advanced and cross-platform JavaScript applications, even today, especially while maintaining robust browser performance. JavaScript can be protected by copyright and obfuscated, but ultimately is delivered to the web browser as unprotected textual content. A clever developer can read your JavaScript code and borrow your great ideas.  And, as stated earlier, users are able to disable JavaScript execution altogether, opting out of a dynamic web browsing experience, even on the best smartphones.

JavaScript is reliably implemented in smartphones and newer mobile devices with rich Internet functionality. It is generally *not* implemented in mainstream mobile browsers on featurephones, although at the time of this writing, mainstream mobile browsers are advancing rapidly. XHTML-MP 1.0 does not support either the `<script>` or `<noscript>` tags used with JavaScript. Those markup tags integrate JavaScript into a web document and are declared only in XHTML-MP 1.1 and 1.2. So, mobile browsers that support only XHTML-MP 1.0  do not support any kind of scripting. (Some older browsers that support subsets of HTML 4 may provide syntactic support for the <script> tag but not for JavaScript.) Full web browsers that render XHTML and HTML on mobile devices generally support JavaScript, but there is variation in their supported events, DOM manipulation functions, and language features.

## ECMAScript Mobile Profile

Just like XHTML-MP and Wireless CSS, there is a mobile-specific subset of JavaScript standardized for implementation in browsers on low-power mobile devices. The Open Mobile Alliance (OMA) created the ECMAScript Mobile Profile (ECMAScript MP) specification in 2004. It defines a scripting language that is a superset of WMLScript, and a subset of the ECMAScript used in desktop browsers. ECMAScript MP has a stricter syntax and leaves many processing-intensive features of ECMAScript as optional, allowing browser vendors to avoid implementing JavaScript features that might impact browser performance.

Here are some important differences between ECMAScript MP and ECMAScript, from the ECMAScript MP specification. In ECMAScript MP:

- The global method `eval()` is optional.
- The `with` keyword is optional.
- Dynamic function construction is optional.
- It is optional to allow property modifications for built-in objects.
- Semicolons must be used to terminate programming statements.
- The DOM is based on JavaScript 1.2 (circa 1997 and predating the ECMAScript standard).

Browse to `http://www.openmobilealliance.org/Technical/release_program/docs/Browsing/V2_3-20050118-C/OMA-WAP-ESMP-V1_0-20040709-C.pdf` to view the ECMAScript Mobile Profile specification in PDF format.

Mobile developers use a device database to check whether a browser supports JavaScript. A device database tracks mobile browser support for JavaScript (and AJAX), but generally does not distinguish between browsers that support ECMAScript MP and JavaScript or provide details about supported APIs or events. That research is left to the mobile development community as an exercise! Fortunately, some browser vendors provide online articles and PDFs that document browser capabilities.

# Embedding JavaScript in a Markup Document

JavaScript scripting is supported in XHTML-MP 1.1 and 1.2 using the same markup syntax as XHTML. Mobile Web documents containing scripting must use a doctype for the appropriate XHTML-MP version to ensure that the markup is valid. Here are the doctypes used for XHTML-MP 1.1 and 1.2, respectively.

```
<!DOCTYPE html PUBLIC "-//WAPFORUM//DTD XHTML Mobile 1.1//EN"
"http://www.openmobilealliance.org/tech/DTD/xhtml-mobile11.dtd">
```

```
<!DOCTYPE html PUBLIC "-//WAPFORUM//DTD XHTML Mobile 1.2//EN"
"http://www.openmobilealliance.org/tech/DTD/xhtml-mobile12.dtd">
```

Chapter 3 contains more detailed information about doctypes and XHTML-MP versions.

In XHTML-MP 1.1 and later versions, the `<script>` and `<noscript>` tags are used in almost exactly the same way as in XHTML to declare inline and external scripts. The `<script>` tag declares inline and external JavaScript content. The `<noscript>` tag provides alternate markup when scripting is not supported. Mobile JavaScript associates event handlers using DOM properties or as lowercased attributes of XHTML elements.

XHTML-MP 1.1 supports ECMAScript MP using either the `text/javascript` or `text/ecmascript` MIME types.

The `<script>` tag can be placed in the header or body of an XHTML-MP 1.1 or 1.2 document. As in XHTML, this tag can contain inline JavaScript or link to an external JavaScript library. The following XHTML-MP snippet is an example of inline JavaScript declaring an event handler function:

```
<script type="text/javascript">
// Function that handles the onload event
function handleOnLoad(event) {
        alert(event.type);
}
</script>
```

Scripts can also be declared as external JavaScript libraries, as in this example:

```
<script type="text/javascript" src="http://learnto.mobi/books/bmwd/05/lib.js" />
```

Browsers supporting JavaScript fire events as users interact with a web document. Details of a browser's event model can vary across device models, especially for mobile-specific use cases like rotating the screen display from portrait to landscape. (See the next section for a discussion of XHTML-MP events.) In XHTML-MP 1.1 and XHTML, events can be bound to JavaScript handler functions using attribute values. The following example binds the handleOnLoad JavaScript handler function declared above to the onload event in the web document:

```
<body onload="handleOnLoad(event)"> … </body>
```

Notice the event parameter in the onload attribute of the `<body>` tag. This parameter is an instance of the built-in Event object (whose members vary between ECMAScript and ECMAScript-MP). It is not necessary to provide the event parameter as a parameter for the event handler function if the function does not use its information.

Scheme-based execution of JavaScript may not be supported in mobile browsers using the script tag. However, the related technique of handling an event using inline JavaScript statements is supported in XHTML-MP 1.1. In this example, the onload event is handled directly by:

```
<body onload="alert('Hello World')"> … </body>
```

DOM-based methods for associating an event handler function in JavaScript may not be supported in mobile browsers. This JavaScript example below assumes the existence of the onload property of the built-in document object, and uses the property to assign a handler function to the event. The document object model in mobile Javascript implementations may not provide supported events as properties of document objects. Use caution when associating events with handler functions using DOM properties, as mobile browsers compliant with the ECMAScript-MP standard need not support this method.

```
window.onload = handleOnLoad;
```

Dynamic function construction is an even riskier method for assigning handler functions to events. Dynamic function construction using the built-in function object is optional in the ECMAScript-MP standard and may not be supported in mobile browsers. The following example JavaScript creates an anonymous function and assigns it as the onload event handler.

```
window.onload = new function() { alert('Hello World'); };
```

Few mobile browsers outside of smartphones support the DOM properties and dynamic function construction features required to associate events with handler functions using the previous two methods. Mobile browsers supporting the entire desktop ECMAScript standard would support all of these approaches.

JavaScript event handler functions can cancel an event, if it is user-cancellable, by returning false from the function. In XHTML-MP 1.1 and later, only the onclick, onreset and onsubmit events are cancellable.

```
<a href="actualpage.html" onclick="return !doThis();">...</a>
```

## Supported JavaScript Events in XHTML-MP 1.1

At a minimum, any browser compliant with the XHTML-MP 1.1 standard must support the mandatory JavaScript events summarized in Table 5-1.

**Table 5-1.** *Mandatory JavaScript Events in XHTML-MP 1.1*

| Event Attribute | Supported XHTML-MP Tag(s) | Event Description |
| --- | --- | --- |
| onload | body | Event fires when the markup document has finished loading. |
| onclick | `Mandatory: a, img, input, object, option, textarea`<br><br>Optional: abbr, acronym, address, b, big, blockquote, body, caption, cite, code, dd, dfn, div, dl, dt, em, fieldset, form, h1, h2, h3, h4, h5, h6, hr, i, kbd, label, li, link, noscript, ol, optgroup, p, pre, q, samp, select, small, span, strong, table, td, th, tr, ul, var | Event fires when a selectable element (such as a link) is selected by the user. If the event is not cancelled by the user, the link target is activated. |
| onsubmit | form | Event fires when form submission is activated. If the event is not cancelled by the user, the form is submitted. |
| onreset | form | Event fires when form reset is activated. If the event is not cancelled by the user, the form is reset to its original state. |

Further, mobile browsers supporting XHTML-MP 1.1 may also enable the additional, optional JavaScript events summarized in Table 5-2.

**Table 5-2.** *Optional JavaScript Events in XHTML-MP 1.1*

| Event Attribute | Supported XHTML-MP Tag(s) | Event Description |
| --- | --- | --- |
| onunload | body | Event fires just before the markup document is removed from the browser. |
| ondoubleclick | Mandatory: a, img, input, object, option, textarea<br><br>Optional: abbr, acronym, address, b, big, blockquote, body, caption, cite, code, dd, dfn, div, dl, dt, em, fieldset, form, h1, h2, h3, h4, h5, h6, hr, i, kbd, label, li, link, noscript, ol, optgroup, p, pre, q, samp, select, small, span, strong, table, td, th, tr, ul, var | Event fires when a selectable element (such as a link) is selected twice by the user within a short period of time. |

| Event Attribute | Supported XHTML-MP Tag(s) | Event Description |
| --- | --- | --- |
| onmousedown | a, abbr, acronym, address, b, big, blockquote, body, caption, cite, code, dd, dfn, div, dl, dt, em, fieldset, form, h1-h6, hr, i, img, input, kbd, label, li, link, noscript, object, ol, optgroup, option, p, pre, q, samp, select, small, span, strong, table, td, textarea, th, tr, ul, var | Event fires when a mobile device's pointing method is activated while the pointer is over an element in the markup document. |
| onmouseup | See onmousedown | Event fires when a mobile device's pointing method is released while the pointer is over an element in the markup document. |
| onmouseover | See onmousedown | Event fires when a mobile device's pointer is moved over an element in the markup document. |
| onmousemove | See onmousedown | Event fires when a mobile device's pointer is moved while over an element in the markup document. |
| onmouseout | See onmousedown | Event fires when a mobile device's pointer is moved away from an element in the markup document. |
| onfocus | a, label, input, select, textarea | Event fires when an element in the markup document is focused. |
| onblur | a, label, input, select, textarea | Event fires when an element in the markup document loses focus. |
| onkeypress | Mandatory: a, img, input, object, option, textarea

Optional: abbr, acronym, address, b, big, blockquote, body, caption, cite, code, dd, dfn, div, dl, dt, em, fieldset, form, h1, h2, h3, h4, h5, h6, hr, i, kbd, label, li, link, noscript, ol, optgroup, p, pre, q, samp, select, small, span,

strong, table, td, th, tr, ul, var | Event fires when a key is pressed and released. |

| Event Attribute | Supported XHTML-MP Tag(s) | Event Description |
|---|---|---|
| onkeydown | See onkeypress | Event fires when a key is pressed. |
| onkeyup | See onkeypress | Event fires when a key is released. |
| onselect | input, textarea | Event fires when text in a text field is selected by the user. |
| onchange | input, select, textarea | Event fires when the value of an input element has changed and the element loses focus. |

An excellent reference that tests actual mobile browser compatibility with JavaScript events is the Mobile Compatibility Tables from QuirksMode at http://www.quirksmode.org/m/table.html.

The large number of optional events and target elements in XHTML-MP 1.1 compounds fragmentation in JavaScript implementations across mobile browser models.  Browsers can implement from four to eighteen events and still claim compliance with the markup standard. The breadth of supported events directly affects the usefulness and complexity of JavaScript features that can be implemented in the browser.

You might notice that the events in Tables 5-1 and 5-2, taken together, may not cover all use cases for mobile user interaction with a web browser. Smartphone mobile browsers commonly extend the XHTML-MP 1.1 supported events with additional XHTML events, adding to JavaScript fragmentation but also providing critical usability improvements for advanced devices. Scripting standards are useful, but JavaScript support in a mobile browser may not perfectly adhere to a standard. Developer workarounds for mobile scripting bugs are common.

## JavaScript Fragmentation in Mobile Browsers

JavaScript implementations in mobile browsers suffer from three types of fragmentation: proprietary API extensions, differences in DOM methods and properties, and varying sets of supported events.

Proprietary APIs extend the JavaScript virtual machine with new functions and objects. In addition to complying with ECMAScript standards, many desktop and mobile browsers implement extra JavaScript functionality in the form of proprietary APIs. This practice is specifically allowed in the ECMAScript-MP specification. In mobile browsers, proprietary APIs provide access to hardware functionality like GPS location and screen orientation. Proprietary JavaScript APIs are not discussed further in this chapter but are mentioned in Chapter 7, when we examine mobile browser models available in smartphones.

The properties and methods available in the DOM vary depending on the level of standards compliance and can include proprietary extensions. At a minimum,

ECMAScript MP defines mandatory implementations of the `document`, `form`, `link`, `text`, `textarea`, `select`, `option`, `password`, `button`, `reset`, `radio`, `submit`, and `checkbox` objects, each with properties and methods derived from components of JavaScript 1.2 and the W3C's DOM Level 2 HTML specification. In particular, forms and form elements support the usual JavaScript properties that allow getting and setting of input field values.

The `document` object provides two mandatory and one optional list of subelements, to make it easier to iterate scriptable components of a web document. After a web document is completely loaded, the `document.forms` array provides access to all of the `form` elements (`<form>` tags) in the document, making iterating the forms in a document as easy as:

```
for (var i = 0; i < document.forms.length; i++) {
        var myForm = document.forms[i];
        // Perform an operation on the form…
}
```

The `document.links` array is a list of all the `link` elements (`<a>` tags) in the web document, ordered from top to bottom of the document. The `document.images` array, an optional component of ECMAScript MP, is a list of all the `image` elements (`<img>` tags) in the web document, ordered like `document.links`.

The DOM in ECMAScript MP provides a subset of the node and element traversal methods from the W3C's DOM Level 2 Core Specification. In particular, ECMAScript MP allows inspection of the document element hierarchy and changing of document data. However, ECMAScript MP-compliant browsers are allowed to forego implementing objects and methods that enable structural changes to the document object hierarchy, as a performance optimization measure for low-power browsers. (Since AJAX features change the structure of a web document, a mobile browser supporting JavaScript may not also support AJAX.)

In particular, the `document` object in ECMAScript MP supports the useful `getElementsByTagName()` and `getElementById()` methods, allowing element traversal by type and lookup by the unique identifier in its ID attribute.

XHTML-MP elements support traversing subelements by type using the `getElementsByTagName()` method. Additionally, element attributes may be retrieved and updated using the `getAttribute()`, `setAttribute()`, and `removeAttribute()` methods. These methods are used in ECMAScript MP because the DOM does not often provide properties for each individual element attribute (as is common in desktop JavaScript and XHTML).

Of course, advanced mobile browsers are free to support more DOM objects and methods than provided in ECMAScript MP. Many smartphone browsers implement the full DOM Level 2 specification and some or all of the DOM Level 3 specification, aligning their JavaScript functionality with that of desktop web browsers. Only OEM specifications and on-device testing will uncover the exact levels of standards-compliance in a mobile browser.

The events supported in the mobile browser may also vary, especially for mobile-specific use cases. Tables 5-1 and 5-2 in the previous section show the bare minimum of event support in XHTML-MP 1.1 and ECMAScript MP. Many smartphones and increasing numbers of browsers on mainstream mobile devices support additional events and event targets in order to provide the richest possible JavaScript programming environment to Mobile Web developers.

JavaScript for mobile devices is a significant advance in Mobile Web interactivity. It and AJAX drive rich Internet applications in a mobile context. This makes Mobile Web sites more useful and attractive to Internet-savvy users who expect advanced functionality and immediate updates while interacting with web pages. Mobile developers must weigh the user experience benefits of incorporating JavaScript into a Mobile Web page with the challenges of overcoming API fragmentation, maintaining adequate browser performance, and conserving battery life for a mobile device running an interactive web application.

## Examples of Mobile JavaScript

The following two mobile JavaScript examples illustrate embedding client-side interactivity into a Mobile Web document in XHTML-MP.

Listing 5-1 is a simple, annotated example of using EcmaScript MP in an XHTML-MP 1.1 Mobile Web document. The listing uses JavaScript to randomly assign a new background color to the <div> element with the ID of theBox when the document loads. The colors array is a list of six possible background images. The handleOnLoad() event handler function is executed after the document loads. This function chooses a random integer between 0 and 5 using Math.floor() and Math.random(), two mathematics methods from EcmaScript MP. This integer becomes the offset into the colors array used to select the background color for theBox. The built-in method getElementById() of the document object provides programmatic access to the div element, whose setAttribute() method is called to update the value of the background-color CSS property for the style XHTML-MP element attribute. Updating this value causes the background color to change.

In the comments at the end of the handler function, notice the two alternative JavaScript approaches for updating the background color style property that are not supported in EcmaScript MP.

Examine the structure of the following link from Listing 5-1:

```
<a href="5-1.php" onclick="location.reload();" >Re-load</a>
```

It contains both an href attribute and an onclick event handler. The inline JavaScript in the onclick event is executed when the link is clicked and causes the browser to reload the current web document. If the JavaScript fails (or returns false, since the event is cancellable), then the browser falls back to the URL provided as the href link target.

Browse to http://learnto.mobi/books/bmwd/05/5–1.php to view Listing 5-1 in a mobile or desktop browser.

**Listing 5-1.** *Annotated Mobile JavaScript in an XHTML-MP 1.1 Document*

```php
<?php
// Set the response content-type
header("Content-type: application/xhtml+xml");
header("Cache-control: no-transform");

// Write the XML declaration
echo '<?xml version="1.0" encoding="UTF-8"?>';
?>
<!DOCTYPE html PUBLIC "-//WAPFORUM//DTD XHTML Mobile 1.1//EN"
"http://www.openmobilealliance.org/tech/DTD/xhtml-mobile11.dtd">
<html xmlns="http://www.w3.org/1999/xhtml">
<head>
<title>Listing 5-1: Example of onload Event</title>
<style type="text/css">
#theBox {
            background-color:#777777;
            margin:5px;
            padding:5px;
            border-width: 1px;
            border-style: solid;
            border-color: #000000;
}
</style>
<script type="text/javascript">
// This is a list of six colors to use as div backgrounds.
var colors = new Array();
colors[0] = '#FF0000';
colors[1] = '#00FF00';
colors[2] = '#0000FF';
colors[3] = '#00FFFF';
colors[4] = '#FF00FF';
colors[5] = '#FFFFFF';

/// This is the onLoad event handler
function handleOnLoad() {
            // Get a random number between 0 and 5
            var random = Math.floor(Math.random() * 6);
            // Change the color of the div
            document.getElementById('theBox').setAttribute('style', 'background-
color: ' + colors[random]);

            // Approaches that are not supported in ECMAScript-MP:
            //document.getElementById('theBox').bgColor = colors[random];
            //document.getElementById('theBox').setAttribute('background-color',
colors[random]);
}
</script>
<noscript><p>Sorry, no script support in this browser.</p></noscript>
</head>
<body onload="handleOnLoad()">
<h1>onLoad Example</h1>
<p><a href="javascript:location.reload();">Re-load</a> this page to watch the background
color change below:</p>
<div id="theBox">
This box changes color.
</div>
```

```
</body>
</html>
```

Figure 5-1 shows the Mobile Web document resulting from the code in Listing 5-1 as displayed in the Palm Pre, Android, and Opera Mini mobile browsers. Notice how the background colors of the box are different in each browser.

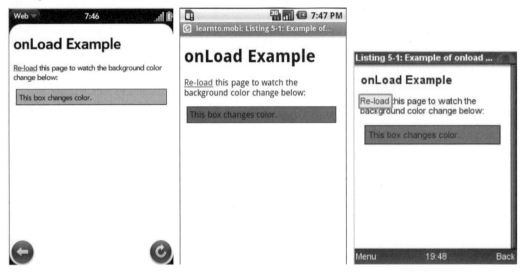

**Figure 5-1.** *The code from Listing 5-1 produces different results in the Palm Pre, Android, and Opera Mini mobile browsers*

Listing 5-2 is a tabbed user interface in JavaScript. Three textual tabs are presented, with one activated and two blurred. The text for each tab is a link. Clicking a tab causes that tab to activate and blurs the other two tabs. In the listing, the `handleOnClick` JavaScript function is the event handler when any of the text links comprising the tabs are clicked. The function parameter `index` provides the zero-based index of the clicked tab. The `index` is used to construct the ID of each tab so it can be referenced using `document.getElementById()` and have the value of its `class` attribute updated to visually reflect an activated or blurred tab. In the XHTML-MP markup, notice how there is no extra whitespace between the `<a>` elements for each tab. This ensures that the tabs are aligned next to each other with no vertical gutters.

Browse to http://learnto.mobi/books/bmwd/05/5–2.php to view Listing 5-2 in a mobile or desktop browser. We will revisit this listing in the next section to dynamically update the content visible in a tab using AJAX.

**Listing 5-2.** *EcmaScript MP Tabs in an XHTML-MP 1.1 Document*

```
<?
// Set the response content-type
header("Content-type: application/xhtml+xml");
header("Cache-control: no-transform");

// Write the XML declaration
echo '<?xml version="1.0" encoding="UTF-8"?>';
?>
```

```
<!DOCTYPE html PUBLIC "-//WAPFORUM//DTD XHTML Mobile 1.1//EN"
"http://www.openmobilealliance.org/tech/DTD/xhtml-mobile11.dtd">
<html xmlns="http://www.w3.org/1999/xhtml">
<head>
<meta name="viewport" content="width=240,user-scalable=no" />
<title>Listing 5-2: Example of onclick Event</title>
<style type="text/css">
.tab {
                padding: 5px 10px 1px 10px;
                margin: 0px;
                background-color:#cccccc;
                border-width: 1px;
                border-style: solid;
                border-color: #666666;
                font-weight: normal;
                font-size: smaller;
                text-decoration: none;
}
.activeTab {
                padding: 5px 10px 1px 10px;
                margin: 0px;
                background-color:#ffffff;
                border-width: 1px 1px 0px 1px;
                border-style: solid;
                border-color: #666666;
                font-weight: bold;
                font-size: small;
                text-decoration: none;
}
#content {
                padding: 10px;
                margin: 0px;
                border-width: 1px;
                border-style: solid;
                border-color: #666666;
}
</style>
<script type="text/javascript">

// This is the onClick event handler for the tab links
// index - the zero-based index of the tab that was clicked
function handleOnClick(index) {
                // Construct the ID of the clicked tab
                var tabId = "tab" + index;
                // Update the style of the active tab.
                document.getElementById(tabId).setAttribute('class', 'activeTab');

                // Update the styles of the inactive tabs.
                if (index != 0) {
                                document.getElementById("tab" + 0).setAttribute('class',
'tab');
                }
                if (index != 1) {
                                document.getElementById("tab" + 1).setAttribute('class',
'tab');
                }
                if (index != 2) {
```

```
                    document.getElementById("tab" + 2).setAttribute('class',
'tab');
                }

                // Do not follow the link
                return false;
        }
</script>
<noscript><p>Sorry, no script support in this browser.</p></noscript>
</head>
<body>
<h1>Example of JavaScript tabs</h1>
<div id="tabs">
<a href="#" id="tab0" class="activeTab" onclick="return handleOnClick(0);">Fruit</a><a
href="#" id="tab1" class="tab" onclick="return handleOnClick(1);">Veggies</a><a href="#"
id="tab2" class="tab" onclick="return handleOnClick(2);">Honey</a>
</div>
<div id="content">Click a name to to activate the tab.</div>
</body>
</html>
```

Figure 5-2 shows the Mobile Web document from Listing 5-2 as displayed in the Palm Pre, Android, and Opera Mini mobile browsers. Notice how the tabs change visual appearance as they are activated and blurred.

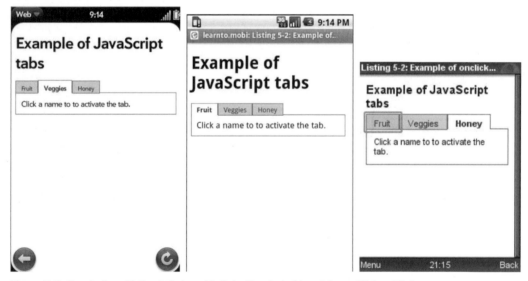

**Figure 5-2.** *Results from Listing 5-2 viewed in Palm Pre, Android, and Opera Mini mobile browsers*

# AJAX in Mobile Browsers

AJAX is commonly used to create dynamic web pages by updating just one portion of the web document, without a complete page reload. This is done by a background process that asynchronously obtains additional data from the web server. A JavaScript-intensive web page with AJAX functionality is commonly referred to as a Rich Internet

Application (RIA), where the term "application" indicates that the page's user interface and functionality are dynamic and driven using scripting logic rather than static markup tags.

AJAX is implemented in advanced mobile browsers and is especially common on smartphones. It has numerous user experience and network efficiency benefits on mobile devices. AJAX reduces bandwidth because only fragments of web documents are transmitted in a network request. It produces web applications that update more quickly than full document refreshes. But mobile browsers also have challenges with AJAX features. AJAX may cause increased processing and can drain battery life due to the additional network requests required to dynamically update web content on frequently updating pages with significant background activity. Mobile Web developers must detect support for AJAX using a device database, and iteratively include web application functionality only for supported browsers. Developers must judiciously incorporate AJAX into a Mobile Web site to reap the benefits of dynamic content updates without incurring additional user download costs or impacting battery life.

Many mobile browsers support AJAX, making it a viable technology for smartphones and other mobile phones with advanced Internet functionality. Android, iPhone, Palm webOS, Internet Explorer Mobile, and Nokia Series 60 (third edition and later) browsers all natively support AJAX. Recent versions of Opera Mobile, Opera Mini, and Access NetFront provide AJAX functionality for smartphone and newer featurephone browsers. However, JavaScript fragmentation makes testing AJAX on actual mobile devices and browsers (not emulators) a priority. Remember, "mobile AJAX" doesn't exist. The "mobile" component and major point of fragmentation is the JavaScript implementation in the mobile browser. AJAX is AJAX in any web browser that supports its prerequisite standards. But, the Mobile Web is a special environment in which AJAX features can be disrupted by network latency, disconnects, request timeouts, and bandwidth issues.

At minimum, mobile browsers providing AJAX functionality must support XHTML-MP 1.1 or later, or XHTML and either ECMAScript MP or JavaScript. The JavaScript engine must include the `XMLHttpRequest` object (or similar; later in this section you will meet a different object used in Microsoft mobile browsers), a special JavaScript object that performs the asynchronous web requests at the heart of AJAX. (An industry acronym for `XMLHttpRequest` is XHR.) Additionally, the JavaScript implementation must also include DOM methods and properties in JavaScript that modify the structure of a web document, especially `document.getElementById()`, `element.innerHTML`, and less commonly, `element.innerText`.

The `innerHTML` property of an XHTML or XHTML-MP element allows setting and getting of the markup inside the element. In practice, setting this property reconstructs the child DOM elements of this markup element. This property is used to update parts of the markup document in response to an AJAX request. For example, consider a markup document that contains the following div element:

```
<div id="article">Hello, World</div>
```

The JavaScript below updates the child markup of the `div` element:

```
document.getElementById('article').innerHTML = '<span class="title">My
Article</span><br/>';
```

Executing the JavaScript statement above rebuilds the child DOM elements of article in the document object model in browser memory. The document markup is not modified, so viewing the source code in a desktop browser does not surface the modified XHTML. In the DOM, the markup for article and child elements is now:

```
<div id="article"><span class="title">My Article</span><br/></div>
```

This simple but powerful technique lets a mobile browser supporting AJAX reload partial markup documents, allowing a web application to update only the dynamic components of a web document, saving network bandwidth and preventing unnecessary retransmission of static document features.

The innerText property of an XHTML or XHTML-MP element allows setting and getting of the text inside the element. Setting this property changes the element's textual content and removes any child DOM elements. For example, consider a markup document that contains the following div element:

```
<div id="article">Hello, World</div>
```

The value of the innerText property for the article element is the string "Hello, World", as illustrated in the example below.

```
// This expression evaluates to true.
(document.getElementById('article').innerText == 'Hello, World')
```

The innerText property is generally available only in mobile browsers that implement the desktop dialect of JavaScript, and it is used less commonly in AJAX transactions than its innerHTML relative. Firefox supports this property as textContent instead of innerText.

After using a device database to ensure that the target mobile browser supports JavaScript and AJAX, the basic implementation steps to include AJAX in a Mobile Web document are:

1. Decide how AJAX should be used to dynamically update part of the web document. Use JavaScript to handle the event that initiates the AJAX transaction.

2. In JavaScript, create an instance of XMLHttpRequest, the AJAX object making asynchronous requests to a web server.

3. In JavaScript, handle XMLHttpRequest state changes to detect errors and capture the web response document. The web response is usually XML, JSON, or an XHTML-MP or XHTML fragment.

4. In JavaScript, use document.getElementById and element.innerHTML to update the dynamic portion of the document.

5. Review the implementation to make sure that AJAX transactions are not used too frequently. Overuse of background web requests can cause browser performance degradation and impact battery life.

Although AJAX originally stood for "Asynchronous JavaScript and XML", it is not very practical to use XML as the web server response format for the third step in AJAX transactions, because this approach requires the mobile browser to parse and interpret XML. Instead, use an XHTML-MP or XHTML document fragment or JSON in the web response for better performance on mobile devices. Potentially, web response document fragments might also be transcoded in a mobile network, but this is an uncommon occurrence. Transcoding is discussed further in Chapter 12.

The first step in an AJAX transaction is to decide how AJAX is used in a web application to dynamically update part of the document. In the example in Listing 5-5, excerpted in Listings 5-3 and 5-4, AJAX initiates when the user activates a tab by clicking. In your Mobile Web application, AJAX can be triggered by user events or a JavaScript timer (if the mobile browser supports desktop ECMAScript).

> **NOTE:** When AJAX transactions are controlled by a JavaScript timer (for periodically updating news headlines and so forth), *always* notify the user about background updates (for example, by using a loading animation), and allow the user to control the timer and choose to disable updates. This courtesy allows the mobile subscriber to control the charges and battery consumption associated with network use.

The second step in an AJAX transaction creates an instance of XMLHttpRequest, the AJAX object making asynchronous requests to a web server. The JavaScript function in Listing 5-3 is a standard method for creating an XHR instance to use in AJAX. Some Microsoft browsers including Internet Explorer Mobile support AJAX via ActiveX objects instead of XMLHttpRequest. The getXHR() function attempts to create an XHR using JavaScript object names supported in all mobile and desktop browsers. The function returns the new XHR instance or null if no such object was created. Notice the use of try and catch blocks to detect object creation errors.

**Listing 5-3.** *JavaScript Function to Obtain an XMLHttpRequest Instance*

```
// Function to obtain an instance of XMLHttpRequest used in an AJAX request
function getXHR() {
    if (window.XMLHttpRequest) {
        return new XMLHttpRequest();
    }
    else try {
        return new ActiveXObject('Msxml2.XMLHTTP');
    } catch(e) {
            try {
                return new ActiveXObject("Microsoft.XMLHTTP");
            } catch(e) {
                return null;
            }
    }
}
```

The third step in an AJAX transaction handles XMLHttpRequest state changes to detect errors and capture the web response document. Listing 5-4 is a JavaScript function that implements an asynchronous web request using AJAX. The updateContent() function first obtains a new XMLHttpRequest instance using the getXHR() function from Listing 5-3. Then it calls the XHR's open() method to specify that the background web request should use the HTTP GET method at the provided URL. The XHR provides progress updates for the request using its onreadystatechange event. The function in Listing 5-4 creates an anonymous callback function as the onreadystatechange event handler. The handler function checks the readyState and status properties of the XHR to decide how to handle the progress update. The readyState property indicates the progress of the web request. Table 5-3 lists the possible numeric values of the readyState XHR property and their meanings. The status property is the status code of the HTTP response, once it is complete. The HTTP response status code of 200 indicates that the server successfully completed the request.

**Table 5-3.** *Possible Values of the readyState Property of XMLHttpRequest*

| Symbolic Value | Numeric Value | Description |
| --- | --- | --- |
| UNSENT | 0 | The XMLHttpRequest object has been created. No web request has been sent. |
| OPENED | 1 | The open() method has been called. The web request has been created but not yet sent. The send() method can be used to submit the request. |
| HEADERS_RECEIVED | 2 | The web request has been sent. All HTTP response headers have been received. |
| LOADING | 3 | The web request has been sent. All HTTP response headers have been received. The response body has started to be received. |
| DONE | 4 | The web request is completed or terminated with an error. |

In Listing 5-4, the anonymous event handler for the onreadystatechange event performs three actions. If the asynchronous web request is in progress, it displays an animated loading image inside the element whose ID is the second function parameter. If the AJAX request completes successfully, the body of the web response is used as the content of the element. If the AJAX request terminates with an error, a textual error message is displayed to the user in the element. The handler function returns true when the AJAX request completes or false if the XMLHttpRequest object could not be instantiated.

**Listing 5-4.** *JavaScript Function to Obtain an XMLHttpRequest Instance*

```
// Global variable that holds the XHR instance.
var req = null;

// Use AJAX to update the page content.
```

```
// Returns true if the AJAX request succeeded, or false otherwise.
function updateContent(url, id) {
    req = getXHR();
    if (req != null) {
        // Create a HTTP get request
        req.open('GET', url);
        // Anonymous callback function to handle state changes for the web request
        req.onreadystatechange = function() {
            // State "4" is response received.
            if (req.readyState == 4) {
                // Check for HTTP 200 - successful response from web server
                if (req.status == 200) {
                    document.getElementById(id).innerHTML = req.responseText;
                } else {
                    document.getElementById(id).innerHTML = 'Could not retrieve data.';
                }
            }
            // For all other states, show an animated gif indicating that content is
loadin
            // This loading animation may also be shown as soon as the AJAX request
starts
            else {
                document.getElementById(id).innerHTML = '<img id="loading"
src="http://learnto.mobi/books/bmwd/05/loading.gif" width="16" height="16"/>';
            }
            return false;
        }

        // Start the AJAX transaction
        req.send('');
    } else {
        return false;
    }

    return true;
}
```

The fourth step in an AJAX transaction uses document.getElementById and element.innerHTML to update the dynamic portion of the document. Listing 5-4 displays the use of these constructs to find the div element with ID content and update its child HTML to reflect the progress of the request or display the document fragment obtained asynchronously.

The fifth step in an AJAX transaction reviews the implementation to make sure that AJAX transactions are not used too frequently. In the case of the AJAX example in Listing 5-5, AJAX is initiated by a user event (clicking to activate a tab), not based on JavaScript timers. AJAX functionality is entirely controlled by the user. If the user does not click a tab, then no AJAX transactions are initiated. Since the non-AJAX implementation of this feature would entail reloading the entire web document when a tab is activated, adding AJAX reduces bandwidth consumption. Herein lies the AJAX network performance efficiency. Transmitting a web document fragment instead of an entire web document means fewer bits across the wire(less).

> **NOTE:** At the time of this writing, the W3C is drafting behavioral standards for XMLHttpRequest
> (even though XMLHttpRequest is already supported in all desktop browsers). See
> http://www.w3.org/TR/XMLHttpRequest/ for more information about the standardization effort.

## Example of AJAX for Mobile Browsers

The mobile AJAX example in Listing 5-5 illustrates using EcmaScript MP and AJAX to
create dynamic tabs in a Mobile Web document in XHTML-MP. As stated earlier, this
web document uses AJAX to dynamically load an XHTML-MP document fragment when
the user clicks to activate a tab in the user interface. Listings 5-3 and 5-4 excerpt
getXHR() and updateContent(), two JavaScript functions used in Listing 5-5. The
handleOnClick() function in Listing 5-5 uses JavaScript to update the visual style of the
active and inactive tabs, as in the non-AJAX version of this example in Listing 5-2. In
addition, handleOnClick()initiates an AJAX request to update the contents of the div
element with ID content with dynamic markup requested from a web server.

In this example, the web documents requested using AJAX are static fragments of
XHTML-MP markup. Browse to http://learnto.mobi/books/bmwd/05/5–5–0.php to view
one of the static fragments. The URL targets of AJAX requests can be static or dynamic
markup fragments, JSON, or XML documents.

It is worth noting the structure of the tab links in Listing 5-5. Each link has both an href
attribute value and an onclick event handler, as in the example below:

```
<a href="5-3-0-static.php" id="tab0" class="activeTab" onclick="return
handleOnClick(0);">Fruit</a>
```

When the AJAX transaction completes successfully, the handleOnClick() function
returns false, canceling the click event. AJAX controls the document updates and the
href is not followed. But when the AJAX transaction fails (in this case, when the
XMLHttpRequest object cannot be instantiated), the handleOnClick() function returns
true and the href is followed, navigating the browser to a new web document. This
pattern of providing both an onclick event handler that implements AJAX and an href
URL to a fallback static markup document is used to gracefully degrade the user
experience when AJAX is unavailable in the mobile browser.

In Listing 5-5, the getXHR() function is embedded in the web document for the sake of
providing a standalone AJAX example. The function could also be included in an
external JavaScript library to maximize code reuse.

Browse to http://learnto.mobi/books/bmwd/05/5–5.php to view Listing 5-5 in a mobile or
desktop browser.

**Listing 5-5.** *Dynamic Tabs using AJAX and JavaScript in an XHTML-MP 1.1 Document*

```
<?
// Set the response content-type
header("Content-type: application/xhtml+xml");
header("Cache-control: no-transform");
```

```
// Write the XML declaration
echo '<?xml version="1.0" encoding="UTF-8"?>';
?>
<!DOCTYPE html PUBLIC "-//WAPFORUM//DTD XHTML Mobile 1.1//EN"
"http://www.openmobilealliance.org/tech/DTD/xhtml-mobile11.dtd">
<html xmlns="http://www.w3.org/1999/xhtml">
<head>
<meta name="viewport" content="width=240,user-scalable=no" />
<title>Listing 5-5: AJAX Tabs</title>
<style type="text/css">
.tab {
                padding: 5px 10px 1px 10px;
                margin: 0px;
                background-color:#cccccc;
                border-width: 1px;
                border-style: solid;
                border-color: #666666;
                font-weight: normal;
                font-size: smaller;
                text-decoration: none;
}
.activeTab {
                padding: 5px 10px 1px 10px;
                margin: 0px;
                background-color:#ffffff;
                border-width: 1px 1px 0px 1px;
                border-style: solid;
                border-color: #666666;
                font-weight: bold;
                font-size: small;
                text-decoration: none;
}
#content {
                padding: 10px;
                margin: 0px;
                border-width: 1px;
                border-style: solid;
                border-color: #666666;
}
#loading {
                padding: 5px;
}
</style>
<script type="text/javascript">
// Global variable that holds the XHR instance.
var req = null;
// Function to obtain an instance of XMLHttpRequest used in an AJAX request
function getXHR() {
    if (window.XMLHttpRequest) {
        return new XMLHttpRequest();
    }
    else try {
        return new ActiveXObject('Msxml2.XMLHTTP');
    } catch(e) {
            try {
                return new ActiveXObject("Microsoft.XMLHTTP");
```

```
                } catch(e) {
                    return null;
                }
        }
    }


    // Use AJAX to update the page content.
    // Returns true if the AJAX request succeeded, or false otherwise.
    function updateContent(url, id) {
        req = getXHR();
        if (req != null) {
            // Create a HTTP get request
            req.open('GET', url);
            // Anonymous callback function to handle state changes for the web request
            req.onreadystatechange = function() {
                // State "4" is response received.
                if (req.readyState == 4) {
                    // Check for HTTP 200 - successful response from web server
                    if (req.status == 200) {
                        document.getElementById(id).innerHTML = req.responseText;
                    } else {
                        document.getElementById(id).innerHTML = 'Could not retrieve data.';
                    }
                }
                // For all other states, show an animated gif indicating that content is
loading
                else {
                    document.getElementById(id).innerHTML = '<img id="loading"
src="http://learnto.mobi/books/bmwd/05/loading.gif" width="16" height="16"/>';
                }
                return false;
            }

            // Start the AJAX transaction
            req.send('');
        } else {
            return false;
        }

        return true;
    }

    // This is the onClick event handler for the tab links
    // index - the zero-based index of the tab that was clicked
    function handleOnClick(index) {
        // Construct the ID of the clicked tab
        var tabId = "tab" + index;
        // Update the style of the active tab.
        document.getElementById(tabId).setAttribute('class', 'activeTab');

        // Update the styles of the inactive tabs. This could also be achieved in a for
loop.
        if (index != 0) {
            document.getElementById("tab" + 0).setAttribute('class', 'tab');
        }
        if (index != 1) {
            document.getElementById("tab" + 1).setAttribute('class', 'tab');
```

```
    }
    if (index != 2) {
        document.getElementById("tab" + 2).setAttribute('class', 'tab');
    }

    // Use AJAX to update the "content" div.
    // Construct the URL to use to retrieve the updated content
    var url = "http://learnto.mobi/books/bmwd/05/5-5-" + index + ".php";
    // If the AJAX request succeeded, do not follow the original link
    if (updateContent(url, "content")) {
        return false;
    }

    // If we are here, then the AJAX transaction failed.
    // Follow the link and load the static page.
    return true;
}
</script>
<noscript><p>Sorry, no script support in this browser.</p></noscript>
</head>
<body>
<h1>AJAX Tabs</h1>
<div id="tabs">
<a href="5-5-0-static.php" id="tab0" class="activeTab" onclick="return
handleOnClick(0);">Fruit</a><a href="5-5-1-static.php" id="tab1" class="tab"
onclick="return handleOnClick(1);">Veggies</a><a href="5-5-2-static.php" id="tab2"
class="tab" onclick="return handleOnClick(2);">Honey</a>
</div>
<div id="content">Click a name to to activate the tab.</div>
</body>
</html>
```

Figure 5-3 shows the Mobile Web document from Listing 5-5 as displayed in the Palm Pre, Android, and Opera Mini mobile browsers. Make sure to view Listing 5-5 in a mobile browser to observe the performance of AJAX transactions on actual mobile devices. Click each tab to view the loading image during the AJAX request and the content of each dynamically loaded document fragment.

**Figure 5-3.** *Viewing the results of Listing 5-5 in Palm Pre, Android and Opera Mini mobile browsers*

# Testing AJAX Support in Mobile Browsers

A device database can help you determine whether AJAX is supported by a mobile browser. Additionally, two public web sites provide Mobile Web tools that test whether a mobile browser supports AJAX. The Frost AJAX tests (http://pwmwa.com/frost/, http://frostlib.org) and the AJAX tests from MobileTech (http://ajax.mobiletech.mobi/) exercise mobile browsers and provide visual results of AJAX compatibility tests. The MobileTech test site saves mobile browser information and test results to include in databases of mobile browsers known to support AJAX.

Or, you can create your own AJAX test tool using the Mobile Web development techniques described in this chapter. Remember, testing that a mobile browser supports only the syntax of AJAX (XMLHttpRequest, <script> tag, and so on) is insufficient. You must also assess mobile network speed and browser performance impacts when deciding whether a mobile device supports AJAX well enough to include support for it in your Mobile Web application.

### EXERCISE 5: DOES YOUR MOBILE DEVICE SUPPORT JAVASCRIPT AND AJAX?

Assess whether your mobile device supports JavaScript and AJAX. Use a device database and the public AJAX mobile browser tests to discover the extent of client-side interactivity supported by the mobile browser(s) on your device.

- Find the user-agent for the browser(s) on your mobile device. See Appendix B for instructions for capturing the User-Agent HTTP request header from a mobile browser.

- Use the web browser interfaces for the DeviceAtlas or WURFL device databases to look up the expected support levels for JavaScript and AJAX in each mobile browser. See Chapter 4 for more about device databases.

- View Listing 5-5 in each mobile browser as an ad hoc test for AJAX and JavaScript support.

- Complete the Frost and MobileTech AJAX tests in each mobile browser.

What were the results of your investigation? Do the browsers installed on your mobile device support JavaScript and AJAX? Answer these questions for each mobile browser:

1.  Do the DeviceAtlas and WURFL device databases show that the browser supports JavaScript and AJAX?

2.  Do the Frost and MobileTech AJAX tests conclude that the browser supports JavaScript and AJAX?

3.  Do the device database and tested support levels for AJAX differ? If so, how? How could you resolve this conflict using the developer community resources in Chapter 4?

4.  How much mobile network latency is observed when activating each tab in Listing 5-5? How does AJAX functionality affect the browser performance?

For extra credit, find Mobile Web sites on the public Internet and assess their usability and performance in the mobile browsers installed on your mobile phone, if the browsers support JavaScript and AJAX.

## Summary

This chapter introduced JavaScript and AJAX for mobile browsers as methods to increase the client-side interactivity of Mobile Web documents and optimize its impact on a mobile network. A mobile browser can support a complete JavaScript implementation customarily available on desktop browsers, or it can support EcmaScript Mobile Profile, a subset of JavaScript functionality targeted specifically for the constrained processing environment of a mobile device. A device database and testing on actual mobile devices are used to determine whether a mobile browser supports JavaScript and AJAX. When these technologies are available in a mobile browser, scripting features should be iteratively developed into a Mobile Web site and tested, to ensure syntax compatibility and assess their impacts on browser performance. Examples of Mobile JavaScript and AJAX features for Mobile Web documents provide syntax examples and implementation details.

The next chapter presents design and usability techniques for Mobile Web pages.

# Advanced Mobile Web Development Techniques

Part 3 introduces advanced development techniques that improve Mobile Web usability and enhance the user experience on smartphone browsers.

Here you'll see how to make the design and usability of your Mobile Web pages even better to help the mobile user easily and rapidly achieve goals. You'll compare smartphone screen dimensions, examine sample page layouts, and learn about design and usability best practices.

Then you'll investigate the advanced features of smartphone browsers. You'll learn how to take advantage of these features by exploring XHTML and JavaScript techniques for enhancing the user experience of Mobile Web applications on a number of smartphone browsers, including the iPhone, Android, Palm webOS, BlackBerry, Nokia Series 60, Opera, and Windows Mobile.

# Chapter 6

# Mobile Web Usability

Mobile Web usability is a measure of how easy (or otherwise) a user finds it to interact with a web site through a mobile device. In this chapter we look at some of the most heavily used Mobile Web sites and show you how to apply best practices and design guidelines to create an effective web site for a mobile device.

As we delve into Mobile Web usability, you should keep one thing in mind: *you are developing for a mobile user*. A mobile user is not someone sitting in front of a computer with undivided concentration, but rather someone who is on the move, waiting for a bus, on his way to work, with friends in a coffee shop, shopping. A mobile user's attention is often divided: she might be listening to music or talking to friends while using the mobile device. A mobile user has a very short attention span and is in a highly interruptible and dynamic environment.

A user visits a web site on a mobile device for a purpose. As a developer, your goal is help her achieve that purpose in the least amount of time. This chapter will help you develop such a Mobile Web site, and is divided into four sections:

**Best Practices for Usable Mobile Web Sites** looks at mobile versions of four popular web sites—Bank of America, CNN, Flickr, and Wikipedia—to see how they satisfy their customer's goal in an effective way.

- **Mobile Browser Layout Comparison** gives you specific information about mobile browsers across popular devices: Android, iPhone, BlackBerry, Palm Pre, Windows Mobile, Nokia Series 60, and Nokia Maemo. This section shows you the screen layouts of all the popular mobile devices and gives a context for your development.

- **Designing Mobile Web pages** dives into different web site categories and show you how to create an effective design for each of them. This section covers the following: news, search, service, portal, and media-sharing web sites with example layouts.

■ **Design Guidelines** are a set of tips and practices that can be used for developing web sites that cater to the maximum number of users. These guidelines can be used as checkpoints while developing your Mobile Web site.

# Best Practices for Usable Mobile Web Sites

In this section we will see how popular Internet brands have created mobile versions of their web sites, and what trade-offs they have made with respect to design and functionality.

We looked into twenty-five popular Mobile Web sites (more details in a later section) and selected these four web sites for our case studies.

■ Bank of America

■ CNN

■ Flickr

■ Wikipedia

Each of these Mobile Web sites represents a particular type of site, each requiring distinctive functionality (see Table 6-1). For example, the Bank of America web site provides continual online service and it demands login authentication. CNN, on the other hand, is a news site that delivers an ever-changing flow of information. Flickr typifies the current trend of media-sharing web sites, while Wikipedia is an encyclopedia, dictionary, and search tool.

We will study each of these web sites carefully, looking for common patterns, and identify the features that determine the design of these Mobile Web sites.

**Table 6-1.** *Popular Mobile Web Sites by Type and Features*

| Web Site | Type | Features | URL |
|---|---|---|---|
| Bank of America | Service | Secure online banking, location lookup, help | `https://bankofamerica.com /mobile/` |
| CNN | News | Dynamic information, headlines, weather | `http://m.cnn.com` |
| Flickr | Media | Media sharing, my account, search | `http://m.flickr.com/` |
| Wikipedia | Encyclopedia | Information database | `http://m.wikipedia.org/` |

# Case Study #1: Bank of America

The Bank of America desktop web site is feature-rich and provides an abundance of services and content to online visitors. A customer can log in and accomplish all banking tasks through the web site, without ever talking to a bank representative. The site provides easy-to-use access to all banking services.

Compared with the desktop version, the Mobile Web site provides only the most-used features. Figure 6-1 shows different versions of the site. The image on the left is the desktop web site and the two figures on the right are mobile renderings. The top-right page is a minimal version of the web site for older mobile phones, and the lower-right page is a smartphone version with a rich user interface and interactivity.

> **Note** By smartphone version, I mean a version for mobile devices with rich features and an advanced web browser with CSS and JavaScript capabilities. The Bank of America web site redirects to the richest possible user interface based on the capability of the device.

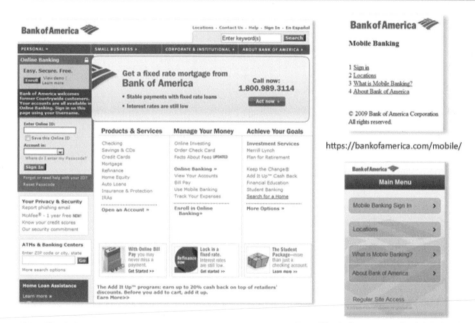

**Figure 6-1.** *Multiple versions of the Bank of America web site for desktops, featurephones, and smartphones*

## Features of the Bank of America Mobile Web Site

The Bank of America site provides great insight into Mobile Web design. The feature-rich site, when moved to a mobile device, becomes a thin, function-based web site. Fewer than 20 percent of the features are ported to mobile versions. The reason is simple:

when a mobile user visits a bank web site, he has a purpose in mind—either to locate an ATM or to check or transfer his balance. The other services available in the desktop web site or a bank branch are not required.

The following characteristics of this example can be useful when designing a similar, service-driven Mobile Web site:

- Only those features needed by a mobile user go into a Mobile Web site.

- Offering versions of a Mobile Web site optimized for mass-market mobile devices and smartphones accommodates more customers.

- The basic mobile version is optimized for bandwidth—plain text with optimized images.

- In the smartphone version, the width of the navigation is not fixed for a particular device but is set at 100 percent to accommodate devices of different dimensions.

- The smartphone version also has a link to the desktop version of the site because the mobile browser is capable of displaying the desktop version, although the user will need to zoom in to find particular information.

- Although the desktop version allows for both English and Spanish renderings, the mobile version, based on the browser locale information, displays only the English version and does not allow for language change.

- The mobile versions use security certificates and the HTTPS protocol.

- The mobile versions also have help on mobile banking to help beginners understand the Mobile Web site.

## Case Study #2: CNN

The next web site we are going to look at is CNN, a news site that is all about change and dynamic information. News is grouped into a number of categories. The home page presents the latest news, and other sections display politics, entertainment, weather, health, technology, travel, and living headlines.

The web site is meant to provide up-to-date information. A user comes to it to check the latest news, or goes straight to a category of his choice and reads further. Visitors can choose to listen to or watch videos of the broadcasts, and some users also come to check weather. The web site also offers user accounts for personalized news.

Figure 6-2 shows the desktop version of the CNN web site (left) as compared to the mobile versions (right). Like the Bank of America site, CNN tries to accommodate multiple devices with separate versions for older mobile phones with limited browser capability (right, top) and for the latest smartphones (right, bottom).

Figure 6-2. *Multiple versions of the CNN web site for desktop, featurephones, and smartphones*

**NOTE:** Both mobile versions of the CNN web site point to the same URL, but render different versions based on the mobile browser capability. Refer to Chapter 4 "Device awareness and content adaptation" for more information about device detection. Also, Chapter 12 includes strategies for switching between desktop and Mobile Web experiences deployed at the same URL.

# Features of CNN Mobile Web Site

The CNN Mobile Web site is made up of category blocks from the desktop web site. The Mobile Web site consists of category headers and the news title, which, when clicked, shows details of that category of news. The Mobile Web site allows users to SMS or e-mail the news to another phone or e-mail address. The smartphone version also lets users share via social network sites, like Facebook, Digg, and the like.

The following design characteristics can be seen in the CNN Mobile Web site:

- Current news is dynamic information and most interesting to the user, so it is always displayed on the landing page in all desktop and mobile versions.

- The web site contains blocks of information that can be displayed individually on the mobile screen, so there's a detail view for each.

- The layout allows the information to flow linearly downward, so the user can scroll down for more news blocks, headlines, and so forth.

- There is no horizontal scroll like the desktop version.

- News is grouped into multiple categories, shown linearly in the normal mobile version and as a dropdown in the smartphone version.

- News follows a standard headline-description pattern that is displayed when the user clicks on a particular headline inside a category

- News is meant for sharing so all versions allow for sharing through email, SMS, and social widgets.

- User account features are not ported to the mobile version.

- There are minimal or no advertisements on the Mobile Web site

- Smartphone versions of the Mobile Web site also have links to the standard desktop version, as well as to the audio/video option where user can hear/watch broadcasts.

## Case Study #3: Wikipedia

Wikipedia comprises a huge collection of articles on almost every subject, written and maintained collaboratively by a self-selected group of volunteers. For an end user, it is a free web-based encyclopedia and provides information in many different languages. Wikipedia allows users to contribute to the information database in an easy-to-use online editor. Anyone with Internet access can write and make changes to articles, but revisions are subject to review and approval by a small editorial group.

Users come to the Wikipedia web site to look for information on a particular person, topic, or event. Typically, they browse or search for the topic, then leave. Volunteer editors add and edit new information, which is immediately available to end users.

Figure 6-3 shows the desktop version of Wikipedia (left) compared to the mobile versions (right).

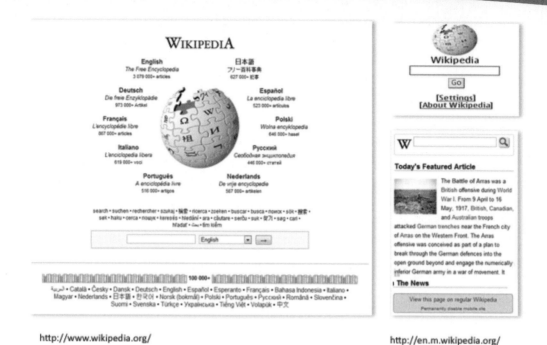

http://www.wikipedia.org/                                    http://en.m.wikipedia.org/

**Figure 6-3.** *Multiple versions of the Wikipedia.org web site for desktop, featurephones, and smartphones*

**NOTE:** Wikipedia.org is a multilingual information site that allows for language selection in both desktop and older mobile versions. In the smartphone version based on the browser language from the HTTP header, it redirects the user to `http://en.m.wikipedia.com` (en for English).

## Features of Wikipedia Mobile Web site

The Wikipedia web site is all about instant information for a visitor. Users all over the world visit the site to get complete details about a particular topic. This functionality, when ported to a mobile version, becomes a simple search.

In the older phones where browser features are limited and the language of the browser may not be known, the web site allows for changing the language through settings. But in a rich smartphone browser, Wikipedia takes the browser language and redirects the user to that language search. It also uses the space to show a featured article along with the search. The featured article, like the CNN web site's latest news, is dynamic information, which makes it interesting.

The mobile Wikipedia web site shows us the following:

- Search functionality, the core of the Wikipedia web site, is ported to mobile version.

- Some functionality, like new user accounts, add new page, edit, and so forth, is not meant for a mobile context.

- Desktop versions of the web site have links to other Wikipedia sites like Wikiquotes and Wiktionary, which are not ported to mobile versions.

- Wikipedia tries to accommodate a wide range of users by having multiple mobile versions of the web site.

- The featured article can be found on the desktop Wikipedia site after selecting a language (see `http://en.wikipedia.org/wiki/Main_Page`).

- The layout allows the information to flow linearly downward, so users can scroll down for more news headlines.

- There is no horizontal scroll like the desktop version.

- The smartphone version width is set to 100 percent to accommodate devices with different dimensions.

- The smartphone version has a link to the main web site.

## Case Study #4: Flickr

Flickr is an online photo- and video-sharing web site. It provides visitors with a photo search and allows users to create accounts and share personal photographs. It is used as a personal photo repository. Flickr also has a paid subscription, which gives users more space for photo and video storage.

The Flickr site provides easy-to-use photo management to subscribed users and free photo search to visitors. Users come to the site to find pictures of a particular person, topic, or event.

Figure 6-4 shows the desktop version of Flickr (left) compared to the mobile versions (right).

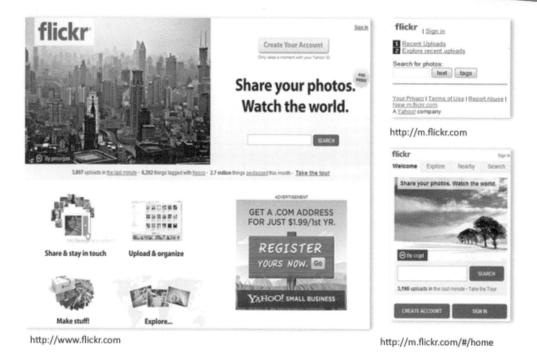

**Figure 6-4.** *Multiple versions of Flickr for desktop, featurephone (right, top,) and smartphones (right, bottom)*

**NOTE:** The numbers 1 and 2 in the old mobile version of Flickr are mapped to the phone keys to make certain functions easily accessible.

## Features of Flickr Mobile Web site

Flickr is about finding, and sharing pictures, so the Mobile Web site allows for user login and search. Based on browser capability, Flickr redirects users to different versions of the web site, but these core functionalities persist.

The desktop site provides a number of additional services, like the ability to make calendars, collages, and so forth from pictures and to get prints, but the mobile version only ports the main functions. The smartphone version also allows new account creation and has a link to the desktop web site.

The mobile Flickr web site shows the following:

- Search and my account functionality exist in the mobile version.
- The smartphone version includes new account creation.
- Maximum display is desired because of the gallery view of pictures.

- The smartphone version is based on the width of the device; the browser adjusts its layout, using a width of 100 percent.

- Flickr accommodates a wide range of users by having multiple mobile versions of the web site.

- Because the featured image is dynamic and interesting, it is displayed on the landing page in both desktop and smartphone versions.

- The layout allows the information to flow linearly downward, so the user can scroll down for more.

- There is no horizontal scroll like the desktop version.

- The smartphone version has a link to the main web site.

These four case studies show us many of the best practices that are followed industry-wide and used by millions of mobile users. They were meant to give you some ideas of what you need to consider when designing your Mobile Web site, what should be the key points, what to do when you have multi-language sites, and how you can accommodate the maximum number of users. As you saw, the smartphone versions always include a link to the desktop version, and using 100 percent-width in smartphone browsers accommodates multiple phones with different screen dimensions. This allows users with advanced mobile devices to choose their experience.

The next section compares the physical layout and dimension details for different phone browsers.

# Mobile Browser Layout Comparison

When you design a web site, you must make sure it displays properly in most browser and screen sizes. A desktop web browser has a screen size of 12-30 inches and a resolution starting at 800 by 600 pixels. Desktops normally have 67 to 130 pixels per inch (PPI).

> **NOTE:** The pixel-per-inch (PPI) count partially determines the display of the image on a screen. Greater PPI values usually mean better quality and depth in the image displayed.

When you create a Mobile Web site, the first thing you need to know is the browser layout details of the target phone you are creating for. To accommodate the largest number of users, you need to know the screen size, resolution, and PPI of all the popular phones. This is also helpful when you plan to create a single smartphone version with a 100-percent width style for multiple devices.

Table 6-2 lists the popular mobile phones with their layout specifications.

**Table 6-2.** *Browser Layout Details for Popular Phones*

| Mobile Phone | Screen size(inch) | Resolution (pixels) | Mode | Pixel Per Inch |
|---|---|---|---|---|
| Android G1 | 3.2 | 320 x 480 | Portrait | 180 |
| BlackBerry Curve | 2.4 | 480 x 360 | Landscape | 165 |
| iPhone | 3.5 | 320 x 480 | Portrait | 163 |
| Nokia Maemo N900 | 3.5 | 800 x 480 | Landscape | 265 |
| Palm Pre | 3.1 | 320 x 480 | Portrait | 186 |
| S60 Nokia 5320 | 2.0 | 240 x 320 | Portrait | 167 |
| Windows Mobile Xperia X1 | 3.0 | 800 x 480 | Landscape | 291 |

Figure 6-5 illustrates the screen resolutions of these devices with respect to each other.

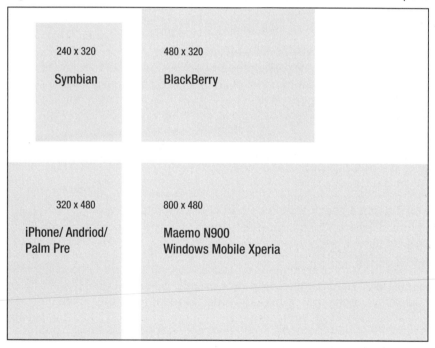

**Figure 6-5.** *Layout comparison of popular phones*

Note that a number of these devices allow both portrait and landscape mode, and a few older phones like the Motorola RAZR have a resolution of 128x160, which still enables Mobile Web browsing. As you can see, many choices are available for end users, so designing web pages—keeping all these devices in mind, planning for screens three times bigger than the smallest one—can be quite challenging, and that's what we are going to talk about next.

# Designing Mobile Web pages

So far we have examined some of the most-used Mobile Web sites, and you have seen the layout, orientation, and screen size of most popular mobile devices. Now we dive into creating web pages for these devices.

There are two simple goals in Mobile Web design—to accommodate the maximum number of users and devices, and to do that with the least amount of effort.

To achieve this, you have to start with a flexible reference design—the bare-minimum functionality you want in your Mobile Web page—and then use a standard layout that will work across the devices. Let's take a closer look at those two concepts.

## Flexible Reference Design

A flexible reference design can be thought of as a baseline for your web site.

We saw in the case studies that most of the web sites have multiple mobile versions; the baseline here is the version meant for the most limited of the mobile phones. This defines the bare-minimum functionality of the web site that you want for your mobile users. Once you have set this minimum, you need to decide what other functionality you want for rich mobile browsers that are capable of complex CSS and JavaScript.

To create a flexible reference design:

1.  List the set of functions from the desktop web site you want to port to the device. My suggestion is to take only the top 20 percent of useful features from the desktop web site to the Mobile Web.

2.  List the most important features for which the mobile user will open the site while on the move; these should be part of the home page. For example, for the Bank of America site, both login to online banking and search for locations are important for a user on the move, so both should appear on the home page.

3.  For information web sites, it is dynamic, up-to-date information that makes the site compelling. Be sure you put that on the home page.

4.  Divide the content into blocks of information or services that can be displayed at once in the mobile screen, and display one at a time.

5.  Allow for vertical scroll if needed.

The next step is to create a standard layout for your web page that adapts easily across multiple devices. There are number of options to either redirect the user to a different page based on the Mobile Web browser or to use the same page with different CSS styles for different browsers, as shown in Figure 6-6.

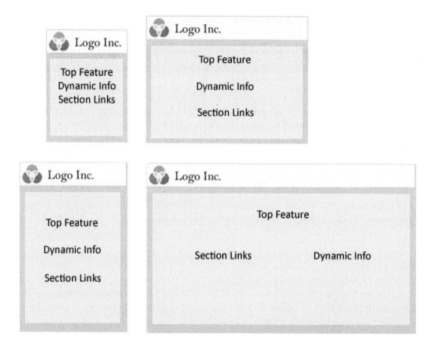

**Figure 6-6.** *A reference design for a landing page that can be used on multiple devices*

> **NOTE:** For older mobile devices, plain text and images might fit well with the basic reference design as shown in the top left in Figure 6-6, but new mobile phones with advanced browser capabilities should use CSS to utilize the device space efficiently, as in the other three layouts.

Now that you have a basic reference design, let's move ahead and see the standard layouts that can be used based on the functionality of the web site.

## Standard Layout

This section will show you standard layouts for different types of sites and describes why a particular layout is preferred. Table 6-3 shows 25 popular desktop web sites from Alexa (an online web-site ranking service) grouped into five categories based on functionality and layout.

**Table 6-3.** *Web Site Categories*

| News | Search | Service (login needed) | Portal | Media-Sharing |
|---|---|---|---|---|
| BBC | Answers | Bank of America | Adobe | Flickr |
| CNN | Ask | Blogger | Amazon | Photobucket |
| Digg | Bing | Facebook | eBay | YouTube |
| MSN | Google | LinkedIn | Microsoft | |
| CNET News | Wikipedia | Monster | Walmart | |
| Weather | | | Yahoo | |

Most of the web sites we come across show characteristics of one or more of these categories. Let's see in more detail what standard layouts can be used for these sites.

## News Web Site

As we saw in Case Study #2, a news web site generally consists of dynamic information grouped into multiple sections. Figure 6-7 shows a standard layout for a mobile version of a news site, which also contains Top Links.

Features of a news web site include:

- Regularly updated latest news, which is most interesting to the user
- Different sections for news with headlines
- A news article with the standard headline, description, and images

**NOTE:** A user interface without a scrollbar is the best experience for the user. However, if the information is more than the display area, a vertical scrollbar is acceptable. Always avoid horizontal scrollbars. These provide a bad user experience in a small device and can be avoided using 100 percent-width.

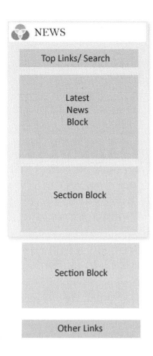
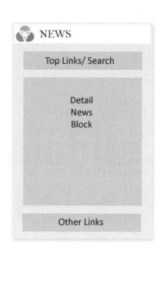

**Figure 6-7.** *A standard layout for a news web site home page (left) and a detail news page (right)*

# Search Web site

The Search web site category includes search engines like Google and Bing as well as sites that aggregate information like Answers.com and Wikipedia.org (Case Study #3). The common pattern here is that most users go to the site to query for particular information, which yields a set of related results from which the user can make a selection and see more details.

Search web sites store information in different categories. For example, Google stores text, images, and video, while Wikipedia stores articles in multiple languages. These options normally become part of settings or initial choices and should be cached, as in the Wikipedia case study where the user-preferred language was cached from settings in the basic mobile version.

Features of the search web sites shown in Figure 6-8 include:

- Standard user interface is a search box and a submit button; avoid a dropdown list.

- Settings need to be saved in cookies or the browser cache.

- Minimal help and about on mobile usage for beginner users.

- Mapping with mobile phone keys for quick results.

**Figure 6-8.** *Standard search and search result features for Mobile Web site*

## Service Web Site

A service web site provides personalized service and lets users log in to their account. Service web sites can be online banking (case study #2 Bank of America), social networking like Facebook, MySpace, blog sites like Blogger, Wordpress, and even online e-mail services. Online service web site always desire new users, so including a link to registration is also becoming a standard practice (see Figure 6-9).

Features of a service web site:

- Login screen on the home page
- Help gives user brief idea about the service usage
- Simple registration to accommodates new users
- Security protocols (https) for authentication

**NOTE:** The registration process can be complex and time consuming on a desktop web site with CAPTCHA (Completely Automated Public Turing test to tell Computers and Human Apart) controls that use a textual image to ensure a human rather than a program is trying to access a site, billing information, and e-mail confirmations. These "extra" features should be avoided in the mobile version. User authentication in a mobile registration process can be achieved by sending a confirmation link via SMS instead of traditional e-mail.

**Figure 6-9.** *Standard Mobile Web layout for a typical service site*

# Portal Web Site

Portal web sites are a combination of news, search, media-sharing, and services web sites and they typically have features of each. They often include search at the top, blocks of information links like news, and sometimes a login (see Figure 6-10).

Portal sites usually have a featured news, product, or service that is promoted. This information is part of the home page and is regularly updated. Portals generally have information grouped into multiple categories, so a drop-down selection for a particular category is used in smartphone versions of the mobile site.

Features of portal web site include

- Search

- Featured item (news, product, and so forth)

- Multiple categories

- Blocks of information

**NOTE:** A mobile portal web site should have a link to the desktop version of the site if possible. Portal users are accustomed to the desktop view of the site and feel more comfortable navigating the original site than the filtered mobile version. This has become standard because a portal is accessed by many users for many different purposes. According to the 80/20 rule, we limit the mobile device to only 20 percent of desktop functionality, and that may well limit the user's choices.

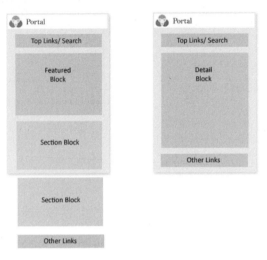

**Figure 6-10.** *Portals use a mix of the news, search, and service templates, depending on the popular features of the site*

## Media-Sharing Web Site

Mobile versions of media-sharing web sites are quite important because of the social nature of the site, which enhances the mobile experience. Moreover, current phones allow for high-quality pictures and videos. Instant sharing of these can be a very attractive and popular feature. A media-sharing site also has traits of service web sites where user can login and view his own gallery (see Figure 6-11).

The standard practice for a mobile media site includes

- Gallery view for maximum display of media

- Login and search on the Mobile Web page

- Device integration for sharing pictures and videos on advanced phones

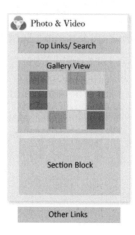
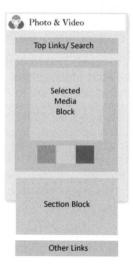

**Figure 6 11.** *Standard template view for mobile media web site*

# Design Guidelines

This section presents some design guidelines for Mobile Web pages. So far we have covered a number of real case studies; we saw the layout specification for different mobile devices and standard templates for different Web site categories. This section will go a step further and give you an objective set of rules for designing and developing Mobile Web pages, including

- Tips for Developing Mobile Web Pages
- Creating a Web Page for the Maximum Number of Users
- Creating a Better Mobile User Experience

## Tips for Developing Mobile Web Pages

The following tips form a handy checklist for designing your Mobile Web site. They are based on my experience.

- **A Mobile Web site needs to be user-driven.** Know why your user visits your web site and provide only those features in the mobile version. Be aware that mobile users need information with minimum interaction.

- **Start with a basic version** for older mobile phone browsers and then add extra features for the smartphone version. This helps you identify the core features of the desktop web site that need to be ported to the mobile version. Use the 80/20 rule (80 percent of the results comes from 20 percent of the features) to identify the top 20 percent of features.

- **Create only two mobile versions,** one for the basic phone and one for smartphones, and then optimize the richer version according to your customer's phone. If you know 80 percent of your users use Nokia phones, optimize the web site for that device and use 100-percent width, which accommodates all other similar devices. Use content adaptation for phones with similar browser capabilities but different dimensions to adapt to a particular device.

- **Restrict your Mobile Web site to three levels of navigation**. A mobile user has a very short span of time; try to get him what he is looking for as fast as possible. Standard search navigation is Search to Result to Detail page. If the user searches for a particular item, the navigation should be Search to Detail page, and at any page the search should be visible for reuse; the user should not need to go back three steps to get to the search.

- **Standard practice for the Mobile Web is using the m subdomain** `http://m.website.com` and the `.mobi` top-level domain, `http://website.mobi`. These are accepted and known by most mobile users, so don't use `http://mobile.website.com` or `http://website.com/mobile`. If your web site is hosted there, at least redirects your `m.websitename.com` subdomain to your current location. Other direct mobile URIs need to be short.

- **Save user settings.** This is very important and gives a better user experience by minimizing user interaction. Use the browser cache effectively to remember the user's last set of configurations.

- **Future-proof your Mobile Web site.** Test the site for both portrait and landscape mode, and make necessary changes to ensure the site displays nicely on both. Often, the proper use of styles (100 percent-width) can solve this issue. This helps make the web site future-proof.

- **Dynamic information** on the home page keeps the web site interesting for the mobile user. If your site is about blogs, news, or information, try to provide something new to the user every time he visits the web site.

- **Testing** should be done on actual devices. The testing can also be done on emulators but that does not give as good indication of how the page loads using different wireless Internet connections like 2.5G, 3G, WiMax, and Wi-Fi. Your tests will depend on your target phone. There are online services like deviceanywhere.com that enable remote testing on different mobile devices. See Chapter 10 for more details on testing.

- **Optimize everything.** Optimize images for size; a PNG image can be a good trade-off between quality and size. CSS and JavaScript should also be optimized for size. A number of online optimization tools are available for this purpose. Don't forget to test after optimization. If you are using JavaScript libraries, try to reduce the size by removing the functions you don't need.

- **Reduce server trips** by using image sprites and merging CSS and JavaScript in the same page, instead of using additional include files. Chapter 8 goes into this subject in more detail.

- **Link to the desktop site.** This has become standard practice for smartphone versions.

- **Make the functions accessible.** Allow maximum interaction—even the basic mobile browser allows for access keys that map the phone keys to the navigation (see case study #4, Flickr). Use them to provide shortcut keys for navigation. We will talk about this in more detail in the next section.

- **Avoid the following**: Pop-up windows, mouse-hover menus, auto refresh, auto redirects, external links, horizontal scrolling, and frames.

- **Ajax functionality**, or progressive enhancement, if used sparingly can give a great user experience.

- **For device detection and device capabilities**, refer to Chapter 4.

> **NOTE:** W3C recommended best practices for Mobile Web can be found at `http://www.w3.org/TR/mobile-bp/`, and the dotMobi resource center is at `http://mtld.mobi/`.

## Creating a Web Page for the Maximum Number of Users

To enable maximum accessibility, allow for all the interfaces or input methods a mobile device can provide. To do this, you need to first understand what the interaction points are (that is, the interface available) for a mobile device.

Here is a list of ways a user interacts with a mobile phone:

- **Phone keyboard.** Most of the old mobile devices have phone keyboards with the standard number keys and multiple letters on each. Entering information using these can be tedious so minimize the number of user inputs on your Mobile Web site.

- **QWERTY keyboard.** Some of the latest smartphone have a miniature QWERTY keyboard, along with numbers and special keys, so utilize this interface in the smartphone version of your Mobile Web site.

- **Virtual QWERTY keyboard.** Touchscreen phones have a virtual QWERTY keyboard interface which pops up on request or during data entry. This virtual keyboard takes some space of its own, so try to put the input box on your web page above the potential space for the virtual keyboard. This gives a better user experience. For example, suppose the home page of a service web site contains a login password box. When designing the web page, based on the device, you can keep these input textboxes above the virtual keyboard location.

- **Finger touch, stylus, and thumb.** Touchscreen phones allow for finger touch, stylus input, and thumb interaction. Each interacts on the screen directly but has slightly different surface area for the touch, with the stylus being the smallest and thumb touch the largest. Based on the phones and the number of functions, allow for the best interaction possible.

- **Multi-touch.** A number of the latest phones, like the iPhone, allow for multi-touch and have special touch-specific events, like *touchstart* and *touchend*. If you are targeting those phones, make sure you use these methods to create a better user experience.

- **Voice.** The latest phones also have voice interfaces that are still evolving, so make sure you are ready to capture the voice interaction when it is available.

## Creating a Better Mobile User Experience

User experience can be defined as the level of satisfaction a user gets from a product with respect to how much the user likes and understands the product and how well he is able to use it. In a mobile context, a better experience is a web page that is easily accessible, understandable, and navigable.

To create a better mobile experience, follow these guidelines:

- **Simplify everything.** Use clear, short, simple words for links, buttons, and menus. Every feature and service on the Mobile Web site should be minimalist. Standard abbreviations are accepted for titles.

- **One idea on one page.** Always focus on one idea on a Mobile Web page. For a news site, a category needs to have a page of its own; don't try to accommodate everything on a single page with a large vertical scroll.

- **Thematic consistency.** Keep some level of consistency with the original web site, like logo and color themes to keep the "feel" of the desktop web site. Don't make drastic changes to the mobile site. If you are targeting a particular phone, use the design guidelines for the phone.

- **Color.** When using color on a Mobile Web page, consider the sun, shade, contrast, and brightness a user might face on the move. Use color not only for style but also for function, such as red for alert. But don't convey important information only by color. For example, even if an error is displayed with red, there should also be text to convey the message.

- **Visual aesthetic.** Make the Mobile Web pages visually pleasing. Use visual cues instead of raw data, spaces between sections, only a few colors. One of the suggestions I give to all is to have a high noise-to-signal ratio as your guiding principle. Noise-to-signal here refers to the contrast between unimportant information (the noise) and the important information (the signal). If your color scheme is drowning your important information amidst the unimportant information, change it. Make the color scheme so that the most important information stands out of the rest. It should be clearly visible and more attractive than the rest of the page.

- **No need for help.** Although service web sites provide a simple help for beginners, a Mobile Web site should be intuitive enough on its own. If you must, keep the help to one page.

- And keep text input to a minimum, replacing them with select items on forms where possible.

## EXERCISE 6: DESIGN A MOBILE WEB SITE

Open your favorite web site and create a mobile version of it based on what you have learned in this section:

- List all the top features you think can be useful to the mobile user.

- Use the 20 percent principle to prune features from the desktop.

- Create a layout based on the design versus functionality trade-off as described in the standard layout section.

- Design a CSS-based XHTML web site with page flow up to 3 levels (10 pages).

- Host the web pages in a free server and test in an actual mobile device

Answer these questions:

1. What is the single most important thing about Mobile Web usability?

2. What are the top two things you should keep in mind while creating Mobile Web page?

3. List five common features you think every Mobile Web site must have.

# Summary

In this chapter, you learned about Mobile Web usability. You studied the features of four of the most popular Mobile Web sites and learned from their implementation. We discussed the standard layouts for popular Web sites and suggested some standard design principles for the Mobile Web. In the exercise, you applied your knowledge to create a Mobile Web site.

In the next chapter, we will examine how to enhance these Web pages.

# Chapter 7

# Enhancing Mobile Web Pages for Smartphone Browsers

The Mobile Web development techniques discussed in all other chapters of this book are portable across mobile devices and browsers. Using a device database and adequate testing enables a mobile developer to enhance a Mobile Web page with advanced features for modern browsers and gracefully downgrade the experience for mass-market browsers—and do so with reasonable confidence that a mobile device will be served the appropriate Web content.

This chapter is all about smartphone browsers. You'll forget about portability and cross-platform Mobile Web development. Instead, you'll dive deep into the feature sets of the most capable mobile browsers and most popular smartphone devices in the market today, using this information to create compelling Mobile Web applications tailored to the strengths of these advanced browsers. However, this chapter is not intended to provide an exhaustive feature list for each smartphone browser. Each smartphone browser merits a book unto itself! Rather, you'll learn about their significant features and limitations, as well as where to find references to developer and OEM documentation for additional reading.

All mobile browsers in this section support XHTML, CSS2, and JavaScript. Most of them also support AJAX, making smartphone browsers suitable platforms for dynamic Mobile Web applications. Your investigation starts by reviewing the common features found across many smartphone browsers and continues with discussions of features found in mobile browsers in iPhone, Android, webOS, BlackBerry, Nokia Series 60, and Windows Mobile devices. The chapter concludes with an overview of the powerful third-party smartphone browser Opera Mobile and its relationship to Opera's other mobile browser, Opera Mini.

# Common Web Techniques for Smartphone Browsers

Smartphone browsers share some common advanced markup techniques. The `Viewport` `<meta>` tag controls the logical dimensions and scaling of the browser viewport window. The JavaScript `onresize` and `onorientationchange` events capture orientation changes in the mobile device (such as when the user rotates between landscape and portrait views). You can use JavaScript to determine the new device orientation after an orientation change.

In addition to technical documentation from OEMs and browser vendors, an excellent reference for JavaScript event and object support in smartphone browsers is Peter-Paul Koch's Mobile compatibility tables, which you can find at his QuirksMode blog at `www.quirksmode.org/m/table.html`.

## Viewport Meta Tag

Many smartphone browsers scale Web pages to a wide viewport width, one appropriate for displaying desktop-optimized markup. These browsers allow the user to zoom in and out of scaled Web pages. For example, Opera Mobile uses a default viewport width of 850 pixels, and the iPhone uses a default width of 980 pixels. The `Viewport` `<meta>` tag allows a Mobile Web developer to set the best viewport size and scaling limits for the Mobile Web document. This `<meta>` tag controls the logical width, logical height, and initial scaling factor of the browser window (or viewport) in iPhone, BlackBerry, Opera Mini, and other mobile browsers. On some smartphones, the `Viewport` `<meta>` tag specifies whether the user can scale the Web page, and if so, to what maximum and minimum scaling factors. The presence of the `Viewport` `<meta>` tag also indicates that the markup document is optimized for mobile devices.

The `content` value of the `Viewport` `<meta>` tag is a comma-delimited list of directives and their values. The following `<meta>` tag lists all directives and example values:

```
<meta name="viewport" content="width=240, height=320, user-scalable=yes,
  initial-scale=2.5, maximum-scale=5.0, minimum-scale=1.0" />
```

The `width` and `height` directives specify the logical width and height of the viewport, respectively. These directives require a value that is either a numeric viewport dimension in pixels or a special token. The `width` directive uses the `device-width` token to indicate that the viewport width should be the screen width of the device. Similarly, the `height` directive uses the `device-height` token to indicate that the viewport height should be the screen height of the device.

The `user-scalable` directive specifies whether the user can zoom in and out of the viewport, scaling the view of a Web page. A `yes` value allows users to zoom, while a `no` value prevents user-controlled zooming and scaling. A Mobile Web developer might disable user scrolling using the `no` value when the Web page is mobile-optimized and designed to be viewed without zooming.

The `initial-scale` directive sets the initial scaling or zoom factor (or multiplier) used for a Web page. The default initial scaling value varies by smartphone browser. Typically, you set the initial value to display the entire page in the browser viewport. A value of 1.0 displays an unscaled Web document.

The maximum-scale and minimum-scale directives set the user's limits for scaling or zooming a Web page. These values can range from 0.25 to 10.0. As with initial-scale, the values of these directives are scaling factors or multipliers applied to the viewport contents.

Virtually all smartphone browsers support the width and user-scalable directives of the Viewport <meta> tag. Notably, Opera Mobile disregards the user-scalable directive, asserting instead that mobile users should always retain the ability to scale Web pages in a mobile browser. The many smartphones browsers using the WebKit rendering engine (see the "WebKit in Mobile Browsers" section of this chapter) support all Viewport directives. You declare viewport size and scaling in a <meta> tag, so browsers that do not support the directives should safely and silently fail, without causing markup validation or well-formedness errors.

The following example <meta> tag directs a mobile browser to set the viewport width to the smartphone screen width (whatever value that might be) and disable user scaling. This <meta> tag is commonly used in mobile-optimized Web pages to allow the user to view and scroll the page contents without zooming:

```
<meta name="viewport" content="width=device-width, initial-scale=1.0,
    user-scalable=no" />
```

Figure 7-1 shows the Mobile Web page from Listing 9-2 in Chapter 9 with and without the previous Viewport <meta> tag example included in the markup, as rendered on the Palm Pre. Notice how the Viewport <meta> tag controls the page scaling and initial usability. Disabling user scrolling and setting a meaningful viewport width precludes the user's need to zoom to view the Web content.

**Figure 7-1.** *Mobile Web Page with and without the Viewport Meta Tag, respectively, displayed on the Palm Pre*

# Detecting Orientation Changes in JavaScript

Many smartphones update the orientation of the screen's display in reaction to physical device manipulation by the user. For example, when a user rotates a smartphone from portrait to landscape mode, the device reacts by switching the screen's orientation. Smartphone browsers surface this event to Mobile Web developers in JavaScript using either the onresize or onorientationchange events of the browser's window object.

Smartphone browsers support one or both of these events, so on-device testing is crucial when deciding which event is best **handled** in the target browser. The iPhone supports both events, and mobile developers generally handle only the onorientationchange event to detect orientation changes. Android and other WebKit-derived browsers support only the onresize event. BlackBerry devices support an onresize event on the document object; however, only a few BlackBerry mobile devices support screen orientation changes.

Inside the event handler for an orientation change event, a developer can use one of two methods to obtain the current screen dimensions and device orientation. iPhone developers can use the built-in window.orientation JavaScript integer property, where the value describes the current browser orientation. Table 7-1 lists the possible values of window.orientation and their meanings.

**Table 7-1.** *Values of the window.orientation JavaScript Property for iPhone*

| Property Value | Description |
| --- | --- |
| -90 | The device orientation is landscape; the screen is rotated clockwise (the device's button is on the left side). |
| 0 | The device orientation is portrait; this is the default property value. |
| 90 | The device orientation is landscape; the screen is rotated counter-clockwise (the device's button is on the right side). |
| 180 | The device orientation is portrait; the screen is turned upside down. (The iPhone doesn't support this option on the iPhone yet, but it might be supported in later firmware versions.) |

The following sample JavaScript code uses the built-in window.orientation property to determine whether the smartphone is in landscape or portrait orientation:

```
switch (window.orientation) {
    case -90:
        // Clockwise landscape orientation
        break;
    case 0:
        // Portrait orientation
        break;
    case 90:
        // Counter-clockwise landscape orientation
        break;
}
```

Alternatively, you can use the built-in `screen.widthy` and `screen.height` JavaScript properties, and perform a simple mathematical calculation to determine the device orientation. If the screen's width is greater than its height, then the device is in landscape orientation. Otherwise, the device is oriented as portrait. The following JavaScript example uses the built-in JavaScript properties to determine the device's orientation:

```
var width = parseInt(screen.width);
var height = parseInt(screen.height);

if (width > height) {
    // landscape orientation
}
else {
    // portrait orientation
}
```

In the previous example, you use the built-in function `parseInt()`to ensure that the screen width and height values are integers, in the event that a mobile browser's JavaScript implementation types the properties as strings.

In some cases, a mobile browser (not a smartphone browser) might not update the `screen.width` and `screen.height` values to reflect an orientation change. Instead, these property values statically keep their values for portrait orientations. This behavior is generally not seen on smartphones, but you can see it on full Web browsers on mass-market mobile devices. On-device testing is encouraged to rule out that you haven't introduced this JavaScript bug in your Mobile Web application.

Listing 7-1 is an example Mobile Web document that is compatible with the iPhone. It handles the `onorientationchange` event to detect and react to orientation change in a mobile browser. The event handler uses `window.orientation` to report the current orientation.

**Listing 7-1.** *Handling Orientation Changes With the onorientationchange Event*

```
<?xml version="1.0" encoding="UTF-8"?>
<!DOCTYPE html PUBLIC "-//WAPFORUM//DTD XHTML Mobile 1.1//EN"
"http://www.openmobilealliance.org/tech/DTD/xhtml-mobile11.dtd">
<html xmlns="http://www.w3.org/1999/xhtml">
<head>
<meta name="viewport" content="width=device-width,user-scalable=no" />
<title>Listing 7-1: Orientation Changes with onorientationchange</title>
<style type="text/css">
#content {
    padding: 10px;
    margin: 10px;
    border-width: 1px;
    border-style: solid;
    border-color: #333333;
}
</style>
<script type="text/javascript">
// Capture the orientation change event
function handleOrientationChange() {
```

```
    // Find the current orientation.
    var orientation = "unknown";
    switch (window.orientation){
        case -90:
        orientation = "Landscape (clockwise)";
        break;
        case 0:
            orientation = "Portrait";
            break;
        case 90:
        orientation = "Landscape (counter-clockwise)";
        break;
    }

    // Add the current screen dimensions.
    var screenSize = screen.width + " x " + screen.height;

    // Update the orientation information for the user
    document.getElementById("content").innerHTML = orientation + ", "
      + screenSize;
}
</script>
</head>
<!-- Here, we also fire the orientationchange event handler on document load,
 to show the user the default orientation of the mobile device. -->
<body onload="handleOrientationChange();"
 onorientationchange="handleOrientationChange();">
<h1>Orientation Changes</h1>
<p>Re-orient the mobile device. Look in the box below to learn about the
 current orientation.</p>
<div id="content"></div>
</body>
</html>
```

In Listing 7-1, the JavaScript function handleOrientationChange is the event handler for the onorientationchange event. It computes the orientation using the window.orientation property. The current orientation is reported to the user by updating the innerHTML of the div element with id content. You can observe the orientation change behavior in Listing 7-1 by viewing http://learnto.mobi/books/bmwd/07/7-1.xhtml in a smartphone browser.

Figure 7-2 shows Listing 7-1 inside the iPhone emulator in both portrait and landscape orientations. Notice that the text inside the div element with ID content reports that the screen dimensions do not change to match the current orientation. Because the iPhone provides the window.orientation property, you can determine the device's orientation without relying on the screen.width and screen.height properties to change values.

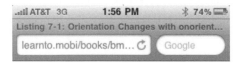

# Orientation Changes

Re-orient the mobile device. Look in the box
below to learn about the current orientation.

Portrait, 320 x 396

# Orientation Changes

Re-orient the mobile device. Look in the box
below to learn about the current orientation.

Landscape (counter-clockwise), 320 x
396

**Figure 7-2.** *Listing 7-1 displayed in the iPhone emulator in portrait and landscape orientations*

Listing 7-2 is an example Mobile Web document that handles the onresize event to
detect and react to orientation changes in a mobile browser. The event handler uses
screen.width and screen.height to compute and report the current device orientation.

**Listing 7-2.** *Handling Orientation Changes with the onorientationchange Event*

```
<?xml version="1.0" encoding="UTF-8"?>
<!DOCTYPE html PUBLIC "-//WAPFORUM//DTD XHTML Mobile 1.1//EN"
 "http://www.openmobilealliance.org/tech/DTD/xhtml-mobile11.dtd">
<html xmlns="http://www.w3.org/1999/xhtml">
<head>
<meta name="viewport" content="width=device-width,user-scalable=no" />
<title>Listing 7-2: Orientation Changes with onresize</title>
<style type="text/css">
#content {
    padding: 10px;
    margin: 10px;
    border-width: 1px;
    border-style: solid;
    border-color: #333333;
}
</style>
<script type="text/javascript">
// Capture the resize event
function handleResize() {

    // Find the current orientation.
    var orientation = "unknown";
```

```
    var width = parseInt(screen.width);
    var height = parseInt(screen.height);

    if (width > height) {
        orientation = "Landscape";
    }
    else {
        orientation = "Portrait";
    }

    // Add the current screen dimensions.
    var screenSize = screen.width + " x " + screen.height;

    // Update the orientation information for the user
    document.getElementById("content").innerHTML = orientation + ", "
      + screenSize;
}
</script>
</head>
<!-- Here, we also fire the orientationchange event handler on document load,
 to show the user the default orientation of the mobile device. -->
<body onload="handleResize();" onresize="handleResize();">
<h1>Orientation Changes</h1>
<p>Re-orient the mobile device. Look in the box below to learn about the
 current orientation.</p>
<div id="content"></div>
</body>
</html>
```

In Listing 7-2, the JavaScript function handleResize is the event handler for the onresize event. It computes the orientation using the screen.width and screen.height properties. As in Listing 7-1, you report the current orientation to the user by updating the innerHTML of the div element with id content. You can observe the orientation change behavior in Listing 7-2 by viewing http://learnto.mobi/books/bmwd/07/7-2.xhtml in a smartphone browser.

Figure 7-3 shows Listing 7-2 in the Android emulator in both portrait and landscape orientations. Notice how the text inside the div element with ID content updates as the orientation changes. This occurs because the screen.width and screen.height property values change to the current device orientation.

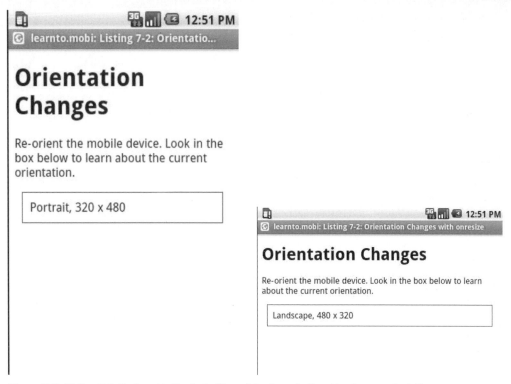

**Figure 7-3.** *Listing 7-2 displayed in the Android emulator in portrait and landscape orientations*

# WebKit in Mobile Browsers

WebKit is a layout and rendering engine for Web browsers that provides strict Web standards compliance without sacrificing page-rendering performance. WebKit was originally authored in C++ and has been ported to several development frameworks in desktop- and mobile-computing environments.

Apple authored the original WebKit browser engine for the Mac OS X version of the Safari desktop Web browser by forking and improving HTML and JavaScript components of the KDE open-source project. In 2005, Apple open-sourced the framework and provided public access to the WebKit source-control system. Since that time, the WebKit Open Source Project (`http://webkit.org/`) has controlled WebKit development. WebKit development can be observed and affected by any developer (including you!). Browse the WebKit Trac timeline at `http://trac.webkit.org/timeline` to view recent changes to the source code. Developers employed by mobile browser vendors such as Apple, Google, Nokia, and Palm contribute source code changes back to WebKit on a daily basis.

The WebKit browser engine consists of two main libraries: WebCore and JavaScript Core. Together, these libraries control Web page rendering and client-side interactivity. The WebKit engine supports these Web standards:

- **Markup**: HTML 4.01, XHTML 1.0, parts of HTML 5

- **Styles**: CSS 2.1 and parts of CSS3

- **Scripting**: JavaScript 1.8, AJAX, and DOM Levels 1, 2, and 3

The Apple Safari and Google Chrome desktop Web browsers use the WebKit rendering engine. Additionally, many smartphone browsers use the WebKit rendering engine and because of this, robustly support the Web markup, style, and scripting standards listed previously. The iPhone, Android, webOS, and Nokia Series 60 Web browsers are all based on WebKit technology.

After reading several chapters reporting discouraging fragmentation trends in the mobile landscape, you might be jumping for joy at the prospect of a consistent implementation of WebKit in smartphone browsers. Unfortunately, mobile browser vendors might base their Web rendering on WebKit, but the development process requires porting the WebKit C++ source code to a mobile-appropriate framework and adapting it to run with adequate performance on the limited resources of a mobile device (after all, smartphones are still limited-computing devices). Consequently, you find variations in WebKit implementations. Peter-Paul Koch, of the well-known QuirksMode blog (www.quirksmode.org), tested 19 WebKit implementations (including 10 WebKit-based smartphone browsers) and discovered slight differences in supported CSS and JavaScript features. You can find Koch's WebKit comparison table at http://www.quirksmode.org/webkit.html. The result: Many smartphone browsers use the WebKit rendering engine, providing an almost, but not entirely consistent mobile development platform for rich Internet applications. As always, make sure to test your Web applications on actual mobile devices to judge syntactic compatibility and rendering performance (see Chapter 10 for more information about testing Mobile Web applications).

WebKit introduces several CSS extensions to allow styles to specify advanced visual effects in the browser. Several WebKit CSS properties are working their way into upcoming releases of CSS standards. Table 7-2 summarizes some of the most widely used WebKit CSS extensions and their effects. While not all WebKit CSS extensions are implemented in all WebKit-derived mobile browsers, the WebKit CSS extensions in Table 7-2 are all supported in Safari Mobile on the iPhone.

Listing 7-3 is an example Mobile Web document that uses some of the WebKit CSS extensions from Table 7-2 to. Browse to http://learnto.mobi/books/bmwd/07/7-3.xhtml to view this listing in a WebKit mobile browser.

**Table 7-2.** *Selected WebKit CSS Extensions*

| Property Name | Property Value | Description |
|---|---|---|
| `-webkit-background-size` | 1 or 2 integer values in pixels | Sets the size of a background image. |
| `-webkit-border-radius` | Integer value in pixels | Specifies a rounded corner for a box element and sets the radius of the rounded corner. |
| `-webkit-box-shadow` | 2 shadow widths in pixels and a color value | Specifies a drop shadow for the image. |
| `-webkit-transform` | One of several CSS transformation functions | Applies a visual transformation to the element (scales, rotates, translates, and so on). |
| `-webkit-text-size-adjust` | Percentage value | Scales the text by the provided percentage to increase or decrease the text size. |

**Listing 7-3.** *Mobile Web Document that Uses WebKit CSS Extensions*

```
<?xml version="1.0" encoding="UTF-8"?>
<!DOCTYPE html PUBLIC "-//WAPFORUM//DTD XHTML Mobile 1.1//EN"
"http://www.openmobilealliance.org/tech/DTD/xhtml-mobile11.dtd">
<html xmlns="http://www.w3.org/1999/xhtml">
<head>
<meta name="viewport" content="width=device-width,user-scalable=no" />
<title>Listing 7-3: WebKit CSS Extensions</title>
<style type="text/css">
#content {
    width: 89px;
    height: 89px;
    padding: 10px;
    margin: 10px;
    border: 2px solid #333;
    -webkit-border-radius: 5px;
    -webkit-transform: rotate(15deg);
}
#tulips {
    width: 79px;
    height: 79px;
    margin: 5px;
}
</style>
</head>
<body>
<h1>WebKit CSS Extensions</h1>
<div id="content"><img id="tulips" src="tulips.jpg" /></div>
</body>
</html>
```

Figure 7-4 shows a screenshot of the example Mobile Web document in Listing 7-3, as viewed in the Palm Pre and Android emulators. Notice how the WebKit CSS extensions improve the mobile-user experience on smartphones by rounding the border corners of the div element and rotating the tulip image.

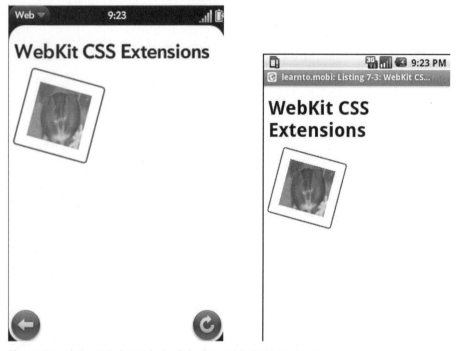

**Figure 7-4.** *Listing 7-3 viewed in the Palm Pre and Android emulators*

Figure 7-5 shows a screenshot of the example Mobile Web document in Listing 7-3, as viewed in Opera Mobile's small screen view, which does not support WebKit CSS extensions. Notice how the Mobile Web page adapts gracefully. The proprietary WebKit extensions are isolated in the style sheet, so the mobile browser simply ignores the unrecognized styles.

## WebKit CSS Extensions

**Figure 7-5.** *Listing 7-3 viewed in the Opera Mobile's small screen view*

# Safari Mobile for iPhone

Safari Mobile is the default Web browser installed on the iPhone. Apple is widely known for eschewing Mobile Web standards on the iPhone and claiming that its browser, unlike any others, supports only Desktop Web standards. It is true that Safari Mobile has no support for the legacy Mobile Web markup language WML, but otherwise Safari Mobile does a good job displaying existing Mobile Web content. This is not a surprise because Safari Mobile uses the same WebKit browser engine that is found in Apple's Safari Desktop Web browser.

The iPhone Dev Center (http://developer.apple.com/iphone/) contains a wealth of information about Web standards, best practices, and Mobile Web development techniques. The iPhone Dev Center requires (free) developer registration to access developer documentation. If you have a Mac OS X computer, you can download and install the iPhone SDK and emulator, which simulates the Safari Mobile browser application. Perhaps the best part about the iPhone Dev Center is the breadth and depth of developer documentation, which indicates a dedication to helping developers understand iPhone design, usability, and technology.

The essential guide to the iPhone for Web developers is the Safari Web Content Guide (http://developer.apple.com/iphone/library/documentation/AppleApplications/Reference/SafariWebContent) in the iPhone OS Reference Library section of iPhone Dev Center. This document provides an iPhone-specific education on Web design, Web development, and the iPhone browser environment. For example, the Safari Web Content Guide shows developers that the iPhone contains ample memory, allowing desktop-style limits on the sizes of Web resources:

- The maximum decoded size of GIF, PNG, and TIFF files is 3MB.
- The maximum decoded size of a JPEG is 32 MB.
- JavaScript, HTML, and CSS files must each be less than 10MB!
- JavaScript can execute for up to ten seconds before being forced to stop.
- Safari Mobile can simultaneously open up to eight Web documents.

**NOTE:** While the iPhone's seemingly limitless upper bounds on Web resource size might be feasible on the device, mobile networks have great difficulty serving Mobile Web content at these sizes. See Chapters 8, 11, 12, and Appendix D for discussions about why serving megabytes of text and binary Web content to a smartphone is unrealistic and impolite on mobile networks and the Mobile Web.

Apple's iPod Touch media player and mobile device is virtually identical to the iPhone, except that it doesn't enable you to access a mobile radio network. Safari Mobile runs identically on the iPhone and iPod Touch. Any iPhone-optimized Web site is also optimized for iPod Touch, provided the Web site recognizes iPod Touch user-agents.

Figure 7-6 shows a screenshot of Safari mobile in the iPhone Simulator, one component of the iPhone SDK.

**Figure 7-6.** *Safari Mobile in the iPhone simulator*

# Browser for Android Mobile Devices

The browser in Android mobile devices uses the Apple version of the WebKit browser engine. (WebKit is described more fully in the "WebKit in Mobile Browsers" section earlier in this chapter.) The WebKit implementation on Android smartphones includes full Web standards support, as well as support for some HTML 5 elements, including local databases, which power offline browsing. All versions of the Android Browser support Google Gears.

Unfortunately for developers, outside of the WebKit documentation available at http://webkit.org, there are few official documents describing the browser functionality in Android OS versions. Developers are left to determine the WebKit version from the device's user-agent string and use this information to deduce the browser's capabilities. Some Android browser documentation is available at the official Android Developers Web site (http://developer.android.com/index.html). This Web site is targeted at developers writing native applications for Android devices, but it does include some useful browser information. Web developers should download and install the free Android SDK to gain access to device and browser emulation.

One of the more helpful Web development tools in the Android SDK is on-device debugging of Mobile Web applications. On-device debugging can be quite useful for resolving JavaScript and AJAX problems that are inconsistent or difficult to reproduce in an emulator.

Install the Android SDK and use the Android Debug Bridge (http://developer.android.com/guide/developing/tools/adb.html) to debug JavaScript running in the browser on an emulator or actual Android mobile device. The Android Debug Bridge connects the Android SDK to a running emulator or mobile device. Once connected, you can view browser debugging and error statements by configuring the Bridge to display debug statements for the WebCore tag. Activate this tag in the Android SDK to cause JavaScript errors and debugging information to output to a console window.

Figure 7-7 shows Google mobile search results in the Android browser in the Android G1 emulator, which is part of the Android SDK.

**Figure 7-7.** *Android browser in the Android G1 emulator*

# webOS Browser for Palm Pre

The webOS browser in the Palm Pre (and Pixi) smartphones uses the WebKit browser engine, which provides broad support for Web standards, as described in the "WebKit in Mobile Browsers" section earlier in this chapter. The webOS browser also supports some HTML5 features, including partial functionality for the canvas element and local databases, the technology that enables offline browsing of Mobile Web applications. In practice, the webOS browser functions similarly to the Safari Mobile browser.

The webOSdev developer community (http://developer.palm.com/) is open to any developer with free registration. You can download webOS emulators and the webOS SDK from the webOSdev community. It also provides documentation and developer blogs about webOS, preinstalled Palm applications (including the webOS browser and mobile development tips), and techniques and best practices. Notably, mobile developers use Web standards to develop native applications for the webOS platform. Your knowledge of XHTML, JavaScript, and CSS Web standards gives you a headstart in learning how to develop rich Web and native applications for webOS devices.

Figure 7-8 shows Yahoo! Mobile search results in the webOS browser in the Palm Pre emulator.

**Figure 7-8.** *webOS browser in Palm Pre emulator*

# BlackBerry Browser

The BlackBerry Browser is embedded in every BlackBerry smartphone. The browser has historically supported only Mobile Web standards (XHTML-MP, WML, and Wireless CSS) and has a reputation for slow performance and delayed innovation. BlackBerry devices are definitely smartphones, but they haven't always had a smartphone-grade browser. That said, Research in Motion (RIM) has done an excellent job of documenting the functionality of the BlackBerry browser for each release of the BlackBerry operating system, so at least the limits of the browser are well-understood.

The BlackBerry Developer Zone (http://na.blackberry.com/eng/developers/) is the mobile developer community for the BlackBerry platform. Research in Motion (RIM) provides extensive platform documentation, tools, emulators, and forums for mobile developers. BlackBerry Browser Documentation (http://docs.blackberry.com/en/developers/subcategories/?userType=21&category=B lackBerry+Browser) is available for several recent platform releases, from version 4.2 to the recently released 5.0 platform.

The BlackBerry Browser has implemented Mobile Web standards since early in the platform's evolution. Until the BlackBerry 4.6 release in 2008, however, full Web standards have been ignored or partially implemented in the browser, causing frustrated mobile developers to route BlackBerry Web requests to streamlined and sparsely featured Mobile Web pages. Even early Mobile Web standards such as Wireless CSS were left partially implemented. If there is a silver lining to this situation, RIM did thoroughly document the partial implementations, allowing interested developers to understand exactly which features were left unsupported.

With the releases of the Bold 9000 in 2008 and the touchscreen Storm 9500 in 2009, version 4.6 of the Blackberry platform includes a browser that finally and fully supports HTML 4.01, JavaScript, DOM Level 2 components, and AJAX. Unfortunately, the relatively recent release of this AJAX-enabled browser for the Blackberry means that many Mobile Web sites still treat all BlackBerry browsers as compliant only with WAP standards.

Despite these issues, the BlackBerry Browser is quite innovative in some ways. For example, since version 4.3, two built-in and proprietary JavaScript objects have provided access to the network type and GPS location of Blackberry devices. The blackberry.network property is a String that specifies the mobile network type currently used by the smartphone. Its value varies according to the connected network, but could be CDMA, EDGE, iDEN, GPRS, or other values. The blackberry.location property is an instance of the Blackberry Location object that provides the GPS coordinates of the smartphones, if GPS is supported on the device. The blackberry.location.GPSSupported property is a Boolean whose value that indicates whether the mobile device supports GPS. The blackberry.location.latitude and blackberry.location.longitude properties provide the GPS coordinates of the smartphone. The Blackberry Location object also provides methods to refresh the GPS location and set the GPS method used to retrieve the handset location. For more details about the blackberry.network and blackberry.location JavaScript objects, review the BlackBerry 4.3 Content Developer's Guide at http://docs.blackberry.com/en/developers/deliverables/1369/BlackBerry_Browser_V ersion_4.3_Content_Developer_Guide.pdf.

Of course, BlackBerry smartphones are designed primarily for enterprise use, so they support many content-delivery protocols that rely on installations of BlackBerry enterprise servers at corporate or mobile network datacenters.

Figure 7-9 shows a screenshot of Google mobile search results in the BlackBerry Browser for the touchscreen BlackBerry Storm 9530; the device runs version 4.7.0 of the BlackBerry mobile platform.

**Figure 7-9.** *Google search results in the Blackberry Storm 9530 emulator for BlackBerry Platform 4.7.0*

## Nokia Web Browser on Series 60 Smartphones

Nokia Series 60 3rd and 5th edition smartphones include the Nokia Web browser that uses a port of the WebKit browser engine to the Series 60 Symbian platform. As mentioned in the "WebKit in Mobile Browsers" section of this chapter, the WebKit browser engine provides Nokia smartphones with rich support for Web standards, including XHTML, JavaScript, AJAX, and Adobe's Flash Lite.

Starting with Series 60 3rd Edition, the Nokia Web Browser has supported Web standards and advanced browsing features such as page layout, scaling, and the ability to open multiple browser windows. AJAX support was added in the Series 60 3rd Edition, Feature Pack 1. Nokia Series 60 5th Edition introduced a touch-enabled user interface, user-controlled page scaling and zooming, full-screen browser display, and browser shortcut keys.

Forum Nokia (http://www.forum.nokia.com) is Nokia's mobile developer community for Web and application development. After registering for the site (which is free), developers can browse and download technical articles, specifications, emulators, and sample code. Nokia Series 60 emulators include all pre-installed mobile applications, including the Nokia Web Browser. You can acquire emulators for each version of the Nokia Series 60 platform (as well as Nokia's other major mobile OS, Series 40).

Look in the Web Technologies (`www.forum.nokia.com/Technology_Topics/Web_Technologies/`) section of Forum Nokia to find information about all Nokia browser technologies, especially the WebKit browser for Series 60 smartphones. The port of WebKit to the Series 60 Symbian platform is an open-source project; you can find project information at http://trac.webkit.org/wiki/S60Webkit. Browse this link to view project status, download the Symbian C++ source code, and learn how to build the WebKit library.

Figure 7-10 shows the Nokia Web Browser running in the Nokia N97 smartphone emulator.

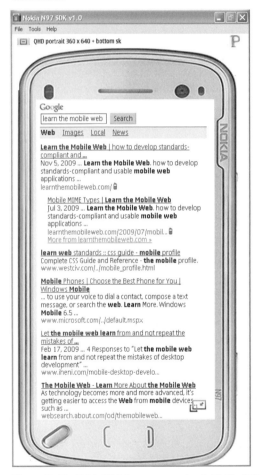

**Figure 7-10.** *Nokia Web browser running in Nokia N97 device emulator for Series 60, 5th Edition Platform*

# Internet Explorer Mobile for Windows Mobile

Internet Explorer Mobile (IE Mobile) is the Web browser installed by default on all Windows Mobile devices. Internet Explorer 6 (which ships with Windows Mobile 6) supports these Web standards:

- **Markup**: HTML 4.01, XHTML 1.0 and 1.1, XHTML MP, XHTML Basic, and WML

- **Style**: CSS 2.1, CSS Mobile Profile 1.0, and Wireless CSS 1.1

- **Scripting**: JScript 5.6 (compatible with ECMAScript 3); DOM 1 and parts of DOM 2 and DOM 3; and AJAX.

- **Other**: Google Gears (IE Mobile 4.01 and later)

Internet Explorer Mobile supports AJAX but handles request object creation in a syntactically different way than other smartphone browsers. For AJAX requests, Internet Explorer Mobile uses the `Microsoft.XMLHTTP` ActiveX object, consistent with other versions of Microsoft Web browsers, but not with non-Microsoft browsers. Internet Explorer Mobile creates an AJAX request object using the following JavaScript statement:

```
var req = new ActiveXObject('Microsoft.XMLHTTP');
```

In contrast to the preceding approach, most mobile browsers create an `XMLHttpRequest` object for AJAX using this JavaScript syntax:

```
var req = new XMLHttpRequest();
```

Listing 5-3 in Chapter 5 shows an example of a cross-browser function that creates an AJAX request using the request object defined for the mobile browser.

The `MobileOptimized` `<meta>` tag is used in Internet Explorer Mobile to indicate that a Web document contains mobile-optimized markup intended for display at a specific screen width. The following example `<meta>` tag sets the preferred screen with to 320 pixels:

```
<meta name="mobileoptimized" content="240" />
```

When Internet Explorer Mobile recognizes the `MobileOptimized` `<meta>` tag, it assumes that the Web document is optimized for mobile devices. It then displays but does not automatically scale the Web page as it would for Desktop Web content. Instead, the browser displays the page in a single column with the width provided in the `content` attribute (see Chapter 12 for more information on the `MobileOptimized` `<meta>` tag, which enables you to indicate that a markup document is optimized for mobile devices.

Microsoft Developer Network (MSDN) provides Internet Explorer Mobile browser documentation and code samples at `http://msdn.microsoft.com/en-us/library/bb159821.aspx`. The MSDN articles cover Internet Explorer Mobile version 6 and earlier.

Increasingly, Windows Mobile devices are shipped to consumers with third-party browsers (such as Opera Mobile) pre-installed as the default browsing application.

Internet Explorer Mobile is still installed on these devices, but it requires the user to navigate a device's application menus to select the browser.

# Opera Mini and Opera Mobile Browsers

Opera is an independent Norwegian software company that develops the Opera desktop browser and two mobile browsers: Opera Mini and Opera Mobile. Opera Mini and Opera Mobile are very different mobile browsers that are targeted at different kinds of mobile devices.

Opera Mini is a thin client browser application written in Java Platform, Micro Edition (Java ME or J2ME) and deployed to mass-market featurephones. The Opera Mini browser is part of a client-server solution that allows mainstream mobile devices to browse any Mobile and Desktop Web site, even when a site uses advanced desktop features that makes it unbrowsable on the device's built-in browser.

The Opera Mini client is widely available for mass-market mobile devices. To the end user, Opera Mini appears to be a desktop Web browser running on her limited mobile phone. However, broad mobile compatibility is possible because Opera Mini is actually a transcoding solution and not a fully functional web-browsing mobile application. The Opera Mini client communicates with an Opera server, which performs the requested Web browsing operation and sends an optimized view of the resulting Web page back to the client. The server translates HTML into Opera Binary Markup Language (OBML— essentially, an image with clickable regions that represent links) and sends the OBML to the client for rendering. Opera Mini supports JavaScript and AJAX, but runs neither on the mobile device. All browser functionality is executed at the server. As you might imagine, this means that Opera Mini supports a JavaScript event model that is limited to events that can be captured and sent to the server for processing. Background processing and timer-initiated JavaScript is not supported.

> **NOTE:** Opera Software has ported Opera Mini to the Android platform. (The Opera Mini application is available for free in Android Market.) In a smartphone context, Opera boasts that its Opera Mini browser saves time and money by using its transcoder to compress Web pages by up to 90%. But in my opinion, a transcoded browser's utility is questionable on Android. This advanced mobile platform includes a powerful WebKit-based mobile browser and typically appeals to smartphone users who are less concerned with bandwidth costs because they pay for flat-rate and unlimited-bandwidth data plans.

Figure 2-19 shows the Web-based Opera Mini emulator available at `www.opera.com/mini/demo/` (requires Java to be installed on the desktop computer). Opera documents JavaScript support in Opera Mini 4 at `http://dev.opera.com/articles/view/javascript-support-in-opera-mini-4/`.

Opera Mobile is entirely different from Opera Mini. Opera Mobile is a standalone, standards-based Web browser for Windows Mobile and Nokia Series 60 mobile devices.

Tabbed browsing, zooming, panning, and touchscreen optimizations make a mobile user's browsing experience fast and familiar. Opera Mobile supports full Web standards, including:

- **Markup**: XHTML 1.0; HTML 4.01 and parts of HTML 5; WML 1.3 and 2.0

- **Style**: CSS 2 and 3

- **Scripting**: JavaScript, DOM Level 2, and AJAX

- **Other**: Google Gears (Opera Mobile 9.5 and later)

Opera does not provide an emulated version of Opera Mobile. If you do not have access to a Windows Mobile or Nokia mobile device, one way to approximate Opera Mobile rendering of Desktop Web pages is to install the desktop Opera browser (www.opera.com/download/). Navigate to a Desktop Web page in Opera and use the View ➤ Small Screen menu command to show the page as rendered by Opera Mobile. Small screen rendering is similar to the actual display in Opera Mobile because the desktop and mobile Opera browsers use the same rendering engine. (Of course, far fewer fonts are available to a mobile browser.)

Figure 7-11 shows a screenshot of Yahoo! mobile search results in the Opera Mini 5 emulator.

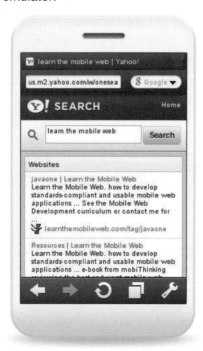

***Figure 7-11.*** *Yahoo! Mobile search results in Opera Mini 5 Emulator*

Figure 7-12 shows an example of Opera's mobile-approximating small screen view of the Learn the Mobile Web desktop site (http://learnthemobileweb.com).

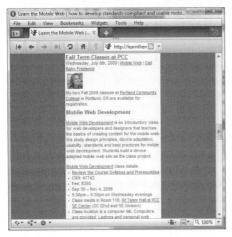

**Figure 7-12.** *Opera's small screen view approximates Web-page rendering in Opera Mobile*

## EXERCISE 7: EXPLORING SMARTPHONE BROWSERS

Use the techniques in the "Common Web Techniques for Smartphone Browsers" and "WebKit in Mobile Browsers" sections of this chapter to enhance an existing Mobile Web page to use Web standards, JavaScript, and CSS extensions supported by the WebKit browser rendering engine. Start with a Web page that complies with mobile standards, and then improve its markup, scripting, and styles with the wider options available in smartphone browsers and WebKit until you are satisfied with its optimized functionality and usability. Try to use some of the WebKit CSS extensions to test their support in mobile browsers. As you go through this exercise, try to do the following:

- View the resulting Mobile Web page on WebKit mobile browsers in iPhone, Android, webOS and Nokia Series 60 devices. Use emulators if actual mobile devices are not available.

- View the resulting Mobile Web page in non-WebKit smartphone browsers such as the BlackBerry browser, Internet Explorer Mobile, and Opera Mobile.

- View the resulting Mobile Web page on WebKit desktop browsers such as Google Chrome and Apple Safari.

Next, answer these questions:

1.  How consistent is the layout and user experience for your Mobile Web page between mobile browsers using WebKit? Between WebKit and non-WebKit mobile browsers? Between mobile and desktop browsers?

2.  How does the use of Web standards and WebKit extensions enhance the usability, performance, and document size of the Mobile Web page?

3.  How gracefully does your smartphone-optimized Mobile Web page display when viewed on mass-market mobile browsers? What changes could you make to safeguard the user experience for these browsers?

# Summary

This chapter introduced you to the advanced features in smartphone browsers that make them especially appealing platforms for rich Mobile Web applications. Smartphone browsers support common markup elements and JavaScript events that enhance the interactivity of Mobile Web content. The powerful WebKit browser engine supports Web standards and is the foundation of the default mobile browsers on many smartphones. The browser engine allows mobile developers to create a single optimized Mobile Web experience that targets iPhone, Android, webOS, and Nokia Series 60 mobile devices.

Mobile browsers on smartphones include varied feature sets and standards implementations. This chapter covered the feature sets of mobile browsers on iPhone, Android, webOS, BlackBerry, Nokia Series 60, and Windows Mobile devices. It explained the differences between two popular mobile browsers by Opera Software: Opera Mini, a transcoded Web experience for mass-market mobile devices; and Opera Mobile, a standards-compliant Web browser for smartphones.

The next chapter discusses post-processing optimizations for Mobile Web markup, styles, scripts, and images to minimize document sizes, maximize performance, and encourage client-side caching in mobile browsers.

# Part IV

# Deploying into the Mobile Ecosystem

By now, your adaptive and standards-compliant Mobile Web site is running, but it may need tuning to ensure the best possible performance on the Mobile Web. Part 4 provides real-world strategies to ensure the survival and adoption of your Mobile Web content.

You'll learn to compress document size, reduce web server transactions, and coerce mobile browsers into caching your Mobile Web content.

You'll validate mobile markup syntax, styles, and overall site readiness using three validation services from W3C and dotMobi.

You'll test your Mobile Web site using mobile browser emulators as well as browsers on actual mobile devices.

You'll deploy your Mobile Web content into the ecosystem and learn how to use a simple script to distinguish between desktop and mobile browser traffic, routing mobile browsers to your optimized Mobile Web site. You'll acquire Mobile Web traffic through search engine submission, advertising, promotions, whitelisting, and mobile SEO.

You'll defensively fortify your Mobile Web site to discourage transcoders from machine-adapting markup that is already optimized for mobile devices. You'll learn to identify when your Mobile Web site encounters traffic from transcoders, and adapt your pages for the device originating the request rather than the transcoder.

Finally, you'll share your Mobile Web and phone expertise by contributing device capabilities, browser test results, and mobile development tips and tricks with the mobile development community.

Chapter **8**

# Optimizing Mobile Markup

By now, you have developed a Mobile Web site that serves mobile markup and adapts content for target mobile devices. After you develop your content, your next step in deploying a real world, Mobile Web application is to optimize the format and delivery of your mobile markup, styles, scripts, and images.

This chapter describes post-processing techniques for mobile markup and Web server optimizations that prepare your Mobile Web content for transmission across mobile networks and maximize the ability of mobile browsers to cache your content. The goal of performing Mobile Web optimizations is to reduce a Web document to its smallest possible file size without disturbing its functionality or introducing extra latency. You also want to deliver the reduced document with caching directives to coerce the mobile browser to cache the file appropriately.

Interestingly, few of the techniques in this chapter are unique to the Mobile Web. You can also use these techniques (except MIME multipart encoding) to optimize desktop Web documents. Advanced desktop Web browsers and broadband Internet connections make such optimizations a nice idea, but unnecessary for all but the most heavily trafficked Web sites. On the desktop, it is simply not sensible to optimize a 40k JPEG image into 10k PNG or a 40k XHTML page into a 10K page; however, on mobile devices, the optimized documents have improved compatibility and performance in mobile browsers and are far more likely to be saved in the browser cache. The simple techniques described in this chapter have immediate benefits on the Mobile Web.

If you are wondering why markup optimizations are necessary on the Mobile Web, especially considering that 3G networks are commonplace and broadband-speed 4G networks are expected in the near future, I will answer by asserting that mobile network bandwidth is limited, costly, and congested. Unsatisfactory latency is routinely experienced on mobile networks. Witness the iPhone effect, the unprecedented level of congestion seen on AT&T's mobile network after record sales of the iPhone. AT&T customers experienced network slowdowns and outages while the operator scrambled to upgrade cell towers and network hardware to handle the dramatic increase in data throughput. Imagine the time savings to iPhone users and cost savings to AT&T if Mobile Web sites serving the iPhone were all optimized to conserve 10% to 25% of the file size of Web documents.

# Post-Processing Techniques for Mobile Markup

Web markup, especially the markup generated by server-side runtime environments (Perl, PHP, Java EE, and so on), is nearly always inflated by unnecessary whitespace, empty tags, unused attributes, duplicated CSS properties, and a large number of linked external resources. Post-processing techniques can distill a Mobile Web document into its essential components and remove extraneous content.

Depending on your choice of runtime framework, these techniques are most likely already available as open-source software libraries. Manually applying post-processing techniques is strongly discouraged due to the likelihood of human error. Instead, you should find or create a software library to post-process your Mobile Web application's markup into its final optimized form.

## Minimize External Resources

The first and most basic optimization for Mobile Web markup documents is to reduce the number of linked external resources. A *linked external resource* is a style sheet, JavaScript library, image, or any other type of file that is embedded into the markup document by linking to the remote file.

Each external resource requires an (expensive and frequently slow) mobile network connection to retrieve the content. Once retrieved, each resource requires browser memory to render and in some cases, file system space to cache.

You can take a handful of steps to minimize the external resources linked to a Mobile Web document:

- Use no more CSS style sheets than absolutely necessary. Ideally, you should use only one.

- Use no more JavaScript libraries than absolutely necessary. Ideally, you should use only one.

- Minimize the number of images in the document and, making sure that every image you use is absolutely necessary for the page design and functionality.

Listing 8–1 provides an example of excessive linking to external resources. It shows a header from the mobile home page for a popular US news magazine. The header links to 10 external CSS files, each of which is less than 1k in file size!

The number of style sheets is not related to the complexity of site design. Using multiple style sheets is a desktop Web development technique that doesn't apply to Mobile Web development. A mobile browser sends ten network requests, one to retrieve each tiny style sheet. (Some mobile browsers open concurrent network requests to speed up downloading of external resources, as you'll see later in this chapter.) Then the browser processes each CSS file, incorporating new and overridden style definitions. The mobile browser might re-render the document after each style sheet is processed, applying the new styles, or it might continue to display the document without styles until all 10 CSS files have been processed.

**Listing 8-1.** *Unoptimized XHTML-MP Header with Linked Stylesheets in Bold*

```
<?xml version="1.0" encoding="iso-8859-1"?>
<!DOCTYPE html PUBLIC "-//WAPFORUM//DTD XHTML Mobile 1.0//EN"
"http://www.wapforum.org/DTD/xhtml-mobile10.dtd">
<html xmlns="http://www.w3.org/1999/xhtml" xml:lang="en">
  <head>

    <link rel="stylesheet" type="text/css" href="css.widget?css=tabpane" />
    <link rel="stylesheet" type="text/css" href="css.widget?css=window" />
    <link rel="stylesheet" type="text/css" href="css.widget?css=slideshow" />
    <link rel="stylesheet" type="text/css" href="css.widget?css=article" />
    <link rel="stylesheet" type="text/css" href="css.widget?css=button" />
    <link rel="stylesheet" type="text/css" href="css.widget?css=menu" />
    <link rel="stylesheet" type="text/css" href="css.widget?css=area" />
    <link rel="stylesheet" type="text/css" href="css.widget?css=list" />
    <link rel="stylesheet" type="text/css" href="css.widget?css=simplelist" />
    <title><!-- Site Name Redacted --></title>
    <link rel="apple-touch-icon" href="apple-touch-icon.png"/>
    <meta http-equiv="Content-Type" content="text/html; charset=iso-8859-1" />

    <link rel="stylesheet" type="text/css" href="css/1008" />
    <script type="text/javascript" src="/scripts/combined.js.h-2010362177.pack"
></script>
  </head>
```

In a mobile browser, processing ten style sheets is up to ten times less efficient than processing a single style sheet. The optimized approach is to centralize all style declarations into a single CSS document and link that as the sole style sheet in the document header.

Listing 8-2 shows the properly optimized header from Listing 8-1. This Web document header centralizes styles in a single external style sheet.

**Listing 8-2.** *Optimized XHTML-MP Header with Linked Style Sheets in Bold*

```
<?xml version="1.0" encoding="iso-8859-1"?>
<!DOCTYPE html PUBLIC "-//WAPFORUM//DTD XHTML Mobile 1.0//EN"
"http://www.wapforum.org/DTD/xhtml-mobile10.dtd">
<html xmlns="http://www.w3.org/1999/xhtml" xml:lang="en">
  <head>

    <link rel="stylesheet" type="text/css" href="styles.css " />
    <title><!-- Site Name Redacted --></title>
    <link rel="apple-touch-icon" href="apple-touch-icon.png"/>
    <meta http-equiv="Content-Type" content="text/html; charset=iso-8859-1" />
    <script type="text/javascript"
        src="/scripts/combined.js.h-2010362177.pack" ></script>
  </head>
```

**NOTE:** Can you find another problem in Listing 8–1? The `<script>` tag is supported starting in XHTML-MP 1.1, a more recent version of the markup format than is declared in the Web document's doctype.

## Remove Whitespace, Comments and Unnecessary Markup

After you've minimize the *number* of external resources in a Mobile Web document, your next step is to optimize the *contents* of Web resources by removing unnecessary comments, whitespace (spaces, tabs, and line breaks), and markup tags and attributes that serve no purpose in the document. Whitespace and comments in Web documents are useful for human readability, but unnecessary for interpretation by desktop or mobile browsers. Often, server-side Web runtime frameworks create unnecessary markup tags and attributes with missing values. XHTML, JavaScript, and CSS documents stripped of unnecessary whitespace, comments, and unused markup function exactly the same in browsers as their human-readable counterparts.

The software industry term for removing unnecessary content from a Web document is *minification*. For example, a CSS document is *minified* when it contains valid syntax and no unnecessary whitespace characters. A *minifier* is a software tool or library that minimizes Web documents by removing unnecessary characters.

Minifiers are available as file-based postprocessors or as core features of the runtime language. For example, the YUI Compressor from Yahoo! (`http://developer.yahoo.com/yui/compressor/`) is a Java tool that minifies CSS and JavaScript. Another popular JavaScript minifier is JSMin from Douglas Crockford (`www.crockford.com/javascript/jsmin.html`); this tool is available in C, C#, Java, Perl, PHP, Objective Caml, Ruby, and even JavaScript. Django templates include a `spaceless` filter that automatically removes whitespace between HTML tags.

**NOTE:** You can find many minifiers available for free on the Web. Search the Web for *minify* and include a file type to find related software libraries. For example you might use the search phrases *minify javascript* or *minify css*.

Whitespace and comments enhance the human-readability of a Web document, improving both the learning and debugging experiences. However, the efficiency costs are high. Whitespace and comments do not affect the structure or presentation of an XHTML document, but they can constitute 30% - 50% of its file size, especially when Web documents are generated by runtime frameworks. On the desktop Web, the developer clarity gained by including whitespace might be beneficial and outweigh efficiency concerns. But on the Mobile Web, unnecessary whitespace and markup, as well as comments of any kind, are extraneous bytes that you should not be transmit across the mobile network.

For XHTML documents, minification means removing all comments and unnecessary whitespace from the document. The following is an example XHTML comment that is functionally unnecessary, but might be helpful to developers. You can remove the comment with no ramifications:

```
<!-- Embed first special directly here. -->
```

The next example shows an XHTML tag with attributes and textual content containing extra whitespace characters:

```
<a      href="#">   market      home     </a>
```

You can minimize this tag to remove the unnecessary whitespace. This simple minification achieves a size savings of 31% by reducing the code from 43 to 28 characters:

```
<a href="#">market home</a>
```

Notice how one character of whitespace is maintained between the words in the link label. A single whitespace character is often intended in text markup elements. Desktop and mobile browsers compress runs of more than one whitespace character to a single character, and so should your optimized markup.

You should also remove line breaks between XHTML tags. For example, you can rewrite the following three lines of unoptimized XHTML markup to remove unnecessary space and line-break characters:

```
<div class="nav">
<a      href="#">   market      home     </a>
</div>
```

Minification causes the XHTML markup to span a single line, achieving a size savings of 27% by reducing the code from 69 to 50 characters:

```
<div class="nav"><a href="#">market home</a></div>
```

Listing 8-3 shows an example of a human-readable and unoptimized XHTML-MP document. It contains line breaks, comments, and extra whitespace for a clean, readable document. From a Mobile Web development perspective, this document contains many unnecessary characters.

**Listing 8-3.** *XHTML-MP Document Before Minification*

```
<?xml version="1.0" encoding="UTF-8"?>
<!DOCTYPE html PUBLIC "-//WAPFORUM//DTD XHTML Mobile 1.1//EN"
"http://www.openmobilealliance.org/tech/DTD/xhtml-mobile11.dtd">
<html xmlns="http://www.w3.org/1999/xhtml">
<head>
<link rel="stylesheet" href="/styles.css" type="text/css" />
<title>Produce Specials</title>
</head>
<body>
<h1 class="hdr">Weekly Specials</h1>
<p>Sunset Farmers&apos; Market has weekly produce specials! Click the image below to see
this week&apos; specials.</p>
<div class="content">
<!-- Embed first special directly here. -->
```

```
<img id="theImg" src="raspberries.jpg" alt="Produce Specials"/>
<div id="theText">$2.50 per pint</div>
</div>
<div class="nav">
<a href="#">   market      home      </a>
</div>
</body>
</html>
```

Listing 8-4 shows the XHTML-MP document from Listing 8-3 after you minify its markup. The documents are functionally identical. Listing 8-4 achieves a 12% size efficiency, reducing the document from 766 to 674 characters. The more bloated the unoptimized document is with comments and whitespace, the greater the size savings you can achieve with minification.

**Listing 8-4.** *XHTML-MP Document After Minification*

```
<?xml version="1.0" encoding="UTF-8"?><!DOCTYPE html PUBLIC "-//WAPFORUM//DTD
XHTML Mobile 1.1//EN" "http://www.openmobilealliance.org/tech/DTD/xhtml-
mobile11.dtd"><html xmlns="http://www.w3.org/1999/xhtml"><head><link
rel="stylesheet" href="/styles.css" type="text/css" /><title>Produce
Specials</title></head><body><h1 class="hdr">Weekly Specials</h1><p>Sunset
Farmers&apos; Market has weekly produce specials! Click the image below to see
this week&apos; specials.</p><div class="content"><img id="theImg"
src="raspberries.jpg" alt="Produce Specials"/><div id="theText">$2.50 per
pint</div></div><div class="nav"><a href="#">market home</a></div></body>
</html>
```

For CSS documents, minification means removing unnecessary comments and whitespace, as well as and limiting style declarations to styles used in the Mobile Web document or application. If your Mobile Web content uses external CSS files, you should include the style declarations used across as many documents in the site as possible. This allows a minimum number of CSS files to be downloaded, cached in the mobile browser, and efficiently shared across multiple markup documents. If your Mobile Web content uses internal style sheets, you should include only the style declarations used in the current Web document. Internal CSS is scoped to the document, so you have no reason to include styles not referenced in the markup.

Minification can also include shortening CSS selectors to lengths of one or two characters. This technique minimizes the amount of XHTML markup used to reference commonly used style names. The following snippet shows an example unoptimized CSS style declaration that spans multiple lines, includes extra whitespace, and has a long name:

```
.myLongStyleName {
    margin: 5px;
    padding: 5px;
    font-size: small;
    font-style: italic;
}
```

In the next example, you minimize the style name and declaration, achieving a size savings of 53% (reducing the code from 96 to 45 characters):

```
.m{margin:5px;padding:5px;font:italic small;}
```

This example markup references the unoptimized style name:

```
<div class="myLongStyleName">...</div><div
    class="myLongStyleName">...</div><div
    class="myLongStyleName">...</div>
```

The markup is more efficient when it references the shortened style name, achieving a size savings of 37% (reducing the code from 123 to 78 characters):

```
<div class="m">...</div><div class="m">...</div><div class="m">...</div>
```

When you implement CSS minification that changes selectors, make sure that you update the style declaration and all markup that references the style by name. Also, be sure to coordinate with your Web designer to ensure a consistent transition to optimized CSS style names in Web application mock-ups and the source code. Finally, you should be aware of conventions used by external JavaScript libraries, which almost always use IDs and class names to select elements.

Listing 8-5 shows an unoptimized CSS style sheet that spans multiple lines and includes extra whitespace.

**Listing 8-5.** *CSS Before Minification*

```
.nav {
    margin: 3px;
}
.hdr {
    margin: 5px;
    font-weight: bold;
}
.content {
    margin: 2px auto;
    text-align: center;
}
// Use for the main image associated with an article
#theImg {
    background-color:#777;
    margin:5px;
    padding:2px;
    border: 1px solid #000;
}
#theText {
    margin:5px;
    padding:5px;
    font: italic small;
}
```

Listing 8-6 minifies the style sheet in Listing 8-5 by removing comments, whitespace and shortening style names. It achieves a 47% savings in file size (reducing from 378 to 201 characters) when compared to Listing 8-5.

**Listing 8-6.** *CSS After Minification*

```
.n{margin:3px;}.h{margin:5px;font-weight:bold;}.c{margin:2px auto;text-
align:center;}#i{background-color:#777;margin:5px;padding:2px;border:1px solid
#000;}#t{margin:5px;padding:5px;font:italic small;}
```

JavaScript minification uses the same techniques as CSS minification. Comments and unnecessary whitespace are removed, and wherever possible, JavaScript function and variable names are shortened to one or two characters.

Minification drastically reduces the human readability of JavaScript, which complicates debugging and can cause scripting bugs to avoid detection. Before minifying, make sure that all JavaScript statements are properly terminated using a semicolon, so that no line breaks are semantically relevant. *You should minify JavaScript only after you've completed functional testing of the unoptimized libraries.* Minification changes variable and function names, so minified JavaScript will have an updated interface, requiring modifications in markup documents that use scripting. A less risky alternative is to minify JavaScript syntax without changing the names of variables and functions. Software libraries that implement JavaScript minification include options for choosing how aggressively to minimize script file size. After minification, you should comprehensively retest the libraries and updated markup on all targeted mobile browsers.

Listing 8-7 shows an unoptimized JavaScript file that includes extra whitespace, line breaks, and human-readable variable and function names.

**Listing 8-7.** *JavaScript Before Minification*

```
// The list of our images
var imgs = new Array();
imgs[0] = "blackberries.jpg";
imgs[1] = "pumpkins.jpg";
imgs[2] = "raspberries.jpg";
imgs[3] = "tulips.jpg";

// The list of special prices.
var specials = new Array();
specials[0] = "blackberries: $2.50 per pint";
specials[1] = "pumpkins: $.45 per lb - this week only";
specials[2] = "raspberries: $4.00 per pint";
specials[3] = "flowers: $5.00 per dozen";

// The number of specials
var numSpecials = 4;

// Index of current special
var currentSpecial = 0;

/// This is the onClick event handler
function handleOnClick() {
        // Increment the current special.
        currentSpecial = (currentSpecial + 1) % numSpecials;

        // Get the new image URL and specials text
        var newSrc = imgs[currentSpecial];
        var newTxt = specials[currentSpecial];

        // Update the image URL and specials text in the document
        document.getElementById("theImg").src = newSrc;
        document.getElementById("theText").innerHTML = newTxt;
}
```

Listing 8-8 minifies the script in Listing 8-7 by removing comments, whitespace, and shortening style names. It achieves a 38% savings in file size (reducing the code from 411 to 255 characters) compared to Listing 8-7.

**Listing 8-8.** *JavaScript After Minification*

```
var is=new Array();is[0]="blackberries.jpg";is[1]="pumpkins.jpg";is[2]=
"raspberries.jpg";is[3]="tulips.jpg";var sp=new Array();sp[0]="blackberries:
$2.50 per pint";sp[1]="pumpkins: $.45 per lb - this week only";sp[2]=
"raspberries:$4.00 per pint";sp[3]="flowers: $5.00 per dozen";var ns=4;
var cs=0;function hoc(){cs=(cs+1)%ns;var ni=is[cs];var nt=sp[cs];document.
getElementById("theImg").src=ni;document.getElementById("theText").innerHTML=
nt;}
```

Listing 8-8 illustrates an important point: if you minimize the CSS, you might also need to update element identifiers such as theText in JavaScript.

The minification techniques explored so far in this chapter optimize Web documents containing a single type of Web content. However, you can also apply minification to an XHTML document that embeds internal CSS and JavaScript. Listing 8-9 is a Mobile Web document that includes markup, styles, and scripting in a single file, while Listing 8-10 implements all the minification techniques described in this chapter to reduce the file size of Listing 8-9 as much as possible.

You can view the effect achieved by Listing 8-9 in a mobile browser at http://learnto.mobi/books/bmwd/08/8-9.xhtml.

**Listing 8-9.** *XHTML-MP Document with Internal CSS and JavaScript Before Minification*

```
<?xml version="1.0" encoding="UTF-8"?>
<!DOCTYPE html PUBLIC "-//WAPFORUM//DTD XHTML Mobile 1.1//EN"
"http://www.openmobilealliance.org/tech/DTD/xhtml-mobile11.dtd">
<html xmlns="http://www.w3.org/1999/xhtml">
<head>
<title>Produce Specials</title>
<style type="text/css">
.nav {
    margin: 3px;
}
.hdr {
    margin: 5px;
    font-weight: bold;
}
.content {
    margin: 2px auto;
    text-align: center;
}
#theImg {
    background-color:#777777;
    margin:5px;
    padding:2px;
    border-width: 1px;
    border-style: solid;
    border-color: #000000;
}
#theText {
    margin:5px;
```

```
        padding:5px;
        font-size: small;
        font-style: italic;
}
</style>
<script type="text/javascript">
// The list of our images
var imgs = new Array();
imgs[0] = "blackberries.jpg";
imgs[1] = "pumpkins.jpg";
imgs[2] = "raspberries.jpg";
imgs[3] = "tulips.jpg";

// The list of special prices.
var specials = new Array();
specials[0] = "blackberries: $2.50 per pint";
specials[1] = "pumpkins: $.45 per lb - this week only";
specials[2] = "raspberries: $4.00 per pint";
specials[3] = "flowers: $5.00 per dozen";

// The number of specials
var numSpecials = 4;

// Index of current special
var currentSpecial = 0;

/// This is the onLoad event handler
function handleOnClick() {
    // Increment the current special.
    currentSpecial = (currentSpecial + 1) % numSpecials;

    // Get the new image URL and specials text
    var newSrc = imgs[currentSpecial];
    var newTxt = specials[currentSpecial];

    // Update the image URL and specials text in the document
    document.getElementById("theImg").src = newSrc;
    document.getElementById("theText").innerHTML = newTxt;
}
</script>
</head>
<body>
<h1 class="hdr">Weekly Specials</h1>
<p>Sunset Farmers&apos; Market has weekly produce specials! Click the image
below to see this week&apos;s specials.</p>
<!-- Embed first special directly here. -->
<div class="content">
<img id="theImg" src="raspberries.jpg" alt="Produce Specials"
onclick="handleOnClick();"/>
<div id="theText">$2.50 per pint</div>
</div>
<div class="nav">
<a href="#">   market      home    </a>
</div>
</body>
</html>
```

Listing 8–10 shows the minified XHTML-MP document from Listing 8-9. It minifies the previous listing's markup, styles, and scripting. It achieves a 37% savings in file size compared to the code in Listing 8-9 (reducing the code from 2074 to 1309 characters), with no loss of functionality or browser compatibility. Listing 8-10 is one long line that wraps across multiple lines when printed in this book. You can view it in a mobile browser at http://learnto.mobi/books/bmwd/08/8-10.xhtml.

**Listing 8-10.** *XHTML-MP Document with Internal CSS and JavaScript After Minification*

```
<?xml version="1.0" encoding="UTF-8"?><!DOCTYPE html PUBLIC "-//WAPFORUM//DTD
XHTML Mobile 1.1//EN" "http://www.openmobilealliance.org/tech/DTD/xhtml-mobile11.dtd">
<html xmlns="http://www.w3.org/1999/xhtml"><head><title>Produce Specials</title><style
type="text/css">.n{margin:3px;}.h{margin:5px;font-
weight:bold;}.c{margin:2px auto;text-align:center;}#i{background-color:#777;
margin:5px;padding:2px;border:1px solid #000;}#t{margin:5px;padding:5px;font-
size:italic small;}</style><script type="text/javascript">var is=new Array();
is[0]="blackberries.jpg";is[1]="pumpkins.jpg";
is[2]="raspberries.jpg";is[3]=
"tulips.jpg";var sp=new Array();sp[0]="blackberries: $2.50 per pint";sp[1]=
"pumpkins: $.45 per lb - this week only";sp[2]="raspberries: $4.00 per pint";
sp[3]="flowers: $5.00 per dozen";var ns=4;var cs=0;function hoc()
{cs=(cs+1)
%ns;var nr=is[cs];var nt=sp[cs];document.getElementById("i").src=nr;
document.getElementById("t").innerHTML=nt;}</script></head><body><h1 class=
"h">Weekly Specials</h1><p>Sunset Farmers&apos; Market has weekly produce
specials! Click the image below to see this week&apos;s specials.</p><div class="c"><img
id="i" src="raspberries.jpg" alt="Produce Specials" onclick=
"hoc();"/><div id="t">$2.50 per pint</div></div><div class="n"><a href="#">
market home</a></div></body></html>
```

Markup, style and scripting minification techniques are powerful and capable of reducing the file-size footprint of Web documents by 50% or more. This simple post-processing technique should be in the toolset of every Mobile Web developer.

# Adapt and Transcode Images

Once you optimize your markup and text resources, the next post-processing step is to review images for adaptation and transcoding opportunities. You can adapt images in two ways. First, you can reduce them to the smallest possible file size. Second, you can transcode them into the best format supported in the mobile browser.

You can take several actions to optimize the format and size of an image. First, you can reduce the dimensions of the image. You should consider the design of your Mobile Web site, evaluating whether the image dimensions are appropriate or you can reduce them without impacting your site's readability or usability.

Second, you can reduce the number of colors you use in your images. Device databases report the number of colors supported by the mobile device display hardware. (See Chapter 4 for information about device databases.) You should use images that contain the same number of colors (or fewer) than supported by the device, and you might consider providing multiple versions of an image to target varied display strengths. An experienced graphic designer can modify the image design to reduce the number of colors, while minimizing the impact to an image's quality.

Third, you can use image compression to reduce the file size. Image manipulation software and/or an experienced graphic designer can remove optional information in the image file (comments, author information, unused palette colors, and so on) and compress the image bytes using compression methods supported by the image format. As image compression increases, image quality decreases, so you must strike a balance between optimizing for file size and visual quality.

Once you optimize your images to reduce their file sizes, you might find you also need to transcode them into the best format supported in the mobile browser. Today's mobile browsers support PNG, GIF, and JPG image formats. If your Mobile Web application targets only recent mobile devices, you most likely do not need to worry about image transcoding. However, older mobile devices, many of which are still used to browse the Mobile Web, might not adequately support all three formats. You can use a device database to determine image format support in mobile browsers.

You can choose static or on-the-fly methods for image resizing and transcoding. Static transcoding means that an image is saved in multiple sizes and formats. The server-side Web runtime language consults a device database to determine the best image format for the device and modifies image URLs to reference the static image in the most appropriate format. Static transcoding is appropriate for images whose contents rarely change, such as logos, headers, and footers.

On-the-fly image transcoding employs a modified version of a caching proxy server (such as the GAIA Image Transcoder at `http://gaia-git.sourceforge.net/` or tinySrc, which you can find at `http://tinysrc.net/`) to transcode a static image into the best format for the mobile browser. The image server transcodes the image and caches the transcoded versions for later reuse. In the Mobile Web document, you restructure image URLs to request an optimized version of a static image from the transcoder by either suggesting a target image format or trusting the proxy server to choose the best format for the device. On-the-fly image transcoding is appropriate for dynamic images, such as news and entertainment photos.

## MIME Multipart Encoding of a Response Document

Many featurephone browsers that implement WAP 2.0 (XHTML-MP and mobile CSS subsets) support MIME multipart, an envelope standard borrowed from email, to encapsulate a markup document and all dependent resources into a single-server response. WAP browsers with lean feature sets might not support Web markup standards or client-side scripting, but they often support MIME multipart as a method of improving browser performance by delivering a Web page together with its dependent resources in a single network request. This optimization reduces network latency and increases browser rendering speed.

Support for MIME multipart depends on the mobile browser. If you implement this featurephone browser optimization in your Mobile Web site, make sure that you use a device database and on-device testing to produce MIME multipart envelopes only for supported browsers (see Chapter 4 for information about device databases and Chapter 10 for information about testing mobile browsers).

MIME multipart encapsulation is a legacy technique used to speed up Mobile Web rendering on older mobile devices, some of which still browse the Mobile Web in significant numbers. MIME multipart is *not* a viable encapsulation technique for smartphone browsers. gzip response compression and client-side caching are preferred for advanced devices (see the next section for more information about gzip response compression).

The content type for a Web page encapsulated with MIME multipart is multipart/related. Some mobile browsers recognize multipart content using the multipart/mixed content type, which is technically incorrect, but more widely seen in Accept request headers from mobile devices. Using the multipart/mixed content type in a multipart server response might bring wider compatibility with mobile browsers, despite the technical incorrectness. RFC 2387 (http://tools.ietf.org/html/rfc2387) defines the structure of a MIME multipart/related content type.

> **NOTE:** An RFC is a technical document governed by the Internet Engineering Task Force (IETF) that defines an Internet standard or best practice.

In a MIME multipart Web response, the Web server sends one of two content types in the Content-Type HTTP response header and includes a token that marks the boundary between encapsulated documents. The following snippets show examples of the two variants of response header using bndry as the boundary token. Of course, only one Content-Type header is allowed in an HTTP response header:

```
Content-Type: multipart/mixed; boundary=bndry
Content-Type: multipart/related; boundary=bndry
```

The HTTP response body contains multiple content documents that you combine into a single Web document. You delimit the boundary between documents using a newline followed by the boundary token on its own line. In this Web response, the delimiter has the following format:

```
--bndry
```

You follow each boundary token with MIME headers describing the document, followed by a newline and the document contents. Table 8–1 lists the MIME headers that are allowed at the top of each document section. For more details about MIME content headers, see documentation at http://www2.roguewave.com/support/docs/leif/sourcepro/html/protocolsug/10-1.html and links to related RFCs.

**Table 8-1.** *MIME Headers Allowed in Sections of MIME Multipart Web Documents*

| HTTP Header Name | Header Value Description | Example Header Values |
| --- | --- | --- |
| Content-Type | MIME type of the resource | text/html<br>image/jpg |
| Content-ID | Unique ID of the resource in the Web response | part100@mydomain.com<br>100 |
| Content-Description | Textual description of the resource | Comments about Sunset Farmers' Market |
| Content-Transfer-Encoding | Encoding of the resource | base64 |
| Content-Location | Local name of the resource: You use this to link across resources in a multipart document. | comments.txt<br>pumpkins.jpg |
| Content-Disposition | Description of how to display the resource in the document: The inline value indicates a mobile browser should display an image normally, while the attachment value indicates the image should be displayed by an external application or user-initiated action. | Inline attachment |

The example that follows is a section in a MIME multipart document that encapsulates a text document. Notice the boundary delimiter, content headers, and text body. You construct a MIME multipart response by appending several document sections into a single Web response. One document links to a resource in another document section using the name provided as the value of the Content-Location MIME header:

```
--bndry
Content-Type: text/plain
Content-ID: 100
Content-Description: Comments about Sunset Farmers' Market
Content-Location: comments.txt
I enjoyed my afternoon at the Sunset Farmers' Market. I found two beautiful
bouquets of flowers to adorn our dining table. The produce was fresh and
bountiful. We enjoyed meeting the farmers directly and even signed up for a CSA!
```

Let's examine a complete Web document and externally linked images encapsulated using a MIME multipart envelope. Listing 8-11 is the example Web document. It is similar to Listing 8-9 but does not include JavaScript for the sake of brevity (this document is wrapped in a MIME multipart envelope in Listing 8-13).

**Listing 8-11.** *Example XHTML-MP Document with Two Externally Linked Resources*

```
<?xml version="1.0" encoding="UTF-8"?>
<!DOCTYPE html PUBLIC "-//WAPFORUM//DTD XHTML Mobile 1.0//EN"
"http://www.wapforum.org/DTD/xhtml-mobile10.dtd">
<html xmlns="http://www.w3.org/1999/xhtml">
<head>
<title>Produce Specials</title>
<style type="text/css">
.nav { margin: 3px; }
.hdr { margin: 5px; font-weight: bold; }
.content { margin: 2px auto; text-align: center; }
.specialImg { background-color:#777777; margin:5px; padding:2px;
 border-width: 1px; border-style: solid; border-color: #000000; }
.specialTxt { margin:5px; padding:5px; font-size: small; font-style: italic; }
</style>
</head>
<body>
<h1 class="hdr">Weekly Specials</h1>
<p>Sunset Farmers&apos; Market has weekly produce specials! Click the image
below to see this week&apos;s specials.</p>
<div class="content">
<!-- First special. -->
<img class="specialImg" src="raspberries.jpg" alt="Raspberries"/>
<div class="specialTxt">$2.50 per pint</div>
<!-- Second special. -->
<img class="specialImg" src="pumpkins.jpg" alt="Pumpkins"/>
<div class="specialTxt">$.45 per lb - this week only</div>
</div>
<div class="nav">
<a href="#">market home</a>
</div>
</body>
</html>
```

Listing 8-12 contains the HTTP response headers sent by an Apache Web server when responding with the document shown in Listing 8-13.

**Listing 8-12.** *HTTP Response Headers for MIME Multipart Envelope*

```
HTTP/1.x 200 OK
Date: Fri, 16 Oct 2009 21:17:58 GMT
Server: Apache/2.0.46 (Red Hat)
X-Powered-By: PHP/5.2.5
Connection: close
Transfer-Encoding: chunked
Content-Type: multipart/mixed; boundary=bndry
```

Listing 8-13 shows the Web document from Listing 8-11 wrapped in a MIME multipart envelope; it combines the markup document and two linked images in a single Web response. You can browse to `http://learnto.mobi/books/bmwd/08/8-13.php` to view Listing 8-13 in a mobile browser that supports MIME multipart.

**NOTE:** For readability, the base-64 encoded image data for `raspberries.jpg` and `pumpkins.jpg` have been truncated in Listing 8-13. You can view the source code of `http://learnto.mobi/books/bmwd/08/8-13.php` to see the complete image encoding.

**Listing 8-13.** *Example XHTML-MP Document in MIME Multipart Envelope*

```
--bndry
Content-Type: application/vnd.wap.xhtml+xml
Content-ID: 100
Content-Location: 8-13.xhtml

<?xml version="1.0" encoding="UTF-8"?>
<!DOCTYPE html PUBLIC "-//WAPFORUM//DTD XHTML Mobile 1.0//EN"
"http://www.wapforum.org/DTD/xhtml-mobile10.dtd">
<html xmlns="http://www.w3.org/1999/xhtml">
<head>
<title>Produce Specials</title>
<style type="text/css">
.nav { margin: 3px; }
.hdr { margin: 5px; font-weight: bold; }
.content { margin: 2px auto; text-align: center; }
.specialImg { background-color:#777777; margin:5px; padding:2px;
border-width: 1px; border-style: solid; border-color: #000000; }
.specialTxt { margin:5px; padding:5px; font-size: small; font-style: italic; }
</style>
</head>
<body>
<h1 class="hdr">Weekly Specials</h1>
<p>Sunset Farmers&apos; Market has weekly produce specials! Click
the image below to see this week&apos;s specials.</p>

<div class="content">
<!-- First special. -->
<img class="specialImg" src="raspberries.jpg" alt="Raspberries"/>
<div class="specialTxt">$2.50 per pint</div>
<!-- Second special. -->
<img class="specialImg" src="pumpkins.jpg" alt="Pumpkins"/>
<div class="specialTxt">$.45 per lb - this week only</div>
</div>
<div class="nav">
<a href="#">market home</a>
</div>
</body>
</html>

--bndry
Content-Type: image/jpeg
Content-ID: 101
Content-Location: raspberries.jpg
Content-Transfer-Encoding: base64
```

/9j/4QRERXhpZgAASUkqAAgAAAAKAA8BAgAGAAAAhgAAABABAgAUAAAAjAAAABIBAwABAAAAAQAAA
BoBBQABAAAAoAAAABsBBQABAAAAqAAAACgBAwABAAAAgAAADEBAgApAAAAsAAAADIBAgAVAAAA2g
AAABMCAwABAAAAAQAAAGmHBAABAAAA8AAAAAAAAABDYW5vbgBDYW5vbiBQb3dlclNob3QgQTgwALQ
AAAABAAAAtAAAAAEAAABQYWludCBTaG9wIFBybyBQaG90byQqOb0iOc9rFgIQSrGu2NS5Fmh/hyx

```
liDShhlves5u5nJ3P//Z

--bndry
Content-Type: image/jpeg
Content-ID: 102
Content-Location: pumpkins.jpg
Content-Transfer-Encoding: base64

/9j/4QRERXhpZgAASUkqAAgAAAAKAA8BAgAGAAAAhgAAABABAgAUAAAAjAAAABIBAwABAAAAAQAAA
BoBBQABAAAAoAAAABsBBQABAAAAqAAAACgBAwABAAAAAgAAADEBAgApAAAAsAAAADIBAgAVAAAA2g
AAABMCAwABAAAAAQAAAGmHBAABAAAA8AAAAAAAAABDYW5vbgBDYW5vbiBQb3dlclNob3QQgQTgwALQ
AAAABAAAAtAAAAAEAAABQYWludCBTaG9wIFBybyBQaG90b09+Fev7Km48i2PnZ1a3Pzz3I2mFxdSzXAP
mSHLEEmtYRUYpIwlLmd7H//Z
```

The MIME Multipart document in Listing 8-13 is divided into three sections. Each is delimited with a line break and the `--bndry` delimiter. After each delimiter token, content headers define the MIME type, ID, filename, and encoding of the content. Next, a line break separates the headers and the content body.

# Web Server Optimizations for Mobile Browsers

Web servers can optimize the delivery of Web content across mobile networks by minimizing the number of bytes transferred for a Web response and using response headers that encourage client-side caching of Web content. Smartphone and other mobile browsers can unpack and display Web documents compressed using `gzip` or `deflate` algorithms. Compressing a text Web document can significantly reduce its file size, thus speeding its transmission across a mobile network. Web servers can also annotate Web documents with caching directives in the HTTP response headers to inform a mobile browser whether and for how long a document should be cached.

## gzip or deflate Response Compression

Apache, IIS and other Web servers can be configured to compress text Web documents using the `gzip` or `deflate` compression algorithms, if requested by the mobile browser. Compressing text documents is extremely effective for optimizing the number of bytes transmitted from server to browser. For the best Mobile Web performance, mobile markup, CSS, scripts, XML, and JSON documents should all be compressed by the Web server. Images, audio, video, and other multimedia documents generally do not benefit from response compression because, for many, compression is intrinsic in their file formats.

A mobile (or desktop) browser requests compressed responses from a Web server using the `Accept-Encoding` HTTP request header. Valid values for the `Accept-Encoding` request header include a comma-delimited list of compression algorithms supported in the browser, which includes the values `gzip` and `deflate`. The `identity` value is optionally used to indicate that uncompressed responses are supported, but this fact is assumed by the Web server. The example that follows is an `Accept-Encoding` request header that declares that the mobile browser supports `gzip` and `deflate` compression. The order of values implies the browser's preference. The browser that provides the request header that follows prefers gzip response compression, but it can also accept deflate compression (gzip compression is much more commonly used):

```
Accept-Encoding: gzip, deflate
```

If a browser requests compression and the Web server is configured to enable it, then the browser might compress the HTTP response using one of the algorithms in the Accept-Encoding request header. Note that the Web server is not obligated to compress the response before sending it to the browser. For example, the server might always send an uncompressed response unless expressly forbidden by the client. The server indicates that a response is compressed by sending a Content-Encoding HTTP response header, the value of which is the compression algorithm used on the response body. The following example shows a response header that indicates the response is compressed using gzip:

```
Content-Encoding: gzip
```

## Apache Web Server Configuration

The Apache 2 Web server enables response compression using the mod_deflate module. You can add mod_deflate to Apache configuration for a virtual host, directory, or location. The mod_deflate module adds a DEFLATE output filter to compress response documents.

To enable response compression by MIME type, you use the AddOutputFilterByType directive to enable the DEFLATE output filter for a list of MIME types. Apache does not distinguish between static and dynamic Web content in mod_deflate configuration; it only cares about the MIME type of the response.

Listing 8–14 shows the Apache configuration used to enable response compression for text file formats in one directory on the http://learnto.mobi web site.

**Listing 8-14.** *Apache 2 Web Server Configuration for Response Compression by URI Location*

```
# Enable response compression for the /books/bmwd/08/compressed directory.
<Location /books/bmwd/08/compressed>
AddOutputFilterByType DEFLATE text/html text/plain text/xml
application/vnd.wap.xhtml+xml application/xhtml+xml text/javascript
application/javascript text/css
</Location>
```

Apache's mod_deflate module provides detailed configuration options. It can selectively disable response compression by file type and for browser user-agents. It can also notify proxy servers that the Web response varies with the Accept-Encoding request header. (For detailed configuration documentation for mod_deflate, see http://httpd.apache.org/docs/2.0/mod/mod_deflate.html.)

To view response compression in action on an Apache 2 Web server, browse to http://learnto.mobi/books/bmwd/08/compressed/8-11.xhtml in a desktop or mobile browser. This document is Listing 8–11 with response compression enabled. The following excerpt from the HTTP response headers indicates that the document is compressed using the gzip algorithm, and that the compressed response size is 620 bytes:

```
HTTP/1.x 200 OK
Server: Apache/2.0.46 (Red Hat)
Content-Encoding: gzip
Content-Length: 620
Content-Type: application/xhtml+xml
```

You can view the uncompressed document at http://learnto.mobi/books/bmwd/08/ 8-11.xhtml. The following excerpt from the HTTP response headers indicates that the document is not compressed, and that the response size is 1136 bytes:

```
HTTP/1.x 200 OK
Server: Apache/2.0.46 (Red Hat)
Content-Length: 1139
Content-Type: application/xhtml+xml
```

gzip response compression reduced the response size by 45% (from 1136 to 620 bytes). This size reduction is comparable to the markup post-processing techniques described earlier in the chapter, but it does require some overhead at the Web server and browser client.

## Microsoft IIS Web Server Configuration

The Microsoft IIS Web server supports gzip and deflate compression algorithms. It separates response compression configuration for static and dynamic Web content. IIS enables compression for static HTML files by default, but it requires manual configuration to compress additional static file types and dynamic Web content.

In IIS, compressed versions of static Web documents are cached in a configurable directory location. This helps to speed up subsequent requests for the compressed file. Compressed versions of dynamic Web documents are not cached to disk on the Web server.

The example that follows is an example of IIS 7.0 command-line configuration for static-response compression. Here, compression is enabled for XHTML-MP documents. You call this command once for each MIME type (in bold) for the desired response compression. You toggle the value of the enabled parameter (in bold) from True to False to enable or disable compression:

```
appcmd.exe set config -section:system.webServer/httpCompression
/+" staticTypes.[mimeType='application/vnd.wap.xhtml+xml',enabled='True']"
/commit:apphost
```

Similarly, the example that follows shows command-line configuration for dynamic response compression for dynamic XHTML-MP documents:

```
appcmd.exe set config -section:system.webServer/httpCompression
/+" dynamicTypes.[mimeType='application/vnd.wap.xhtml+xml',enabled='True']"
/commit:apphost
```

For screenshots and additional details about configuring response compression in IIS 7.0, see www.iis.net/ConfigReference/system.webServer/httpCompression. To

configure response compression in IIS 6.0 using the metabase, start at
http://search.microsoft.com and search for *Using HTTP Compression for Faster Downloads*. The page you want is called, "Using HTTP Compression for Faster Downloads (IIS 6.0)."

> **NOTE:** The deflate compression algorithm is specified in RFC 1951
> (http://tools.ietf.org/html/rfc1951). See www.zlib.net/feldspar.html for a
> helpful explanation of the algorithm. The gzip compression format is derived from the deflate
> standard. For more information about the gzip algorithm, see
> www.gzip.org/algorithm.txt.

# Caching Directives in HTTP Response Headers

The HTTP 1.1 standard defines headers that specify whether you can cache certain Web documents and indicates when cached documents expire. To optimize the delivery of Mobile Web content, you can control the response headers (sent from a Web server to a browser or proxy server client) that specify whether and for how long a Web document should be cached by the browser. Caching headers by server and client properly reduces the number and size of expensive network round-trips required to display a Mobile Web document. On the other hand, some mobile browsers with AJAX functionality aggressively cache documents obtained asynchronously, forcing developers to use caching headers to forbid the caching of dynamic server responses.

This section specifies the HTTP response headers sent by a Web server to declare caching rules to a client. The next section investigates the implementations of client caches in smartphone browsers.

## The Date HTTP Header

The Date header in an HTTP response simply reports the date and time of the server response. Web clients can use the Date response header in cache expiration calculations for Web content. It is included automatically in every Web response in IIS and Apache Web servers.

This Date response header example shows the date in HTTP-date format. All dates in HTTP response headers must be specified in Greenwich Mean Time (GMT):

```
Date: Sat, 17 Oct 2009 01:44:49 GMT
```

## The Last-Modified HTTP Header

The Last-Modified header in an HTTP response reports the date and time that the response document was last modified. Its value is an HTTP-date in the same format that the Date header uses. The meaning of the last-modified date can vary according to the Web content. For static documents, the date used is the last-modified date of the file on the Web server's file system. For dynamic Web documents, the date used could be the current system time or the most recent date that a component of the document was changed. The Last-Modified header is included automatically in every Web response in IIS and Apache Web servers. Web clients can use the response header in cache expiration calculations.

The following Last-Modified example is for a document where the contents have not changed since 1989:

```
Last-Modified: Mon, 02 Oct 1989 22:49:17 GMT
```

## The Expires HTTP Header

The Expires header in an HTTP response that sets the date and time after which the response document is considered stale and must be revalidated or removed from a client cache. The only valid header value is an HTTP-date in the same format that the Date header uses, as in this example:

```
Expires: Sun, 18 Oct 2009 00:00:00 GMT
```

The Expires header is not included automatically in HTTP responses. You must configure it for use in the Web server or generate it programmatically in the Web runtime framework. To use the Expires header to prevent caching of Web content, set its date to a point in the past.

Some Web servers use the Expires header and provide an (invalid) numeric value, generally 0 or -1. This is meant to indicate that a response should not be cached. Although a non-date value is invalid for the Expires header, this technique does comply with the HTTP 1.1 standard. According to the standard, invalid values for the Expires header indicate that the document is already expired and must not be cached. The following example shows how to expire a Web document using this response header technique:

```
Expires: -1
```

For caching purposes, the presence of a Cache-Control header with a max-age directive overrides the date value in the Expires header.

## The Cache-Control HTTP Header

The Cache-Control header is the primary response header used to set caching directives for a Web document. A caching directive is a declaration that, according to HTTP 1.1 standard, must be obeyed by downstream caching proxy servers and browser clients. You can use the Cache-Control header in an HTTP request or response. This section discusses how Web servers can use the header in HTTP responses to declare caching rules to a browser.

One important purpose of HTTP caching directives is to prevent downstream proxies and clients from interfering with the functionality of Mobile Web content by caching documents past their declared expirations. Another important purpose of these directives is to optimize network traffic by preventing unnecessary requests for unexpired Web content. Both are important on the Mobile Web. The directives explained in this section emphasize encouraging mobile browser clients to cache appropriately and prevent unnecessary use of the mobile network.

You construct the `Cache-Control` response header value by combining one or more caching directives into a comma-separated list. The following example response header illustrates how to use commas to separate caching directives. This `Cache-Control` header uses directives to prevent clients from storing, transforming, or caching the Web document:

`Cache-Control: no-cache, no-store, no-transform`

Table 8-2 describes the caching directives used in the `Cache-Control` response header.

**Table 8-2.** *Caching Directives for the Cache-Control HTTP Response Header*

| Caching Directive | Description |
| --- | --- |
| Public | The HTTP response is public and may be cached by shared and private caches. This is the default visibility of a Web document. |
| Private | The HTTP response is private and intended for a single user. The response can only be cached by a private cache. A shared cache (such as a proxy server) may not cache the document. |
| no-cache<br>no-cache="<*token*>" | When <*token*> is not provided, this directive indicates that a cache *may store* this HTTP response, but *may not use* the response to satisfy later requests without first revalidating the document by contacting the Web server.<br><br>When <*token*> is provided, the directive indicates that a cache *may store* this response document and *may use* it to satisfy later requests for the document, but *must remove* the response header(s) listed in <*token*> from the cached response. This directive is used to allow caching of the response, but prevent certain headers from being sent when the cached response is reused. |
| no-store | The HTTP response contains sensitive information and may not be stored in the file system of a cache. The cache should make its best effort to remove the response from memory as soon as possible. |
| no-transform | The HTTP response must not be modified, optimized, transformed, or otherwise changed by a cache.<br><br>Some caching proxy servers modify and transform Web documents. The most prevalent (and in my opinion, the worst) example of this on the Mobile Web is a transcoder, a proxy server that machine-optimizes markup for mobile devices. See Chapter 12 for a discussion of transcoders and defensive programming techniques (such as using this directive) that discourage transcoding of mobile-optimized markup.<br><br>Use of this directive for Mobile Web documents is strongly encouraged to prevent downstream "optimization" by misbehaving transcoders. |

| Caching Directive | Description |
|---|---|
| `must-revalidate` | When the HTTP response expires from a cache, it must be revalidated by contacting the Web server before it can be used to satisfy later requests for the document. Some Web caches ignore document expirations. The purpose of this directive is to force all caches to re-validate the HTTP response at expiration, regardless of cache configuration. |
| `proxy-revalidate` | This directive is similar to `must-revalidate`, with the exception that only proxy servers are forced to revalidate the HTTP response at expiration. Private browser caches are not required to revalidate. |
| `max-age="<seconds>"` | This directive specifies the maximum age (which you specify in `<seconds>`) that the HTTP response can attain in a cache before expiration. The `max-age` directive overrides expiration dates specified in the `Expires` response header. |
| `s-maxage="<seconds>"` | This directive is similar to `max-age`, but it applies only to shared proxy caches, not to private browser caches. When this directive is provided, its expiration age overrides values in both the `max-age` directive and the `Expires` response header. |

## The Pragma HTTP Header

You use the `Pragma` header with a value of `no-cache` to indicate that the response should not be cached, as shown in this example response header:

```
Pragma: no-cache
```

It is included here as a reminder to Mobile Web developers to avoid its use. The `Pragma` response header is not sufficient to indicate that a Web document is not cacheable! `Pragma` is an optional header component of the HTTP 1.1 protocol, which means it can be ignored by Web servers, caches, and clients. Instead, you should use the `Cache-Control` header to indicate that a response is not cacheable:

```
Cache-Control: no-cache
```

## The Vary HTTP Header

The Vary header lists request headers that might cause the Web response document to change. The value of the `Vary` header is a comma-separated list of request header fields where the values might affect the content of the Web response. This information is used by a caching proxy to limit reuse of a cached document to only those browser clients that provide request headers with the same values as the original request.

You can use the `Vary` response header to identify adaptive and dynamic Mobile Web content to caches. For example, a Mobile Web page that has content tailored to mobile devices and browser versions might provide this `Vary` response header:

```
Vary: User-Agent, Accept
```

The Vary header indicates to caches that the Web response should be reused only in the cache for Web browsers that provide identical values of the User-Agent and Accept request headers—in other words, the Web response should be used only for the same versions of the mobile device.

> **NOTE:** For a detailed explanation of every request and response header defined in the HTTP 1.1 specification, see www.w3.org/Protocols/rfc2616/rfc2616-sec14.html.

## Examples of Caching Directives in HTTP Response Headers

To understand how you can combine response headers to set caching rules for Web content, it might help to analyze a few examples of response headers.

Listing 8–15 provides Expires and Cache-Control headers that restrict all storage, reuse, and modification of this document in any Web cache. The Expires header with a value of -1 indicates that the document is already expired and should not be cached, although this usage is not a best practice. The values in the Cache-Control header indicate (respectively) that the document is private and should not be cached by intermediate servers, should not be used as a cacheable response, should not be stored in memory or on the file system, and must not be modified.

The headers in Listing 8–15 prevent all downstream caching of the HTTP response. This configuration might be appropriate for dynamic Mobile Web documents, but opting out of all Web caching, including the browser cache, comes at the price of increased traffic across the mobile network. Mobile users will pay a performance penalty when you use such a strong caching directive. The Web server is contacted for every document request, even when the user navigates forward and backward through the browser history.

**Listing 8–15.** *HTTP Response Headers that Prevent Response Caching*

```
Date: Sun, 18 Oct 2009 00:00:00 GMT
Last-Modified: Sun, 18 Oct 2009 00:00:00 GMT
Expires: -1
Cache-Control: private, no-cache, no-store, no-transform
```

Listing 8–16 provides more reasonable caching headers for dynamic Mobile Web content. The directives in the Cache-Control header declare that the document can (respectively) be cached by any cache; cached for up to five minutes; and at expiration, must be revalidated by contacting the Web server. This header configuration allows proxy servers to cache high-traffic dynamic content for short periods, reducing traffic to the originating Web server, while still frequently refreshing the document to ensure updated content.

**Listing 8–16.** *HTTP Response Headers that Prevent Response Caching*

```
Date: Sun, 18 Oct 2009 00:0:00 GMT
Last-Modified: Sun, 18 Oct 2009 00:00:00 GMT
Cache-Control: public, max-age=300, must-revalidate
```

The headers in Listing 8–14 are suitable for Mobile Web documents with time-sensitive information, such as news headlines or sports scores. Alternatively, the max-age directive could be replaced with an Expires response header that sets an absolute date and time for document expiration.

Listing 8–17 provides Expires and Cache-Control headers that encourage permanent storage of the Web response document.

**Listing 8–17.** *HTTP Response Headers for a Static Web Document*

```
Date: Sun, 18 Oct 2009 00:00:00 GMT
Last-Modified: Mon, 1 Jun 2009 00:00:00 GMT
Expires: Mon, 1 Jun 2029 00:00:00 GMT
Cache-Control: public, no-transform
```

In Listing 8–17, the Cache-Control header declares that the document is cacheable by any Web cache, but must not be modified. The Expires header sets document expiration for 20 years in the future, effectively requesting permanent storage and reuse by caches. The Date and Last-Modified headers show that the document has not changed in more than four months, so an earlier version of the document might also be reused in the cache.

The headers in Listing 8–17 encourage proxy servers and browser caches to permanently store and reuse static Web documents such as images and style sheets. (Of course, caches can remove unexpired documents for other reasons, such as disk-space constraints, so a request for permanent caching does not prevent all subsequent requests for the document.) If a static, permanently cached document must be updated in the future, versioning or otherwise changing its URL is an effective method for circumventing the caching directives. For example, if a cached style sheet at /sunset/resources/styles.css changes as part of a site update, it could be relocated to /sunset/resources-1.1/styles.css or /sunset/resources/styles.css?v2 and served with the same headers requesting permanent caching.

## EXERCISE 8: OPTIMIZE MOBILE MARKUP AND WEB RESPONSES

Evaluate the mobile markup and HTTP response optimization techniques described in this chapter. Choose one page from a popular Mobile Web site, then download the markup and linked resources (such as images, CSS, and JavaScript libraries). Apply each optimization technique to the Mobile Web page; be sure to save file versions before and after you apply optimizations. Note changes in file size, content, and page load times in mobile browsers.

Try these optimization techniques:

- Reduce the number of linked resources in the markup document.

- Remove unnecessary whitespace and comments in the markup document.

- Encode the document in a MIME multipart envelope.

- Compress the markup document using gzip (do this on a desktop computer if a Web server is not available).

- Add HTTP caching directives appropriate to the type of Web content.

Answer these questions:

1. How do post-processing optimizations affect file size and content, download times in mobile browsers, and the human-readability of the final document? Use the Firebug (https://addons.mozilla.org/en-US/firefox/addon/1843) or YSlow (https://addons.mozilla.org/en-US/firefox/addon/5369) Firefox browser extensions to discover the interplay between document caching and network speed.

2. How can you employ Web server optimizations using Web frameworks?

3. Which optimizations are testable without using a mobile browser? Why?

## Summary

This chapter optimizes Mobile Web content to improve the quality of the mobile user experience, employing post-processing techniques and Web server configuration to reduce the amount and size of Web documents and encourage client-side Web caching.

After reducing the number of linked resources in a Web document, you remove unnecessary whitespace and comments to optimize the size of the remaining files. You optimize performance on older mobile browsers using a MIME multipart envelope to encapsulate markup and linked resources into a single Web response. For modern mobile browsers, you compress HTTP responses using gzip compression to achieve more than 50% savings in the byte size of textual Web documents. You use caching directives in HTTP response headers to direct mobile browsers to cache.

The next chapter details mobile markup validation and methods to evaluate the mobile-friendliness of Web documents.

# Chapter 9

# Validating Mobile Markup

Markup validation is the practice of machine-checking that a Web document complies with syntax rules and adheres to the dialect of the document format in use. As you develop your Mobile Web application, you can use validation to check whether your markup and style sheet documents are well-formed and valid. During the testing cycle, you should thoroughly validate every Mobile Web document in your project to ensure strict adherence to Web and Mobile Web standards.

You first learned about the merits of valid and well-formed mobile markup in Chapter 3. This chapter provides you with tools to validate your markup, diagnose validation errors, and ensure that, at least syntactically, your markup is appropriate for display in a mobile browser.

You perform markup validation by providing a document URL, an entire Web document, or a document fragment to a public validation service on the Web. Table 9-1 lists several markup and style sheet validation services on the public Internet. A validation service analyzes the document and reports validation results. If the document is invalid or not well-formed, the validation service might display several pieces of information for each syntax error, such as its markup snippet, file location, and clarifying details for resolving the problem. If the document is valid, the service reports the document's validity and might even display congratulations.

In addition, many IDEs check whether your documents are well-formed and valid as you type, using cached copies of the document DTD or schema. Markup and style validation in IDEs and offline tools are not discussed further in this chapter.

The public markup validation services discussed in this chapter offer source code downloads or application programming interfaces (APIs) for local installation and/or offline use. Developers use offline validation to maintain the privacy of new Mobile Web services by avoiding uploading sensitive URLs to a public service. Local installation of markup validation services provide better performance for heavy usage than uploading content to the public Internet. Also, local installations of markup validation services are scriptable, which enables you to integrate validation into a software development or quality assurance (QA) tool chain.

All public Web validators check markup syntax. Some validators targeting Mobile Web documents might also measure the mobile-friendliness of Web documents by evaluating criteria such as page weight (the size of your markup document and all linked resources) and adherence to mobile industry best practices. These mobile validators evaluate your Mobile Web document for suitability for transmission across mobile networks, user cost to download, and expected usability in mobile browsers.

# Importance of Valid Markup on the Mobile Web

On the desktop Web, only 4% of (X)HTML documents use valid markup and style sheet syntax, according to a 2008 study by Opera. Markup validation is encouraged; however, it isn't mandated for desktop Web documents or required by Web browsers. The relaxed syntax rules of HTML permit lenient development practices. For many, it is simply not a Web development priority to produce syntactically compliant Web pages. Further, desktop browsers are often smart enough to identify invalid markup, determine author intent, and circumvent or correct the faulty markup.

On the Mobile Web, valid style sheet and markup syntax is essential. Developers must achieve 100% compliance with markup and style sheet standards in Mobile Web documents to ensure compatibility with a broad range of Mobile Web browsers. Of course, no standards organization has announced that Mobile Web pages must be valid at all costs, but the reality is that invalid or poorly-formed markup adversely impacts your document's compatibility with mobile browsers in ways that are far more destructive than with desktop Web browsers. Mobile browsers are advancing rapidly, but generally are not designed to scour a Web document for invalid markup and to render the document as *intended* by the developer. The mobile browser displays the markup document as written. An invalid Mobile Web document might be incompletely or poorly displayed in the browser. Or, the mobile browser might waste cycles attempting to render the faulty document, causing the browser to perform poorly.

Vigilance in validating mobile markup has a direct effect on mobile traffic levels. The mobile user often pays a significant performance penalty for browsing an invalid Mobile Web document—a penalty that might deter the visitor from returning. Current and older mobile browsers that adhere only to WAP standards might crash, or worse, cause the phone to restart when encountering malformed markup. Mobile browsers supporting full Web standards provide a more forgiving user experience by incompletely rendering the invalid page. However, mobile users quickly learn to avoid Mobile Web sites that perform poorly, fail to display, or crash their phone's browsers. Also, mobile search engines might penalize or exclude mobile sites with invalid markup.

Listing 9-1 shows an invalid XHTML-MP Mobile Web document. It contains three XHTML-MP and CSS syntax errors. Can you find them? Listing 9-2 is the validated and corrected version of the XHTML-MP document. Review the code in bold in Listing 9-2 to find the differences between the documents.

Figures 9-1 and 9-2 show the invalid and valid markup as displayed in the Android, Palm Pre, and iPhone emulators.

**Listing 9-1.** *Invalid XHTML-MP Markup and Wireless CSS*

```
<?xml version="1.0" encoding="UTF-8"?>
<!DOCTYPE html PUBLIC "-//WAPFORUM//DTD XHTML Mobile 1.0//EN"
"http://www.wapforum.org/DTD/xhtml-mobile10.dtd">
<html xmlns="http://www.w3.org/1999/xhtml">
<head>
<meta name="HandHeldFriendly" content="true" />
<meta name="viewport" content="width=320,initial-scale=1.0,user-scalable=no"/>
<title>Invalid Mobile Markup</title>
<style type="text/css">
.hdr {
  text-align: center;
  font-variant: small-caps;
  font-size: large;
  margin: 2px 0px 4px 0px;
}
.ad {
  margin: 8px;
  text-align: center;
}
.adImg {
  border: 0px solid;
  margin-bottom: 2px;
}
.adtext {
  margin: 0px;
}
.intro {
  font-size: small;
  margin: 4px 2px;
}
ol.menu {
  list-style-type: none;
  margin: 0px;
  padding: 0px;
  text-align: left;
}

ol.menu li {
  margin: 2px;
  padding: 2px 6px;
  background-color: #aaffaa;
  color: #000000;
}
.ftr {
  text-align: center;
  font-size: small;
  margin: 4px 0px 2px 0px;
}
</style>
</head>
<body>
<h1 class="hdr">Sunset Farmers&apos; Market</h1>
<div clas="ad">
<a href="#"><img class="adImg" src="berry_ad.jpg" width="200" height="40"
 alt="Fresh Raspberries This Week" /></a><br/>
<a class="adtext" href="#">fresh raspberries this week</a>
</div>
```

```
<div class="intro">Visit us every Wednesday afternoon in the city center
 for farm-fresh fruit, vegetables and plants.</div>
<ol class="menu">
<li><a href="#">About the Market</a></li>
<li><a href="#">Seasonal Favorites</a></li>
<li><a href="#">Hours &amp; Directions</a></li>
<li><a href="#">Our Local Farmers</a></li>
<li><a href="#">Stall Map</a></li>
</ol>
<div class="ftr">Call <a href="tel:+15035551234" class="ctc">503-555-1234 for
 market info</div>
</body>
</html>
```

Figure 9-1 displays the invalid markup from Listing 9-1 in mobile browser emulators. Notice how the smartphone browsers vary the display of an invalid document. The iPhone and Palm Pre browsers surface XML errors in the document to the developer in the emulator. In this figure, all browser emulators silently fail the CSS syntax error, as is also the case in the browsers in actual devices. Mobile browsers in actual mobile devices might also suppress markup errors to the end user.

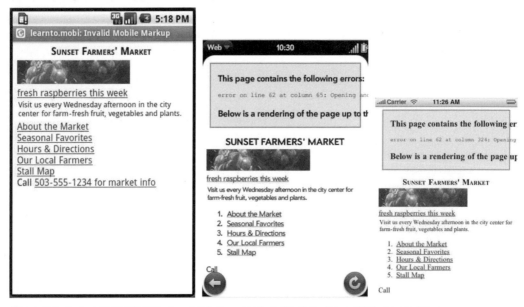

**Figure 9-1.** *An Invalid Mobile Web document viewed in Android, Palm Pre, and iPhone emulators*

**Listing 9-2.** *Valid XHTML-MP Markup and Wireless CSS with Bolded Corrections*

```
<?xml version="1.0" encoding="UTF-8"?>
<!DOCTYPE html PUBLIC "-//WAPFORUM//DTD XHTML Mobile 1.0//EN"
"http://www.wapforum.org/DTD/xhtml-mobile10.dtd">
<html xmlns="http://www.w3.org/1999/xhtml">
<head>
<meta name="HandHeldFriendly" content="true" />
<meta name="viewport" content="width=320,initial-scale=1.0,user-scalable=no"/>
<title>Valid Mobile Markup</title>
<style type="text/css">
```

```css
.hdr {
  text-align: center;
  font-variant: small-caps;
  font-size: large;
  margin: 2px 0px 4px 0px;
}
.ad {
  margin: 8px;
  text-align: center;
}
.adImg {
  border: 0px solid;
  margin-bottom: 2px;
}
.adtext {
  margin: 0px;
}
.intro {
  font-size: small;
  margin: 4px 2px;
}
ol.menu {
  list-style-type: none;
  margin: 0px;
  padding: 0px;
  text-align: left;
}
ol.menu li {
  margin: 2px;
  padding: 2px 6px;
  background-color: #aaffaa;
  color: #000000;
}
.ftr {
  text-align: center;
  font-size: small;
  margin: 4px 0px 2px 0px;
}
</style>
</head>
<body>
<h1 class="hdr">Sunset Farmers&apos; Market</h1>
<div class="ad">
<a href="#"><img class="adImg" src="berry_ad.jpg" width="200" height="40"
 alt="Fresh Raspberries This Week" /></a><br/>
<a class="adtext" href="#">fresh raspberries this week</a>
</div>
<div class="intro">Visit us every Wednesday afternoon in the city center for
 farm-fresh fruit, vegetables and plants.</div>
<ol class="menu">
<li><a href="#">About the Market</a></li>
<li><a href="#">Seasonal Favorites</a></li>
<li><a href="#">Hours &amp; Directions</a></li>
<li><a href="#">Our Local Farmers</a></li>
<li><a href="#">Stall Map</a></li>
</ol>
<div class="ftr">Call <a href="tel:+15035551234" class="ctc">503-555-1234</a>
```

```
for market info</div>
</body>
</html>
```

Listing 9-2 makes three changes to correct the syntax errors in the invalid Mobile Web document:

- The style definition for ol.menu properly closes using the } character.

- The first div in the document corrects the spelling of the class attribute.

- The last div in the document completes the click-to-call link with an </a> close tag.

Figure 9-2 displays the validated markup from Listing 9-1 in mobile browser emulators. Notice how valid markup causes the smartphone browsers to display the document more (but not entirely) uniformly.

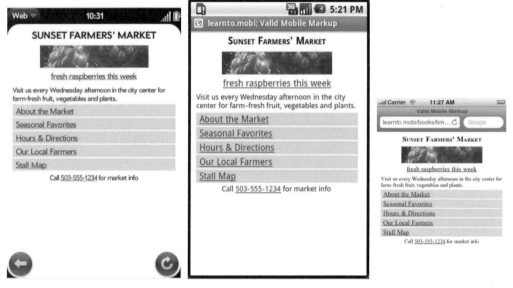

**Figure 9-2.** *A Validated Mobile Web document viewed in Android, Palm Pre, and iPhone emulators*

# What Validation Does Not Test

Validators decide whether your markup documents are syntactically and grammatically correct and comply with Web standards. However, valid markup does not solve all Web-development problems. A valid Web document can be poorly structured and can render poorly in mobile browsers. This excerpt from the W3C Markup Validation Service's help document (http://validator.w3.org/docs/help.html#validandquality) succinctly summarizes the relationship between validity and quality:

*Validity is one of the quality criteria for a Web page, but there are many others. In other words, a valid Web page is not necessarily a good Web page, but an invalid Web page has little chance of being a good Web page.*

Validators do not judge markup quality and efficiency. With the exception of W3C MobileOK checker and mobiReady, validators also do not evaluate a document's suitability for display in Mobile Web browsers. Bloated and imprecise markup can be syntactically correct and fail miserably on an actual mobile device. During the development process, you should keep in mind that validity is necessary but not sufficient to ensure your markup documents are suitable for mobile browsers.

# Public Markup Validators

Public markup validators allow anonymous online users to check the syntax of Web documents. Many of these validators provide source code or APIs that enable local installation of markup validation services. Table 9-1 introduces five public validators and summarizes the breadth of their validation services.

**Table 9-1.** *Public Markup Validators*

| Validator | Validation Scope | URL | Source Code |
|---|---|---|---|
| W3C Markup Validation Service | Markup syntax for HTML, XHTML, and other Web markups.<br><br>Validates any XML-based Web document that specifies a DTD, enabling XHTML-MP and WML validation. | http://validator.w3.org/ | http://validator.w3.org/source/<br><br>Source code is available through CVS. Linux RPMs are provided.<br><br>Validator is written in Perl with CSS, HTML and JS support files. |
| W3C CSS Validation Service | CSS syntax. Checks grammar, property names, and values from CSS 2.1 standard. | http://jigsaw.w3.org/css-validator/ | http://jigsaw.w3.org/css-validator/DOWNLOAD.html<br><br>Source code is available through CVS.<br><br>Validator is written as a Java EE servlet. |

| Validator | Validation Scope | URL | Source Code |
|---|---|---|---|
| W3C MobileOK Checker | Checks for conformance with MobileOK basic tests, a machine-verifiable subset of the W3C Mobile Web Best Practices. | http://validator.w3.org/mobile/ | http://dev.w3.org/cvsweb/2007/mobileok-ref/<br><br>Source code is available through CVS.<br><br>Validator is written as a Java SE library. |
| mobiReady | Checks HTML, XHTM, and XHTML markup syntax.<br><br>Checks for conformance with MobileOK basic tests.<br><br>Checks markup characteristics for mobile-friendliness. | http://ready.mobi/ | http://mobiforge.com/testing/story/getting-started-with-ready-mobi-api<br><br>API access is in beta at the time of this writing. |
| Validome | HTML, XHTML, and WML markup. | http://www.validome.org/ | Source code is not available. |

> **NOTE:**  Markup validators check CSS grammar and syntax. However, there is no public validator for the restricted grammars of mobile CSS subsets. When developing to the Wireless CSS or CSS Mobile Profile standards, developers must manually ensure that they use only supported property names and values.

## W3C Markup Validation Service

The W3C Markup Validation Service (http://validator.w3.org/) is a free and public validator that checks the syntax of Web markup documents. It validates HTML, XHTML, and Web documents in any XML dialect, including XHTML-MP and WML, provided that a DTD is declared in the document.

The W3C Markup Validation Service accepts a markup document as input through URI, file upload, and direct input. It automatically detects the document's markup type and character encoding, or it gives you the option of setting these manually. It also checks markup syntax for Web documents and provides detailed error messages, code snippets, and suggestions for fixing markup problems.

Optionally, the validator will reformat and correct your Web document using HTML Tidy (http://tidy.sourceforge.net/), a software library that corrects common HTML errors and improves HTML formatting and readability. HTML Tidy was originally conceived by the W3C and is now managed as an open-source software project at SourceForge (`http://www.sourceforge.net`).

Figure 9-3 shows W3C Markup Validation Service output for the invalid XHTML-MP markup from Listing 9-1. The figure displays the document URI, character encoding, document type, and the number of validation errors.

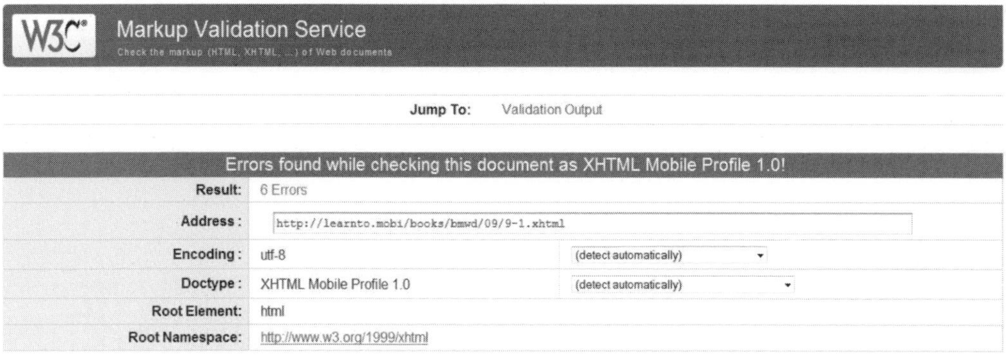

**Figure 9-3.** *W3C Markup Validation Service output for a Valid XHTML-MP Document*

Figure 9-4 reports details of validation errors from the W3C Markup Validation Service. The validator provides the line number and code snippet identifying each error, as well as an explanation of the error and suggestions for resolving it.

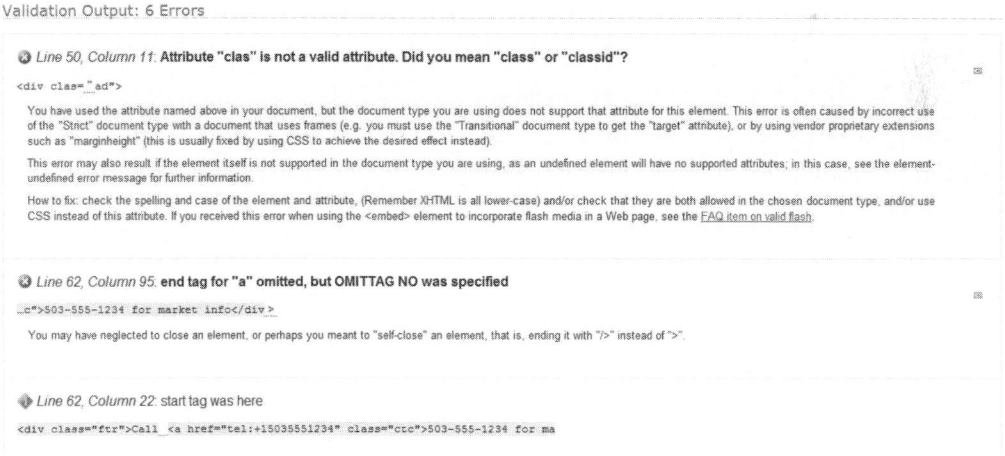

**Figure 9-4.** *A list of document-validation errors from the W3C Markup Validation Service*

Figure 9-5 shows W3C Markup Validation Service output for the valid XHTML-MP document from Listing 9-2. In addition to showing the document URI, character encoding, and document type, the validation output clearly identifies that the document has validated successfully.

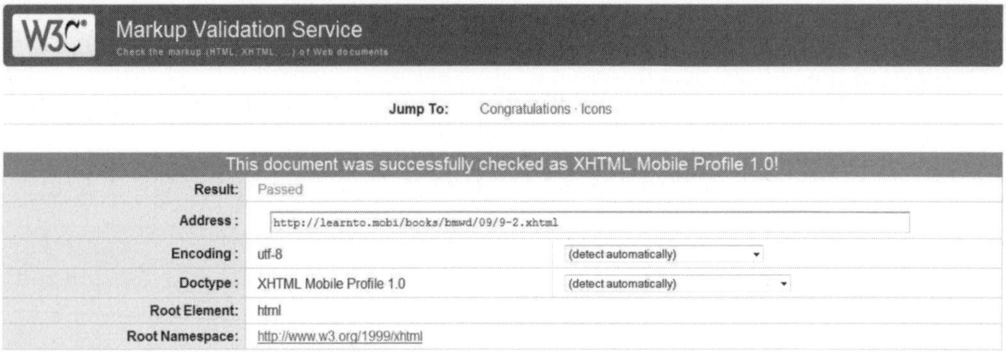

**Figure 9-5.** *W3C Markup Validation Service output for a Valid XHTML-MP Document*

# W3C CSS Validation Service

The W3C CSS Validation Service (http://jigsaw.w3.org/css-validator/) is a free, public validation service that checks for valid syntax, property names, and property values in Cascading Style Sheets. The validation service supports the CSS 2.1 standard.

The W3C CSS Validation Service accepts HTML or XHTML documents with internal CSS or CSS documents for validation. These files might be provided by URI, file upload, or direct input. Optionally, you can select the level of warnings to display with validation output and the target CSS profile for validation. However, in my testing, I found that selecting the *mobile* profile validated against CSS 2.1 instead of CSS Mobile Profile.

> **NOTE:** The W3C CSS Validation Service accepts HTML or XHTML documents with CSS or CSS files as validation input. At the time of this writing, it does *not* support XHTML-MP documents with CSS as validation input. To validate CSS in XHTML-MP documents, provide a direct link to an external CSS file or copy and paste CSS into the validation input field.

Figure 9-6 shows W3C CSS Validation Service output for an invalid CSS document. Error messages are less clear and less helpful than the W3C Markup Validation Service, but the output is enough to pinpoint the location of the CSS error. CSS parsing failed at the declaration of ol.menu li; the error is a missing } in the preceding style declaration for ol.menu.

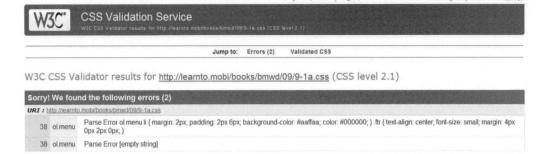

**Figure 9-6.** *W3C CSS Validation Service output for an invalid CSS document*

The W3C CSS Validation Service lists the CSS styles that validated successfully in the document. Figure 9-7 shows validation output that lists all valid style names and definitions.

Valid CSS Information

```
.hdr {
    text-align : center;
    font-variant : small-caps;
    font-size : large;
    margin : 2px 0 4px 0;
}

.ad {
    margin : 8px;
    text-align : center;
}

.adImg {
    border : 0 solid;
    margin-bottom : 2px;
}

.adtext {
    margin : 0;
}

.intro {
    font-size : small;
    margin : 4px 2px;
}
```

**Figure 9-7.** *A list of valid CSS style definitions in W3C CSS Validation Service output*

Figure 9-8 shows the validator output when a CSS document is syntactically correct and validation succeeds.

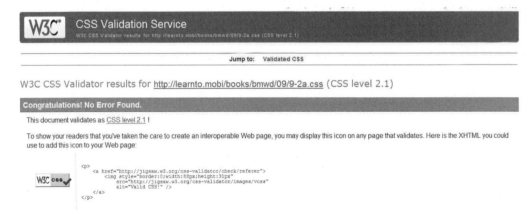

**Figure 9-8.** *W3C CSS Validation Service output for a valid CSS document*

# W3C mobileOK Checker

The W3C mobileOK Checker (http://validator.w3.org/mobile/) is a free, public validation service that measures the mobile-friendliness of a Web page or site using a machine-verifiable subset of tests from the W3C's Mobile Web Best Practices 1.0 guidelines ( www.w3.org/TR/mobile-bp/).

The W3C Mobile Web Best Practices guidelines provide a list of 60 best practices for improving the user experience of the Web when accessed from browsers on mobile devices. Of the best practices, 24 are machine-verifiable. This subset of best practices is tested using the W3C mobileOK Basic Tests 1.0 (www.w3.org/TR/mobileOK-basic10-tests/).

The W3C mobileOK Basic Tests check for mobile-friendly markup. It tests for several criteria, including the following:

- HTTP responses and/or markup document must include cacheing directives.

- Markup must be valid XHTML, XHTML Basic, or XHTML Mobile Profile.

- The number of external resources (images, style sheets, libraries, and so on) should be fewer than 10 and must be fewer than 20.

- Image maps must not be used.

- Images must specify `height` and `width` attributes.

- Frames must not be used.

- Pop-up windows must not be used as link targets.

- Style sheets must be used for presentation.

The W3C mobileOK Checker implements W3C mobileOK Basic Tests to judge the mobile-friendliness of a markup document. The Checker assigns a score from 0 to 100 to the markup document. Larger scores indicate greater mobile-friendliness.

Figure 9-9 is a W3C mobileOK Checker report for an invalid XHTML-MP document. The report displays the mobile-friendliness score (82 of 100), the document size, and the number of network requests required to render the document and all dependent resources.

**Figure 9-9.** *W3C mobileOK Checker output for an invalid XHTML-MP document*

The W3C mobileOK Checker provides a list of test failures, each of which is a potential mobile markup flaw, HTTP issue, or problem in external resources that caused reductions in the mobile-friendliness score. The Checker describes each issue and its severity in impacting delivery of Mobile Web content to mobile browsers. Figure 9-10 displays a list of test failures for an invalid XHTML-MP document.

Figure 9-10. *A list of W3C mobileOK Checker test failures for an Invalid XHTML-MP document*

Figure 9-11 shows the improved mobile-friendliness score for a valid XHTML-MP document, where the only mobileOK Basic Test failure consists of an HTTP response header that is served without caching directives.

Figure 9-11. *W3C mobileOK Checker showing an improved mobile-friendliness score*

> **NOTE:** The W3C provides more validators, broken link checkers, and other quality assurance tools at www.w3.org/QA/Tools/.

# mobiReady

The mobiReady (`http://ready.mobi/`) validation and testing tool evaluates the mobile-friendliness of a Web document using markup validation, W3C mobileOK Basic tests, dotMobi's compliance tests for all domains registered on the .mobi top-level domain, and other helpful guidelines.

dotMobi's mobiReady is a Mobile Web test tool that evaluates the content and size of a Mobile Web document, its MIME type and HTTP response headers, and the estimated speed and cost to download across mobile networks. mobiReady assigns a tested Web document an overall mobile-readiness score from 1 to 5, with 5 indicating the best adherence to Mobile Web standards and best practices. mobiReady's colorful and graphical validation output is easy to review. It provides detailed explanations of the mobile-friendliness tests and notes whether the document under review passed each test. mobiReady can also test an entire Mobile Web site by following internal links from a start page, providing validation details for all encountered pages.

Figure 9-12 shows mobiReady's summary of a validation test performed on an XHTML-MP document with invalid syntax, but which otherwise meets many criteria for mobile-friendliness. The summary displays the document URI, mobile-readiness score, file size, and estimated cost and speed to download across geographies and types of mobile networks.

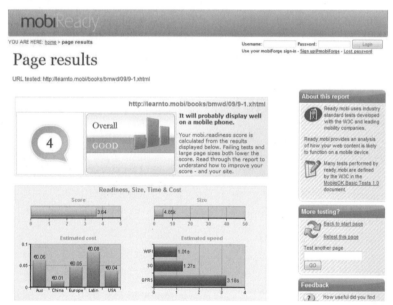

**Figure 9-12.** *mobiReady summary for an invalid XHTML-MP cocument that meets other mobile-friendliness criteria*

Figure 9-13 shows the number of validation tests performed and whether the document passed or failed each test. You can see an explanation of the failed XHTML-MP validation test beneath the test summary. The test Web document from Listing 9-1 declares XHTML-MP as the markup format, but does not contain valid markup. The *help me fix it* links in mobiReady validation results connect developers to technical articles that describe defenses against each type of validation or mobile-friendliness error.

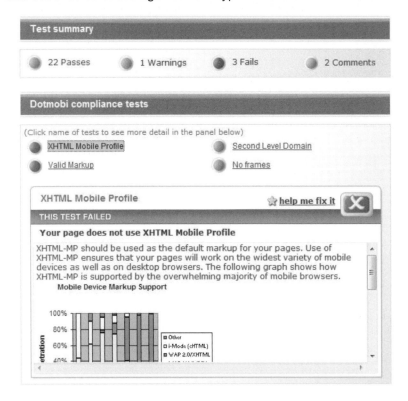

**Figure 9-13.** *mobiReady summary of validation and mobile-friendliness test results*

Figure 9-14 shows details for more mobile-friendliness tests performed by mobiReady. The XHTML-MP document has invalid syntax and is not served with HTTP response headers providing caching directives; however, it otherwise meets mobile-friendliness criteria.

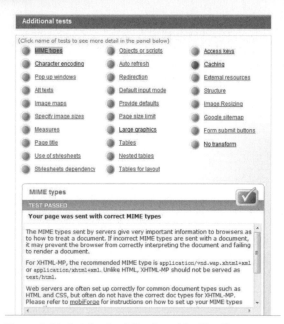

**Figure 9-14.** *Details of mobiReady mobile-friendliness tests*

# Validome

Validome (`http://www.validome.org`) is a free, public, and closed-source validator for HTML, XHTML, and WML documents. It checks for compliance with W3C markup standards, as well as best practices in cross-browser desktop Web development. Validome provides extremely accurate validation output.

Optionally, Validome allows you to choose from several desktop Web browser user-agents to use in validation, displays HTTP response headers, and shows a tree view of the markup document.

Figure 9-15 shows Validome output for an invalid XHTML-MP document. It displays the document type, character set, and a link to the validation output.

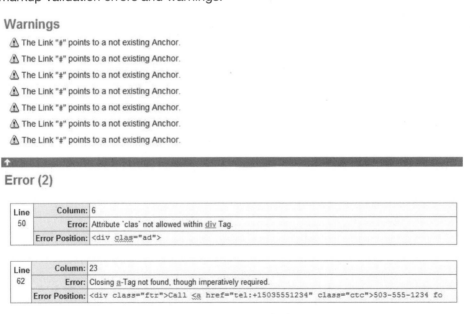

**Figure 9-15.** *Validome output for an invalid XHTML-MP document*

When the markup document is invalid, Validome shows validation errors and warnings. Validome's error messages are terse but informative and include the line number, code snippet, and a description of the error. Figure 9-16 shows Validome output that lists markup validation errors and warnings.

### Warnings

⚠ The Link "#" points to a not existing Anchor.

⚠ The Link "#" points to a not existing Anchor.

⚠ The Link "#" points to a not existing Anchor.

⚠ The Link "#" points to a not existing Anchor.

⚠ The Link "#" points to a not existing Anchor.

⚠ The Link "#" points to a not existing Anchor.

⚠ The Link "#" points to a not existing Anchor.

### Error (2)

| Line 50 | Column: | 6 |
|---|---|---|
| | Error: | Attribute `clas` not allowed within div Tag. |
| | Error Position: | `<div clas="ad">` |

| Line 62 | Column: | 23 |
|---|---|---|
| | Error: | Closing a-Tag not found, though imperatively required. |
| | Error Position: | `<div class="ftr">Call <a href="tel:+15035551234" class="ctc">503-555-1234 fo` |

**Figure 9-16.** *Validome output listing XHTML-MP markup-validation errors*

Figure 9-17 shows the Validome output after it validates that a markup document is syntactically correct.

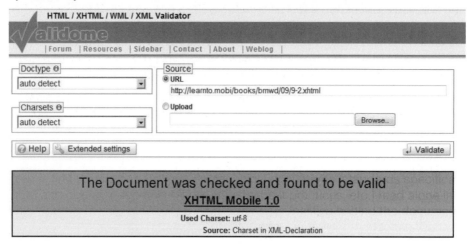

**Figure 9-17.** *Validome output for a valid XHTML-MP document*

# Summary

This chapter focuses on markup validation for Mobile Web documents. You learned the importance of well-formed and valid markup on the Mobile Web. You also learned that mobile browsers might not be as adept at circumventing markup problems as their desktop counterparts. You also explored the features and scope of five public markup validators, including some that also measure the mobile-friendliness of a Web page.

Validity is one of many indicators of markup quality, but in isolation it does not indicate that a Web document provides an adequate user experience in mobile browsers. For this reason, some markup validators check for compliance with Mobile Web best practices, in addition to validating document syntax.

The next chapter covers testing strategies for Mobile Web sites.

# Chapter 10

# Testing a Mobile Web Site

Testing a Mobile Web site can be complicated and expensive. Comprehensive testing means using a wide variety of mobile devices and operators to access the Internet across radio networks and Wi-Fi and to exercise the features of the Mobile Web site. Mobile Web testing requires access to many mobile devices or, less effectively, simulation of the mobile devices and as much of the mobile ecosystem as is feasible: the mobile browser running on device hardware, with bandwidth-limited network access, through the private services of the operator network, and finally out to the public Internet to retrieve Mobile Web content.

Some developers have cabinets full of hundreds of mobile devices that run on all the operators in their geography to use for testing Mobile Web sites. But many developers do not have this luxury. Even with a slew of mobile devices, it is quite likely that a Mobile Web development project has customers outside its coverage areas. Using actual mobile devices *is* the gold standard for testing, but it is not necessary to make a huge investment in hardware to test on actual devices. It is possible to test Mobile Web content on devices without ever holding a mobile phone in your hand. Operators, OEMs, and technology companies rent web-based access to mobile devices running in geographies around the world. This "virtual device" technology allows a developer to operate a device in a geographic location (a Nokia 5800 on Vodafone in Germany, for example), reserving the device for only as long as necessary to test the Mobile Web site.

If actual devices are unavailable, the next best Mobile Web site testing method is to use browser and device simulators to mimic the functionality of a mobile device as it browses the Web. Simulators are sometimes accurate enough in emulating mobile device behavior to determine basic browser support for the design, styles, and scripting on a Mobile Web page. But simulators are not perfect replications of mobile browser or device behavior. They are especially poor at mimicking the memory and processing constraints of actual devices. This means a simulator can't show that a Mobile Web page renders slowly or leaks memory and destroys browser performance due to misbehaving JavaScript. Simulators are also not available on all desktop environments. A PC-based Mobile Web developer may be able to test mobile markup on many smartphone emulators, but her Mac-using UI designer may only be able to emulate the iPhone.

The effectiveness of emulator testing is increased when emulated Web requests are routed through the mobile operator's private network, better replicating the communication path of an actual mobile device. However, proxy access to the operator network is usually restricted to companies with established business relationships. Frustratingly, emulator effectiveness may also be decreased in this situation if the emulator's user-agent is not known to the mobile operator, which may reject its Web requests or present it a poor or transcoded user experience.

The least effective method for testing Mobile Web content is to use a desktop web browser. Firefox, Safari, and other desktop browsers can be configured to mimic the request headers of a mobile device, but that is where the similarities end between the two platforms. Display algorithms, tolerance for invalid syntax, caching limits, and scripting performance are all advanced enough in a desktop browser to lull the Mobile Web developer into a dangerous, false sense of compatibility for the Mobile Web pages under test. Desktop browser testing should be used only as a sanity-check during active development.

I'll start by describing how mobile browsers access the Internet across the mobile operator network. Successful Mobile Web site testing simulates mobile browsers, devices, and networks. Next, I'll present strategies for testing on actual mobile devices, including using a device remoting service and acquiring rental and loaner devices from developer programs. As noted above, when on-device testing is not possible, you can test a Mobile Web site using browser and device emulators, which provide a marginally accurate representation of the site on a mobile device. Finally, I'll delve further into why testing Mobile Web content in a desktop browser is a useful developer tool, but does not provide a realistic assessment of site performance or usability on mobile devices.

# Mobile Web Testing Methodology

To understand how best to test a Mobile Web site, you need to know how and where web traffic flows between a browser on a mobile device and a Web server on the public Internet. Emulator testing most accurately simulates a Web request from an actual mobile device when it follows the same path to the Internet that the device follows, on the operator network, or as close as possible to the same path. Figure 10-1 shows a simplified view of the possible communications paths between a mobile browser and a Web server.

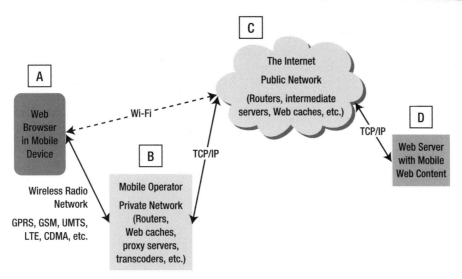

**Figure 10-1.** *How mobile devices access the Internet*

Component A is the mobile browser running on device hardware, generally a mobile phone or netbook. Mobile Web testing exercises the mobile browser within the hardware constraints, including limited memory, storage, and processing power. Mobile Web testing also includes operating the browser using all user input and navigation methods on the device, such as hardware or software keyboards, dial pads, D-pads, joysticks, roller balls, and stylus or finger gestures.

Component B is the mobile operator's private network. It filters, caches, and sometimes modifies web traffic between the Internet and a mobile device. The operator network also provides valuable services to mobile subscribers and approved web partners, including unique user identification and centralized billing for premium services.

Component C is the public Internet, which routes web traffic through intermediary servers and caches toward its destination. Intermediary servers cache web responses but rarely or never filter and modify traffic.

Component D is the destination Web server whose content is requested by the mobile browser.

It is important to understand Mobile Web traffic flow for testing because, in the absence of using actual mobile devices running on operator networks and in all target geographies, testing involves simulation of mobile browser capabilities (A), mobile device constraints (A), the path its Web request takes to get to the public Internet (B, or routes that circumvent B), and the possible modifications to the request and response caused by its path to the Internet (B).

When a mobile device (A) connects through the mobile radio network, its request is routed through intermediary services owned by the operator (B) before reaching the Internet (C). The web response is routed in reverse, from the public Internet (C), through operator services (B) and across the radio network back to the mobile device (A).

The private services on an operator network (B) include firewalls, proxy servers, web caches, and transcoders, each of which has the opportunity to block, filter, and modify a Web request or response. Operator services usually perform valuable bandwidth-saving tasks that benefit mobile subscribers. However, misbehaving or misconfigured operator services can wreak havoc on the mobile user experience, blocking subscriber access to legitimate Mobile Web sites and reformatting markup that is already optimized for mobile. See Chapter 12 for more information about transcoders and defensive programming techniques to discourage them from modifying your mobile-optimized markup.

## Mobile Browser Testing Considerations

When a mobile device connects via Wi-Fi instead of the radio network, its Web request is *not* routed through the operator network. Instead, it connects directly to the ISP controlling the Wi-Fi service and from there reaches the public Internet. Wi-Fi connectivity is much faster than a 3G mobile network and circumvents the operator network (unless the operator also owns the Wi-Fi network and treats mobile browser requests over Wi-Fi similarly to radio connections).

When testing mobile devices with Wi-Fi capability, it is important to use both Internet access methods when testing a Mobile Web site, because the choice of access method may change the substance of the Web request or response. Other Internet access methods are available for some mobile devices (including sharing desktop Internet access when the device is tethered to a computer), but they are not relevant from a testing perspective and therefore are not discussed further in this book.

When testing with actual mobile devices is not possible, successful testing simulates as much of the mobile browser, mobile device, and mobile network as possible, focusing on these areas:

- Functionality of the mobile browser
- Constraints and modalities of the mobile device
- Internet access method and its modifications to the Web request and response, including interruptions to Internet access

(Of course, it is not necessary to simulate the public Internet or Web server, because they are accessible and operate consistently using any Internet access method.)

## Choosing Mobile Devices to Use in Testing

Comprehensive Mobile Web testing targets multiple mobile browser versions, device models, operating systems, and mobile networks. An early challenge in Mobile Web testing is choosing a small number of test mobile devices that provide adequate test coverage. It isn't feasible to test your Mobile Web site on every mobile device, so choosing a broad subset is crucial. Follow this process to choose the set of mobile devices to target for site testing:

1. Start with all the mobile devices targeted for support on the Mobile Web site. Depending on the goals of the Mobile Web site, this list could be broad (for example, all devices supporting XHTML-MP) or narrow (only Blackberry devices for an enterprise Web application or mass-market devices for a dating or youth site).

2. Organize the devices by content adaptation groups, as defined in Chapter 4. Select at least one device per content adaptation group to use in testing.

3. Organize the devices by mobile browser version. Inspect the user-agent or consult a device database to learn the browser version. Select at least one device per mobile browser version to use in testing.

4. Organize the devices by mobile operating system and version. Select at least one device per major OS version to use in testing.

5. Organize the devices by modality and input method. Separate touchscreen and non-touch devices, devices with QWERTY keyboards and keypads, and so forth. Choose one device from each modality and input method to use in testing.

6. Choose the strongest and weakest devices from the list of all supported devices, where "strong" and "weak" are your subjective evaluations of browser performance and device capabilities. (For example, the weakest device may have the earliest release date, smallest heap size, and smallest screen size. The strongest device may be a recent smartphone.) Select both devices to use in testing.

7. Collect the list of devices selected in Steps 2-6. These are the devices to use in Mobile Web site testing.

8. Make sure the test devices in Step 7 are supported by an adequate number of target mobile operators. If not, add in extra devices from Steps 2-6 until all target operators are equally represented. Consider testing how crawlers from mobile search engines view the Mobile Web site. For more information about crawlers and mobile search engines, see Chapter 11.

# Testing on Actual Mobile Devices

The three areas of simulation focus I listed in the "Mobile Browser Testing Considerations" section of this chapter show the superiority of Mobile Web testing using actual mobile devices. Testing on devices obviates the need to simulate any component of the mobile device or network. Mobile Web testing can focus exclusively on the compatibility and performance of the Mobile Web site on the device's browser. Testing on devices is the single best way to assess Mobile Web site functionality and usability.

## Acquiring Mobile Devices

The main challenge with a testing strategy that uses actual mobile devices, after selecting the mobile devices to include in the test group, is affordably acquiring the mobile devices and operator subscriptions for testing. One perfectly valid approach is to invest hundreds or thousands of dollars in purchasing mobile devices and service plans. But this approach is too expensive for many Mobile Web developers, especially independent developers and small companies. Instead, developers can gain access to discounted mobile device rentals or remote device access through developer and partner programs in the mobile ecosystem.

Mobile developer and partner programs are offered through device manufacturers, mobile OS manufacturers, and mobile operators. The mobile industry's recent focus on third-party applications increased the documentation, technical support, and accessibility of mobile developer programs. Today, many US and European mobile operators and OEMs provide third-party developers with API documentation, browser documentation, and some degree of openness about the private services available on an operator network.

One benefit of enrolling in mobile developer and partner programs is increased access to mobile devices. Partner programs with paid enrollment may provide discounts for purchasing mobile devices or free loaner devices. Developer programs with free enrollment often provide access to a Virtual Developer Lab with web-based access to actual mobile devices used in testing. Virtual Developer Lab access is sometimes free but generally requires payment. Remote access to mobile devices is a cost-effective way to test your Mobile Web site using actual devices running in mobile networks around the world.

One provider of device remoting services is Mobile Complete, makers of the DeviceAnywhere (http://deviceanywhere.com/) mobile application testing platform. DeviceAnywhere provides remote access to actual mobile devices running on operator networks in the US and Europe, charging a monthly fee for access to device packages (usually per operator), and an hourly rate for service access. Users remotely control mobile devices using a desktop application that allows full control of the device. Users can press buttons, view the screen, perform touchscreen gestures, navigate device menus, view videos, and listen to sounds emitted from the device. A competitive service from Perfecto Mobile (http://perfectomobile.com/) provides a similar device remoting product, though at the time of this writing, audio access is not available to remoted mobile devices.

Figure 10-2 shows DeviceAnywhere providing remote access to the Samsung Jack. I used the DeviceAnywhere client on a Windows desktop computer to launch Internet Explorer Mobile and browse to http://learnthemobileweb.com.

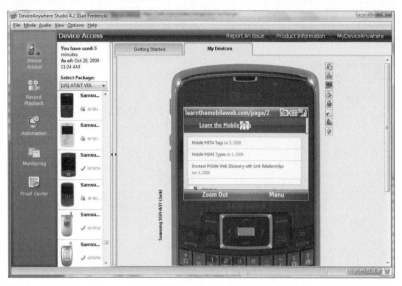

**Figure 10-2.** *Remote access to AT&T mobile devices using DeviceAnywhere*

# Developer Programs

Developer and partner programs also provide technical support, browser documentation, forums, and opportunities to interact with the sponsoring company at technical and industry events. Table 10-1 lists developer programs and the availability of test devices at major mobile device manufacturers.

**Table 10-1.** *Developer Programs at Mobile Device Manufacturers*

| Manufacturer | Developer Program | Discounted Devices? | Rent or Borrow Devices? | Virtual Devices? |
| --- | --- | --- | --- | --- |
| Nokia | Forum Nokia http://www.forum.nokia.com/ | Yes, with invite-only access to Forum Nokia PRO.<br><br>http://www.forum.nokia.com/Premium_Services/ | No | No |
| Motorola | MOTODEV<br><br>http://developer.motorola.com/ | No | No | Yes, powered by Device Anywhere.<br><br>http://developer.motorola.com/fasttrack/deviceanywhere/ |
| Samsung | Samsung Mobile Innovator<br><br>http://innovator.samsungmobile.com | No | No | Yes, in-house Virtual Device Laboratory, Lab.dev. Free access to all members.<br><br>http://innovator.samsungmobile.com/bbs/lab/labplatform.do |

| Manufacturer | Developer Program | Discounted Devices? | Rent or Borrow Devices? | Virtual Devices? |
|---|---|---|---|---|
| LG | LG Mobile Developer Network  http://developer.lgmobile.com/ | No | No | Yes, powered by Device Anywhere.  http://www.deviceanywhere.com/lg/welcome.htm |
| Palm | webOSdev  http://developer.palm.com | No | No | No |
| Research in Motion (BlackBerry) | BlackBerry Developer Zone  http://na.blackberry.com/eng/developers/  BlackBerry Alliance Program  http://partners.blackberry.com/ | Yes, in Alliance Program. | Yes, loaners available in Alliance program. | No |
| Apple | Apple Developer Connection  http://developer.apple.com/ | No | No | No |
| Sony Ericsson | Sony Ericsson Developer World  http://developer.sonyericsson.com/ | No | Yes, loaners available in invite-only Premier Partner program. | Yes, powered by Device Anywhere.  http://www.deviceanywhere.com/sonyericsson/welcome.htm |

Table 10-2 lists developer programs and the availability of test devices at major mobile OS manufacturers.

**Table 10-2.** *Developer Programs at Mobile OS Manufacturers*

| Mobile OS | Developer Program | Discounted Devices? | Rent or Borrow Devices? | Virtual Devices? |
|---|---|---|---|---|
| Windows Mobile (Microsoft) | Windows Mobile for Developers  http://developer.windowsphone.com | Yes, with Mobile Solutions competency in the Microsoft Partner Program for Windows Mobile.  http://www.microsoft.com/windowsmobile/en-us/business/partners/partner-overview-login.mspx | No | No |
| Android (Google) | Android Developers http://developer.android.com | No. Can purchase the Android Dev Phone 1, which allows complete OS modification. | No | No |

| Mobile OS | Developer Program | Discounted Devices? | Rent or Borrow Devices? | Virtual Devices? |
|---|---|---|---|---|
| BlackBerry (Research in Motion) | See entry in Table 10-1. | | | |
| iPhone (Apple) | See entry in Table 10-1. | | | |
| webOS (Palm) | See entry in Table 10-1. | | | |
| Symbian (Symbian Foundation, formerly Nokia) | Symbian Developer Community http://developer.symbian.org/ | No | No | No |

Table 10-3 lists developer programs and the availability of test devices at US and European mobile operators.

*Table 10-3. Developer Programs at US and European Mobile Operators*

| Operator | Developer Program | Discounted Devices? | Rent or Borrow Devices? | Virtual Devices? |
|---|---|---|---|---|
| AT&T (US) | devCentral http://developer.att.com/ | No | No | Yes, powered by DeviceAnywhere. http://www.deviceanywhere.com/ |
| T-Mobile (US) | T-Mobile Partner Network http://developer.t-mobile.com | No | No | Yes, powered by DeviceAnywhere. http://www.deviceanywhere.com/tmobile/welcome.htm |
| Verizon (US) | Verizon Developer Community http://vzwdevelopers.com | No | No | Yes, powered by DeviceAnywhere. http://www.deviceanywhere.com/vz/signup.htm |
| Sprint (US) | Sprint Application Developer Program http://developer.sprint.com | No | No | Yes, powered by DeviceAnywhere. http://www.deviceanywhere.com/sprint/welcome.htm |

| Operator | Developer Program | Discounted Devices? | Rent or Borrow Devices? | Virtual Devices? |
|---|---|---|---|---|
| Orange (EU) | Orange Partner Program http://orangepartner.com | No | No | Physical access to devices at Orange developer centers in San Francisco, New York, UK or China. |
| Vodafone (EU) | Betavine Open Mobile Application Community http://www.betavine.net/ | No | No | Yes, powered by Perfecto Mobile. http://www.perfectomobile.com/ |

# Testing in Mobile Emulators

When testing with mobile devices is not possible, emulator testing can provide a reasonably accurate, though imperfect, measure of compatibility with modern smartphones, mobile devices, and mobile browsers. Emulators can test that a Mobile Web page complies with markup standards and document size limits supported on the device. Emulated browsers provide a closer approximation of the display and usability of web content on the device than a desktop browser. However, testing demands precise and accurate rendering of Mobile Web content, so accepting a "close approximation" too often leads to uncaught bugs and hidden browser incompatibilities.

Referring to the three focus areas for simulation testing of a Mobile Web site in the "Mobile Browser Testing Considerations" section of this chapter, mobile device and browser emulators provide some simulation of the mobile ecosystem, but lack the precision necessary to be used as the only tool for mobile browser testing. Emulators do mimic the features of a mobile browser, and some emulators even attempt to simulate the hardware constraints of a mobile device. Since emulators run on a desktop computer, in practice, simulation of hardware constraints is unreliable. Emulators are always faster and more powerful than their corresponding mobile devices. This makes emulators an inappropriate choice for testing browser and scripting performance.

Mobile emulators attempt to simulate mobile user input and navigation modalities, but have drawbacks when testing on touchscreen-only devices. Mouse movements in an emulator are unnatural equivalents to finger or stylus touches and gestures on a phone's touchscreen. Emulator testing can be appropriate for preliminary usability checks, but generally must be followed with on-device testing to ensure that a Mobile Web page is easy to use.

It is possible to configure an emulator to access the Internet using a proxy server, which could provide access to the operator's private network. However, proxy access is generally restricted to web partners with existing business relationships and not widely available to Mobile Web developers.

**NOTE:** Adventurous mobile developers could connect an emulator or desktop browser to the mobile operator network using a desktop computer and a wireless modem with appropriately configured access points (APNs). This is difficult to set up but, when successful, routes Web requests through the mobile radio network, allowing you to view source or sniff packets to inspect the changes that proxy servers and transcoders on the mobile network make to Mobile Web content. Only a few mobile networks look deep enough into this kind of network connection to realize that the emulator is not a real mobile device.

Or, you can connect a real mobile device to the desktop computer via Wi-Fi, configuring the computer to act as a transparent HTTP proxy into the wireless modem's radio network. You can then use the desktop computer to view the headers and bodies of HTTP transactions between the mobile device and the web site.

These testing approaches allow in-depth observation of the Mobile Web requests and responses used in advanced mobile development and QA.

# Testing in Desktop Browsers

By now, it should be clear that testing Mobile Web sites in desktop browsers is a poor substitute for either on-device or emulator testing. Desktop browsers provide little or no simulation of the mobile browser or ecosystem. Referring back to the three focus areas for simulation testing of a Mobile Web site in the "Mobile Browser Testing Considerations" section of this chapter, desktop browsers make no attempt to emulate mobile browser features or mobile device constraints and modalities. Since the browser used for testing resides on a desktop computer, it is also not possible to mimic the mobile user experience. Proxy or modem access to the operator's private network would allow simulation of mobile network access, but these access methods are restricted to web partners with existing business relationships.

However, desktop browsers do play an important role in providing imprecise but quick feedback during Mobile Web development. Web developers can and should use desktop browsers for basic compatibility testing of a Mobile Web document. Firefox, Safari, and other desktop browsers can be configured to impersonate a mobile device (as you learned in Chapter 2). Desktop browsers can enforce standards compliance and provide developers with loose feedback about mobile markup syntax and presentation.

Figures 10-3 and 10-4 show the rendering variations between Firefox and the Palm Pre emulator for two popular mobile web sites. Figure 10-3 displays the Mobile Web site for the New England Patriots, an NFL team (http://patriots.mobi), which Firefox and the Pre render quite similarly—but not identically. Notice the subtle font and spacing variations.

**Figure 10-3.** *Similar display of Mobile Web content in Firefox and the Palm Pre emulator*

Figure 10-4 shows the Mobile Web site for AccuWeather (http://www.accuweather.com/m/), which is drastically different between desktop and mobile browsers. One major variation in the display is the lack of a Viewport META tag that would have provided a scaling cue to the Palm Pre browser.

**Figure 10-4.** *Different display of Mobile Web content in Firefox and Palm Pre emulator*

> **NOTE:** Use your knowledge of smartphone optimizations for Mobile Web markup to guess a possible cause for such different rendering between Firefox and Palm Pre browsers in Figure 10-3.

## EXERCISE 10: PLAN A TESTING STRATEGY FOR YOUR MOBILE WEB SITE

Use the information in this chapter to plan a testing strategy for your Mobile Web site. Start by writing a one-page document that summarizes the purpose of the Mobile Web site, the use cases implemented on the site, and the behavior of major site features. In this document, detail your approach to on-device testing:

- Review the list of mobile devices, browsers, and networks targeted for the Mobile Web site. You created this list when you selected markup language(s) and designed the site's content adaptation features.

- From the list of target devices, choose a subset of mobile browsers, mobile devices, and mobile networks to use in testing.

    - Select a variety of browser models, mobile OSes, and device manufacturers.

- Decide whether testing will be performed using actual mobile devices, simulators, or desktop browsers.

    - If testing with actual mobile devices, choose a strategy for acquiring the devices.

These ad-hoc tests may help frame your device-testing strategy:

- Browse your Mobile Web site using a mobile device with radio and Wi-Fi access to the Internet. Inspect the HTTP request and response headers on the Web server. Do headers change with the Internet access method, and if so, how? How do header changes affect the functionality of your Mobile Web site?

- Choose a mobile device supported on the Mobile Web site. View the Mobile Web site using a desktop browser impersonating the mobile device, the device's emulator, and the actual mobile device. How does the rendering of the site change using the three kinds of browsers? Are the site features easy to access using the navigation and input modalities on the actual device?

Review your test strategy document with other project developers and designers. Gather feedback to improve the breadth and depth of testing on your Mobile Web site.

# Summary

This chapter examines Mobile Web testing strategies. Starting with an understanding of how mobile devices access the Internet, I presented a Mobile Web testing methodology that selects test devices to maximize browser, device, and network test coverage. You learned about the pros and cons of Mobile Web testing using actual browsers on mobile devices, emulated browsers, and desktop browsers. One cost-saving approach for testing on actual devices is to use a device remoting service, which allows remote control of mobile phones in US and European geographies. When testing on actual devices is not feasible, emulator testing is a reasonable alternative, but does not provide a completely accurate assessment of mobile browser compatibility or performance. Mobile Web testing using desktop browsers is wildly inaccurate and should only be used by Mobile Web developers for ad-hoc testing during active development.

The next chapter describes how to deploy a Mobile Web site to the public Internet and acquire traffic from mobile devices.

# Chapter 11

# Deploying a Mobile Web Site

The strategies in this chapter can help you deploy your Mobile Web site to the public Internet and acquire traffic. Mobile switchers are helpful tools used to co-locate Mobile and Desktop Web sites on a single domain. You can write your own switcher using a device database or implement an off-the-shelf product.

Once your Mobile Web site is live, on-site and off-site traffic acquisition strategies attract mobile users to your service. An on-site traffic acquisition strategy is implemented in the source code of your web site. This chapter discusses several on-site strategies, including standard Mobile Web site naming, link relationships in META tags, mobile sitemaps, and mobile-appropriate search engine optimization (SEO) techniques. An off-site strategy is one that is implemented externally. Search engine registration and adding link relationships into a companion Desktop Web site are off-site strategies that help improve your Mobile Web site's discoverability and position in mobile search engine rankings.

## Routing Mobile Traffic to a Mobile Web Site

Before deploying a Mobile Web site, you must choose its domain name. You might use a new, mobile-specific domain, or you can co-locate the site on the same domain as its companion Desktop Web site. If you decide to co-locate on the same domain, you may then choose either to isolate your Mobile Web content using a new path on the domain, or to integrate it with Desktop Web content on the same URL. All are valid deployment strategies.

Figure 11-1 summarizes deployment options for a new Mobile Web site.

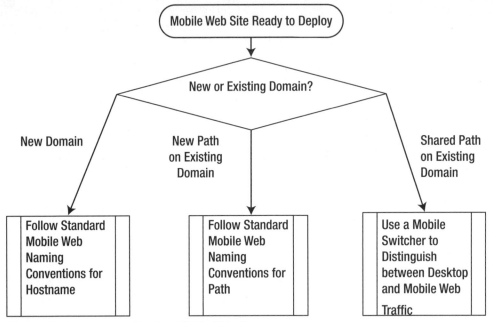

**Figure 11-1.** *Deployment options for a Mobile Web site*

If you choose a new domain name or a new path on an existing domain, it is important to select a name that matches industry-standard Mobile Web naming conventions. Following the naming conventions is one effortless way to announce your site's mobile-friendliness to the mobile ecosystem. This practice reduces the risk of double-transcoding. (See Chapter 12 for information about transcoders.)

If you choose to deploy on an existing path and domain name, you should implement a mobile switcher to distinguish between desktop and mobile traffic, routing each to its optimized web site. Mobile switchers are also used when developers deploy Desktop and Mobile Web sites on one domain and wish to route web traffic from the top-level domain to the most appropriate experience for the web client. A more advanced mobile switcher also considers the domain name point of entry and the user's choice of experience. Mobile switchers are easy to develop (see examples in Chapter 4) and are also available as off-the-shelf products.

## Standard Mobile Web Domain and Pathnames

If you deploy your Mobile Web site to a new, mobile-specific domain or pathname, you should follow industry standard naming conventions. The conventions were created as a mechanism for web crawlers, robots, and transcoders to identify Mobile Web content by inspecting only the URL.

The .mobi TLD (top-level domain) is the most prominent example of a Mobile Web domain naming convention. This TLD is managed by dotMobi (http://mtld.mobi/). Domains ending in .mobi may be purchased from domain registrars. If a .mobi domain hosts web content, the site *must* provide mobile-optimized markup for mobile browsers or risk revoked registration. This rule is enforced by dotMobi, which validates that all registered .mobi domains provide mobile-friendly web content.

Table 11-1 lists conventions and frequently chosen names for Mobile Web domains. With the exception of the .mobi TLD, all naming conventions relate to subdomains, prefixes for an existing domain name. In addition to the conventions listed in this table, the prefix i.* is increasingly popular for hosting iPhone-optimized Mobile Web sites.

**Table 11-1.** *Mobile Web Domain Name Conventions*

| Domain Name | Subdomain or TLD? | Example |
| --- | --- | --- |
| *.mobi | TLD | learnto.mobi |
| m.* | subdomain | m.facebook.com |
| mobile.* | subdomain | mobile.yahoo.com |
| wap.* | subdomain | wap.getjar.com |
| iphone.* | subdomain | iphone.mydomain.com |
| wireless.* | subdomain | wireless.mydomain.com |
| wml.* | subdomain | wml.mydomain.com |
| pda.* | subdomain | pda.mydomain.com |
| xhtml.* | subdomain | xhtml.weather.com |

Table 11-2 lists conventions and frequently chosen names for paths to Mobile Web content. Pathname conventions may be used when deploying your Mobile Web site on an existing domain name. Like the emerging i.* domain name convention, the /i/ path is a popular shortening of /iphone/ for hosting iPhone-optimized Mobile Web sites.

**Table 11-2.** *Mobile Web Path Conventions*

| Path | Example |
| --- | --- |
| /m/ | mydomain.com/m/ |
| /mobile/ | mydomain.com/mobile/ |
| /iphone/ | mydomain.com/iphone/ |
| /wireless/ | mydomain.com/wireless/ |
| /gmm/ | mydomain.com/gmm/ |
| /portable/ | mydomain.com/portable/ |

As the Mobile Web developer, you or your company control the choice of domain and pathnames used to host your Mobile Web site. It is advantageous to follow the naming conventions in this section, but you can ultimately choose any names you wish for your site.

## Mobile Switching Algorithms

If you co-locate Mobile and Desktop Web sites on the same domain, you may need to use a mobile switcher to route web traffic to the more appropriate of the two sites for the browser. Mobile switchers are web runtime scripts that conditionally redirect web clients to different destinations based on browser and device characteristics. Generally, switchers distinguish between desktop and mobile browsers, but they could also distinguish *among* mobile browsers. Switchers can redirect web clients by issuing an HTTP 302 redirect to a destination URL, by selecting a script to execute locally, or by performing any other appropriate action in the runtime language. Web developers often provide links that allow users to choose the preferred mobile- or desktop-optimized web experience, remembering this choice in a cookie so the switcher can later respect this user preference. Indeed, respecting a mobile user's choice of optimized web experience is a Mobile Web best practice.

It is easy to write your own mobile switcher using a device database and its companion web runtime API. A mobile switcher might use any device database characteristics (web standards support, browser characteristics, hardware capabilities, and so forth) as criteria for routing web traffic to one of several Desktop and Mobile Web sites.

Chapter 4 contains sample code for two simple switchers in Listings 4-5 and 4-8. Each switcher separates web traffic from desktop and mobile browsers, sending each to an optimized web site. A more realistic mobile switcher implementation would redirect to a variety of Desktop and Mobile Web content based on browser, device capabilities, and user preference.

Listing 11-1 is sample code for a more robust switching algorithm. It redirects to several web locations by separating web traffic into the following groups:

1. Desktop web browsers

2. Legacy mobile browsers that support only WML

3. iPhone and iPod Touch mobile devices

4. Touchscreen mobile devices (except for iPhone and iPod Touch)

5. Mobile devices without touchscreens

This algorithm checks device capability in order to weed out devices with browsers in groups 1 and 2 that should not receive Mobile Web content in XHTML-MP or XHTML. When a device meets the group criteria, it is immediately redirected to the best web location. The remaining mobile devices fall into Groups 3 through 5 according to capability. Apple mobile devices in group 3 are redirected to a Mobile Web site optimized for Safari Mobile. Touchscreen mobile devices in group 4 are redirected to a touch-optimized Mobile Web Site. The remaining devices are group 5, which are redirected to a lean Mobile Web site suitable for featurephones and smartphones. Listing 11-1 does not consider or save user preferences.

You can view Listing 11-1 by browsing to `http://learnto.mobi/books/bmwd/11/11-1.php` in a desktop or mobile browser. Impersonate browsers from each of the five groups to exercise the full functionality of the mobile switcher.

**Listing 11-1.** *Mobile Switcher Using WURFL Device Database*

```php
<?php
// This script is a mobile switcher that redirects a Web request to one of several
destinations, depending on device capabilities.

// Desktop browsers are redirected to this URI:
$desktopRedirect = "/books/bmwd/11/desktop.php";

// WML-only browsers are redirected to this URI:
$wmlRedirect = "/books/bmwd/11/legacy.wml";

// iPhone/iPod Touch browsers are redirected to this URI:
$iphoneRedirect = "/books/bmwd/11/iphone.php";

// Touchscreen browsers
$touchRedirect = "/books/bmwd/11/touch.php";

// All remaining mobile browsers (non-touch devices that support XHTML-MP) are
redirected to this URI:
$mobileRedirect = "/books/bmwd/11/mobile.php";

// Initialize WURFL
require_once('../04/wurfl-php-1.r1/WURFL/WURFLManagerProvider.php');
$wurflConfigFile = "/home/webadmin/learnto.mobi/html/books/bmwd/04/wurfl/wurfl-
config.xml";
$wurflManager = WURFL_WURFLManagerProvider::getWURFLManager($wurflConfigFile);

// Get the device making the HTTP request
$device = $wurflManager->getDeviceForHttpRequest($_SERVER);

// Check device capabilities and redirect as soon as criteria is met, to minimize device
database lookups.

// Bug Workaround: When WURFL identifies some desktop web browsers, it provides an array
for this capability. Choose the first value of such an array.
$isWireless = $device->getCapability('is_wireless_device');
if (is_array($isWireless)) {
        $isWireless = $isWireless[0];
}

// Group 1: Is this device a desktop browser?
$isDesktop = ($isWireless == "false");
if ($isDesktop) {
    header("Location: " . $desktopRedirect);
        exit;
}

// Group 2: Does the device support only WML?
```

```php
$preferredMarkup = $device->getCapability('preferred_markup');
$isWml = (strpos($preferredMarkup, 'wml') === 0);
if ($isWml) {
    header("Location: " . $wmlRedirect);
        exit;
}

// Group 3: Is this device an iPhone or iPod Touch?
// In WURFL, all iPhones and iPod Touch devices are descendents of the device with ID
"apple_iphone_ver1". Ascend the device hierarchy and test device IDs to find the parent
Apple device ID.
$isAppleParent = false;
$appleParent = "apple_iphone_ver1";
$ancestor = $device;
while ($ancestor != null) {
        $isAppleParent = ($ancestor->id == $appleParent);
        if ($isAppleParent) {
            break;
        }

        // An exception is thrown when we ascend past the top of the device hierarchy.
        try {
            $ancestor = $wurflManager->getDevice($ancestor->fallBack);
        } catch (Exception $e) {
            $ancestor = null;
        }
}
if ($isAppleParent) {
    header("Location: " . $iphoneRedirect);
        exit;
}

// Group 4: Does the device have a touchscreen?
$isTouchscreen = ($device->getCapability('pointing_method') == "touchscreen");
if ($isTouchscreen) {
    header("Location: " . $touchRedirect);
        exit;
}

// Group 5: Otherwise, the browser is on a non-touchscreen mobile device and supports
XHTML-MP
header("Location: " . $mobileRedirect);
exit;
?>
```

The first section of Listing 11-1 identifies the redirect URLs for each of the five groups of devices. Next, the WURFL device database and API are initialized. Then, the device database criteria for each group are evaluated using the WURFL API. If the requesting device is determined to belong to a group, an HTTP 302 redirect is immediately returned that directs the client to the appropriate web location.

# Mobile Switching Products

If you don't want to write your own mobile switcher, there are open-source and commercial alternatives.

The co-creator of the WURFL device database, Luca Passani, provides The Switcher (http://www.passani.it/switcher/), a commercial switcher for Java, PHP, and .NET that redirects between one desktop and one mobile URL. The Switcher is completely independent from the WURFL device database.

Idel Fuschini created the Apache Mobile Filter (http://www.idelfuschini.it/it/apache-mobile-filter-v2x.html, http://sourceforge.net/projects/mobilefilter/), an open source software library in Perl that is meant for use with the Apache web server with mod_perl2 extension module. The Apache Mobile Filter identifies the mobile device and adds WURFL device characteristics to Apache environment variables, making them available to any Web runtime framework that integrates with Apache. In addition, Apache configuration files can be used to tell the Apache Mobile Filter to redirect Web traffic from desktop browsers, mobile browsers, and transcoders to different destination URLs.

Listing 11-2 is a sample Apache and mod_perl2 configuration that allows the Apache Mobile Filter to function as a mobile switcher. This listing should be added to Apache's httpd.conf configuration file.

**Listing 11-2.** *Apache Mobile Filter Configuration for Mobile Switching*

```
# Configuration Group 1: Basic Apache Mobile Filter Configuration
# WURFLFilter configuration
PerlSetEnv MOBILE_HOME <path to Apache Mobile Filter installation>
PerlSetEnv CacheDirectoryStore /tmp
PerlSetEnv WurflNetDownload true
PerlSetEnv DownloadWurflURL  http://downloads.sourceforge.net/wurfl/wurfl-latest.zip#
PerlSetEnv CookieCacheSystem true # used only in production
PerlModule Apache2::WURFLFilter
PerlTransHandler +Apache2::WURFLFilte


# Configuration Group 2: Redirect Targets for Desktop, Mobile and Transcoder Requests
# Redirect URL for desktop browsers
PerlSetEnv FullBrowserUrl http://www.fullbrowsersite.com
# Redirect URL for mobile browsers
PerlSetEnv MobileVersion http://www.mobilesite.com
# Redirect URL for transcoders
PerlSetEnv RedirectTranscoder true
PerlSetEnv RedirectTranscoderUrl http://www.transcodersite.com
```

The first group of mod_perl2 configuration directives in Listing 11-2 set the basic configuration for the Apache Mobile Filter. This includes providing a path to the software installation, enabling caching, and choosing whether the Filter automatically downloads updated versions of the WURFL device database.

The second group of configuration directives sets the destination redirect URLs for web requests from desktop browsers, mobile browsers, and, optionally, transcoders.

# Mobile SEO and Traffic Acquisition

Once your Mobile Web site is deployed on the public Internet, the next challenge is acquiring traffic from mobile users. The tips in this section help drive mobile traffic to your site by increasing your site's discoverability and SEO. Registering your Mobile Web site with mobile search engines is one off-site method to encourage your site's inclusion in search results targeted to mobile devices. Several on-site traffic acquisition techniques increase mobile site discoverability and associate related Desktop and Mobile Web sites. Metadata in mobile markup can express link relationships that tell search engines that your site is mobile-optimized. Mobile sitemaps advertise the pages of your Mobile Web site and provide entry points for mobile crawlers. On-page mobile SEO techniques improve search rankings without bloating the size of your markup documents.

This section does not discuss marketing techniques to boost the visibility of your Mobile Web site to mobile users. Books and web sites on web and mobile marketing are great resources for learning traffic acquisition techniques using online, print, and guerilla marketing campaigns.

## Mobile Search Engines and Crawlers

Mobile search engines are search engines that crawl and index web documents optimized for mobile devices. When accessed from a mobile browser, many Internet search engines provide mobile-specific search results, generally in a category named Mobile Web. In addition, there are now several new search engines that provide search results for mobile devices only.

You may notice mobile search engines attempting to answer the search query before or instead of generating the traditional search results "list of blue links". This optimization saves mobile users the effort, cost, and risk of clicking search result links that may not provide the desired information. For example, if a mobile user searches for "patriots score", the mobile search engine may display the score from the latest New England Patriots NFL football game in a more prominent location than search result links.

Figure 11-2 is a screenshot of Yahoo! mobile search results on a Nokia 96 for the "patriots score" search query. Notice how the team name is recognized and the Patriots' win/loss record, latest score, and official Web site are provided above any other links to web pages.

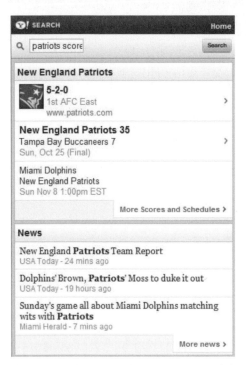

**Figure 11-2.** *Yahoo! search results on the Nokia N96 for the "patriots score" search query*

A traffic acquisition strategy for the Mobile Web starts with submitting your Mobile Web site to mobile search engines. Site submission allows you to provide the site URL and sometimes other metadata including the target geography. On the Mobile Web, site submission makes a difference because crawler discovery of mobile-optimized Web sites is more difficult. A mobile crawler has trouble discovering the entire Mobile Web because it is decidedly less cross-linked than the Desktop Web. Entry points for mobile-optimized web sites are not simply domain names. As we saw in the "Standard Mobile Web Host Domain Names and Pathnames" section, mobile entry points can reuse domains from Desktop Web sites and may introduce new pathnames. This makes it difficult to discover Mobile Web sites using zone files of registered domains.

Table 11-3 lists major mobile search engines that should be your targets for site submission.

Make sure that crawlers for mobile search engines (called mobile crawlers) are allowed to access your Mobile Web site. Both device databases mentioned in Chapter 4 identify mobile crawlers from major search engines, allowing your mobile switcher to route them specifically to your Mobile Web content.

**Table 11-3.** *Major Mobile Search Engines*

| Search Engine Name | URL |
| --- | --- |
| Google Mobile | http://www.google.com/m |
| Yahoo! Mobile | http://m.yahoo.com/ |
| AOL Mobile | http://wap.aol.com/ |
| Ask.com Mobile | http://m.ask.com/ |
| Bing Mobile | http://m.bing.com/ |
| Taptu | http://m.taptu.mobi/ |
| Find.mobi | http://find.mobi |

# Using Link Relationships for Mobile Site Discovery

In XHTML and XHTML-MP, the `<link>` tag is used to express link relationships between web pages. It has a variety of uses, including referencing external style sheets, as seen in Chapter 3. If your Mobile Web site has a companion Desktop Web site, the `<link>` tag can be used to increase Mobile Web site discovery. Embed a specially formatted `<link>` tag in a Desktop Web page to advertise the URL of the page's mobile-optimized version.

The `<link>` tag has the following format, where RELATIONSHIP is a token identifying the nature of the link relationship, MEDIA is the media type of the external content, and URL is the URL of the external content:

```
<link rel="RELATIONSHIP" media="MEDIA" href="URL" />
```

If a page in your Desktop Web content has an equivalent page that is mobile-optimized, embed the `<link>` tag in the Desktop Web page with a relationship of alternate, media type of handheld, and provide the URL to the Mobile Web page.

For example, Yahoo! News on the desktop uses the URL http://news.yahoo.com/. Its mobile equivalent for featurephones is http://us.new.m.yahoo.com/w/ynews on the Mobile Web. The Yahoo! News desktop home page might embed this `<link>` tag to express its relationship to the Yahoo! Mobile News site:

```
<link rel="alternate" media="handheld" href="http://us.new.m.yahoo.com/w/ynews" />
```

This technique targets page-to-page relationships (that is, home-page-to-home-page, article-to-article), not relationships between site entry points on the Desktop and Mobile Web.

One benefit of this technique is that transcoders may elect to forward mobile browsers to the mobile-optimized target of the link relationship when the mobile browser requests a desktop-oriented web document.

# Mobile Sitemaps

Sitemaps are XML files used by webmasters to advertise the list of URLs available on a web site to search engine crawlers. Webmasters submit sitemap URLs manually using HTTP pings to search engines, or by including sitemap URLs in a `robots.txt` file placed in the root directory of a web server. (Learn more about `robots.txt` and the Robot Exclusion Standard at `http://www.robotstxt.org/`.)

A well-behaved search engine crawler reads the `robots.txt` file to determine whether the content owner allows it to crawl web site content on the domain. A special `Sitemap` directive in the `robots.txt` file is used to provide sitemap URLs to search engine crawlers.

For example, the last line of the `robots.txt` file at `http://learnthemobileweb.com/robots.txt` advertises a sitemap URL to Web crawlers:

```
Sitemap: http://learnthemobileweb.com/sitemap.xml
```

An XML sitemap file provides a list of URLs, last modified dates, relative priority among site URLs, and the expected frequency at which the URL content changes. (Learn more about the Sitemap standard at `http://sitemaps.org/protocol.php`.)

Listing 11-3 is a snippet from the Learn the Mobile Web sitemap at `http://learnthemobileweb.com/sitemap.xml`. Notice that metadata is provided for each URL using the `<loc>`, `<lastmod>`, `<changefreq>` and `<priority>` elements.

**Listing 11-3.** *Example Sitemap from LearnTheMobileWeb.com*

```xml
<?xml version="1.0" encoding="UTF-8"?>
<urlset xmlns="http://www.sitemaps.org/schemas/sitemap/0.9">
<url>
        <loc>http://learnthemobileweb.com/</loc>
        <lastmod>2009-10-17T22:23:27+00:00</lastmod>
        <changefreq>daily</changefreq>
        <priority>1.0</priority>
</url>
<url>
        <loc>http://learnthemobileweb.com/2009/07/mobile-meta-tags/</loc>
        <lastmod>2009-07-31T19:29:32+00:00</lastmod>
        <changefreq>monthly</changefreq>
        <priority>0.6</priority>
</url>
</urlset>
```

Google extended the Sitemap standard to create Google Mobile Sitemaps (`http://www.google.com/support/webmasters/bin/answer.py?answer=40348&topic=9346`). A Google Mobile Sitemap is an XML file with the same structure as a Sitemap, adding a new XML namespace to convey that site URLs are optimized for mobile. Google Mobile Sitemaps must contain *only* URLs to Mobile Web content. Since mobile sitemaps are sitemaps, their URLs may be added to `robots.txt` files for discovery by any mobile crawler.

Google Mobile Sitemaps use the additional XML namespace
`http://www.google.com/schemas/sitemap-mobile/1.0` with the `mobile` prefix and create
a single XML element in that namespace. Each `<url>` element in a mobile sitemap
whose URL is Mobile Web content (which should be all `<url>` elements) contains the
child XML element `<mobile:mobile/>` to note that the URL is intended for mobile
devices.

Listing 11-4 is an example Google Mobile Sitemap containing two mobile-optimized
URLs. Google's mobile extensions to the Sitemap standard are bolded. Notice the
additional namespace declared in the `<urlset>` element and the `<mobile:mobile/>`
element marking each URL as mobile-optimized.

**Listing 11-4.** *A Google Mobile Sitemap*

```
<?xml version="1.0" encoding="UTF-8"?>
<urlset xmlns="http://www.sitemaps.org/schemas/sitemap/0.9"
xmlns:mobile="http://www.google.com/schemas/sitemap-mobile/1.0">
<url>
  <loc>http://www.google.com/xhtml</loc>
  <lastmod>2004-10-01T23:05:32+00:00</lastmod>
  <mobile:mobile/>
</url>
<url>
  <loc>http://www.google.com/wml?site=local</loc>
  <mobile:mobile/>
</url>
</urlset>
```

Create a Google Mobile Sitemap and link to it in `robots.txt` to provide your Mobile Web
site URLs to mobile search engines. Many mobile search engines read Google Mobile
Sitemaps to discover mobile-optimized web pages.

# SEO for the Mobile Web

Some traditional SEO techniques are also appropriate for Mobile Web sites. I have
already discussed mobile site submission as the first step in mobile SEO. Markup
validity, adherence to industry best practices, and ensuring that your Mobile Web
content is publicly accessible are basic mobile SEO principles that can reap dividends.

Markup validation is discussed in detail in Chapter 9. The mobile-readiness, syntactic
validity, and adherence to industry best practices of your Mobile Web site are very
important to mobile SEO, much more so than on the Desktop Web. Crawlers for mobile
search engines must differentiate between desktop-optimized and mobile-optimized
web pages in order to include only Mobile Web content in search results. Mobile
crawlers must judge the level of mobile optimization in your Mobile Web documents.
Valid and obviously mobile-optimized markup, served with a mobile MIME type, makes
it easy for the crawler to conclude that your pages are intended for the Mobile Web.

Furthermore, your Mobile Web pages must be available on the public Internet and
spiderable by mobile search engine crawlers. I cannot stress this point enough. If you

deploy a mobile switcher, web clients identified as mobile crawlers must be redirected to mobile-optimized content. Keep in mind that mobile crawlers may mimic the user-agents of actual mobile devices, to determine the degree to which the web site adapts content to mobile browsers. Nothing reduces web site discoverability better than excluding search engine crawlers from your web site. Use the features of your selected device database to identify web traffic from mobile crawlers and route the traffic to your Mobile Web site. Your site's robots.txt file, discussed earlier in this section, can also be used to explicitly allow or exclude spidering from mobile crawlers.

Search rankings and discoverability will also improve when your Mobile Web site focuses on providing the best possible mobile user experience. Use the language features of XHTML-MP or XHTML to embed textual metadata in the document header. Display Mobile Web content in the mobile markup language and centralize presentation details in CSS. Do target search keywords for your web document.

On the Mobile Web, search keyword use is different. Because text entry is difficult, mobile search keywords are shorter than desktop searches. Mobile users are also frequently searching for nearby locations. Make sure your mobile search keywords identify the location of Mobile Web content (for example, "portland") and your Mobile Web site category (such as "coffee") to target your site for location-aware search keywords like "coffee portland" (or even simply "coffee" when the mobile user's location is determined to be Portland, Oregon).

Embed search keywords into your mobile markup document's title, header, and body. Keyword use is also appropriate in anchor text for internal links.  However, remember the small screens of mobile devices and short attention spans of mobile users. Keyword stuffing provides a poor user experience, frustrates impatient mobile users, and increases abandonment rates for your Mobile Web pages. So, use keywords judiciously. Focus instead on providing a great user experience. Simple, user-centered web programming practices will reap SEO benefits.

Of course, SEO for the Desktop and Mobile Web is a moving target. Mobile SEO in particular is constantly evolving. Even mobile search engines are experimenting with mobile SEO techniques. It is important for Mobile Web developers and marketers to keep current with best practices in mobile SEO because the landscape is rapidly changing.

## SEO Practices to Forget

Many traditional on-site SEO practices try to increase search rankings by repeating keywords over and over again in a web document. Relentless keyword stuffing degrades the user experience and inflates the size of the web document. Both effects are especially detrimental on the Mobile Web, where users want compact, snackable information and the fastest possible download speeds while browsing. Remember, the typical session length for Mobile Web users is only 3-5 minutes. Mobile Web users want to achieve their browsing goal and move on with their daily lives.

In particular, the desktop SEO practice of keyword stuffing is a very bad idea for the Mobile Web. The examples below of `<a>` and `<img>` tags in XHTML uncover attributes that are frequently used for keyword stuffing. Here, desktop SEO suggests repeating search keywords in the TITLE, LINK_TEXT, ALT, and LONGDESC attribute values:

```
<a href="HREF" title="TITLE">LINK_TEXT</a>

<img src="HREF" alt="ALT" title="TITLE" longdesc="LONGDESC" />
```

This technique does increase the search keyword density in the web document, and without degrading the user experience, but it does so at the cost of inflating the size of the web document. Document size matters on the Mobile Web. Mobile users see a real difference in browsing performance when downloading large markup documents (documents over 15KB). Keyword stuffing using the attributes above provides no presentation gains for mobile browsers and just unnecessarily bloats the document and slows download speeds across mobile networks. Skip keyword stuffing entirely for Mobile Web content.

## EXERCISE 11: ASSESS SEO FOR POPULAR MOBILE WEB SITES

This exercise evaluates the effectiveness of on-page SEO techniques for a popular web site with versions optimized for both desktop and mobile browser. Choose any web site to evaluate. Most social networking, news, entertainment, weather, and travel web sites provide desktop and mobile versions.

- Browse the desktop-optimized version of the web site in any web browser. View its source code.

- Impersonate a mobile device in Firefox. Browse the mobile-optimized version of the web site. View its source code.

- Using mobile search engines (listed in Table 11-3), search for pages on web site. Vary the keywords you use to find the web site. Look for results in the Mobile Web section of the mobile search results page.

Answer these questions:

1. How discoverable is the Mobile Web site in search engines?
2. How does the web site promote discovery of its mobile-optimized version?
3. Does the web site use a sitemap? A Google Mobile Sitemap?
4. How many of the on-page mobile SEO techniques discussed in this chapter are used in the Mobile Web site?
5. Can you infer new mobile SEO strategies from the mobile search results that you encountered?

Answers to these questions may provide insights for deploying your own desktop and mobile-optimized web sites or suggest a new mobile SEO technique.

# Summary

This chapter focuses on deploying your Mobile Web site and attracting traffic from mobile users. Naming conventions for domains help advertise your site URL as containing Mobile Web content. Mobile switchers separate Desktop and Mobile Web traffic using device characteristics, routing each to an optimized user experience. Mobile switchers are easy to write in any web runtime language, but there are also commercial and open-source product alternatives. On-site mobile SEO techniques, such as establishing link relationships between Desktop and Mobile Web content and using a mobile sitemap advertise your Mobile Web site URL to search engine crawlers. Some SEO techniques from the Desktop Web can be reused to optimize Mobile Web content, but many inappropriately bloat document size. Instead, simple, new Mobile SEO principles assist in page optimization.

The next chapter provides survival tips for your Mobile Web site in the mobile ecosystem and describes how you can safeguard your site from undesired transformation by transcoding proxy servers.

# Chapter 12

# How to Play Well in the Mobile Ecosystem

With your Mobile Web site deployed to the public Internet, an important and ongoing consideration is good citizenship in the mobile ecosystem. The mobile ecosystem is the collection of industry players who control subscriber access to the Mobile Web, provide web-based services for mobile subscribers, and shape user behavior on the mobile Internet. Mobile network operators, Mobile Web developers, OEMs, mobile software companies, and infrastructure providers (including transcoder vendors) are all examples of players in the mobile ecosystem. You are also a citizen in the mobile ecosystem. Given the explosive pace of Mobile Web expansion, a single savvy Mobile Web developer can influence the industry, so do not underestimate your ability to make a difference.

In a nutshell, this chapter is about identifying and resolving the ecosystem challenges that affect whether and how mobile users can access your Mobile Web site. Even a standards-compliant and publicly available Mobile Web site can lose users due to ecosystem interference, so it is critical for developers to vigilantly advocate for open access to the Mobile Internet.

## Operators, Transcoders, and Proxies, Oh My!

The challenges that mobile subscribers face in gaining unrestricted access to the Mobile Web are of particular concern to Mobile Web developers. Mobile user access to your Mobile Web site can be disrupted in many ways. Discoverability is a challenge. Mobile Web sites may be deployed and available, but subscribers may not know how to find them, especially for long-tail sites or sites whose domain names differ from their desktop Web equivalents. Mobile users may make mistakes or grow frustrated when typing a long URL into the mobile browser. A user may search using a mobile search engine, but fail to find your Mobile Web site due to crawling problems or a poor search experience. Also possible, but less likely in today's mobile ecosystem, is for a mobile operator to block access to your Mobile Web site using a blacklist. More likely, a mobile operator deploys a transcoding proxy through which all Mobile Web traffic flows, and this transcoder reformats your markup to provide an "optimized" view of your site to the user. The "optimized" view may or may not be an improvement for your mobile users.

Just a few years ago, it was more common for operators to gate access to the public Internet using whitelists and blacklists of allowed and restricted domains. This measure was intended to ensure a safe and adequate user experience for early adopter subscribers tiptoeing onto the early Mobile Web. Operators also attempted to steer Mobile Web traffic to preferred partner sites. Today, such restrictive measures seem draconian. Open access to the Internet is the norm for most mobile operators. However, occasionally blacklists are discovered to be in use and almost always, it is up to the Mobile Web developer to advocate for the removal of their domains from the blacklist.

Procedures for petitioning to modify a blacklist vary widely among mobile network operators. Mobile Web developers should start by contacting the operator through business development channels or using the operator's developer or partner program. (See Table 10-3 in Chapter 10 for a list of developer programs for US and European mobile operators.)

A more common way that mobile subscribers might be impeded in accessing your Mobile Web site, assuming the subscriber knows your site's URL and enters it correctly into the browser, is interference from a transcoding proxy server, known simply as a transcoder. A transcoder is a proxy server deployed by an operator (or a mobile portal or search engine) that intercepts web requests from mobile devices, modifies HTTP request headers, and transforms the markup in the web response to ensure syntactic compatibility with the mobile device. Here, the term "transform" is a euphemism for machine modification of your site's web markup.

In reality, a transcoder has an impossible directive. The purpose of transcoders is to bring the rich Desktop Web to mobile browsers and broaden the featurephone handset catalog that is capable of browsing the Desktop Web. Transcoders ensure that Desktop Web markup is syntactically compatible with limited mobile browsers, preventing the browser crashes and power cycling seen when desktop markup is fed unmodified into these browsers.

Machine adaptation of desktop-optimized markup for mobile browsers almost never results in an adequate user experience. Transcoded web pages may be unlikely to crash a finicky mobile browser, but the resulting user experience may also be crippled and frustrating. Content from the transcoded web page is spread across several Mobile Web pages, requiring multiple clicks and network round-trips to view the original page in its entirety. Forms and other interactive features of the original web page may also be disabled or broken.

Mobile operators tout the benefits of transcoders, including increasing subscriber access to the Web. Here are two excerpts from Verizon Wireless introducing its transcoding service:

> *[The transcoder] … will optimize the format of a web site so that it is quick to render on the mobile device and easy for subscribers to view*

*and navigate…. [The transcoder] allows subscribers to use their wireless devices to view full HTML sites …*

*The integrity of the website will remain intact as the service is only intended to optimize the presentation of the content for delivery in a format manageable for mobile devices.*

Browse to `http://www.vzwdevelopers.com/aims/public/OptimizedViewOptout.jsp` to view the entire discussion of the *Optimized View for Mobile Web* transcoder deployment.

The following excerpts are from Sprint introducing its Open Internet Browsing Optimization Solution transcoder:

*Since a large number of the Sprint Nextel CDMA subscribers navigate the off-portal open Internet using mobile devices and browsers that may not presently support all "Open Web" content, the need increases to improve the user experience through network-level protocol and content adaptation mechanisms for certain traffic using the HTTP web protocol.*

*While these adaptation mechanisms are important to improve the customer experience through content rendered using mobile web browser applications, it is also important to ensure that other users are not negatively affected. To this end, some of the key considerations … include ignoring sites and content known to be mobile-friendly as well as only optimizing traffic from specific sources or user-agents.*

Browse to `https://developer.sprint.com/getDocument.do?docId=98354` to find the Sprint Application Developer Network technical document describing the implementation of the dynamic content adaptation service.

Both the Verizon Wireless and Sprint discussions position transcoders as optimization services that bring the promise of the Desktop Web to limited mobile browsers, with no negative effects on the "integrity of the web site".

> **NOTE**: Mobile operators generally configure transcoders not to intercede in requests from web-capable smartphone browsers. Operators rightly allow unmodified access to the Web and Mobile Web for smartphones and increasingly, for other kinds of devices with web-capable browsers.

A well-behaved transcoder allows limited mobile browsers to safely view desktop-optimized web sites, albeit at the cost of a degraded user experience. A well-behaved transcoder does not modify mobile-optimized web documents or any requests from web-capable mobile browsers. Further, a well-behaved transcoder respects mobile users and content owners by allowing them to opt out of content transformation (using techniques described later in this chapter).

A poorly behaved or misconfigured transcoder can wreak havoc on the Mobile Web, transcoding markup that is already optimized for mobile devices (called "double transcoding"), thus providing a degraded user experience for both Desktop and Mobile Web sites.

Here's where the lawyers perk up. Some transcoders deployed on the Mobile Web today have been observed not only double-transcoding mobile markup but also substantially reformatting Mobile Web content and even inserting external headers, footers, and advertising, all without consideration of copyrights or permission from content owners.

Revisit Figure 10-1 in Chapter 10. This diagram traces web requests from a mobile device through the mobile network, across the public Internet, and to the destination web server. Transcoders can be placed in one of two locations in this figure:

- A transcoder deployed by a mobile operator is positioned in Component B, the operator's private network. The transcoder is a caching and transforming proxy through which some or all Mobile Web traffic is routed.

- A transcoder deployed by a mobile search engine or portal (or any other Mobile Web site) is positioned in Component C, the public Internet. This transcoder is still a transforming proxy, but its impact is limited to transcoding web content linked from its related Mobile Web site.

## Transcoders on the Public Internet

Table 12–1 lists several transcoders available on the public Internet. In the transcoder URL, replace <URL> with the (escaped) URL to the Desktop or Mobile Web page to view after transcoding. For example, browse to `http://skweezer.com/s.aspx?q=http://learnthemobileweb.com` to view the transcoded version of the Learn the Mobile Web desktop Web site in Skweezer.

**Table 12–1.** *Transcoders on the Public Internet*

| Transcoder | URL | Description |
| --- | --- | --- |
| Google Wireless Transcoder | `http://www.google.com/gwt/n?u=<URL>` | Transcodes Google search results for mobile devices. |
| Infogin | `http://d2c.infogin.com/en-us/lnk000/=<URL>` | Transcodes mobile search results for Bing. |
| Skweezer | `http://skweezer.com/s.aspx?q=<URL>` | Public transcoder. |
| Openwave OpenWeb | `http://webeeze.net/<URL>` | Public transcoder. |

The transcoders in Table 12–1 can be used to view adapted versions of Desktop and Mobile Web sites. The exercise at the end of this chapter explores how public transcoders adapt web sites for mass-market mobile devices and smartphones.

Let's examine how public transcoders adapt an example Desktop Web site. Figure 12–1 shows an original, untransformed web page from the Learn the Mobile site, (http://learnthemobileweb.com/2009/07/mobile-meta-tags/).

**Figure 12–1.** *Original, untransformed Learn The Mobile Web desktop web site*

Figures 12–2 and 12–3 show the same web page transcoded using the Google Wireless Transcoder, Infogin, Skweezer, and OpenWeb transcoders. Review Figures 12–1, 12–2, and 12–3 to find similarities and differences in presentation, usability, and content preservation between the original and transcoded versions of the web page.

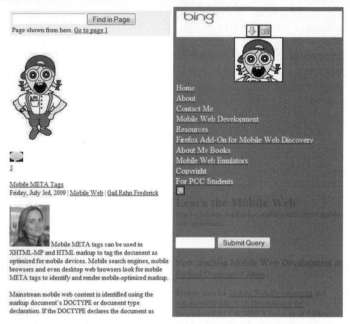

**Figure 12–2.** *Transcoded views of Learn the Mobile Web desktop web site using Google and Infogin transcoders*

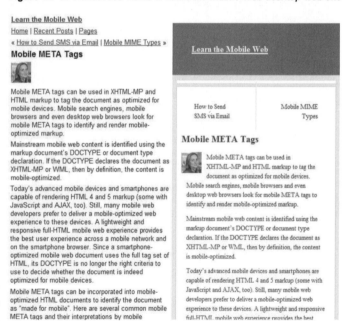

**Figure 12–3.** *Transcoded views of Learn the Mobile Web desktop web site using Skweezer and OpenWeb transcoders*

# Standardizing Transcoder Behavior

The behavior of transcoders is not standardized. At the time of this writing, two mobile industry organizations have proposed guidelines for transcoder behavior in the mobile ecosystem.

The W3C's Mobile Web Initiative is drafting the *Guidelines for Web Content Transformation Proxies* document (`http://www.w3.org/2005/MWI/BPWG/Group/TaskForces/CT/editors-drafts/Guidelines/latest`), guidance for transcoding proxies about the conditions under which content adaptation should be performed. This effort is an Editor's Draft and currently has no official standing as a W3C recommendation or proposed standard. It includes written contributions from invited W3C experts and transcoder vendors. With this effort, the W3C is working with transcoding companies and select Mobile Web developers to set guidelines for common transcoder behavior that aims to ensure a functional user experience while respecting the rights of content owners.

Luca Passani and the WURFL developer community have drafted an alternative document, Rules for Responsible Reformatting: A Developer Manifesto (`http://wurfl.sourceforge.net/manifesto/`). The Manifesto suggests transcoder behavior that respects content owner rights and avoids disrupting device recognition for transcoded Mobile Web traffic.

The W3C draft guidelines and Manifesto differ in many significant ways. Here are some of the most high-profile disagreements about transcoder behavior in the mobile ecosystem:

- Transcoders might modify the request headers from the mobile device originating the request. The transcoder identifies itself to the web site, instead of the mobile device, and provides the original device headers under modified header names.

    - **W3C**: Transcoders should not modify the values of most headers. Exceptions include `User-Agent`, `Accept`, `Accept-Charset`, `Accept-Encoding`, and `Accept-Language`. The original values of modified request headers must be copied to the corresponding `X-Device` header. (That is, move original user-agent to `X-Device-User-Agent` header. Modify transcoder user-agent as `User-Agent` header value.) Do not delete header fields.

    - **Manifesto**: Do not modify existing request headers. OK to add extra headers.

- Some transcoders rewrite HTTPS links and reformat the content of HTTPS documents, breaking end-to-end security between the secure web site and the mobile browser.

- **W3C**: Intercepting HTTPS transactions is strongly not recommended. If a transcoder intercepts and reformats HTTPS content, it must advise the end user and provide a bypass mechanism.

- **Manifesto**: Do not disrupt the end-to-end security of HTTPS. Do not rewrite HTTPS links or reformat HTTPS documents.

- Transcoders might transform mobile markup. This generally occurs because the transcoder fails to identify the original markup as optimized for mobile devices.

  - **W3C**: Transcoders should not transform documents served with mobile doctypes, mobile MIME types, or mobile URL patterns.

  - **Manifesto**: Do not transform documents served with mobile doctypes, mobile MIME types, or mobile URL patterns. Do not adapt web pages under 30KB.

- Transcoders modify web pages even when the content owner forbids the transformation.

  - **W3C**: Do not transform requests or responses using the `Cache-Control: no-transform` HTTP header.

  - **Manifesto**: Do not transform document served with the `Cache-Control: no-transform` HTTP response header.

- Transcoders do not allow users to opt out of transformation, or don't remember user preferences. Instead, transcoders might require users to opt in for transformation services, rather than assuming transcoding is desirable and requiring user action to view the original web document.

  - **W3C**: Transcoders must respect and remember user preference to opt out of transformation.

  - **Manifesto**: Allow users to opt in for transformation instead of forcing them to opt out.

You might have strong opinions about at least some of these issues. If you want to influence the debate about transcoder behavior on the Mobile Web, contact the W3C Mobile Web Initiative at `public-bpwg-ct@w3.org` and the WURFL developer community at its WMLProgramming Yahoo! Group, `http://tech.groups.yahoo.com/group/wmlprogramming/`.

The rest of this chapter presents defensive programming techniques Mobile Web developers can use to reduce the likelihood their mobile markup is transcoded.

# Defensive Programming for the Mobile Web

Now that you understand the promise and reality of transcoders in mobile networks, you'll want to know how you can best confront this challenge. This section provides several practical web development techniques for declaring your markup as optimized for mobile devices, and therefore reducing the likelihood it will be transcoded.

Transcoders are closed-source proxy servers that are not yet governed by any particular standards, so it is impossible to provide an authoritative list of techniques that completely prevent content transformation by any transcoder. These techniques will greatly minimize your site's exposure to unwanted transcoding. In addition, the techniques are helpful for convincing mobile search engine crawlers that your Mobile Web markup is indeed optimized for mobile devices.

## Declaring Your Markup as Mobile-Friendly

The goal of defensive programming for the Mobile Web is to forcefully declare that your markup is optimized for mobile devices. Earlier chapters of this book have introduced several techniques to indicate that a document is Mobile Web content, including:

Complying with industry standards for the site domain name and/or path to mobile content (Chapter 11).

- Using a mobile markup language—XHTML-MP or WML (Chapter 3). Desktop markup languages (HTML and XHTML) are transcoding targets.

- Including the XML doctype declaration in the mobile markup document (Chapter 3).

- Serving mobile markup documents using a mobile MIME type (Chapter 2).

Desktop MIME types (such as text/html) are transcoding targets.

### Using a Self-Referencing Link Relationship

Chapter 11 discussed using the `<link>` tag in XHTML and XHTML-MP to express a thematic relationship between desktop- and mobile-optimized versions of the same web content to improve Mobile Web content discovery. A similar technique can be used as defensive programming against transcoders.

To reinforce that a Mobile Web document is indeed optimized for mobile devices, a self-referential `<link>` tag may be embedded into the document header to declare "I am the mobile-optimized version of this content." To achieve this, use the `alternate` link relationship, the `handheld` media type, and the self-referencing URL to the Mobile Web document. The example below illustrates this technique for the home page of the learnto.mobi Mobile Web site:

```
<link rel="alternate" media="handheld" href="http://learnto.mobi" />
```

## Using META Tags

Two uses of the `<meta>` tag in XHTML and XHTML-MP indicate that the document contains markup intended for mobile devices.

The `HandheldFriendly` `<meta>` tag was originally used to identify mobile content in AvantGo browsers, but has now become a general convention for tagging Mobile Web markup documents. This example shows the usage of the `HandheldFriendly` `<meta>` tag:

```
<meta name="HandheldFriendly" value="true" />
```

The `HandheldFriendly` `<meta>` tag should be used as shown, with no changes to the `name` or `value` attributes.

The `MobileOptimized` `<meta>` tag is used to indicate that the document contains mobile markup intended for display at a specific screen width. This `<meta>` tag was originally used by the Pocket Internet Explorer browser in Windows Mobile devices to force a web document to display in a single column layout at a fixed width. Over time, its use has been generalized to tag mobile-optimized markup. The `value` attribute of this `<meta>` tag should be the screen width for which the Mobile Web document is targeted, or the screen width of the requesting mobile device. The example below shows the `MobileOptimized` `<meta>` tag for a mobile device whose screen width is 320 pixels:

```
<meta name="MobileOptimized" value="320" />
```

## Using Response Headers and Document Size

The `Cache-Control` and `Vary` HTTP response headers, introduced in Chapter 8, are meant to control proxy server and browser caching of the web document, but can also be used to forbid transcoding of a document or image. Use the `no-transform` value of the `Cache-Control` header to direct transcoders not to modify the document, and identify the document as varying the content with values of the `User-Agent` request header, as in the following example:

```
Cache-Control: no-transform
Vary: User-Agent
```

Finally, lightweight mobile markup documents are less likely to be adapted by a transcoder. Keep the file size of Mobile Web markup documents under 15KB. Transcoders may conclude that larger web documents are not intended for mobile devices.

# Identifying Requests from Transcoders

For better or worse, some transcoders modify HTTP request headers when proxying web requests from a mobile device to a web server. A device database helps a Mobile Web developer identify requests from transcoders. When most transcoders rewrite request headers, they prefix some existing mobile device headers with `X-Device` and add new headers with the original names to identify the transcoder. Not every transcoder follows this convention, but many do.

Table 12–2 lists the names of modified request headers that generally identify the mobile device originating the web request. It is a good defensive practice for Mobile Web developers to detect and manage traffic from transcoders. Use a device database to identify web traffic from transcoders and check the alternate headers to identify mobile device information. Identifying the source mobile device and serving transcoders mobile markup increases the chance that the transcoder will pass your markup back unaltered.

**Table 12–2.** *Request Headers Commonly Modified by Transcoders*

| Header Name in Mobile Device Request | Header Name in Request Proxied Through Transcoder |
| --- | --- |
| User-Agent | X-Device-User-Agent |
| Accept | X-Device-Accept |
| Accept-Charset | X-Device-Accept-Charset |
| Accept-Encoding | X-Device-Accept-Encoding |
| Accept-Language | X-Device-Accept-Language |

In addition to overwriting the values of common request headers, transcoders may also identify themselves using the Via or X-Mobile-Gateway headers. The example request headers below identify that the request was proxied through the Novarra transcoder used at Verizon Wireless:

```
Via: 1.1 Novarra (Vision/7.3)
X-Mobile-Gateway: Novarra-Vision/7.3 (VZW; Server-Only)
```

Listing 12–1 is example PHP code that identifies a transcoded Mobile Web request using the WURFL device database API and request headers commonly modified by a transcoder.

**Listing 12–1.** *Transcoder Identification using the WURFL Device Database API*

```
// This snippet decides whether the web request is transcoded and, where possible,
// identifies the source mobile device.

// Initialize WURFL
require_once('wurfl-php-1.r1/WURFL/WURFLManagerProvider.php');
$wurflConfigFile = "/home/webuser/learnto.mobi/html/books/bmwd/04/wurfl/wurfl-
config.xml";
$wurflManager = WURFL_WURFLManagerProvider::getWURFLManager($wurflConfigFile);

// Get the device making the HTTP request (without regard for transcoding, yet)
$device = $wurflManager->getDeviceForHttpRequest($_SERVER);

// Find the user-agent for the device in a possibly transcoded request.
$userAgent = null;
```

```php
// Check whether WURFL identifies the device as a transcoder
$isTranscoder = $device->getCapability('is_transcoder');
if ($isTranscoder == "true") {
    // Get the user-agent from the header recommended by WURFL
    $headerName = $device->getCapability('transcoder_ua_header');
    if ($headerName != null) {
        // Transform header name into a format required by PHP
        $headerName = str_replace(' ', '_', $headerName);
        $headerName = str_replace('-', '_', $headerName);
        $headerName = strtoupper($headerName);
        // If the user-agent was found in this header, use it.
        if (isset($_SERVER['HTTP_' . $headerName])) {
            $userAgent = $_SERVER['HTTP_' . $headerName];
        }
    }
}

// Check for the X-Device-User-Agent header value.
// If it exists, it is the device originating the request.
if ($userAgent == null) {
    if (isset($_SERVER['HTTP_X_DEVICE_USER_AGENT'])) {
        // Save the device user-agent.
        $userAgent = $_SERVER['HTTP_X_DEVICE_USER_AGENT'];
    }
}

// If we can't find a transcoded user-agent, then the request is untranscoded.
if ($userAgent == null) {
    $userAgent = $_SERVER['HTTP_USER_AGENT'];
}

// Get the originating mobile device using the user-agent value
// found in one of many headers.
$device = $wurflManager->getDeviceForUserAgent($userAgent);
```

The code in Listing 12–1 starts by initializing the WURFL device database (using the method explained in Chapter 4). Next, the device is identified in WURFL using the original HTTP request headers. This step allows the developer to use WURFL to determine whether the request is from a transcoding proxy server. The script then attempts to find the user-agent of the mobile device originating the transcoded web request.

The WURFL property is_transcoder has the string value true when the web request is proxied through a transcoder. WURFL tracks a modified header location for the user-agent of the mobile device originating the request in the transcoder_ua_header property. Listing 12–1 checks the value of this header for the device's user-agent.

If the user-agent of the originating device can't be determined using WURFL device properties, the script checks the X-Device-User-Agent header, a common header location for the user-agent in transcoded web requests. The script uses this user-agent, if it exists.

If the user-agent of the originating device can't be determined using WURFL or from alternate HTTP request headers, the request does not originate from a transcoder so the User-Agent header is used to find the user-agent of the requesting mobile device.

Listing 12–2 is example PHP code similar to Listing 12–1 that identifies a transcoded Mobile Web request using the DeviceAtlas device database API and request headers commonly modified by a transcoder.

**Listing 12–2.** *Transcoder Identification Using the DeviceAtlas Device Database API*

```php
// This script decides whether the web request is transcoded and, where possible,
// identifies the source mobile device.

// Initialize DeviceAtlas
require_once('deviceatlas/Mobi/Mtld/DA/Api.php');
$tree = Mobi_Mtld_DA_Api::getTreeFromFile("deviceatlas/20091028.json");

// Find the user-agent for the device in a possibly transcoded request.
$userAgent = null;

// DeviceAtlas does not have device database properties that identify requests from
// transcoders, so we only manually check in the X-Device-User-Agent header fo
// an alternate user-agent.

// Check for the X-Device-User-Agent header value.
// If it exists, it is the device originating the request.
if ($userAgent == null) {
    if (isset($_SERVER['HTTP_X_DEVICE_USER_AGENT'])) {
        // Save the device user-agent.
        $userAgent = $_SERVER['HTTP_X_DEVICE_USER_AGENT'];
    }
}

// If we can't find a transcoded user-agent, then the request is untranscoded.
if ($userAgent == null) {
    $userAgent = $_SERVER['HTTP_USER_AGENT'];
}

// Get all DeviceAtlas properties for the device.
$props = Mobi_Mtld_DA_Api::getProperties($tree, $userAgent);
```

The code in Listing 12–2 starts by initializing the DeviceAtlas device database. (See Chapter 4 for more about DeviceAtlas.) The script then looks for the user-agent of the mobile device originating the transcoded web request. It then checks the X-Device-User-Agent header and uses this as the mobile device's user-agent, if its value is not null.

If the user-agent of the originating device can't be determined from the alternate HTTP request header, the request does not originate from a transcoder, so the User-Agent header is used to find the user-agent of the requesting mobile device.

The user-agent is used to identify the mobile device in the DeviceAtlas API and obtain device properties.

A developer might conclude that the code in Listings 12–1 and 12–2 requires some effort to determine the User-Agent of the actual mobile device originating a transcoded web request. This kind of new logic is required on any Mobile Web site wanting to identify the underlying mobile device motivating a request from a transcoder.

## EXERCISE 12: EVALUATING TRANSCODERS ON THE PUBLIC INTERNET

Mobile Web transcoders should reformat web content optimized for desktop browsers to improve its usability on mobile devices. Transcoders should leave mobile-optimized content intact and respect the rights of content owners to disallow machine optimization.

A simple experiment in Firefox allows you to evaluate the usability of transcoded web pages.

- Configure Firefox to impersonate a mobile device using the User-Agent Switcher and Modify Headers add-ons.
- Use the public transcoders listed in Table 12–1 to view the transcoded versions of Desktop and Mobile Web sites.

Answer these questions:

1. How does the markup, navigation, page structure, and usability change between the original and transcoded versions of the site?

2. How does the behavior of web forms and other client-server interactivity change for the transcoded version of the site?

3. How does the transcoder preserve and respect the site content?

4. Is it possible to navigate past the transcoder to view the original site?

5. How does the transcoder handle requests from smartphones? Does it adapt Desktop and/or Mobile Web sites when the requesting mobile browser is web-capable?

6. What to you are the pros and cons of browsing the Web using a transcoder?

Make sure to vary the impersonated mobile devices to evaluate how transcoders behave with mass-market mobile devices and smartphones.

# Summary

This chapter familiarizes you with the mobile ecosystem and the struggle between operators, transcoder vendors, and independent developers to understand and shape user behavior on the Mobile Web.  I presented several reasons why mobile users have difficulty discovering and navigating to a Mobile Web site. You learned why transcoders are deployed on a mobile network, how transcoders affect the web browsing behavior of mobile users, how to detect web traffic from transcoders, and how to uncover the mobile devices originating the requests. Defensive programming techniques reduce the risk of your already mobile-optimized Web page being double-transcoded for ostensibly improved compatibility with mobile devices.

The next chapter explores the future growth of the Mobile Web and changes in mobile subscriber and usage patterns. You'll meet expert Mobile Web developers and architects who share their opinions and projections about the future of the Mobile Web and mobility in general.

# Chapter 13

# The Future of the Mobile Web

This final chapter explores the future of the Mobile Web, including its expected near-term growth, changes in subscriber patterns, and industry projections.

Mobile Web subscriber and content growth is exploding and expected to continue its aggressive gains. Mobile subscribers are browsing the Mobile Web in ever greater numbers and upgrading to more powerful mobile devices with standards-compliant full Web browsers.

The number of mobile subscribers choosing smartphones is expected to dramatically increase. In a June 2009 report about the Palm Pre, the Yankee Group, an independent technology research and consulting firm in Boston, Massachusetts, found that 41% of consumers are likely to choose a smartphone as their next mobile phone purchase. Smartphone volume will grow to 38% of all handsets by 2013, representing the largest growth opportunity within mobile devices. (By 2013, a majority of mobile subscribers are still expected to *not* be using smartphones, though the devices they do use might contain mobile browsers compliant with Web standards.) Browse to
`http://www.yankeegroup.com/pressReleaseDetail.do?actionType=getDetailPressRelea se&ID=2458` to read the press release for the Yankee Group report.

A February 2009 survey by Nielsen and Tellabs polled 50,000 US and European mobile subscribers and found that, despite the global recession, mobile Internet use and mobile data adoption are expected to spike through 2010. Twenty-five percent of consumers who do not currently use mobile data services intend to start using them shortly. Consumers intend to dramatically increase the use of mobile data services over the next two years—with a significant ramp-up by February 2010. Up to 71% of consumers anticipate daily use of services such as mobile Internet. But, these consumers remain concerned about cost, speed, reliability, and quality of service. Browse to
`http://www.tellabs.com/news/2009/index.cfm/nr/53.cfm` to read press release for the Nielsen and Tellabs survey.

These statistics support the continued explosion of Mobile Web content and users, and suggest that the amount of traffic on the Mobile Web will continue its aggressive growth. For Mobile Web developers, growing audiences mean greater appetites for Web-based mobile services and improved revenue opportunities.

# Mobile Web Experts on the Future of Mobility

In the second half of 2009, I conducted a series of email interviews with a panel of technology experts, each with a long history on the Mobile Web, to find out what they thought about the advancement of the Mobile Web and the effects of standards and standards bodies on Mobile Web technologies. I also asked these "gurus" to provide advice and guidance to new Mobile Web developers. For many developers, the Mobile Web is first understood through dry technical documents (standards specifications, OEM and operator documentation, industry best practices, etc.) read alone in an office. This interview highlights the individuals and personalities behind the documentation to uncover the thriving, dynamic, and controversial aspects of the Mobile Web.

The roundtable participants, each with a long history on the Mobile Web, are forthcoming with their opinions and ideas about the future of mobile devices and the Mobile Web. They assess the impact of Web 2.0 and 3.0 technologies on the Mobile Web, offer advice to new Mobile Web developers, and discuss the evolution of mobile devices, mobile browsers, and the Mobile Web.

Andrea Trasatti was most recently the Directory of Technology Strategy at dotMobi. He has been deeply involved in mobile device recognition and content adaptation on the Mobile Web, first as the co-creator of the WURFL device database and more recently as the designer and lead developer for dotMobi's DeviceAtlas device database.

Bennett Marks is Senior Architect for Compatibility and Industry Cooperation at Nokia. As a former member of the Open Mobile Alliance, Marks has been involved with standardizing mobile browser technologies since 1997.

François Daoust is the Mobile Web Initiative specialist at W3C. (The Mobile Web Initiative oversees all W3C standards and recommendations efforts for the Mobile Web.) Formerly of MotionBridge and Microsoft, Daoust now maintains the W3C mobileOK checker and is an online tutor for the W3C Mobile Web Best Practices.

Luca Passani is the other co-creator of the WURFL device database and API. Formerly of Openwave and AdMob, Passani now leads WURFL development and advocates for the rights of content owners and developers on the Mobile Web.

## ROUNDTABLE INTERVIEW WITH MOBILE WEB EXPERTS

FREDERICK: What is the most remarkable thing about the Mobile Web today? The most frustrating? How will these perks and problems change in the near future?

TRASATTI (dotMobi): The Mobile Web is part of the Web, and of course its most remarkable achievement is [its] reach. Accessing the Web has been made very easy and the amount of information available is almost immeasurable. Mobile access to the Web is still in its infancy despite the fact that we've been trying to make it real for the last 10 years, but soon it will be ubiquitous.

The most frustrating part is the quality of the content that you can consume on the Web. Let's forget for a moment the distinction between Web and Mobile Web, in fact this distinction is a technicality, to consumers [it is] all one big thing and that's the way it should be. Today, the vast majority of sites cannot distinguish a mobile device from a desktop PC and a lot of sites are hardly usable even on netbooks (that are supposed to be PCs, not mobile devices). As a user, I think the biggest frustration is the uncertainty of the content they will receive when visiting a site, and if it will even work.

Luckily, after many stale years, things are now moving fast again, and what is making this even faster is that both Web site owners and mobile device vendors are converging. Easier and cheaper ways to produce mobile content are emerging while vendors are selling devices with bigger screens, more comfortable input methods and better browsers. The combination of the two forces, plus lower access prices from operators, is making the Mobile Web "happen."

MARKS (Nokia): Just seeing the realization of the dream that we were all talking about almost 15 years ago is amazing to me. The problems of small screen, lack of CPU … were well understood even 10 years ago. To truly have "the Internet in your pocket," with the democratizing value that it represents blows me away. I guess the most remarkable things for me are cultural. Kids incorporate it effortlessly into their lives. Browsers on phones are making the Internet available to 1 or 2 billion people that have not had access before.

I continue to be frustrated by the UI limitations that we face. They are to some extent self imposed by our narrow thinking about how we interact with these devices. As long as the bandwidth and attention requirements remain the same, there will be strong limitations to what we can do with these devices. I await better visual interfaces (direct eye projection?) and better input mechanisms.

As we arrive at critical mass for the location-aware mobile Internet, there will be a fundamental shift in expectations about interpersonal communications. This is already happening. Knowing "everything" about someone is an opportunity to do good or bad. The definitions of security and privacy are being turned upside down. I still marvel at the difference between how I perceive privacy and how my 18-year-old child views it.

DAOUST (W3C): The most remarkable thing is the diversity of modalities to experience the Web. Mobile constraints forced engineers to innovate, leading to touch screens, zoomable user interfaces, augmented reality browsers, etc.

The most frustrating part is fragmentation, coupled with the difficulty of testing content on a wide range of mobile devices. This is the plague of the mobile world. It prevents "normal" people from authoring content that truly works on mobile devices.

Fragmentation is diminishing at a slow and steady pace, thanks to the Web stack of standard technologies being more consistently implemented in mobile devices, initiatives such as device description repositories (DDR), e.g., WURFL or DeviceAtlas to make Mobile Web developers life easier, and thanks to standardization efforts.

PASSANI (WURFL): At the cost of sounding banal, the most remarkable thing about the Mobile Web is the Web itself, the fact that everyone with a mobile phone will be able to access a subset of the full Web that has high enough value for mobile users to access it when they are not in front of a PC.

My work has always been in the area of empowering content authors to make their content available to mobile users. This is not a simple task, because the Web as we know it is not built to work on mobile devices. Developers need to figure what is relevant to mobile users and "mobilize" that part. In this context, the most frustrating part is, needless to say, device fragmentation: there is simply no device like another!

Device fragmentation has added a completely new dimension to the problem[s] of content authors: you cannot take the properties of the mobile device for granted, which is something that you can do with traditional Web development (at least as a first approximation). Mobile developers need new programming paradigms which accept the fact that clients may vary wildly.

In my opinions, this problem will not change. Device fragmentation is here to stay. Different people like different phones. That's just like different people like different cars. Some love SUVs that make them feel safe. Some love small cars that are easy to park in big cities. Some love Ferraris and can afford them. Others love Ferrari, too, but can only afford a Fiat Punto. If someone asked you which car is going to win over all others, the answer would be simple: none. There will still be plenty of different kinds. The measure of success is decimals of market share. Mobile phones are [no] different. Device fragmentation is here to stay and there is not much that "standards" can do about it.

FREDERICK: How will mobile devices and Mobile Web technologies evolve in the next five years?

TRASATTI (dotMobi): If I had to use just one word, it would be "convergence". Mobile devices are turning into mini-computers. The growing ease of access is making our life more and more connected. Synchronization is a very important topic and I'm not thinking about contacts and calendars only, I am talking about being able to access all my resources from everywhere. We are moving from having one PC for everything to having one PC at work, one at home, a netbook, and one or more devices. BlackBerrys and iPhones prove that users want to be able to do as much as they can with each device.

Devices will therefore evolve to become more connected and interoperable.

Touch is big in hype today and is probably an ideal input method if you want to manage windows and very different content, but I would not rule out keyboards and dialpads as they can be more compact and more efficient. I doubt any of these technologies will disappear, although touch is definitely growing at the cost of the others.

MARKS (Nokia): We are still in a device-centric mode. Changes, such as embedded projectors, better sensors, faster graphics engines, and indoor GPS will define the directions of applications development for the next five years. I hope that there will be one or more ID interaction technologies that will finally pan out in the marketplace. So far RFID, barcodes, and BT buoys have not been practical enough for general deployment. Maybe Bocodes? (`http://www.newlaunches.com/archives/bocodes_a_replacement_for_traditional_barcodes.php`)

When we truly have continuous positional, situational, and motivational awareness transmitted to our mobile device, we will see a whole new class of applications that today are only hinted at. The other thing that will drive the direction in the next five years is the move to ubiquitous HSDPA and LTE (radio network technologies). There will be reliance in the car and elsewhere on applications that today require a fast WiFi connection. I don't think that this will spawn many new applications, per se, but rather bring us to the point where we will rely on certain applications that we cannot today rely on outside of the house.

DAOUST (W3C): A mobile device is a magic wand. It's an all-in-one gadget that features a phone, a camera, a GPS, accelerometers, a list of contacts, an agenda, micropayments facilities through one's mobile operator, etc. The current trend is to enable access to these capabilities directly from the browser, using Web technologies like JavaScript. That is the work of the newly created Device APIs and Policy Working Group within W3C (http://www.w3.org/2009/dap/).

It is a switch from regular Web pages to Web applications and relates to the ongoing efforts to standardize widgets (http://www.w3.org/2008/webapps/wiki/PubStatus#Widgets_Specifications).

PASSANI (WURFL): Faster hardware. More bandwidth. More WiFi. All together this will mean more people browsing the Mobile Web and more companies mobilizing their Web content. Last week, my friend who has known me for more than six years finally asked me if I could configure the Internet on his phone. It's happening slowly. But it's happening.

FREDERICK: How do you see the Mobile Web adopting and affecting Web 2.0 and Web 3.0 technologies and methods? How does Web 2.0 and Web 3.0 adapt for mobile?

TRASATTI (dotMobi): It seems like the Web 2.0 as it happened on the desktop is not able to migrate smoothly to the mobile. UIs used on the Web hardly fit on mobile and cooperation as it happened on sites like Digg has not migrated to the Mobile Web.

On the other hand, the new trend of providing APIs to access and edit information in a machine-to-machine fashion might be the door to allow Web 2.0 to happen on mobile devices. I think that Web 3.0 is the missing link to open the dam to cooperation on Mobile Web. Once you have an easy API that you can use to access and modify data in the cloud, you can create specialized UIs and applications and optimize for the mobile context. Not just the use on a mobile device, but also the immediacy that is needed for a user on the move.

MARKS (Nokia): The notion of a mashup (at this point a very 2007 concept) must be revisited, not as a way to integrate multiple data sources on the internet side, but rather as an integration of data on the client and Web side as equal partners. Indeed, I would go one step further, and say that the notion of traditional client and server roles in applications has outgrown its usefulness. The device is an equal partner now, providing data alongside Web sources and integrated together to find, filter, and present relevant information. That is why we are seeing such a standards battleground developing around the "Web runtime API." That is also why we are seeing some mobile devices showing up with Web servers in them. It's an easy way to turn the tables.

We are seeing some Web 3.0 adaptation already in HTML 5 and children of "Google Gears," where there are a set of standard facilities for both sharing the compute tasks, and for doing it with intermittent connectivity. Solving the intermittent connectivity problem in a robust and standard way will be the big Web 3.0 win.

DAOUST (W3C): Mobile devices used to be late, trying to provide support for things that already existed in the desktop world. While constraints still restrict some of the possibilities, mobile devices now introduce new features and needs that affect the development of Web technologies:

- Access to the device capabilities through the development of standardized APIs.

- More semantics within the markup to help identify the roles of parts of the content, and provide new ways to display the information to users (while focused on accessibility, the ARIA specification also matches some of the preoccupations of mobile devices: http://www.w3.org/TR/2009/WD-wai-aria-20090224/).

- New interaction methods that change the way information is processed by users (gestures, speech, movements, augmented reality).

PASSANI (WURFL): I don't know what Web 2.0 is, nor do I know what Web 3.0 is. I hit Wikipedia and found some kind of explanation, but I am still confused. All I see is that there are Web sites. Web sites may have user-generated content. User-generated content may obviously take advantage of offering a mobile UI to user who is mobile. Spending a lot of effort in deriving higher truths out of these simple facts is an exercise which does not particularly excite me. I'll gladly leave it to others.

FREDERICK: How do you see the Mobile Web and native mobile applications evolving in the next five years? Will they converge?

TRASATTI (dotMobi): Companies like Google would like everything to happen on the Internet. I think that both the Web and native applications have their advantages; there will definitely be some convergence with applications using more and more the network, but they will remain separate entities and should continue taking advantage of their differences.

A dark horse that sits in the middle between the two is widget technology, recently approved in its version 1.0 by the W3C. Widgets try to take the best of both worlds. It will be interesting to see how they evolve and how developers take advantage of this new technology.

MARKS (Nokia): Assuming that native application development will always be more expensive than Web development, it reduces to a financial decision where the cost of native development is taken as the cost of protecting your critical applications space. When this equation fails, as I think it will in three to five years, then convergence will happen quickly.

DAOUST (W3C): There will always be specific needs to native mobile applications, but we believe the Web will be *the* platform for mobile applications in the future. Native mobile applications are de facto specific to a certain class of devices. This means the resulting application cannot address the whole market. Support for Web technologies will vary from device to device, but the advice mentioned above apply here as well: ubiquitous Web applications should work everywhere, and then content adaptation should make it possible to improve user experience on more specific classes of devices.

PASSANI (WURFL): I don't think they will converge at all. Usability is a key factor for users to decide that they want to use the mobile internet. No matter how good and fast a mobile device is going to be, the full Web will always be a pain to use on a mobile device. This is certainly true in a 5 year perspective, but probably quite a bit longer than that. What we will see is a proliferation of tools that makes it easy to create mobile content, as well as tools which empower developers to easily "mobilize" their own existing Web content.

FREDERICK: Is the standards-based Web browser the killer app for mobile devices? If not, then what is?

TRASATTI (dotMobi): The killer app is the interoperability, the ability for users to access the same resources they use in a different context from their mobile device. If the browser becomes the enabler, then it will be the killer application. I see a future where there will be many applications that are important in the day-to-day life of a mobile user, but hardly a single application that wins over all the others.

MARKS (Nokia): The killer app was, is, and will remain VOICE. The standards-based Web browser is what levels the playing field for data applications. Lowering the cost-to-entry barrier for getting on the mobile device is critical but not how I define a killer app.

DAOUST (W3C): The Web is a killer platform. It does not necessarily have to stay within the "browser app." Web technologies may be part of other apps. Widgets are one example. Yes, the underlying Widget engine is a browser, but it is slightly different from a real browser application.

PASSANI (WURFL): There is no such thing as the killer app. Or, there are many killer apps. The killer function in mobile is communication. SMS is the killer app. Email is another killer app. WA-based chat is also a killer app. Social networking introduces new aspects, but it is still about communication.

Communication has such high-value for consumers that they think 10 Euro cents is an acceptable price to deliver 160 bytes of information (i.e., the length of one text message).

FREDERICK: What is the role of transcoders in the mobile ecosystem? How do transcoders affect Mobile Web browsing patterns? How will their role change in the next five years? Is content adaptation by proxy the future of the Mobile Web?

TRASATTI (dotMobi): Five years is a very long time in this space. I don't think that content adaptation by proxy is the future of the Mobile Web, but it will definitely remain as a technology. There are millions of sites on the Internet that have not been updated in 5 or 10 years. Some users still access them, and although they probably do not cater all the traffic alone, altogether they do account for a lot of traffic. Proxies will be important to allow users to access any content they wish without being concerned if it will work.

Transcoding proxies use a holistic approach and try to do a good job on any possible site. This is nearly impossible, of course, and the content they produce is often less than perfect. Usability is probably what suffers the most. Nevertheless, they have the great advantage of removing the concern from the user about the accessibility of a Web site. This should be considered an advantage of transcoding proxies. With the advancement of mobile device technology and the creation of Web sites that are optimized for users on the move, the importance of transcoders will diminish. They will likely continue to exist to cover all those niche sites that never bothered to get updated.

MARKS (Nokia): I hope transcoders are an affectation of a technology in transition. My experience is that transcoders are a tradeoff between the short-term gains they present and the long-term problems they generate. I don't think that content adaptation by proxy is the future of the Mobile Web, at least I hope not.

DAOUST (W3C): The Internet has always been about "smart ends, dumb core." Things start to evolve there, and lots or research projects are being conducted to design smarter cores. Transcoders could be viewed as such an attempt. They were introduced to bridge the gap for old devices that do not have full support for Web technologies. In theory, that means a larger portion of the Web is accessible from mobile devices, that's a very good thing!

Transcoders trigger many concerns in practice, from basic technical issues to tricky control, privacy, and security issues, most of them being grounded on the fact that transcoders are "in the middle," with limited control from Web authors and from end users. The Mobile Web Best Practices working group is working on a set of guidelines for transcoders (http://www.w3.org/TR/ct-guidelines/).

Some mobile browsers have also been developed with a small client and a transcoding component that runs on the company's servers (e.g., Bolt, Skyfire, Opera Mini). The transcoding component cannot be bypassed. Secure content (think user credentials and credit card number) are thus decrypted on the company's servers.

Issues are likely to show up in the "usual" desktop world as well, c.f. Opera Turbo:

```
http://labs.opera.com/news/2009/03/13//
```

Content adaptation is useful for a variety of reasons (e.g., to transcode on the fly a video to a mobile user that does not currently have enough bandwidth) and is likely to stay around. More semantics are needed to flag content that may be transcoded, and more generally speaking to have the different pieces of the delivery chains talk and understand each other.

PASSANI (WURFL): I could answer this question in two ways. That transcoding has such a huge potential for destruction of the mobile ecosystem that operators should stay away from it, regardless of the small increase of data usage they may obtain when they launch it. For transcoders, Web content is cannon fodder. They chop up whatever comes in their way, irrespective of the effort that the content owner may have made to recognize mobile users and provide a mobile-optimized experience for them.

On the other hand, I can try to see the big picture and provide a more compromising answer. Transcoders are necessarily launched together with relatively cheap flat-fee data plans for users. This is good, because it finally delivers a good message to consumers: don't be afraid to give the Mobile Web a try. If, in addition to this, operators decide to respect the rules of the Manifesto for Responsible Reformatting (http://wurfl.sourceforge.net/manifesto/) when they deploy their transcoders, then there is potential for an upside to transcoders, too. But, respecting the mobile ecosystem is key.

FREDERICK: What is the role of organizations like the W3C, OMA, dotMobi, and the WURFL community in shaping Mobile Web technologies and practices?

TRASATTI (dotMobi): While there have been some small struggles between OMA and W3C about who should lead the development of Web technologies on the Mobile Web, I think that both have now cleared what their position should be. The W3C is focusing on Web-related technologies while the OMA is focusing more on network layers and communication protocols. This is a positive development where the W3C can continue doing what it has done well in the past years and the OMA can focus on the technologies that define how operators and devices interoperate. The OMA will likely remain less visible to the public.

WURFL is, of course, a great project that offers an entry point to the Mobile Web. It should continue its amazing work in the open source world, trying to make it always easier to create content and help remov3 the problem of device detection while empowering developers to create interfaces that optimize the access to content.

MARKS (Nokia): Each has a different role in the ecosystem. My friend Luca Passani started WURFL as a way to solve market incompatibilities between browsers in an effort driven by developers. I chaired the OMA UAProf (User Agent Profiling) working group in OMA, to solve some of the same issues, but from a manufacturer's point of view. In OMA, and subsequently W3C, we attempted to plug holes in the standards themselves to increase interoperability. But this is a long-term process, and sometimes driven by market forces that these organizations cannot control.

W3C has published a number of Web best practices documents. Dan Applequist from Vodafone has been a champion of this type of activity for a long time. However, here too, there are market forces that tend to drive "best practices" in different directions. That is why the W3C document reads as "apple[quist] pie and motherhood," stating the obvious but not giving detailed advice for any particular situation.

DAOUST (W3C): One role is to tackle fragmentation, and thus move away from a Mobile Web restricted to a few mobile experts and create a Mobile Web that regular Web authors can play with. Reducing fragmentation also includes reducing discrepancies between desktop and mobile worlds that are just two facets of the same Web. A second role is to educate people. That is one of the goals of the Mobile Web Best Practices standard. A third role is to enable new possibilities that originate from the mobile world. Standardized device APIs are required to make things possible without running into new fragmentation nightmares.

PASSANI (WURFL): I don't see that any of these organizations have much in common. For the W3C, I think they had a chance to be a significant player in the mobile industry, but they badly blew it. One thing that the mobile industry badly needs is someone to trust. Someone that has the credibility to say, "I am not here for the money, so you can trust me to do the right thing for the industry as a whole." Someone in that position would be able to "police" industry players and call out those who don't go far enough in implementing basic standards or do not abide by certain industry ethics.

W3C had a chance to occupy that position, but execution was poor and the lack of vision displayed by whoever was running that initiative was disappointing. First, W3C did not come to terms with a very simple idea: either you give citizenship to all devices (and then you need to accept and ratify mobile fragmentation) or you state that devices without this and that feature (say, 3G, big screen, JavaScript, CSS, and so on) are outside of the scope of the initiative. W3C did not take a decision. They preferred to keep the waters cloudy and hope to get away with redefining the Mobile Web, making it appear like an instance of the full Web and proceed to claim ownership on standards for the new area. This was very shortsighted, if you ask me. Not getting rid of this basic ambiguity backfired on W3C's plan badly.

The W3C Mobile Web Best Practices has very limited value to developers, who typically end up turning elsewhere for advice.

But W3C also managed to do worse than this. W3C did not see the potential for destruction that transcoding could bring to the Mobile Web. They allowed transcoder vendors to create a W3C task force to ratify bad transcoding practices with the Content Transformation Guidelines. These guidelines bless transcoding hacks and allow them to appear as compliant with a standard. Consider that transcoders hide a device make and model from HTTP requests, break HTTPS end-to-end security, remove banners advertisements (and income!) from the original site and repurpose the content of a site without authorization from the content owner. It is not surprising that many find W3C's endorsement of these practices to be disgusting.

OMA is the organization that started WAP. So, they did have a role in the history of the Mobile Web. In my perception, OMA is no longer as relevant as it used to be. I think they suffered the same problem as W3C: OMA did not have the credibility to be the sheriff and enact a fair vision for everyone. Pushed by different sides, things moved too slowly and confusingly. Internet standards eventually took over in many areas. In spite of this, the Mobile Web still means XHTML-MP in most cases, so they did leave a mark.

I never had any particular feelings for or against dotMobi's introduction of a .mobi domain. After all, from a technological viewpoint, the actual domain makes no difference at all. Also, in the beginning, I appreciated dotMobi's effort to create tools and documentation for developers. In 2007, dotMobi disappointed me, though. While many individuals at dotMobi fully recognized the danger that transcoders represented for developers, the organization ended up supporting the W3C transcoder task force.

WURFL is neither an organization nor a standards body. WURFL is an open-source project and a community of people who have adopted it. Yet, I think you are right that the WURFL name can be mentioned side-by-side with organizations that attempt to create standards in this area. WURFL was founded on the concept that device fragmentation is here to stay. WURFL is all about supporting developers who want to manage device fragmentation, rather than sticking their heads in the sand and hoping it disappears.

For this reason, WURFL is the de facto standard when it comes to mobile device capability detection. But that's not it. WURFL is also about its large community of real mobile developers. The community was created 10 years ago and it has constantly been packed with practitioners who need to make the Mobile Web work in the face of all the screwups by device manufacturers, gateway makers, and network operators. It is not surprising that people on the WMLProgramming Yahoo! group are opinionated and always ready for a fight.

The WURFL community has grown strong over the years. And respected. This respect has become clear when the community first complained loudly about transcoders and then proceeded to create a very clear and actionable set of rules for operators and transcoder vendors, the so called "Manifesto for Responsible Reformatting." This initiative has taught tens, or even hundreds, of operators around the planet how to deploy transcoders (if they really have to) without pissing off the totality of their ecosystem in one shot. This is a great example of where the WURFL community has stepped forward and played the role that neither W3C, nor OMA, nor .mobi were able to play for the lack of spine, lack of independence, lack of honesty, or a combination of the three.

FREDERICK: Pitch the importance of your organization's best practices documents. Is any single best practices document authoritative for the Mobile Web? Why or why not?

MARKS (Nokia): As I alluded to earlier, the core universal "best practices" are useful, but do not address situations in enough detail to be prescriptive. Just look at an iPhone, Nokia N97, and the BlackBerry of your choice. How can you have a single set of universal best practices for a capacitive multitouch, a resistive fine-point touch and a QWERTY device? Furthermore, each of these has a different UI and different browser interaction model. Nokia spends significant money on end-user interaction modeling. We think we are right for our devices. Apple clearly has a strong model, and they have it right for the segment that that they target.

DAOUST (W3C): When work on the Mobile Web Best Practices standard was started in 2005, Web technologies were already there, but Web authors had no real reference to follow to make their content work on mobile devices, making it difficult for them to start to enter the mobile playground. Best practices were needed. The Mobile Web Best Practices standard is the result of a couple of years of discussion among the main actors of the mobile scene. The best practices it contains were thoroughly checked and agreed upon. Its goal is to serve as a reference for Web authors who want to go mobile.

PASSANI (WURFL): After spending a few months with the W3C group which delivered the Best Practices, I finally realized that there was no way anything good for developers could come out of that initiative. So, I walked out and created the guidelines the way they should have been. Of course, I called on the community to contribute to the effort. This gives the Global Authoring Practices for the Mobile Web (http://www.passani.it/gap/) a credibility which the W3C and the dotMobi work is lacking.

FREDERICK: What are the four most important facts that new developers should learn about the Mobile Web?

TRASATTI (dotMobi): Device diversity, open standards, agile development, and pragmatism.

MARKS (Nokia): In the short term, given that the development community is all about making money, developers need to understand in a fundamental way how mobility affects their application for the user, and what is required to leverage it. Secondly, developers need to understand what web-side or cloud-based architecture means to their applications. Thirdly, developers need to study the issues around compact, space-limited UI design.

DAOUST (W3C): First, a functional user experience on a vast majority of devices (both desktop and mobile) can be achieved through a clean and ubiquitous design. Separate content, layout, and control and degrade or enhance gracefully. The Mobile Web Best Practices, while targeting "mobile" devices, contain practical ubiquitous recipes. Existing tools may help developers assert they follow some of these best practices, seen in particular in the mobileOK mark, automatically testable using checkers such as the W3C mobileOK Checker (http://validator.w3.org/mobile/).

Second, more carefully crafted user experiences can be achieved on top of the ubiquitous design through content adaptation. Beware: such content is more time-constrained (mobile devices and accessible technologies change over time), targets specific classes of devices, and is costly to develop (testing required!). More carefully crafted user experiences may include a dedicated "mobile"" version that matches the preoccupations of users on the go.

Third, focus on content. There is no room for superfluous on devices with limited screens, limited bandwidth, and limited interaction methods. The above use of "limited" should be seen as a positive constraint, one that fosters innovation.

PASSANI (WURFL): First, given an existing Web site, identify all the functions offered by it. Select the top 20% which users may want to access while they are mobile and mobilize those. Second, come to terms with device fragmentation. Some will tell you that device fragmentation will become a problem of the past eventually. This is false. Third, once you have come to terms with device fragmentation, figure out the cheapest way for you to deal with it in your Mobile Web application.

FREDERICK: How does your organization nurture Mobile Web developers and act as a steward of the Mobile Web?

MARKS (Nokia): Early on, Nokia invested a lot of money and effort in boot-strapping the whole notion of the Mobile Web. Today we participate in W3C, dotMobi, and a number of different organizations. But our biggest stewardship is simply our commitment to following the standards, and to providing much of the work we do to the open source community.

Nurturing Mobile Web developers is in the self-interest of all device manufacturers. We nurture the development community to gain mindshare in that community. We have Forum Nokia (http://www.forum.nokia.com/) that provides developers with tools, code, documentation, devices, etc. We also purchased Qt, which is one of the premier UI SDKs for the Web, mobile or otherwise (https://qt.nokia.com/products).

DAOUST (W3C): Within the W3C, the Mobile Web Initiative was created in 2005 to make browsing the Web from mobile devices a reality. Achievements include the Mobile Web Best Practices standard, the mobileOK mark and Checker and the Device Description Repositories Simple API that provide guidance to Web authors willing to learn what the Mobile Web is all about. The Mobile Web Initiative also runs training courses on the Mobile Web Best Practices (http://www.w3.org/Mobile/training/).

XHTML Basic 1.1 (published by W3C) and XHTML Mobile Profile 1.2 (published by OMA) marked the convergence between both organizations, and the end of a separate stack of Web technologies between the mobile world and the desktop world. The work now naturally shifts from Web pages to Web applications, with ongoing work on device APIs and widgets, and on a new set of best practices for the development of Mobile Web Applications.

# Summary

This chapter gave you a look at the future of the Mobile Web, including projections for subscriber growth and increased smartphone adoption. You met Mobile Web technology experts who discussed their experiences, ideas, and opinions about the current and future Mobile Web, offering guidance and suggestions to programmers who are new to Mobile Web development. One important outcome from the interview is that even in the inner circle of experts, there is still no consensus about the future direction of the Mobile Web. Its path is hotly debated. But the experts recognize the importance of educating new Mobile Web developers and through their organizations empowering developers with online training, best practices, and technology documentation.

Now, off you go, to your adventures in developing usable and adaptive Mobile Web applications for smartphones and other mobile devices!

# Part V

# Appendixes

Part 5 contains a range of reference material to give you a leg up on learning Mobile Web development.  You'll find user-agents, browser information, and HTTP request headers supplied for many types of mobile devices, especially smartphones. There's a glossary to help you decipher mobile industry acronyms, technical terms, and jargon. And a case study takes you under the hood as it describes an experiment that uncovers the actual caching and concurrency behavior of mobile browsers.

# Sample User-Agents from Mobile Devices

## User-Agents from Mobile Devices

This appendix lists user-agents and browser information for the default browsers in several models of mobile phones. This information is used to impersonate a mobile device for testing Mobile Web pages. You can consult the browsable DeviceAtlas and WURFL device data repositories in Chapter 4 for user-agents for virtually all mobile devices in the market today.

## LG VX-9100

**Listing A–1.** *User-Agent for LG VX-9100*

```
LGE-VX9100/1.0 UP.Browser/6.2.3.2 (GUI) MMP/2.0
```

**Table A–1.** *Device Information for LG VX-9100*

| Make | Model | Screen Size | WML | XHTML-MP | HTML | JavaScript | AJAX |
|------|-------|-------------|-----|----------|------|------------|------|
| LG | VX-9100M | 320x194 | Yes | Yes | No | No | No |

## Nokia 5310b XpressMusic

**Listing A–2.** *User-Agent for Nokia 5310b XpressMusic*

```
Nokia5310XpressMusic/2.0 (05.91) Profile/MIDP-2.1 Configuration/CLDC-1.1
```

**Table A–2.** *Device Information for Nokia 5310b XpressMusic*

| Make | Model | Screen Size | WML | XHTML-MP | HTML | JavaScript | AJAX |
|------|-------|-------------|-----|----------|------|------------|------|
| Nokia | 5310b | 240x320 | Yes | Yes | Yes | Yes | No |

# SonyEricsson C905

**Listing A–3.** *User-Agent for SonyEricsson C905*

SonyEricssonC905/R1BA Browser/NetFront/3.4 Profile/MIDP-2.1 Configuration/CLDC-1.1
JavaPlatform/JP-8.4.0

**Table A–3.** *Device Information for SonyEricsson C905*

| Make | Model | Screen Size | WML | XHTML-MP | HTML | JavaScript | AJAX |
|------|-------|-------------|-----|----------|------|-----------|------|
| SonyEricsson | C905 | 240x320 | Yes | Yes | Yes | Yes | Yes |

# Motorola Droid

**Listing A–4.** *User-Agent for Motorola Droid*

Mozilla/5.0 (Linux; U; Android 2.0; en-us; Droid Build/ESD20) AppleWebKit/530.17 (KHTML, like Gecko) Version/4.0 Mobile Safari/530.17

**Table A–4.** *Device Information for Motorila Droid*

| Make | Model | Screen Size | WML | XHTML-MP | HTML | JavaScript | AJAX |
|------|-------|-------------|-----|----------|------|-----------|------|
| Motorola | Droid | 480x854 | No | Yes | Yes | Yes | Yes |

# Motorola Cliq (MB200)

**Listing A–4.** *User-Agent for Motorola Cliq*

Mozilla/5.0 (Linux; U; Android 1.5; en-us; MB200 Build/CUPCAKE) AppleWebKit/528.5+ (KHTML, like Gecko) Version/3.1.2 Mobile Safari/525.20.1

**Table A–4.** *Device Information for Motorila Cliq*

| Make | Model | Screen Size | WML | XHTML-MP | HTML | JavaScript | AJAX |
|------|-------|-------------|-----|----------|------|-----------|------|
| Motorola | MB200 | 320x480 | No | Yes | Yes | Yes | Yes |

# Android G1 Developer Edition

**Listing A–4.** *User-Agent for Android G1 Developer Edition*

Mozilla/5.0 (Linux; U; Android 1.5; en-us; Android Dev Phone 1 Build/CRB21)
AppleWebKit/528.5+ (KHTML, like Gecko) Version/3.1.2 Mobile Safari/525.20.1

**Table A–4.** *Device Information for Android G1 Developer Edition*

| Make | Model | Screen Size | WML | XHTML-MP | HTML | JavaScript | AJAX |
|------|-------|-------------|-----|----------|------|-----------|------|
| T-Mobile | G1 | 320x480 | Yes | Yes | Yes | Yes | Yes |

# Palm Pre

**Listing A–5.** *User-Agent for Palm Pre*

```
Mozilla/5.0 (webOS/1.0; U; en-US) AppleWebKit/525.27.1 (KHTML, like Gecko) Version/1.0
Safari/525.27.1 Pre/1.0
```

**Table A–5.** *Device Information for Palm Pre*

| Make | Model | Screen Size | WML | XHTML-MP | HTML | JavaScript | AJAX |
| --- | --- | --- | --- | --- | --- | --- | --- |
| Palm | Pre | 320x480 | Yes | Yes | Yes | Yes | Yes |

# Apple iPhone

**Listing A–6.** *User-Agent for Apple iPhone*

```
Mozilla/5.0 (iPhone; U; CPU iPhone OS 2_2_1 like Mac OS X; en-us) AppleWebKit/525.18.1
(KHTML, like Gecko) Version/3.1.1 Mobile/5H11 Safari/525.20
```

**Table A–6.** *Device Information for Apple iPhone*

| Make | Model | Screen Size | WML | XHTML-MP | HTML | JavaScript | AJAX |
| --- | --- | --- | --- | --- | --- | --- | --- |
| Apple | iPhone | 320x480 | No | Yes | Yes | Yes | Yes |

# Blackberry Curve 8310

**Listing A–7.** *User-Agent for Blackberry Curve 8310*

```
BlackBerry8310/4.2.2 Profile/MIDP-2.0 Configuration/CLDC-1.1 VendorID/102
```

**Table A–7.** *Device Information for Blackberry Curve 8310*

| Make | Model | Screen Size | WML | XHTML-MP | HTML | JavaScript | AJAX |
| --- | --- | --- | --- | --- | --- | --- | --- |
| Blackberry | Curve 8310 | 320x240 | Yes | Yes | Yes | Yes | No |

# How to Capture the User-Agent for a Mobile Device

You find the User-Agent in the HTTP request headers sent when a mobile device connects to a web server. To capture the user-agent for a mobile device, follow the instructions in Appendix B for capturing request headers from the device. Look for the value of the User-Agent request header.

A mobile device model might use different User-Agent values, depending on the firmware installed on the device and the microbrowser used to browse the Mobile Web. If any user-agent associated with the device is sufficient for your purposes, it can also be obtained by finding the device model in a mobile device database. There, you can inspect all the user-agents that others have discovered for the device.

# Sample Request Headers from Mobile Devices

## Request Headers from Mobile Devices

This appendix lists the full HTTP request headers sent by the default browsers for several models of mobile phones. These request headers were obtained from a Web server on the learnto.mobi domain, so they might include request headers added by mobile operator proxies and headers specific to the Web request. You can use HTTP request headers to impersonate a mobile device for testing Mobile Web pages.

### LG VX-9100

**Listing B–1.** *HTTP Request Headers for LG VX-9100*

```
X-Wap-Profile: "http://uaprof.vtext.com/lg/vx9100/vx9100.xml"
Cos-Name: 5
Accept: application/vnd.phonecom.mmc-xml, application/vnd.wap.wmlc;type=4365,
application/vnd.wap.wmlscriptc, application/vnd.wap.xhtml+xml,
application/xhtml+xml;profile="http://www.wapforum.org/xhtml", image/bmp,
image/gif, image/jpeg, image/png, image/vnd.wap.wbmp, image/x-up-wpng,
multipart/mixed, multipart/related, text/html, text/plain,
text/vnd.wap.wml;type=4365, audio/midi, audio/qcelp, audio/vnd.qcelp,
audio/mid, audio/x-midi, audio/x-mid
Accept-Charset: utf-8
Accept-Encoding: deflate, gzip
Accept-Language: en; q=1.0, en, *; q=0.5
Connection: Close
Host: learnto.mobi
Referer: http://learnto.mobi/
User-Agent: LGE-VX9100/1.0 UP.Browser/6.2.3.2 (GUI) MMP/2.0
Via: 1.1 Comverse 4.5
```

# Nokia 5310b XpressMusic

**Listing B–2.** *HTTP Request Headers for Nokia 5310b XpressMusic*

```
Host: learnto.mobi
Accept: application/vnd.wap.wmlscriptc, text/vnd.wap.wml,
application/vnd.wap.xhtml+xml, application/xhtml+xml, text/html,
multipart/mixed, */*
Accept-Charset: ISO-8859-1, ISO-8859-2; Q=0.8, US-ASCII,
UTF-8; Q=0.8, ISO-8859-15; Q=0.8, ISO-10646-UCS-2; Q=0.6,
UTF-16; Q=0.6
Accept-Language: en-US
DRM-Version: 2.0
Cookie2: $Version="1"
Accept-Encoding: gzip, deflate
User-Agent: Nokia5310XpressMusic/2.0 (05.91) Profile/MIDP-2.1
Configuration/CLDC-1.1
x-wap-profile: "http://nds1.nds.nokia.com/uaprof/N5310XpressMusicr100.xml"
```

# SonyEricsson C905

**Listing B–3.** *HTTP Request Headers for SonyEricsson C905*

```
Accept: multipart/mixed, application/vnd.wap.multipart.mixed,
application/vnd.wap.xhtml+xml, application/xhtml+xml,
text/vnd.wap.wml, text/html, */*
Accept-Charset: utf-8, utf-16, iso-8859-1, iso-10646-ucs-2,
Shift_JIS, Big5, GB2312
Accept-Language: en
x-wap-profile: "http://wap.sonyericsson.com/UAprof/C905R101.xml"
Host: learnto.mobi
User-Agent: SonyEricssonC905/R1BA Browser/NetFront/3.4 Profile/MIDP-2.1
Configuration/CLDC-1.1 JavaPlatform/JP-8.4.0
Accept-Encoding: deflate, gzip
Referer: http://learnto.mobi/
Connection: keep-alive
```

# Motorola Droid

**Listing B–4.** *HTTP Request Headers for Motorola Droid*

```
Host: learnto.mobi
Accept-Encoding: gzip
Referer: http://learnto.mobi/
Accept-Language: en-US
User-Agent: Mozilla/5.0 (Linux; U; Android 2.0; en-us; Droid Build/ESD20)
AppleWebKit/530.17 (KHTML, like Gecko) Version/4.0 Mobile Safari/530.17
Accept: application/xml,application/xhtml+xml,text/html;q=0.9,
text/plain;q=0.8,image/png,*/*;q=0.5
Accept-Charset: utf-8, iso-8859-1, utf-16, *;q=0.7
```

# Motorola Cliq (MB200)

**Listing B–4.** *HTTP Request Headers for Motorola Clip (MB200)*

```
Host: learnto.mobi
Accept-Encoding: gzip
x-wap-profile: http://uaprof.motorola.com/phoneconfig/MotoMB200/profile/MotoMB200.rdf
Accept-Language: en-US
Accept: application/xml,application/vnd.wap.xhtml+xml,
application/xhtml+xml,text/html;q=0.9,text/plain;q=0.8,image/png,*/*;q=0.5
User-Agent: Mozilla/5.0 (Linux; U; Android 1.5; en-us; MB200 Build/CUPCAKE)
AppleWebKit/528.5+ (KHTML, like Gecko) Version/3.1.2 Mobile Safari/525.20.1
Accept-Charset: utf-8, iso-8859-1, utf-16, *;q=0.7
Referer: http://learnto.mobi/
X-Via: Harmony proxy
```

# Android G1 Developer Edition

**Listing B–4.** *HTTP Request Headers for Android G1 Developer Edition*

```
Host: learnto.mobi
Accept-Encoding: gzip
Accept-Language: en-US
Accept: application/xml,application/xhtml+xml,text/html;q=0.9,
text/plain;q=0.8,image/png,*/*;q=0.5
User-Agent: Mozilla/5.0 (Linux; U; Android 1.5; en-us;
Android Dev Phone 1 Build/CRB21) AppleWebKit/528.5+ (KHTML, like Gecko)
Version/3.1.2 Mobile Safari/525.20.1
Accept-Charset: utf-8, iso-8859-1, utf-16, *;q=0.7
Referer: http://learnto.mobi/
```

# Palm Pre

**Listing B–5.** *HTTP Request Headers for Palm Pre*

```
Host: learnto.mobi
Accept-Encoding: deflate, gzip
User-Agent: Mozilla/5.0 (webOS/1.0; U; en-US) AppleWebKit/525.27.1
(KHTML, like Gecko) Version/1.0 Safari/525.27.1 Pre/1.0
Accept: text/xml,application/xml,application/xhtml+xml,text/html;q=0.9,
text/plain;q=0.8,image/png,*/*;q=0.5
Referer: http://learnto.mobi/
Accept-Language: en-us,en;q=0.5
X-Palm-Carrier: c019-00
```

# Apple iPhone

**Listing B–6.** *HTTP Request Headers for Apple iPhone*

```
User-Agent: Mozilla/5.0 (iPhone; U; CPU iPhone OS 2_2_1 like Mac OS X;
en-us) AppleWebKit/525.18.1 (KHTML, like Gecko) Version/3.1.1
Mobile/5H11 Safari/525.20
Accept: text/xml,application/xml,application/xhtml+xml,
```

```
text/html;q=0.9,text/plain;q=0.8,image/png,*/*;q=0.5
Accept-Language: en-us
Accept-Encoding: gzip, deflate
Connection: keep-alive
Host: learnto.mobi
```

## Blackberry Curve 8310

**Listing B–7.** *HTTP Request Headers for Blackberry Curve 8310*

```
Accept-Language: en-US,en;q=0.5
x-wap-profile:
"http://www.blackberry.net/go/mobile/profiles/uaprof/8310/4.2.2.rdf"
Host: learnto.mobi
Accept-Charset: ISO-8859-1,UTF-8,US-ASCII,UTF-16BE,
windows-1252,UTF-16LE,windows-1250
User-Agent: BlackBerry8310/4.2.2 Profile/MIDP-2.0
Configuration/CLDC-1.1 VendorID/102
Accept: application/vnd.rim.html,text/html,application/xhtml+xml,
application/vnd.wap.xhtml+xml,text/vnd.sun.j2me.app-descriptor,
image/vnd.rim.png,image/jpeg,application/x-
vnd.rim.pme.b,application/vnd.rim.ucs,image/gif;anim=1,
application/vnd.wap.wmlc;q=0.9,application/vnd.wap.wmlscriptc;q=0.7,
text/vnd.wap.wml;q=0.7,*/*;q=0.5
profile: http://www.blackberry.net/go/mobile/profiles/uaprof/8310/4.2.2.rdf
Via: BISB_3.4.0.56, 1.1 pmds166.bisb1.blackberry:3128 (squid/2.7.STABLE6)
Cache-Control: max-age=259200
Connection: keep-alive
```

# How to Capture Headers from a Mobile Device

Capturing HTTP request headers from mobile devices gives you the information required to simulate the device in Firefox or a microbrowser emulator. Do the following to capture request headers from a mobile device:

1.  Browse to http://learnto.mobi on the mobile device.

2.  Select **View Request Headers**.

3.  View the HTTP request headers on the Mobile Web page and remember the four-digit number shown at the top and bottom of the page.

4.  Browse to the same location in a desktop browser.

5.  Enter the saved number to view the HTTP request headers from the mobile device.

6.  Save the headers for use in Firefox and mobile emulators.

# Glossary

### AJAX (Asynchronous JavaScript and XML)

AJAX is a method that uses JavaScript to asynchronously update the data displayed on a Web page. The acronym AJAX implies that XML is the response format from the Web server. In practice, however, the Web server might respond with textual or binary data in any format. XML, XHTML, JSON, HTML, and plain text are common response formats used to implement asynchronous Web requests. (Some clever Web developers vary the final letter in the AJAX acronym to indicate the format of the response document: AJAH, AJAJ, and so on.)

### CHTML (Compact HTML)

CHTML is Compact HTML, a subset of HTML for Japanese i-mode browsers. CHTML is used only in Japan. It is considered technically superior to WML and was submitted to W3C, but never standardized. CHTML is gradually being replaced by XHTML-MP in the Japanese market.

### CSS (Cascading Style Sheets)

CSS is a text-based language that describes the presentation of XHTML-MP and HTML documents. CSS applies style information to HTML elements in the HTML document or preferably, in externally-linked style sheets. In desktop CSS, style properties can be inherited. Some versions of CSS used in mobile devices simplify browser rendering by making style inheritance optional.

### CSS Mobile Profile (or CSS MP)

CSS Mobile Profile is a W3C candidate recommendation for a subset of CSS2 intended for use in mobile devices. The CSS Mobile Profile 1.0 recommendation was released in 2002. An updated recommendation, CSS Mobile Profile 2.0, was released in 2008 and is a subset of CSS 2.1 for mobile phones and other resource-constrained devices.

Microbrowsers that conform to the Open Mobile Alliance's Wireless CSS specification are capable of interpreting style sheets in CSS Mobile Profile. The organizations are working to align CSS Mobile Profile 2.0 with OMA Wireless CSS 1.2.

## D-Pad (Directional Pad)

The D-Pad is a set of five hardware keys on a mobile device that allow the user to select elements and navigate up, down, left and right.

## Desktop Web

The Desktop Web is the collection of markup documents on the Internet that are coded and optimized for display and usability on notebooks, desktop computers, and servers.

## Device Database

The device database is a database of identifying and descriptive characteristics of mobile devices. Mobile Web developers use a device database to identify Web traffic from mobile devices and to adapt mobile markup to device capabilities.

## Device Description Repository

Device Description Repository (DDR) is W3C terminology for a device database. The W3C specifies and recommends the DDR-Simple API (http://www.w3.org/TR/DDR-Simple-API/) for accessing device repositories.

## Emulator

An emulator is a desktop software program that simulates the features and behavior of mobile software and mobile devices. Emulators are available from mobile-device manufacturers and software vendors. Emulators encourage mobile-software development by allowing developers to test mobile software on a desktop computer during the development process. Emulators are almost always free to mobile developers.

Mobile web developers generally have several emulators installed on their computers. One emulator is installed for each targeted phone OS or mobile browser.

Emulators are excellent development tools, but they are insufficient for formal testing of mobile software. Nothing substitutes for testing on actual mobile devices.

## Featurephone

A featurephone is a low-cost, mass-market mobile phone with few features.

## Hard Key

A hard key is a single-purpose and labeled hardware key on a mobile device. Examples of hard keys include volume controls, keypad and keyboard keys, and a dedicated back key.

## HDML

Handheld Device Markup Language (HDML) is the oldest markup language intended for display on mobile devices (it was created circa 1996). HDML has a very simple syntax, and it was never standardized. Nevertheless, it proved influential in the development of WML; it is no longer used on mobile devices.

## HTML

Hypertext Markup Language(HTML) is the standard markup language of the Web. Web documents are coded overwhelmingly with this markup language. All desktop and many mobile browsers can render Web documents in HTML.

## HTTP

Hypertext Transfer Protocol (HTTP) is a standardized protocol for transferring Web documents from a Web server to a browser. HTTP is the underlying protocol used in mobile and desktop web browsers.

## Hybrid Application

A hybrid application is a native mobile application that incorporates a Web browser and Web content to add dynamic application features.

## i-mode

i-mode is a proprietary wireless Internet service developed by Access Company for NTT DoCoMo. i-mode provides access to Web, email, and packet data for only Japanese mobile devices. The markup languages used in i-mode services are CHTML or XHTML-MP.

## IDE

An integrated development environment (IDE) is one or more software applications used by computer programmers to develop software. An IDE facilitates software design, development, execution, debugging, and packaging. The simplest IDE combines a text editor and command prompt. GUI environments can also be extremely effective tools for Web and application development.

Many open and proprietary IDEs are available for Web development and adapt well to Mobile Web development. Popular Web development IDEs include Eclipse (www.eclipse.org), NetBeans (http://netbeans.org) and Microsoft Visual Studio (www.microsoft.com/visualstudio/).

## JavaScript

JavaScript is an object-oriented, client-side scripting language used in Desktop and Mobile Web browsers. JavaScript uses syntax similar to the Java programming language, but simplified to appeal to a wider audience of Web developers and designers. JavaScript is standardized as ECMAScript by Ecma International (www.ecma-international.org/), a European information-standards association.

## Microbrowser or Mobile Browser

A microbrowser is a native Web browser application on a mobile device. Microbrowsers have fewer features and support new and different markup languages than those supported by Desktop Web browsers. The microbrowser application is burned into the mobile device's firmware and is not updatable for the life of the mobile device, except for smartphones with updatable operating systems.

Third-party downloadable microbrowsers are the newest members of the microbrowser ecosystem. These browsers are versioned independently from the mobile OS and are freely downloadable and installable on supported mobile devices. Third-party microbrowsers aim to provide a compelling user experience for Mobile and Desktop Web pages.

## MIME Type (or Media Type, Content Type)

A MIME type is a text file type identifier for Web documents. The text identifier consists of type and subtype components with optional parameters, in this format:

```
<type>/<subtype>
```

Examples of common MIME types include `text/html`, `image/gif`, and `application/xhtml+xml`.

The MIME acronym stands for Multipurpose Internet Mail Extensions. MIME types were originally invented to describe the file types of nontext-based email content.

The Internet Assigned Numbers Authority (IANA) controls the registration of MIME media types. See www.iana.org/assignments/media-types/ for more information and a directory of registered media types.

## Minification

Minification is the process of optimizing the file size of Web documents by removing comments, whitespace, and other unnecessary characters.

## Mobile Web

The Mobile Web describes the collection of markup documents on the Internet that are coded and optimized for display and usability on mobile devices.

## Native Application

A native application is mobile software that is compiled into binary executable format, stored in memory, and run locally on the device. Examples of native mobile applications include an email reader, contacts application, or microbrowser.

## OEM

An original equipment manufacturer (OEM) is the manufacturer of mobile-device hardware and, sometimes, the mobile device's operating system.

## OTA

Over the Air (OTA) is mobile industry jargon for transferring data across a mobile network.

## RFC

A Request for Comments (RFC) is a document that defines an accepted or proposed Internet standard or standard practice in computer engineering. The Internet Engineering Task Force (IETF, http://ietf.org) governs RFC documents. RFCs are initiated as draft documents; after significant public review, they are finalized and accepted as a standard.

## Simulator

Simulator is a synonym for *emulator*. See the emulator entry for more information.

## Smartphone

A smarthphone is a high-end mobile phone with integrated Internet features such as email and desktop-capable Web browsing.

## Soft Key

A soft key is a hardware key on a mobile device where the label and functionality are determined by the mobile OS and/or an application running on the device. Many mobile devices provide right- and left-soft keys.

## Software Keyboard

A software keyboard is a keyboard on a touchscreen-mobile device that is drawn on the screen and used with finger- or stylus-input methods. Software keyboards are controlled by the mobile OS.

## User Agent Profile

A User Agent Profile (UAProf) is an XML file in the Resource Description Framework format (RDF, www.w3.org/RDF/) that describes the characteristics of a mobile device and its default Web browser. The URL to a UAProf document is the value of the X-Wap-Profile HTTP request header sent by many, but not all, mobile browsers.

## WAP

Wireless Application Protocol (WAP) is an open standard for network communication allowing mobile devices to access the Internet. It is a lightweight protocol providing support for basic Internet connectivity.

Some constituencies blame WAP for splitting the Web into Desktop and Mobile Web variants. Many Mobile Web developers and designers reject this claim and embrace adapting Web content to client capabilities as a core tenet of effective service delivery. Two facts to keep in mind:

■ The markup language associated with **WAP 1.x** is WML.

■ The markup language associated with **WAP 2.x** is XHTML-MP.

## WBMP

Wireless bitmap (WBMP) is a monochrome-image format. It is supported by WML-only microbrowsers and was widely used in WAP 1.x Web sites intended for used on black-and-white mobile devices. WBMP is not a suitable image format for the modern Mobile Web. (Instead, consult a device database to find image formats supported on a target mobile device.)

## Web Application

A Web application is a remote application that is accessed on the Internet using a desktop Web browser or microbrowser. The remote application runs on a Web server. The application consists of server-side functionality and markup documents rendered in the browser. Web applications require neither binary compilation nor persistent local storage (except for browser caching).

## Wireless CSS (or WAP CSS)

Wireless CSS is a subset of CSS2 with mobile-specific extensions that is standardized by the Open Mobile Alliance (formerly WAP Forum). The 2001 version 1.0 of the specification created the term, *WAP CSS*. The 2006 revision to 1.1 updated the terminology to *Wireless CSS*. The Wireless CSS 1.2 specification was released in 2007.

Microbrowsers that conform to the Wireless CSS specification are also capable of interpreting style sheets in the related, but independent CSS Mobile Profile standard adopted by W3C. The organizations are working to align CSS Mobile Profile 2.0 with OMA Wireless CSS 1.2.

## WML

WML is an XML-based markup language for mobile phones. Its simple and strict syntax includes a JavaScript-like scripting language. WML is considered legacy markup for mobile devices. WML is generally not an appropriate language for smartphone Web development (instead, use XHTML-MP or HTML). WML implements the WAP (Wireless Application Protocol) specification.

## XHTML

XHTML uses the tag set of HTML and strictly enforces XML syntax rules.

## XHTML Basic

XHTML Basic is a subset of HTML targeted for mobile devices, pagers, and set-top boxes. It is a precursor to and subset of XHTML-MP. XHTML Basic is standardized by the W3C.

## XHTML Mobile Profile (XHTML-MP)

XHTML-MP is a superset of XHTML-Basic authored by the Open Mobile Alliance industry group. XHTML-MP implements the WAP 2 specification. It is a popular markup language for mobile devices. XHTML-MP is equally suitable for mobile-optimized Web pages targeting featurephones and smartphones.

# Case Study: Testing Mobile Browser Caching and Performance

In Chapter 8, you learned techniques for optimizing mobile markup, including how to use HTTP response headers to encourage mobile browsers to cache Web documents. Effective caching of Mobile Web content also requires a mobile browser with a cache of sufficient size. But, how do you know which mobile browsers implement caches? To what extent do caching mobile browsers respect caching directives? What kinds of Web documents are actually cached in mobile browsers?

To investigate these questions, you examine a mobile browser test created by Cloud Four (http://cloudfour.com), a mobile technology company in Portland, Oregon.Two cofounders of Cloud Four, John T. Keith and Jason Grigsby, created the Mobile Browser Concurrency Test (www.cloudfour.com/36/mobile-browser-concurrency-test/) to test caching and performance characteristics of mobile browsers.

The Mobile Browser Concurrency Test observes mobile browser behavior from the Web server. The test calculates three pieces of mobile browser performance data:

- The number of concurrent HTTP connections made by the browser (per domain and overall).
- Whether the browser supports GZIP response compression.
- Whether the browser supports caching when the Expires response header is set to a far future date.

Cloud Four's Mobile Browser Concurrency Test is a public contribution to the mobile development community. Anyone can contribute to the test by browsing to http://cloudfour.com/mobile/ using a mobile device. The test aims to collect data from mobile browsers on the widest possible range of devices.

Figure D-1 shows a screenshot of the Mobile Browser Concurrency Test running in a mobile browser.

**Figure D-1.** *Screenshot of Mobile Browser Concurrency Test in a Palm Pre Emulator*

Figure D-2 shows the interactions between the mobile browser and Web server during the concurrency test.

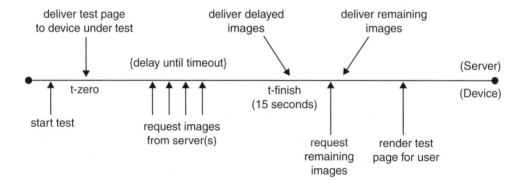

*Figure D-2. Communication between Mobile Device and Web Server in a Mobile Browser Concurrency Test*

The methodology of the Mobile Browser Concurrency Test is detailed at www.cloudfour.com/mobile/methodology.html.

At the time of writing, Keith and Grigsby have collected test results from 2081 unique user-agents, about one third of which are from mobile devices. Test results reveal stark differences in concurrency across mobile browsers:

- Many browsers opened multiple concurrent connections for the first domain and queued requests for the second, third, and fourth domains.

- Smartphone browsers are the most likely to open concurrent connections across multiple domains.

GZIP response compression was found to be widely compatible with mobile browsers:

- GZIP response compression can reduce file size and download time up to 75%.

- GZIP was supported on 83% of tested mobile browsersa—better than expected.

Test results also show that many mobile browsers do not cache Web content:

- Caching was supported on 65% of tested browsers—worse than expected.

- Files under 25K are candidates for client-side caching.

Keith summarizes the Mobile Browser Concurrency Tests in this way: "When we set out to do this test, we were looking at mobile browser performance through the lens of the Yahoo! Exceptional Performance (http://developer.yahoo.com/performance/) research on desktop Web browser performance. They developed and refined basic tenets for improving Web performance as perceived by the end user of the site:

- Reduce the page size (such as compact representation)

- Reduce the size of data transferred (gzip)

- Reduce the number of HTTP connections (consolidate external references)

- Maximize concurrent HTTP connections

- Enable caching (far future expires and size considerations)

"We wanted to understand how mobile device browsers fared in comparison to the desktop browsers previously evaluated, and ultimately wanted to fine-tune the Yahoo! performance recommendations for Mobile Web development."

"Our device testing shows that mobile browsers are less likely to universally support concurrent connections across multiple domains. . . . Mobile Web document retrieval is more likely to be serialized, which might make sense for low speed mobile connections, where total bandwidth is an issue anyway, but not necessarily for mobile devices operating on high-speed mobile networks or across Wi-Fi connctions. If mobile devices are not taking advantage of multiple domain concurrency, then it is less efficient to require more DNS lookups for no good reason. Mobile devices, in general, have more constraints on concurrency, so limiting the number of individual page elements makes even more sense for mobile browsers.There is much to be gained by knowing what kind of device you're talking to and tailoring your content delivery to match."

Several mobile browser performance recommendations are drawn from the concurrency test results:

- Minimize the number and size of files on a Mobile Web site.

- Include only one external CSS style sheet and JavaScript library.

- Browser functionality varies widely, so you should do performance testing on actual mobile devices.

- Include CSS externally or in the page header instead of inline in the style attribute.

- Optimize JavaScript performance by reducing the number of referenced DOM elements; include JavaScript libraries at the bottom of a Mobile Web document.

- Use the compact serialization of JSON in AJAX requests instead of XML.

- Reduce DNS lookups and maximize concurrent download benefits by referencing only 2 to 4 domains per Mobile Web page.

- Use the Expires response header and set its value far into the future.

- Examine Web server logs to confirm that browser caching works as expected.

Test results and raw data are available to the mobile development community under the Creative Commons license at www.cloudfour.com/mobile/summary.php.

# Index

**P**

# X

# Y

# Z